MAOIST
INSURGENCY
SINCE VIETNAM

MAOIST INSURGENCY SINCE VIETNAM

THOMAS A. MARKS

Academy of the Pacific
Honolulu, Hawaii

FRANK CASS
LONDON • PORTLAND, Or.

First published 1996 in Great Britain by
FRANK CASS & CO. LTD
Newbury House, 900 Eastern Avenue, Newbury Park,
London IG2 7HH, England

and in the United States of America by
FRANK CASS
c/o ISBS
5804 N. E. Hassalo Street
Portland, Oregon 97213-3644

British Library Cataloguing in Publication Data

Marks, Thomas A.
Maoist Insurgency Since Vietnam
I. Title
321.094095

ISBN 0–7146–4606–7 (cloth)
ISBN 0–7146–4123–5 (paper)

Library of Congress Cataloguing-in-Publication Data

Marks, Thomas A.
    Maoist insurgency since Vietnam/Thomas A. Marks.
      p. cm.
    Includes bibliographic references and index.
    ISBN 0-7146-4606-7 (cloth) -- ISBN 0-7146-4123-5 (paper)
    1. Insurgency--Thailand. 2. Thailand--Politics and government.
3. Insurgency--Philippines. 4 Philippines--Politics and
government--1946- 5. Insurgency--Sri Lanka. 6. Sri Lanka--Politics
and government--1978- 7. Insurgency--Peru. 8. Peru--Politics and
government--20th century. I. Title.
DS586.M37 1996
959.05--dc20   95-5364
                                                  CIP

Chapters 1, 2, and 5 (partial) first appeared in the journal *Small Wars &*
Insurgencies, Vols. 3&4 (1992 and 1993), and Chapter 3 in *Low Intensity*
Conflict and Law Enforcement, Vol.1, No.3 (Winter 1992).

Printed in Great Britain by
Bookcraft (Bath) Ltd., Midsomer Norton, Avon

For a soldier –

Major Robert C. MacKenzie, SCR, BCR
Killed in action, 24 February 1995, Sierra Leone

Contents

List of Maps

List of Figures

Introduction

Mao Tse-tung's campaign to capture state power in China has long served as the premier illustration of revolutionary warfare for scholars and would-be practitioners alike. Indeed, the vast scope and sheer numbers involved in the Chinese Civil War (1927–49) have served to all but dwarf possible rivals. Of these latter, though, the Vietnam War (1955–75) — also known as the Second Indochina War — certainly succeeded in capturing the world's attention and analysis in a way the Chinese episode could not. Not only was the leading global power, the United States, more directly involved in Vietnam (together with a host of more modest yet nonetheless still formidable players), but the conflict occurred in an era when mass communications were able to publicize its vicissitudes in a fashion simply not possible for the Chinese case. Thus it is Vietnam which has influenced the most recent scholarly generation concerned with revolution.

Still, it is Maoist 'people's war' that has remained the inspiration for would-be revolutionaries. For all the uniqueness of the Vietnamese approach, it is not possible to separate it from its Chinese predecessor — the debt owed in both strategic and tactical particulars is substantial. So, too, is this the case with follow-on episodes. The years since the 1975 end of the Vietnam War have seen four benchmark instances of revolutionary warfare consciously modelled after Mao. These have occurred in Thailand, the Philippines, Sri Lanka, and Peru. In all four, the insurgents have not only claimed to be 'making a revolution' but have held up Mao's approach as that providing guidance for their campaigns. Three of the battles, those of the Philippines, Sri Lanka, and Peru, continue at this writing; the fourth, Thailand, has all but disappeared. Regardless of precise status, none of these four has occasioned adequate scholarly attention.

This is a mistake. It may not, in a sense, be surprising. So much, after all, has been written concerning Maoist insurgency that there would seem little left to add. Such an attitude, however, is shortsighted, because *the form* remains with us still — and is likely to for years to come. This alone should spark our interest. Revolutionary wars which look to the Maoist model are not going to disappear.

The reasons are both pragmatic and ideological. Pragmatically speaking, the Maoist approach offers the most highly developed construct available for 'making a revolution'. Hence there is little need for would-be revolutionaries to look elsewhere for a template. Ideologically speaking, the apparent Maoist appeal to a communion with the masses is compatible with all political philosophies which purport to find legitimacy in those same masses. Hence it is seductive enough to capture adherents across the spectrum. Only the content of 'democracy' need be adjusted to fit the circumstances.

This, in fact, is precisely what has happened in the years since Mao's triumphant 1949 entry into Peking. His approach has been used by insurgents of all persuasions — predictably. For when all is said and done, Maoist insurgency is a *technique* for purposive (i.e., deliberate) action. It is a means to an end, political power; political power to be seized for the purpose of overthrowing the existing order. It is not, as so many of its misguided adherents have claimed, an alternative form of democratic governance. To the contrary, as will become clear in the course of this work, only democracy offers a realistic counter to the Maoist approach.

Analytical Perspectives[1]

In Vietnam the West faced the first post-Chinese Civil War variant of Maoist insurgency. The aftermath of that conflict remains with us still. What were the lessons learned? How should they guide the West in its foreign policy endeavors? Yet like the proverbial blind men and the elephant, the responses seem to depend upon that part of the conflict a particular scholar has examined. At times, to paraphrase President John F. Kennedy, an observer is led to ask, in exasperation, 'You all are talking about the same war, are you not?'[2] United States involvement in Southeast Asia irrevocably changed the face of America and a host of other countries, but how little appears to have been learned from the painful episode.

Can any area be more illustrative of this than the study of revolution, 'Maoist' or otherwise? Certainly, Vietnam has been the most significant revolutionary episode since China, at least as far as the West is concerned. And it has left a painful legacy of division. But in history and political science it is too often a shadowy legacy. Few scholars state explicitly the inspiration for theoretical constructs that are advanced as if sprung from a vacuum — even when they appear most obviously to be a reaction to one or another facet of the Vietnam experience. This we should expect, since the conflict fits neatly into no one's categories. Clearly, it was not the 'invasion' of the South by the North. Just as clearly, however, the Southern struggle was not a free-standing, indigenous peasant rebellion matched in David and Goliath fashion against the power of the United States. It was a revolution and all that is entailed in and implied by that term.

Here we come face to face with our shortcoming. What is the relationship between what went on during the war and what transpired after 'victory' for the Vietnamese communists? What can we learn that is valuable in attempting to understand revolution as a phenomenon? Too little work has been done to pursue such lines of inquiry. It would seem obvious that the most salient topic for examination would be the relationship between the would-be revolutionaries and the revolution that ultimately occurred. How much, for instance, was the former responsible for the latter? Did the communists *make* a revolution? Or did they simply step in at the right time and win virtually by default? Put in terms of that timeless query: do men make history, or does history make men?

Such questions are of more than passing importance. Around the globe, thousands continue to lose their lives as rebel groups struggle 'to make' revolutions, continue to lose their lives as those in power struggle to crush the strategies of those who would seize the state. Are the results ever really in question? Or is the deck stacked from the first draw by structural considerations of which most men are only dimly aware? Do 'victory' and 'defeat', in a hundred minor and major skirmishes and battles, make one whit of difference in the ultimate outcome of the struggle? Or are the contestants only prolonging or hastening that which is already written in the stars?

In the end, we return to the debate which, in the West, has not even begun to be settled: could the United States and its allies have won in Vietnam? Did their various strategic and tactical gambits matter at all in the ultimate outcome?[3] Clarification depends upon how the respondent answers the questions in the previous paragraph. To put my own biases on the table, I see nothing as 'written'. Man is constrained by circumstances, but in the end nothing is real unless man makes it so. Of course history makes men; but just as certainly, men shape history.

This is a philosophy shared by those such as Mao who would 'make' a revolution. They can be termed rebels or revolutionaries or any of a dozen possible labels. Yet the one most appropriate is insurgents; namely, those who wage insurgency. Insurgency itself, as with revolution (to be considered in detail shortly), remains an ill-defined term. Desai and Eckstein have attempted to clarify matters somewhat by offering the following:

> ...insurgency is a syncretic phenomenon — one that joins diverse elements in an explosive mix. It combines three elements: first, the 'spirit' of traditional peasant 'rebellion'; second, the ideology and organization of modern 'revolution'; and third, the operational doctrines of guerrilla warfare.[4]

Useful though it may be, this effort still leaves the observer puzzled as to what precisely the goal of an insurgency is. Consequently, for our purposes here, let me coin the following definition: Insurgency is violence in support, *strategically*, of a political goal, *operationally*, of a political infrastructure, *tactically*, of local political domination. Such a definition recognises both the political nature of the insurgent campaign and its symbiotic relationship with force. Put in slightly different terms, an insurgency, then, is a political campaign backed by 'muscle'; that is, by threatened or actual violence. It has its most readily recognizable civil counterpart, at least in *form*, in the activities of criminal syndicates such as the Mafia or the triads. The goals of these two, however, are not political but economic.

An insurgency, in contrast, is about politics, about reshaping the process of who gets what. It is the conscious effort to supplant one political structure with another. Taken to its logical end, insurgency becomes that which Mao and the Vietnamese communists claimed to be waging, *revolutionary war*, the conscious effort 'to make' a revolution by seizing state power using politico-military means.

And what is a revolution? Even at this late date, sources seem unable to agree upon a basic definition.[5] The popular press, in particular, often equates revolution with successful rebellion. Nothing, of course, could be further from the meaning most accepted by the social sciences (and insurgents), namely that 'by "revolution" we now understand, in addition to the political aspects, a fundamental challenge to the legitimacy of social structures, including patterns of hierarchy or stratification, and titles to economic ownership or control.'[6]

A revolution, in other words, is not simply the exchange of personnel or roles but rather a fundamental overturning of what was. Hagopian, in his basic political science text, *Regimes, Movements, and Ideologies*, draws extensively upon the work of Max Weber to elucidate this development. If all reality can be divided, as Weber does, into three 'systems of social stratification' — economic, political, and status — then a revolution, Hagopian observes, reorders those systems.[7] To achieve such a reordering is the goal of insurgents engaged in revolutionary warfare.

One goal in this book, then, in examining Maoist insurgency since Vietnam, is to understand the relationship between these insurgents, in their deliberate quest to make a revolution, and the larger process of revolution itself, the overturning of the world as it is. In particular, we wish to understand the relationship between insurgent strategic vision and revolutionary outcome. Do the choices made by insurgents matter? And, in particular, is their ideological template of moment? Does a communist ideology, for instance, to use Vietnam again as an illustration, add to the revolutionary conjuncture a crucial element without which events might play themselves out differently? Or is ideology irrelevant?

Given America's decades of involvement in Vietnam, particularly the battle with the guerrilla network of the Vietcong, it is frustrating to realize how little (if any) general theory there is upon which to draw. Indeed, insurgency as a phenomenon has been academically peripheral in recent years. Instead, scholarship concerning revolutions and would-be revolutions has emphasized the importance of structural factors over deliberate (purposive) action.[8] 'Revolutions are not made; they come', writes Theda Skocpol (quoting Wendell Phillips) in her seminal *States and Social Revolutions.*[9] Groups, in other words, do not *make* revolution. Rather, they contend within a revolutionary crisis characterized by state breakdown and widespread peasant rebellion. Such emphasis leads researchers to focus upon the 'deeper' causes of revolutionary conjunctures rather than upon the ideological designs of those who would be king.

If the structural perspective — the so-called 'Third Generation' of revolutionary scholarship[10] — can be said to be the dominant paradigm at the moment, there is nevertheless an emerging groundswell of reaction, one which is dissatisfied with the relegation of deliberate action to the background.[11] Since it is certainly humans who must act within any structural matrix of factors, runs the argument, there must be a role for strategic action. Were this not so, how are we to explain, in acknowledged revolutions, the frequent capture of state power by those very groups who claim to be making revolution?

An example will clarify this point. The anti-French movement in Indochina was comprised of numerous contending groups. Only one, the Vietminh, emerged victorious. Structurally, the Vietminh were the beneficiaries of an alignment of forces which stacked the deck against the French. Nevertheless, this does not explain why the Vietminh were able to benefit from these forces to the extent that they emerged controlling the state, from which vantage point they could carry out their ideologically motivated revolution. Such an explanation can only be gained by examining various strategic and tactical features. This would reveal that the approach adopted, embracing as it did the all-encompassing mechanics of organization and terror, was a key factor.[12]

Scholarly work on Vietnam has not pursued this lead, focusing in the main on other aspects of the conflict.[13] Recent analysis of the Chinese revolution, however, has been helpful.[14] Studies of specific areas demonstrate that much of the Chinese Communist Party (CCP) approach was tactical response to local conditions and exploitation of existing societal institutions — an approach which was adopted as frequently by *Kuomintang* (KMT) forces as by those of the CCP. That the communists were able to emerge victorious stemmed from a superior strategic vision for harnessing operational and tactical gambits. Structure, then, did indeed set the parameters for action, but both of the main contenders for power were able to maneuver as chessmen are moved about the board, a play embracing myriad strategic variations.

The point, of course, is that it is men who comprise a revolution. Structural circumstances mean nothing save they are made real through human action. To venture into the specifics of the CCP campaign just mentioned, or of any similar endeavor, requires that we explore *insurgency*. External manifestations of the campaign, *terror* or *guerrilla war* or *mobile war*, are all only tools to accomplish the political end, the remaking of the political system.

The precise level of force required to achieve this depends upon the strength of the system under attack. Guerrilla warfare may suffice in one case; full-fledged conventional action may ultimately prove necessary in another. Likewise, the correct strategy to be followed will depend upon the particulars of the case at hand. Regardless, that which links strategy to the tactical use of force is the operational utilization of political infrastructure.

Thus the *raison d'être* of insurgent military power, in whatever form, lies in the projection and protection of this infrastructure, leading ultimately to victory.[15] How exactly to achieve this has been related by various revolutionaries whose names are familiar. Mao Tse-tung, for instance, whose doctrines so influenced the Vietnamese, set forth a three-step process (strategic defensive, stalemate, and offensive) and found it necessary, in the end, to transform his guerrilla armies into massive conventional forces to remove the last vestiges of KMT power.[16] Fidel Castro, in contrast, found a Cuba so decayed that minimal guerrilla action was all that was needed to bring the edifice crashing down.[17]

Regardless of the force level required to achieve the political aim in China or Cuba, the critical point is that it was — and is — dictated by the demands for protection of the alternate political system being constructed to carry out a revolution, not by military concerns *per se*. This, to be sure, is the ideal. Numerous other mundane factors, such as logistics or ecological realities, will impact upon insurgent capabilities for force maintenance and projection. Yet it is the inspiration that is important. Step by step, the revolutionaries in China and Cuba created an alternative political movement, then used it to seize power. Having done this, they implemented far-reaching changes — revolutionary changes.

This description has its implications. In particular, it imputes that insurgents, as they gathered strength, were forced to make specific strategic and tactical decisions that were crucial not only to their advancement but also to their very survival. It also implies that the only viable decisions were those that made use, subjectively, of objective revolutionary conditions. This much is true on any battlefield. And certainly 'to make revolution' is to wage war. Consequently, as on the battlefield, we face the reality that victory or defeat is never preordained, no matter how the scales may be weighted in favor of one outcome or the other. The course adopted by the insurgents, as contestants for power — their strategy for waging insurgency, in other words — is crucial.

Ideological Blueprint for a New Regime

Mao's strategy itself did not spring full-grown from his mind. To the contrary, only by fits and starts did it mature. As such, it really has several parts, and the relationship between them is not always appreciated. Specifically, during the Jiangxi (Kiangsi) Soviet period, 1930-34, techniques of small unit warfare and for dealing with the masses were developed. Yet these proved insufficient to prevent the Jiangxi Soviet from being crushed by Chiang Kai-shek's Five Encirclement Campaigns.[18] Subsequently, during the Yenan period, that which followed the Long March of 1934–35, but prior to full-scale war with Japan (7 July 1937), further 'mass line' techniques were developed. Only with the Japanese occupation, however, could a synthesis between guerrilla warfare and mass organization emerge which we would recognise today as 'Maoist insurgency'.

Despite the controversy over the role peasant nationalism played in the mobilization process, Chalmers Johnson is obviously correct in judging that without the Japanese occupation there would not have been Maoist insurgency.[19] One need not even enter into the debate as to whether it was nationalism or social action which activated the peasantry. Both were important and played varying roles depending upon the specific region in question; the real key was the destruction of the *Kuomintang* resource and manpower base by the Japanese, a reality which meant the state — incomplete and inefficient though it was, even after the Northern Expedition of 1926–28 — was no longer able to muster the power which had previously proved quite sufficient to crush the communists, most tellingly in the Fifth Encirclement Campaign (1933-34). Indeed, it is not an overstatement to observe that without the Japanese invasion of 1937 onwards, there might well have been no Mao. The collapse of the KMT in the 1945–49 civil war was an anticlimax. The Nationalist cause was mortally wounded before the battle was joined.[20]

Finally, from the struggle against the Japanese came Mao's actual 'people's war' framework. Here we see all of the diverse pieces fit together to form a picture. What was crucial was that in Mao's final product his earlier 'techniques' were subsumed by the larger strategic approach which rested upon a very particular worldview, that of the insurgent battling within the imperialist context. Absent that, the pieces did not necessarily hang together. This, too, was to pose problems for those who would seek to use the model.

Let us look at this more carefully. It is generally agreed that while Marx outlined the communist critique of political economy, it was Lenin who understood the realities of making a revolution. By perfecting the notion of the clandestine party of revolutionaries, he removed the Marxian revolution from its position as a course of action open only to advanced capitalist societies and placed it within the realm of possibility for any state, provided a revolutionary situation existed and a revolutionary party could guide the population towards consciousness. Mao took this lesson and applied it to China, producing a movement far more grounded in the masses than had been envisaged by Lenin. Mao thus demonstrated the need for revolutionaries to bend Marxism to their particular situation, rather than attempting to fit the situation to Marxism.[21] It was a lesson, we shall see, that would-be revolutionaries frequently overlooked.

Mao's greatest contribution was to recognize that in a country where the working class was unavailable or unable to participate in the revolutionary movement, other classes — in a relationship with the dominant class similar in quality and nature to that between the proletariat and the bourgeoisie — might have class consciousness and, therefore, revolutionary potential. In China the class Mao specifically had in mind was the peasantry, the overwhelming majority of the Chinese population. The revolution, to be sure, would still have to be guided by the representatives of the working class, the party, but the relationship between the party and the masses was to be far more symbiotic than proposed by Lenin. Even as the party raised the consciousness of the peasants, it was to learn from the people and thus to modify its approaches. Only by pursuing such a process of interaction could a correct strategy be developed.

This 'going to the masses' is often mistaken as democratic action. It was anything but that. Rather it was a technique to maximize mobilization of manpower by using a carrot rather than a stick. The masses needed to be brought into decision-making, but their deliberations would be guided in the direction chosen by the party. Early efforts to build revolutionary power upon a proletarian base had foundered upon the most logical of explanations: there was insufficient human material in the urban centers of proletarian concentration to build a potent movement. The peasantry was where the bodies were.

Mao's recognition of the need to mold Marxism to fit the unique circumstances of China had a profound effect in another area, that of the analysis of the revolutionary situation. While agreeing with Lenin that there were major and minor contradictions in a society, Mao recognized that there might arise special circumstances so extreme in their character that there was the chance that the very society which gave rise to the contradictions — and therefore the opportunity for revolutionary action — might be eliminated. The special circumstances would thus have to take priority over the contradictions; that is, the special circumstance in itself became the major contradiction, and all other contradictions became minor.[22]

China, at the time Mao wrote this analysis, was caught up in two great contradictions, that of feudalism versus the masses of the people, and that of China versus imperialism, as represented by Japan. The contradiction between China and Japan had been principal, because the Japanese invasion threatened to wipe out Chinese society. Thus the nature of class relations was changed, since all classes were faced with the issue of survival. The need to resist the common threat made possible bonds which could not have existed previously. The struggle against imperialism had to take priority; and since this was a struggle of the Chinese people as a whole, the entire population could be viewed as a revolutionary class.

Mobilization of this class required a united front against the imperialists. This was also not a new concept,[23] yet in the Leninist context the united front had been a stratagem. For Mao it became much more. He obviously was influenced by the conception of 'democracy of a new type', or 'new democracy', articulated by the Bulgarian communist leader and Comintern general secretary Georgi Dimitrov (1882–1949), wherein a popular front government rested upon a broad anti-fascist popular movement, with all parties included in the popular front as participants.[24] Mao himself welcomed into his united front all except 'enemy classes'. To ensure harmony within the front, certain concessions not involving 'issues of principle' were made. Most significantly, the goal of a 'workers' and peasants' republic' was broadened to include all allied elements in a 'people's republic'.[25]

Hence, while Mao recognized that China, as a precapitalist country, would have to pass through the bourgeois-democratic and socialist stages of revolution to achieve communism, and while the first upheaval would take the form of 'new democracy' as outlined by Dimitrov, he was adding a new slant to the united front concept. The leadership of the 'new democracy' by the 'joint revolutionary democratic dictatorship of several revolutionary classes' was an innovation which extended the limits of the 'dictatorship of the proletariat' concept. He even saw the possibility that the Chinese bourgeoisie might prove capable of assuming the responsibility for driving out Japanese imperialism and introducing democratic government. Here, 'Mao was already groping towards the "people's dictatorship" he was to proclaim in 1949'.[26]

The united front, therefore, had become for Mao an integral step in a process of societal transition, rather than a mere maneuver, to use Trotsky's term, to be utilized for advantage under certain circumstances. It was not a 'temporary makeshift'. Through it the revolution could be propelled to a new stage. In greatly expanding the scope of popular participation in the revolutionary process, Mao echoed the calls of the German female communist Rosa Luxemburg (1870–1919) for a similar strategy. Still, within the Chinese context, this necessarily meant work principally not among the urban proletariat but among the peasantry. Mao was under no preconceptions that actual power could be gained without the support of China's masses. Even while participating in a united front, the communist party was directed to proselyze, to win over to its way of thinking 'the middle forces'. It was within this context that Mao was able to create the mass organization that ultimately allowed him to defeat the *Kuomintang*.

This mass organization had three important aspects: (a) the 'mass line'; (b) emphasis on 'self-reliance'; and (c) a three-phase periodization of the 'protracted war'.[27] The 'mass line' was the formal enunciation of the attitude mentioned above, Mao's conviction that the relationship between the party and the masses had to be one of constant interaction. As Mao wrote:

> All correct leadership is necessarily from the masses, to the masses. This means: take the ideas of the masses (scattered and unsystematic ideas) and concentrate them (through study turn them into concentrated and systematic ideas), then go to the masses and propagate and explain these ideas until the masses embrace them as their own, hold fast to them and translate them into action, and test the correctness of these ideas in such action. Then once again go to the masses so that the ideas are preserved in an endless spiral, with the ideas becoming more correct, more vital and richer each time. Such is the Marxist-Leninist theory of knowledge, or methodology.[28]

Such a philosophy went a ways towards addressing the concerns voiced by Luxemburg that a communist party formulated along the lines proposed by Lenin would inevitably drift into the dictatorship of a few.[29] By insisting upon the mass line's implementation, Mao proposed to avoid ideological dogmatism. It is worth reiterating, though, that this was intended as a feedback mechanism, not as a form of democracy (though left-wing admirers, particularly in the West, were to interpret it as such).

Closely related to the mass line was Mao's emphasis on self-reliance. Not only were the masses the ultimate source of revolutionary rectitude, but upon them the revolutionaries in China depended for their sustenance. There were no foreign sanctuaries as had sheltered Lenin and his compatriots. Neither did the Chinese bourgeois state seem to be in straits as desperate as those into which Russia entered after three years of martial defeat in World War I. We now know this part of Mao's reasoning to be inaccurate in one sense: the Japanese intrusion, in fact, had shattered the KMT state. Nonetheless, in the immediate matter of military confrontation, the 'diehard forces' (i.e., the anti-communist forces) remained powerful *vis-à-vis* the communists. To counter them it was necessary for Mao to engage the third aspect of his approach, the 'protracted war'.

The strength of the national bourgeoisie, and later also the strength of the Japanese imperialists, was overwhelming initially compared to that of the communists. This meant that the party was faced with two tasks: (a) the construction of a viable military apparatus; and (b) with this apparatus to engage in a protracted war of 'three stages': the 'period of the enemy's strategical offensive, the period of the enemy's strategical defense and of our preparations for counter-offensive, and the period of our strategical counter-offensive'. It is not necessary here to examine in detail these phases. Suffice to say they became the more well-known portions of Mao's approach to 'revolutionary warfare', or 'people's war' (i.e., war among and by the people for the purposes of 'national liberation').

This aspect of Mao's contribution was to have enormous impact upon liberation movements throughout the Third World. As he struggled to continue the revolution and to create a new society in post-1949 China, Mao viewed the primary threat to the Chinese revolution no longer as the Japanese but as the Americans. His answer to the threat lay in people's war. Though not authored by

Mao himself, Marshal Lin Piao's 'Long Live the Victory of People's War',[30] published in 1965 to commemorate the twentieth anniversary of Japan's World War II defeat, certainly had his approval. With remarkable clarity, it documented the need for self-reliance and the organic as opposed to expedient role the united front was to occupy in the process. More to our point, a cardinal theme that ran through the work was that, just as the invasion of China by the Japanese imperialists had caused a transformation of the principal and secondary contradictions, so the situation in an Asia ripe for revolution had been transformed by America's assumption of the Japanese imperial role. During the national-democratic revolutionary phase, 'imperialism and its lackeys' were thus the principal enemy. American imperialist aggression presented the Asian communist parties with the opportunity 'to rally all anti-imperialist patriotic forces, including the national bourgeoisie and all patriotic persons', in an anti-imperialist united front. Those from the exploiting classes who joined the struggle against the imperialists thereby played a progressive historical role and transcended their own reactionary essence.

In short, analyzed Lin Piao and Mao, the strategic setting was ripe for seizure of the initiative; and through the united front against the imperialists, the communists of Asia would be able to mobilize their countrymen in such a way as to advance the revolution itself, just as Mao had done in China. Thus the intervention of American imperialism was not a setback but a boon, for it created the historical conditions for the realization of the national united front. Just as importantly, this intervention was not a chance occurrence; rather it was a stage in the historical decline of capitalism, a permanent reality which was to be overcome and utilized to further the revolution.

What Mao had done, in essence, was to redefine revolution as revolutionary warfare and to provide a blueprint for its execution. As can be seen, though, the techniques, while conceivably viable when taken in isolation, were intended to function within a very special context. In particular, the mobilization of the oppressed depended upon two necessities: (a) carving out liberated areas (i.e., soviets) of such size that the alternative society could function to mobilize the masses; and (b) convincing these same masses that the feedback mechanisms of the Leninist structure were a sufficient form of democracy. Absent either of these, the only realistic alternative to effect mobilization was terror. This, in fact, became increasingly prominent in movements which sought to utilize Maoist insurgency. They were to be caught in a strategic misjudgement, because Mao's assessment of the situation, grounded as it was in the economic determinism of Marxism, failed to discern the larger structural dynamic at work, the growth of popular demand for democratic governance.

Small wonder that those adopting the Maoist model, rather than recognizing this strategic reality, fell into an emphasis upon the techniques. Most such students copied from afar, absorbing a filtered view of the Maoist strategy.

Still not completely understood, though, and thus discussed but little in this work, is the extent to which the Chinese sought to pass on *directly* their understanding of what they were about in making revolutionary war (as opposed to imparting technical training, particularly in cadre procedures and military tactics). In all of the cases examined here — Thailand, the Philippines, Sri Lanka, and Peru — it is now established that cadre either actually trained in China or were in contact with Chinese personnel posted abroad. We have long known of the instruction given to Thai communists in China; but it is only more recently that information has surfaced on numerous training trips made to China by Philippine and Peruvian insurgents. The picture is incomplete as concerns the Sinhalese component of the Sri Lankan uprising, though contact did occur with overseas Chinese representatives. What remains yet to be researched is the precise balance struck in this training between technique and approach, which is to say, the relative weight given to tactical, operational, and strategic components of the Maoist vision.

Be this as it may, the model being used by these would-be revolutionaries seemed sound. How then to account for the errors we will see the insurgents commit in this book? Very simply, their approach was flawed, inappropriate to the new circumstances of a world embracing popular rule and rejecting, perhaps only temporarily, dictatorial forms. The trend toward democracy meant Maoist insurgency was still potent as a tactic but could succeed strategically only if the state blundered or was critically weakened by external assault. None of these occurred in the four cases at hand, though certainly Sri Lanka and Peru remain in turmoil. Still, even there, strategic initiative rests with Colombo and Lima after well over a decade of armed struggle in both countries.

Regardless, we have not seen the last of revolutionary warfare.

My examination, it needs to be emphasized, is not intended to be a history of all Maoist insurgencies since Vietnam. An argument could certainly be made that other important post-1975 insurgencies (e.g., the Khmer Rouge in Cambodia since 1979 and the Kurdish PKK since 1984 in Turkey) than those analyzed in this book qualify for attention. Rather I seek to illuminate Maoist insurgency as a strategic approach by examining in detail what I judge to be four premier cases that have occurred in the past several decades. By so doing, we will gain greater insight not only into a strategy still used by virtually all insurgents but also into the only realistic counter to it, democratization.

NOTES

1. Versions of this introduction have been used in two of my previous works: 'Making Revolution: *Sendero Luminoso* in Peru', *Small Wars and Insurgencies* [London], 3/1 (Spring 1992), pp.22–46; and *Making Revolution: The Insurgency of the Communist Party of Thailand in Structural Perspective* (Bangkok: White Lotus Press, forthcoming).
2. President John F. Kennedy's exact comment was, 'You two did visit the same country, didn't you?' See Neil Sheehan, *A Bright Shining Lie: John Paul Vann and America in Vietnam* (NY: Random House, 1988), p.365. Kennedy was addressing the diametrically opposed reports delivered to him on the situation in South Vietnam by Victor 'Brute' Krulak and Joseph Mendenhall.
3. Useful counterpoint concerning this subject may be found by examining, for the affirmative, William Colby, *Lost Victory: A Firsthand Account of America's Sixteen-Year Involvement in Vietnam* (NY: Contemporary Books, 1989); and, for the negative, Gabriel Kolko, *Anatomy of a War: Vietnam, the United States, and the Modern Historical Experience* (NY: Pantheon Books, 1985).
4. Raj Desai and Harry Eckstein, 'Insurgency — The Transformation of Peasant Rebellion', *World Politics*, 42/4 (July 1990), pp.441–65. Elsewhere in their piece (p. 464), the authors observe that insurgency is 'the mix of millenarian zeal, revolutionary ideology and organization, and guerrilla warfare'.
5. A very short but useful discussion of the issue may be found in Thomas M. Magstadt and Peter M. Schotten, *Understanding Politics — Ideas, Institutions, and Issues* (NY: St. Martin's Press, 1988), pp.395–6; cf. Ch. 17, 'Revolution', pp.394–418.
6. J.C.D. Clark, *Revolution and Rebellion — State and Society in England in the Seventeenth and Eighteenth Centuries* (NY: Cambridge UP, 1986), p.4; cf. Ch.1, 'Introduction', pp.1–5.
7. Mark N. Hagopian, *Regimes, Movements, and Ideologies — A Comparative Introduction to Political Science* (NY: Longman, n.d.), esp. Ch. 6, 'Society and Polity', pp.223–58, and Ch.7, 'Social Movements and Revolution', pp.259–300. Cf. Mark N. Hagopian, *The Phenomenon of Revolution* (NY: Dodd, Mead, 1974).
8. Cf. Jack A. Goldstone, 'Theories of Revolution: The Third Generation', *World Politics*, 32/3 (April 1980), pp.425–53. The basic themes discussed in this article appear in expanded form, with readings, in Goldstone (ed.), *Revolutions: Theoretical, Comparative, and Historical Studies* (Chicago: Harcourt Brace Jovanovich, 1985). A benchmark work is Theda Skocpol, *States and Social Revolutions* (NY: Cambridge UP, 1979). Also useful is Walter L. Goldfrank, 'Theories of Revolution and Revolution Without Theory: The Case of Mexico', *Theory & Society*, 7 (1979), pp.135–65.

9. Skocpol (note 8), p.17. The author attributes the precise phrase to Wendell Phillips but notes (fn.43, p.298) that she extracted it from an unreferenced use by Stephen F. Cohen in his *Bukharin and the Bolshevik Revolution* (NY: Knopf, 1973), p.336.
10. Cf. Goldstone, 'Theories of Revolution: The Third Generation', cited in note 8. The emphasis upon structure is a fundamental shift from the 'Second Generation' and its focus upon revolutionary process. The detailed analysis of structural relationships is also considerably removed from the descriptive but largely atheoretical perspective of the 'First Generation'. Among the key works considered representative of the 'Second Generation' approach are: James C. Davies, 'Toward a Theory of Revolution', *American Sociological Review*, 27/1 (Feb. 1962), pp.5–19; Ted Robert Gurr, *Why Men Rebel* (Princeton, NJ: Princeton UP, 1970); Chalmers Johnson, *Revolutionary Change* (NY: Free Press, 1963); and Charles Tilly, *From Mobilization to Revolution* (Reading, MA: Addison-Wesley, 1978). Illustrative 'First Generation' books are: Crane Brinton, *The Anatomy of Revolution* (Englewood Cliffs, NJ: Prentice-Hall, 1938); Lyford P. Edwards, *The Natural History of Revolution* (Chicago, IL: Univ. of Chicago Press, 1927); and Pitrim A. Sorokin, *The Sociology of Revolution* (Philadelphia, PA: Lippincott, 1925).
11. Early works in reaction to Skocpol's structural perspective are representative: Cf. Bruce Cumings, 'Interest and Ideology in the Study of Agrarian Politics', *Politics & Society*, 10/4 (1981), pp.467–95; Jerome L. Himmelstein and Michael S. Kimmel, 'Review Essay: *States and Social Revolutions*: The Implications and Limits of Skocpol's Structural Model', *American Journal of Sociology*, 86/5 (March 1981), pp.1145–54; Elizabeth J. Perry, 'Book Review: *States and Social Revolutions*', *Journal of Asian Studies*, 39/3 (May 1980), pp.533–5; and Elizabeth Nichols, 'Skocpol on Revolution: Comparative Analysis vs. Historical Conjuncture', draft for *Comparative Social Research*, Vol.9 (1986).
12. This issue is discussed explicitly in Truong Buu Lam, *Resistance, Rebellion, Revolution: Popular Movements in Vietnamese History* (Singapore: Inst. of SE Asian Studies, 1984). See esp. Ch.5, 'The Viet Minh Movement', pp.37–48.
13. A useful exception is Greg Lockhart, *Nation in Arms: The Origins of the People's Army of Vietnam* (Boston, MA: Allen and Unwin, 1989).
14. Illustrative works are Elizabeth J. Perry, *Rebels and Revolutionaries in North China, 1845-1945* (Stanford, CA: Stanford UP, 1980); Yung-fa Chen, *Making Revolution: The Communist Movement in Eastern and Central China, 1937–1945* (Berkeley, CA: Univ. of California Press, 1986); Kathleen Hartford and Steven M. Goldstein (eds.), *Single Sparks: China's Rural Revolutions* (Armonk, NY: M.E. Sharpe, 1989).
15. Clarification of this point with respect to Vietnam may be found by consulting what remain the most outstanding works on the subject, those of Douglas Pike: *Viet Cong: The Organization and Techniques of the National Liberation Front of South Vietnam* (Cambridge, MA: MIT Press, 1966); and *PAVN: People's Army of Vietnam* (Novato, CA: Presidio Press, 1986), esp. Chs.9 and 10 of Sect. IV, 'Strategy'. These works are relevant for an understanding of insurgencies in general.
16. For the theory of Mao Tse-tung, see his *Selected Military Writings of Mao Tse-tung* (Peking: Foreign Languages Press, 1968). To compare with Vietnamese thinking on the subject, see Vo Nguyen Giap, *People's War, People's Army* (NY: Bantam Books, 1968).
17. Che Guevara is generally credited with origination of Castro's strategy for seizing power. For his thought, see Che Guevara, *Guerrilla Warfare* (Lincoln, NE: Univ. of Nebraska Press, 1985). Perhaps better known is Guevara (*et al.?*) as synthesised by Regis Debray. Debray's own analysis of revolutionary theory and praxis makes for fascinating reading; see his *A Critique of Arms* (Middlesex, UK: Penguin Books, 1977); additional analysis in Hartmut Ramm, *The Marxism of Regis Debray* (Lawrence, KS: Regents Press of Kansas, 1978). For the Cuban Revolution in general, see Ramon Eduardo Ruiz, *Cuba: The Making of a Revolution* (NY: Norton, 1968).
18. Numerous works are available on this early period. Among the most useful, in dis-

cussing soviet formation, are Linda Grove, 'Creating a Northern Soviet', *Modern China*, 1/3 (July 1975), pp.243–70; and Shinkichi Eto, 'Hai-lu-feng — The First Chinese Soviet Government', Parts I & II, *China Quarterly*, No. 8 (Oct.–Dec. 1961), I: pp.161–83; 9 (Jan.–March 1962), II: pp.149–81.

For the Jiangxi period in general, cf. Philip C.C. Huang, Lynda Schaefer Bell, and Kathy Lemons Walker, *Chinese Communists and Rural Society, 1927–1934*, Chinese Res. Monograph No.13 (Berkeley, CA: Center for Chinese Studies, 1978). Particularly good for Jiangxi specifics are two works by Stephen C. Averill, 'Party, Society, and Local Elite in the Jiangxi Communist Movement', *Journal of Asian Studies*, 46/2 (May 1987), pp.279–303; and 'Local Elites and Communist Revolution in the Jiangxi Hill Country', Ch.11 in Joseph W. Esherick and Mary Backus Rankin (eds.), *Chinese Local Elites and Patterns of Dominance* (Berkeley, CA: Univ. of California Press, 1990), pp.282–304. One may also profitably consult Mao Tse-tung's own *Report From Xunwu*, released in a new edition, Roger Thompson, ed. and trans. (Stanford, CA: Stanford UP, 1990); his introduction is useful.

In dealing with the KMT counterinsurgency, no work approaches that of William Wei, *Counterrevolution in China: The Nationalists in Jiangxi During the Soviet Period* (Ann Arbor, MI: Univ. of Michigan Press, 1985). Though he incorporates his previous research into his text, his individual articles which led up to the book are worth reviewing on their merits, particularly for the insight they give into the state's response to Maoist insurgency: 'The Role of the German Advisors in the Suppression of the Central Soviet: Myth and Reality', in Bernd Martin (ed.), *The German Advisory Group in China: Military, Economic, and Political Issues in Sino-German Relations, 1927–1938* [or *Die deutsche Beraterschaft in China 1927–1938]* (Düsseldorf: Droste, 1981); 'The Guomindang's Three Parts Military and Seven Parts Politics Policy', *Asian Profile* [Hong Kong], 10/2 (April 1982), pp.111–27; 'Warlordism and Factionalism in the Guomindang's Encirclement Campaigns in Jiangxi', in *Illinois Papers in Asian Studies 1983, Pt. II: Kuomintang Development Efforts During the Nanking Decade* (Urbana, IL: Center for Asian Studies, Univ. of Illinois, 1983), pp.87–120; 'Law and Order: The Role of Guomindang Security Forces in the Suppression of the Communist Bases During the Soviet Period', Ch. 2 in Hartford and Goldstein (note 14), pp.34–61; 'Five Encirclement and Suppression Campaigns (1930–1934)', in Edwin Pak-wah Leung (ed.), *Historical Dictionary of Revolutionary China, 1839–1976* (NY: Greenwood Press, 1992), pp.121–3; and 'Insurgency by the Numbers: A Reconsideration of the Ecology of Communist Success in Jiangxi', *Small Wars and Insurgencies* [London], 5/2 (Autumn 1994), pp.201–17.

19. The debate was started by the publication of Chalmers Johnson, *Peasant Nationalism and Communist Power in China* (Berkeley, CA: Univ. of California Press, 1962). For a critique of his approach, see Donald G. Gillin, 'Review Article: "Peasant Nationalism" in the History of Chinese Communism', *Journal of Asian Studies*, 23/2 (Feb. 1964), pp.269–87. Johnson himself considers the controversy and discusses his point further in 'Peasant Nationalism Revisited: The Biography of a Book', *China Quarterly*, No. 72 (Dec. 1977), pp.766–85.

For presentation of the Yenan approach, cf. another Johnson critic, Mark Selden, *The Yenan Way in Revolutionary China* (Cambridge, MA: Harvard UP, 1971). Also useful is his earlier 'The Guerrilla Movement in Northwest China: The Origins of the Shensi-Kansu-Ninghsia Border Region', Parts I & II, *The China Quarterly*, No.28 (Oct.-Dec. 1966), I: pp.63-81; No.29 (Jan.-March 1967), II: pp.61–81. Carl E. Dorris suggests modification of the 'Yenan thesis' in his interesting 'Peasant Mobilization in North China and the Origins of Yenan Communism', *China Quarterly*, No.68 (Dec. 1976), pp.697-719.

20. An excellent work on the damage inflicted upon the KMT by the Japanese invasion is Hsi-sheng Ch'i, *Nationalist China at War* (Ann Arbor, MI: Univ. of Michigan Press, 1982). For the civil war period cf. Suzanne Pepper, *Civil War in China* (Berkeley, CA:

Univ. of California Press, 1978). Fine consideration of the KMT regime, its strengths and weaknesses, is in two works by Lloyd E. Eastman: *The Abortive Revolution: China Under Nationalist Rule, 1927–1937* (Cambridge: Harvard UP, 1974); and *Seeds of Destruction: Nationalist China in War and Revolution, 1937–1949* (Stanford, CA: Stanford UP, 1984).

21. This discussion is based principally upon *The Selected Works of Mao Tse-tung* [hereafter, SWM], 5 vols. (Peking: Foreign Languages Press, various publication dates); Stuart Schram, *Mao Tse-tung* (Middlesex, UK: Penguin Books, 1966); and Schram, *The Political Thought of Mao Tse-tung*, rev. ed. (NY: Praeger, 1976).

22. Mao: '...two contradictory things can be united and can transform themselves into each other, but in the absence of these conditions, they cannot constitute a contradiction, cannot coexist in the same entity and cannot transform themselves into each other'. See 'On Contradiction' (Aug. 1937), SWM I, pp.311–47.

23. For background see my 'The Maoist Conception of the United Front, With Particular Application to the United Front in Thailand Since October 1976', *Issues & Studies*, 16/3 (March 1980), pp.46–69.

24. Cf. Georgi Dimitroff [sic], *The United Front — The Struggle Against Fascism and War* (San Francisco, CA: Proletarian Publishers, 1975).

25. Cf. Lyman P. Van Slyke, *Enemies and Friends — The United Front in Chinese Communist History* (Stanford: Stanford UP, 1967).

26. Schram, *Mao Tse-tung* (n.21), 216.

27. Cf. Chalmers Johnson (n.19), as well as Johnson, 'The Third Generation of Guerrilla Warfare', *Asian Survey*, 8/6 (June 1978), pp.435–47.

28. 'Some Questions Concerning Methods of Leadership' (1 June 1942), SWM III, pp.117–22.

29. Cf. Rosa Luxemburg, 'Leninism or Marxism?', in William Lutz and Harry Brent (eds.), *On Revolution* (Cambridge, MA: Winthrop, 1971), pp.263–75.

30. For a complete text see Lin Piao, 'Long Live the Victory of People's War', *Peking Review*, No.32 (4 Aug. 1967), pp.14–35.

1 Maoist Miscue I: The Demise of the Communist Party of Thailand, 1965–1983

In one of the final scenes of the 1983 film 'Under Fire', Nick Nolte, as journalist Russell Price, joins in the celebration as the Sandinistas march triumphantly into Managua. To his disgust, he finds beside him a mercenary acquaintance who, throughout the film, has kept popping into his life, alternately amusing and shocking him. Price wants nothing to do with the man and makes his exit. As he does, though, the mercenary calls out after him, 'See you in Thailand'.

It is a sentiment that was shared by more than a few over the years. Early on in the Vietnam War, books began to appear with titles such as *Thailand: Another Vietnam?* and *Thailand: The War That Is, The War That Will Be* ('A first-hand report of another Vietnam in the making', read the subtitle). It was only a matter of time, such analyses predicted, before the next domino found itself wobbling. The scriptwriters for 'Under Fire' obviously agreed with them.

Still, the film barely had time to hit the theaters before Thailand had won its war with communist insurgents and was on the verge of an economic boom. Today, Bangkok is being heralded as the next 'Asian miracle'. The Communist Party of Thailand (CPT) is still around and still dreaming of the day its 'people's war' will culminate in a Marxist victory. Yet it has become a shrill voice with no audience — and a minimal number of followers willing to remain in the field.

The reasons for this stunning development have not yet been studied in detail. This is a mistake, because the Thai insurgency provides an exceptionally useful window for examining one of the more recent episodes of 'political war' to play itself out. Furthermore, since the efforts by the insurgents to 'make a revolution' were ultimately unsuccessful, there are practical as well as theoretical lessons to be learned. Ironically, in the end, it was government-led 'people's war' that ended the Maoist-inspired effort by the communists to seize state power.

Growth of the Communist Opposition to the Old-Regime

One of the few states to avoid the loss of its independence in the nineteenth/early twentieth century imperial scramble that divided up the globe, Thailand nonetheless emerged from the episode a greatly changed society. Not only was its economy integrated into the world market, but its political system, following the 1932 over-throw of the absolute monarchy, institutionalized rule by the bureaucratic elite — dominated by the military — a form of gov-ernance which has been termed a bureaucratic polity. (That is, political interplay took place within the bureaucracy itself.) In its geographic boundaries, this polity had shrunk considerably, as both the French and British had lopped off outlying areas. This lat-ter circumstance, though, was a plus, because it made the kingdom more ethnically and culturally homogenous. Thus its basic socio-cultural orientation remained traditionally Buddhist and Thai, both formally and in reality. In the kingdom there was a common thread of belief in Buddhist conceptions of life and correct con-duct, as well as agreement on the legitimacy of the established order, the old-regime, to use the phraseology of political science.

At the apex of that order was the king, who, despite having lost his position as an absolute monarch in 1932, regained, in the decades that followed, prominence in both social life and politics through his role as one who could stand above the fray and serve the interests of Thailand alone. Similarly, the notion that the Thai government ruled with the blessing of the king — even at his plea-sure — increasingly became a political fact which no coup group could ignore, the coup having become, in the post-1932 world of Bangkok, the accepted method for a change of government. To be perceived as having failed to obtain royal assent was to ensure fail-ure.

In addition to his resurgent political position, the king was for-mally the chief patron and protector of the Buddhist religion, which was represented by a vibrant order of monks (*Sangha*). The *Sangha* impacted upon all levels of Thai society, and there was scarcely a major village in the kingdom which did not have within its boundaries a *wat*, or temple, with a small group of monks in residence. The monks were an important element in the continual renewal of culture, because they comprised a transient group, moving in and out of the population. It was considered every young man's duty to spend at least a three-month period in the saffron robe.[1] Members of the *Sangha* were present at all major government functions, and the king himself engaged in activities dictated by the religion as giving strength and unity to the kingdom.

The result was to intertwine integrally religion and polity. This was not merely a formal relationship. Numerous anthropological studies found a community of belief and practice which linked all classes and groups.[2] The value structure was shared by both elites and the populace at large. Among the more central elements were a shared perception that position was a function of *merit* accumulated in past lives; that it was the duty of those more well off to share with and care for those not as well endowed (this was a major tenet of ubiquitous patron-client relationships); and that all members of the polity were at the most basic level members of a unique community linked by that which was 'Thai'.

Beliefs such as these served qualitatively to shape the impact of 'modernization' even while, structurally, conditions grew during the twentieth century which were fraught with conflict. Increasingly, as the bureaucratic polity stifled the constitutive system,[3] forces of the left offered radical solutions to issues of policy, of which there were many, ranging from increasing poverty and landlessness to lack of avenues for political participation. Ultimately, after World War II, the Communist Party of Thailand (CPT) emerged as the primary opposition to the Royal Thai Government's (RTG) socio-economic-political policies. As such it challenged the legitimacy of the Buddhist-sanctioned order.

Communism had long been viewed by the Thai government as a threat. The Russian Revolution had served as an early example of the menace of the philosophy, involving as it did regicide, attacks on religion, and assaults upon the existing order. What damned Marxism still more was its association with the Chinese immigrant problem: the earliest communist proselytism was carried out amongst the Chinese community by agents sent from China. Similarly, other communist activities involved resident foreign communities. Vietnamese communist cadre, for instance, worked amongst the Vietnamese refugee groups in the Thai northeast; and Ho Chi Minh made a secret visit to the kingdom in 1928 as the Comintern's Southeast Asia representative. For a time, in fact, when French pressure became intense during the 1931-33 period, the Vietnam Communist Party (VCP) temporarily shifted its headquarters to the Thai northeast.[4]

Still, it was a schism within the ethnic Thai community that led to the 1933 promulgation of an anti-communist statute. The over-throw of the absolute monarchy in 1932 had occurred in response to, and amidst, economic and social crisis brought on by world-wide depression. Yet the coup plotters had no coherent plan for dealing with this crisis. When Pridi Panomyong, a brilliant mem-ber of the inner coup group, produced an economic strategy that, it was claimed, advanced 'socialist' principles, he was attacked. The plan served as the catalyst for factionalism, and ultimately Pridi found it discreet to leave the country for a time. So broad was the resulting '1933 Act Concerning Communism' that all radical thought was effectively outlawed. So it was, in the years which led up to World War II, that communism was suppressed.

It was only during the worldwide struggle that Thai commun-ism was able to gather momentum. Then, fascinated by the Fascist phenomenon, the military-led regime appropriated many of the notions and trappings of the ideology — to include adoption of the name 'Thailand' in place of Siam — and formally sided with the Japanese after the kingdom was invaded by them in December 1941. The declaration was at best a half-hearted exercise, howev-er, and government officials maintained regular contact with the resistance movement led by Pridi. The communists, too, organized as the Communist Party of Siam (CPS) and the Communist Youth of Siam (CYS), participated in this resistance, though the entire business remained rather low-key. In December 1942 ethnic Chinese communists, joined by some Thai of the CPS, met in what was later called the First Party Congress. Among the various out-comes of this gathering was the formation of the party Politburo (termed at the time the 'Executive Committee').

Such was the focus of the party upon the Chinese community, that it was forced to operate as two sections, one for Chinese, the other for non-Chinese Thai. It was this 'Thai Section' that later became the Thai Communist Party (TCP). At the 1952 Second Party Congress the name was formally changed to the Communist Party of Thailand (CPT); it was there that the Maoist influence became clear. Given Mao's victory in China and the model his approach presented, this was hardly surprising. Furthermore, the CPT hierarchy, especially the Politburo and the Central

Committee, was almost exclusively Sino-Thai in ethnic composition. In the wake of the Second Congress, talk about 'liberation forces' became standard CPT fare. During the late 1950s Thai were for the first time taken out of the country for training in China, North Vietnam, and Laos.

By the Third Party Congress in 1961, the Maoists within CPT ranks were firmly in control, supporters of the Soviet Union having been banished. A formal resolution was passed which declared that armed struggle was the proper strategy for revolution in Thailand. Plans were laid to implement the resolution. These included the 1962 establishment of a Northeast Region Jungle Headquarters, together with front organizations to support the guerrilla forces, such as the Farmer's Liberation Association. The clandestine CPT radio, 'Voice of the People of Thailand' (VOPT), also began broadcasting in 1962, and, virtually until the end of the insurgency, would serve as a principal means for dissemination of party directives and theory. In 1963 VOPT commenced issuing CPT statements designed to foster the impression that a budding united front (a key component of the Maoist approach) was forming. The first clash between government and CPT forces occurred in the northeast on 7 August 1965, subsequently celebrated annually by the CPT as 'Gun Firing Day'.

The insurgency grew in step with the war in Vietnam. Indeed, Bangkok was so concerned with the strategic threat that it committed major forces to ground combat in both Laos and South Vietnam, with smaller numbers seeing covert action in Cambodia. In Thailand, conflict was centered in three major areas: the northeast, north, and south. Each of these areas possessed local features that fostered unrest. Throughout the history of the insurgency, though, the northeast was to remain the primary area of conflict, because CPT campaigns in the north and south attracted mainly ethnic minorities who did not pose the same threat to the government as did action among the Thai-*Isan* of the northeast. Significantly, while the government viewed the insurgency as an integral part of China's strategy for 'liberating' Southeast Asia — and North Vietnam as an instrument to that end — the thrust behind the CPT, whatever the region, in reality originated from within the kingdom itself, in those 'internal contradictions' which existed. Most of the rank and file individuals involved were not communists, therefore, but rather persons who for a variety of reasons were alienated from the existing system. Government repression was the CPT's best recruiting tool.

Of importance in considering these three main areas of conflict was the fact that little evidence could be found of coordination or even liaison between them below the strategic level. That geography played a role in this was undoubtedly so; but the inability of the CPT to surmount obstacles to unified effort led to an ever-expanding reliance for support upon external sources and a constant danger of degeneration from indigeneously-supported insurgency to externally-supported partisan warfare.[5]

Yet initially external links were salutary. The CPT's longstanding ties with the stronger communist parties in the region gave it access not only to the usual training and propaganda assistance but also to the formal mechanisms of support developed to fuel the 'liberation' of Indochina. Of these, the most important was the western portion of the Ho Chi Minh Trail system under the auspices of the 35th PL/95th NVA [Pathet Lao/North Vietnamese Army] Combined Command. Apparently already in existence by 1961–62, this logistics network had possibly been constructed as early as the end of World War II. Its expansion went on simultaneously with the improvement of the main routes of the Ho Chi Minh Trail dedicated to the support of operations in South Vietnam.

Nevertheless, their common purpose notwithstanding, neither the Chinese nor the Vietnamese/Lao were willing to allow the other to encroach into their self-proclaimed spheres of influence. The 35th PL/95th NVA Combined Command, for instance, served the northeastern insurgency, while the conflict in the north was supplied by the Chinese using World War II-era infiltration routes and a newly constructed road network in northern Laos (see Map 1).[6] Regular troops of both sides were so positioned as to stake out their preserves. The south was so far away that it was all but forced to become self-reliant and so remained something of a backwater throughout most of the insurgency. In the main theaters of operation, the north and the northeast, the Sino-Vietnamese rivalry limited the amount of support which reached the CPT and hampered its coordination efforts within Thailand itself.

Thus the growth and intensity of the insurgency were in many respects dependent upon the machinations of these outside supporters, because 'in-country' the communists consistently failed to achieve inroads — among the lowland population of the kingdom's central core — capable of making the movement self-suffi-

MAP 1: COMMUNIST BASES AND SUPPLY ROUTES, THAILAND 1965–1979

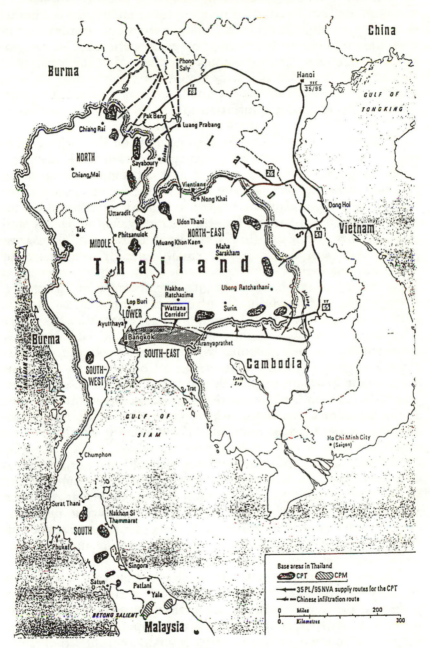

Sources: See Chapter 1 endnote 6 (page 75).

cient. By 1970 internal sources, in fact, were incapable of meeting minimum logistics needs, and, from that date, external sources of weaponry predominated in the CPT supply system.[7] Obviously, the revolutionary conjuncture posited by communist doctrine as necessary for the overthrow of the government had yet to arrive.

Construction of the CPT Infrastructure

This lack of absolute success did not mean the CPT insurgency was not a relative threat. To emphasize a point: The CPT had long sought to engage in revolutionary action and finally did so in the post-World War II years. Maoist 'people's war' was adopted as its strategy. In this conception the greater military power of the state was to be negated by mobilizing the people against it. This was to be done through the creation, using insurgency, of an alternative political organization which eventually would become strong enough to contend directly for power.

Power, then, was the strategic goal of the insurgents. Tactically, this was sought through local guerrilla operations that challenged government control of specific areas. Operationally, the link between the two was a political infrastructure. Indeed, the principal purpose of insurgent armed force was to protect and to facilitate the expansion of this infrastructure. Conversely, for the Thai government seeking to retain state power, to combat revolutionary warfare was to combat the insurgent infrastructure — those mechanisms whereby the populace was organized in an alternative polity (first, as a 'shadow government', eventually, as a 'liberated zone').

Where there is mobilization, in other words, there can be countermobilization. Hence, we have insurgency and counterinsurgency. Neither springs full blown from the circumstances. Both must be painstakingly constructed. As concerns the insurgent effort, we are faced with the classic analyst's riddle: have societal causes produced activism, or has activism taken advantage of societal causes? Opponents of the status quo normally opt for the former, proponents for the latter. In a sense, the query itself is irrelevant, and the distinction in causation need not be made: the two processes are complementary rather than mutually exclusive. As James Scott has perceptively noted,[8] all insurgent movements necessarily contain two elements: leadership ranks comprised of members drawn from society's elite, followers taken from the masses. The same 'causes' motivate them but in very different ways. The leadership normally perceives injustice and attempts to deal with it by ideological solution. The followers, in contrast, who historically have been drawn overwhelmingly from the peasantry,[9] attempt to deal with injustice by correcting those immediate wrongs that are identified.

Insurgent movements, therefore, involve a continuous process whereby the two elements, the leadership and the followers, establish links and interact with each other. Societal causes are a necessary but not sufficient factor for the insurgency. First, the causes must lead to the alienation of both potential leadership and potential insurgent manpower. Second, the two must establish a relationship. Only when this has been accomplished does a potential insurgency exist. But there is a constant tension present. If the ideological approach of the leadership is able to hold sway, insurgency will result. The movement will go on to pursue political goals, normally the effort to remake the system (i.e., to make a revolution). If, however, the resolution of immediate grievances wins out, as normally desired by the manpower, then rebellion will result.[10]

Scale is important in this process, as is the changing relationship over time between three elements: terror, recruitment, and infrastructure. The more vast a country, particularly its rural areas, the more marginal areas there are in which revolutionary political activity can operate with minimal fear of government intervention. The effect of this physical space is often magnified by the 'political space' created through government miscues or omissions. As time goes on, and the infrastructure becomes more established, often using terror to stifle opposition, the original grievances assume less importance. Instead, the mechanisms of organization become paramount. At one extreme, potential recruits see the movement as a viable alternative for social participation; at the other, they simply recognize that it, effectively, has become the state and thus must be obeyed. It socializes and controls.

As with all organizations, the CPT had to have a beginning. Its foreign origins have already been noted — it was an ethnic Chinese and Vietnamese creation. Party members were not originally targeted against Thai society but sent to raise funds amongst their ethnic compatriots for the liberation movement in the motherland. Consequently, the CPT was from its inception very much attuned to the strategic designs of other regional communist parties. It remained so-oriented throughout the struggle. Its Secretary General at the time hostilities broke out (1965), in fact, Thong Chaemsiri, was a Thai-Vietnamese who had come to the kingdom as a refugee from North Vietnam in 1930s. When he was arrested in 1968 (he was later released in 1974 and rejoined the Politburo), his place was taken by Charoen Wanngarm, a Chinese who immigrated to Thailand in the years just before World War II.[11] Four other members of the seven-man ruling Politburo — Deputy Secretary General Wirat Angkathavorn, Song Nopakhun, Udom Srisuwan, and Damri Ruangsutham — were also Sino-Thai.[12] All came from what we may term elite backgrounds. Charoen, for example, first joined the CPT in 1945 and then worked for two years on the editorial board of *Mahachon*, a Bangkok socialist newspaper.[13] Similarly, Udom first gained notoriety as a writer for the economic newspaper *Sethisarn*, 'whose articles served to inspire activists and intellectuals of the period'.[14]

Though some of these top-ranking CPT figures joined the party in the post- World War II years — Udom, for instance, was arrested and held without trial during a 1958 roundup of communist suspects; he did not flee into the jungle until his release seven years later — it was the war and the anti-Japanese resistance that provided the political space for the CPT to emerge from the shadows. Too much should not be made of the party's wartime resistance activity. Thadeus Flood, for example, claims a massive organization supported by widespread popular mobilization,[15] a contention few scholars would support. Still, the foundations for later expansion were laid.

Developments in Trang and Phatthalung Provinces in the south were typical.[16] Following the First Party Congress in December 1942, the CPT (though it had not yet adopted the title) mobilized Sino-Thai for work against the Japanese. When the fighting ended, some of these individuals remained with the party's forces, which then set about expanding. In Trang, for example, particular organizational efforts were carried out in Muang, Kantang, and Palian Districts. These included the abortive formation of a labor union (later ordered by the party to disband) and of a farmers' association, as well as having a party member openly stand as a parliamentary candidate in the 1957 general elections (he was not elected). Significantly, in this two-province effort, several personalities were active who in later years would become important CPT figures, notably Wirat Angkathavorn, future Deputy Secretary-

General.

Following the 1961 decision of the Third Party Congress to opt for 'people's war', additional cadre were sent to the rural areas with instructions to develop further the covert infrastructure; others left for training in North Vietnam. As proselytizing bore fruit, the CPT established three camps: North (07 Area), further divided into two sites, Rai Mai Camp and Khao Kaeo Camp; Central (09 Area); and South (08 Area). Their actual locations changed frequently, to avoid detection, but manpower grew steadily from the initial batch of 16 persons who were housed at the Central Camp after fleeing into the jungle to avoid government actions. Ultimately, strength apparently reached nearly 500.

So it went throughout peripheral areas of the kingdom: the north, northeast, and south. Though not particularly large, neither was the kingdom small. Its 514,000 sq. km. (198,500 sq. miles) and 28 million population (1962) put it in the same league with a unified Vietnam (Thailand was smaller in population but larger in area), which ultimately absorbed a very considerable war. As a tool for CPT expansion, terror was an essential ingredient, but it was selective, generally aimed at recalcitrant villagers or symbols of government authority (e.g., village headmen and schoolteachers). Appeal to grievances was the linchpin of the CPT approach. Consequently, as might be expected, CPT activity was concentrated in areas of rural poverty and political estrangement, above all in the northeast.

That the northeast was susceptible to revolutionary action was due to economic, cultural, and political characteristics which distinguished it from the other regions of Thailand.[17] It was the kingdom's largest and most populous yet poorest area, a fact owing principally to the physical environment. The carrying capacity of the land was so minimal as to make even subsistence agriculture a haphazard operation.[18] As a result, though most northeasterners were owner-operators,[19] poverty was the norm. Per capita income was substantially less than the rest of Thailand.[20] Debt, generally in the form of credit accounts, was widespread, and at least one survey found that annual living expenses for an average family regularly exceeded available resources.[21]

Isan (or *Isaan* or *Isarn*) was also culturally distinct from Thailand's other regions. It was Thai-Lao in orientation, even though the population was far from homogeneous. Northeasterners thought of themselves as part of the Thai king-

dom and looked to Bangkok as the locus of a Thai culture which
in some respects, surveys showed, they regarded as superior to
their own. Yet they retained their sense of regional identity and
local pride.[22] This recognition by northeasterners of their region as
a unique entity manifested itself in the political arena.
Consolidation of national control by Bangkok was only achieved
during the reign of King Chulalongkorn (r.1868–1910). This led
to the imposition of central officials and brief uprisings of a millenarian nature. The creation of a parliament following the overthrow of the absolute monarchy in 1932 presented a forum for the
expression of regional concerns by members of the displaced traditional northeastern aristocracies, as well as by other *Isan* politicians. They quickly established a reputation as an opposition group
with 'leftist' leanings, a stance which led to their repression by the
ruling powers after Phibun Songkhram's conservative regime
established itself in April 1948. In the 'Kilo 11 Incident' (March
1949) four prominent northeastern politicians were assassinated.

> In the subsequent period these four men became symbols of growing
> sentiments shared by a large part of the northeastern populace that
> they were discriminated against as a whole by the Central Thai and
> the central government. The death of these prominent northeastern
> leaders was a major catalyst in the development of Isan regional polit-
> ical identity and purpose for it demonstrated most dramatically the
> attitudes of the central government towards those who were identified
> with Isan political aspirations. In addition, however, Northeasterners
> also began to feel that Central Thai political discrimination was but a
> symptom of more basic economic and cultural discrimination. In the
> next decade these feelings of economic, political, and cultural dis-
> crimination were fired even more as a larger number of
> Northeasterners had increased contact with Central Thai.[23]

Even with the threat of violence in the air, emerging northeastern regional identity could not be stilled. Northeastern members of
parliament 'continually raised the charge of economic discrimina-
tion of the government against the [n]ortheast.'[24] In April 1958 all
northeastern MPs in the pro-government party presented a set of
four demands[25] which they urged be acted upon within 15 days. If
these were not met, they announced that they would bolt the
group and form a separate Northeast Party in collusion with northeastern leftist MPs. The demands were not met, and no *Isan* party
resulted, but the attempt added to government fears of growing

regional identity. The fact that the radical movement in the kingdom at the time was predominantly a northeastern product,
together with the active role played by northeastern delegates in
fostering neutralist sentiments,[26] caused the ruling elite to look
with jaundiced eye at regional demands.

> Officials in the government close to General Sarit [military comman-
> der-in-chief and later prime minister] viewed the pressures exerted
> primarily by northeastern representatives, for 'socialistic' programs to
> improve the economic position of the Northeast, for greater tolera-
> tion of leftist political action within the country, and for a neutral for-
> eign policy with grave apprehension. They were beginning to feel that
> if given free rein the activities of the northeastern MPs could serious-
> ly threaten the security of Thailand. There was a growing awareness
> among these government leaders of the need to deal with what they
> considered a 'northeastern problem'. After Sarit inaugurated a new
> period of military rule in late 1958 [he was to rule until his death in
> December 1963] this 'problem' and its 'solutions' were to become a
> major preoccupation of the Thai government.[27]

The 'northeastern problem' was of particular concern to Thai
policymakers when it was considered within the context of other
events in Southeast Asia. Thai foreign policy during this period
was predicated largely upon an analysis of how best to safeguard
Thailand's security in the face of a perceived dual threat of communist aggression and subversion. The Laotian Crisis of 1959-61,
which involved people with whom *Isan* inhabitants had close affil-
iations, together with the growing conflict in South Vietnam,
heightened fears that northeastern political dissent was part of a
larger communist-led conspiracy to detach the northeast from the
kingdom and to threaten the government. Thus Bangkok moved
directly against the threat. and in 1958-62 those labelled as communists were suppressed.[28] In such an atmosphere many opposition figures, particularly in the northeast, went underground and
linked up with the covert apparatus of the CPT.

The CPT, as we have already seen, had long been active in the
northeast. The activities of the Vietnamese community have been
recounted. As early as 1936, for instance, the communists, many
of them Vietnamese, had paraded openly in Khon Kaen Province;
and during 1949-52 cadres were sent by the CPT to the northeast
to proselytize. With cadres having already been sent abroad for
training in the late 1950s, and with the network of the 35th

PL/95th NVA Combined Command in place to provide logistics support for insurgent action, it was logical that it was the northeast chosen for the 'jungle headquarters' established in response to the Third Party Congress announcement that armed struggle was the proper strategy for liberation. Despite such preparation, the CPT's Sino-Thai elite remained relatively isolated until the political events detailed above offered up the manpower it needed to form a viable movement.

A key incident was the execution, on 31 May 1961, of Krong Chandawong, a longtime northeast activist.[29] A former underground leader in the northeast during World War II, and later a respected MP, Krong had thrice been arrested for alleged subversive activities in the years following the war. His efforts to have parliament repeal the Anti-Communist Act and to adopt a neutralist foreign policy aroused the ire of authorities, but apparently he sealed his doom when he founded the *Samaki Tham* (United in Dharma) movement, 'a loose grassroots organisation [*sic*] to promote self-help and development among northeastern villages'. Viewing the organization as a communist front, the authorities had him arrested and executed, together with another northeast activist, by a police firing squad. An estimated 200 members of the *Samaki Tham* were also seized.

This action had predictable consequences. Hundreds of supporters fled and joined the only viable force capable of resisting the repression, the CPT. Among these fugitives were Krong's children, one of whom, his daughter Kruankhrong, became something of a revolutionary cult figure under the alias 'Rassamee'. Though she actually was a medic rather than a guerrilla fighter as portrayed in propaganda, two of her brothers did rise to provincial-level positions in the insurgent organization (much later they were to surrender to the government).

It was the political space created by repression, then, that allowed the CPT to tap the latent grievances already present as a result of social and ecological realities.[30] To focus the resulting outburst, the CPT constructed an infrastructure which followed standard Leninist lines. At the apex was the seven-man Politburo (Political Bureau). It purportedly represented a 25-man Central Committee (insurgent movements are actually constructed from top down, not the other way around, so those in the lower organ have normally been selected by those in the higher). Central Committee members performed various staff functions, among the most important being overseeing the military apparatus and attempting to build a united front as called for by Maoist ideological thought. Additionally, they often served as heads of Party Provincial (*changwad*) Committees. These oversaw CPT District (*amphoe*) Committees that, in turn, guided 'township' (*tambol*) and village (*muban* or *ban*) party structures. The precise combination of these elements at any particular time was problematical. Villages and hamlets, of course, were particular social and physical entities, but CPT 'districts' and 'provinces' frequently did not correspond to their government equivalents. More often than not, the most standard nomenclature for identifying a particular area of CPT activity was to designate it a 'zone'. As such, a zone could embrace anything from a village to a province.[31]

This structure was a political entity. Its purpose was to further the communist goal of revolution. Robert F. Zimmerman, a US official with long experience in Thailand, has provided a good look at its basic component, the village:

> The party's greatest strength...lies in its elaborate organization at the village level in those areas where Communist insurgents are strongly entrenched. An excellent illustration of this organization at its best is the infrastructure that existed in Ban Nakham village, Ubon Ratchathani Province, in 1966. Although government Communist suppression operations destroyed this infrastructure, there is little reason to doubt that it remains typical of Communist practice in areas where the insurgents are in control. The Ban Nakham village organization was headed by a village committee consisting of a chairman, two assistant chairmen, and four other members, with one of the assistant chairmen and the four ordinary members responsible for directing the activities of eight specialized committees of 15-30 members dealing with such matters as youth and military affairs, political propaganda, labor and business, women's affairs, etc. This structure functioned within the village but was responsible to a 'zone commander' and two assistant commanders based in the jungle. Through this apparatus operating at the local level, the Communists have been able not only to recruit and motivate active adherents but also to mobilize sufficient popular support in the major insurgent areas to generate sources of manpower, food, shelter, and finances (in part through local tax levies), and to develop an effective intelligence network. They have also benefited from a certain amount of illicit 'assistance' in the form of accommodation or even bribes offered by government officials or by private construction firms engaged in building roads into the insurgent areas...[32]

How extensive this infrastructure became is reported by another US official, former CIA officer Ralph W. McGehee:

> Using all the index cards and files, I wrote a final report. I prepared name lists of all cell members, including their aliases, by village. In this district the list contained the names of more than 500 persons. Those 500 persons did not appear anywhere in the Agency reporting at the time. The CIA estimated there were 2,500 to 4,000 Communists in all of Thailand. But our surveys showed the Communists probably had that many adherents in Sakorn Nakorn Province alone.[33]

Though not discussed in McGehee's work, it appears he and his superiors were attempting to compare apples and oranges. The 2,500-4,000 figure would seem to be the then-current estimate of armed guerrillas, while the 500 individuals in the district in question were part of the mass base. To wit, as a village came under control of the CPT 'shadow government', its mobilization included providing manpower for a militia. The best members of this body joined the actual guerrillas in the CPT's base areas, located in inaccessible areas. Thus, at any given time, the actual number of individuals involved in the movement far outnumbered those bearing arms. These arms, it must be added, according to the romantic vision of the guerrilla put forth in much literature, were to come from the government itself, captured mainly in raids and combat. But as we have already noted, a significant proportion of CPT weapons and equipment came from foreign communist sources.

Nevertheless, with supplies and training from abroad used to outfit manpower thrown up by repression at home, the CPT was able to expand steadily. By the early 1970s, a majority of the provinces in the kingdom had been classified as 'infiltrated', meaning some sort of CPT activity was present.[34] Still, this activity remained confined to areas outside the heartland, beyond the central plain which was the social, economic, and political locus of Thailand. Penetration there would have to wait for later events.

Government Response to the CPT[35]

As we would expect in a polity wherein coercive power had created the political space for insurgency, the Thai government during these early years responded to the CPT challenge in an inappropriate fashion. True, in December 1965, the highest levels of the Thai military government moved to deal with the communist problem by ordering the formation of the Communist Suppression Operations Command (CSOC), later to become the Internal Security Operations Command (ISOC). And, true, they placed in charge of it a respected officer who had a background that included covert operations in Laos against the communists, Saiyud Kerdphol. But what the powers-that-be had in mind was better management of the anti-guerrilla campaign, not counterinsurgency.

Saiyud has observed:

> The RTA [Royal Thai Army] then was run by 'the old school', the pre-World War II officers. They had tremendous difficulty understanding counterinsurgency, rebellion, and the fundamental causes which fed revolt. Praphas [former Deputy Prime Minister and the 'muscle' behind the government which ultimately fell in 1973], for example, named CSOC the 'suppression command'. He could understand that the fight had to be coordinated — that's why he set up CSOC — but he wasn't talking about CPM [civil-police-military; essentially the coordinated application of all resources to the insurgent problem, as done by the British to defeat the communists in Malaya during the Emergency]. The younger generation of officers, though, at least some of them, were more attuned to reality. Among them was Prem [later Prime Minister].
>
> We understood that what we were dealing with was a political problem. We applied CPM to the problems of the northeast, yet we knew more was needed than simply a response. Coordination is the key to winning, but all must look at the problem through the same eyes. You need a common blueprint upon which to base the plan.
>
> Two things were obvious: there was nothing worse than to fight the wrong way, and the key is the people. We had to ask ourselves, why do the people have a problem, why are they taking up arms? We did a lot of mechanical things, such as setting up Village Defence Corps and special training centers through which we could run all regular companies. The crucial point, though, more than numbers, is orientation. You have to keep analyzing a target area. You have to keep asking yourself, 'What are the reasons for popular discontent? What are the problems?' Figure out the solutions, then implement and coordinate.[36]

Saiyud's conception was that CSOC would do this. To establish the nature of the problems, he did two things. First, an intelligence analysis center was set up with branches in the field. Copies of all government reports (and any other data which could be gathered up) were fed into the system, then analyzed with the aid of borrowed computer time, a novel methodology for Thailand at the time. This allowed typical bureaucratic misstatement and inaccuracy to be weeded out and a definitive assessment of the problem to be distributed. Second, an extensive research and analysis branch began to function under the brilliant and at-times controversial scholar Somchai Rakwijit. It soon produced comprehensive assessments based upon sound data. In particular, it sent researchers into the field, often alone, to conduct studies of insurgent-infested areas.

Using this data, Saiyud directed his response, a mix of civil and military measures. It was classic counterinsurgency, the sort of approach textbooks outline: identify the problem; move in with solutions using the military to shield the effort; send specially trained forces to harry and kill the guerrillas. In retrospect, it seems a logical enough strategy. Yet it encountered considerable difficulties. CSOC was at first given command authority only over the small CPM task forces deployed to insurgent-affected areas. Guided by a comprehensive intelligence network set up by Saiyud, these began to show promise by 1967 in uncovering and dealing with the CPT infrastructure. But when CSOC asked for more units, military opponents, jealously guarding their own turfs, demurred. Hence, authority over field units was transferred back to regional army commanders. Thereafter, the counterinsurgency program became largely ineffective. Most commanders simply did not deploy their forces in what was viewed as a secondary mission. Instead, they concentrated upon political and economic concerns. When called upon to actually move against insurgent forces, they did so in military fashion, 'search and destroy'.

Nowhere was this more obvious than in the north. There, land quarrels in Chiangrai and Nan Provinces between H'mong tribesmen and Thai exacerbated longstanding lowlander-hill dweller tensions. December 1967 saw the beginning of a series of incidents, first in Tung Chang District of Nan Province, later in Chiang Kam and Terng Districts of Chiangrai Province, as well as Mae Sod District of Tak Province. Others occurred in the three provinces of Petchabul, Loei, and Phitsanulok.[37] Initial Thai response was heavy-handed and succeeded primarily in making enemies. The security forces responded to ambushes with artillery and air strikes, which destroyed villages and threw still more recruits to the insurgents. A flood of refugees resulted, and the economy of a large area in the north was completely destroyed.[38] Attempts by more enlightened officials to adopt alternative means of addressing the problem were mired in red tape and lacked resources.

Realizing the inappropriateness of suppression, Saiyud fought to implement his CPM strategy. As detailed in his manuscript, *The Struggle for Thailand, Section II, A Solution for the North*, Saiyud saw counterinsurgency among the hill tribes as consisting of three stages. In Stage 1 development would take place in an attempt to ward off attempted subversion. This failing, Stage 2, suppression, would begin. Once Stage 2 had been handled correctly, Stage 3, rehabilitation, could occur. The key, though, as Saiyud pointed out, was the development activities of Stage 1.[39]

Saiyud's approach was not accepted by key government officials. Consequently, little came of it. 'Body count' remained the order of the day throughout the 1960s. The heavy-handed (and, in many cases, ham-handed) official approach only increased the ability of the insurgents to recruit. As the number of villages destroyed grew, so, too, did the number of guerrillas. Some CPT propaganda sessions reportedly involved as many as 200 armed guerrillas. Though its strength in the north was only an estimated 3,000 by 1973, the guerrilla movement managed to make life there extremely unsettled in many areas.[40]

Pointless 'search and destroy' culminated in January 1972 when some 12,000 security forces personnel engaged in Operation *Phu Kwang*, the biggest such exercise ever conducted in Thailand. Its aim was to dislodge several hundred H'mong based in the rugged Tri-Province area (Vietnam had its Parrot's Beak threatening Saigon; Thailand had a Laotian equivalent bordered by three Thai provinces and pointing like a dagger towards the central Thai heartland). The operation ended after some two months, with nothing to show for its efforts except 60 troops dead and another 200 wounded, virtually all to booby traps. Most of the insurgents monitored the operation from Laos, to which they had withdrawn as the logistical buildup for the large maneuver became obvious months ahead of time. Once the assault ended, they reinfiltrated into Thailand.[41]

This remained the general pattern of events. Although many Thai appeared to comprehend the socio-economic nature of the northern insurgency, the government response was such as to ensure its failure. At the root of the problem lay the fact that the target population, the H'mong, was not comprised of ethnic Thai. Hence, its members were treated as second-class citizens by many, if not most, Thai. There were few qualms felt in the use of force against a 'non-Thai' population in revolt against the legal government. The racial attitudes carried by the average Thai soldier were difficult to overcome and frequently translated into hostile actions against the population. Suppression thus became a double-edged sword.

The CPT was able to use this sword. As one former H'mong insurgent recounts:

> The communists were Miao [the Thai term for the H'mong, still much in current use], though some cadre were Thai. Some people wanted to resist them, but the army policy then was that the Miao should not be trained in weapons, only development. But the communists took some young Miao and trained them to use arms. Then the BPP [Border Patrol Police] had conflict with young Miao, especially over girls. The communists took those who had conflicts with the BPP and trained them. They then sent them back to attack. The communists came and burned the school down and established themselves. Those Miao associated with foreigners or the government had to leave to seek safety.[42]

Safety, too, was a prime concern in motivating many such as Nuyua Sayang (age unknown) to join the communists:

> I was just a member of the mass base. The communists said they could give us better lives. The young men believed them, but the old men didn't. Safety was the prime factor [why we joined]. People sided with whomever they thought could guard them. You just try to go on with your life.[43]

Reflecting what it was that led some young to throw in their lot with a movement committed to attacking the government, certainly a dangerous undertaking, Laopao Sasong, 40 years of age and a CPT village militia member for more than a decade before his surrender, observes, 'I joined because the communist propaganda said if they liberated the country, every race would be treated equally.'[44]

Here we see a variety of motives but all culminating in the individuals concerned becoming a part of the CPT infrastructure. Once inducted, new members could gradually work their way up to higher positions. Yet in its infancy, the insurgency followed the

classic leader-follower division outlined by Scott. It was the struc-
turing of grievance through the infrastructure that channeled anger
in support of the effort to make a revolution.

Certainly the H'mong status as a minority group influenced
Thai behavior in its efforts to put down rebellion. Still, military
action in the north was not dissimilar to that undertaken elsewhere
in the kingdom. For the first decade of the declared insurgency,
force remained the principal methodology for dealing with the
CPT's political movement. It is noteworthy, however, how contingent support was for the insurgents in those areas where the CPT
was active. Villager loyalty, regardless of structural conditions, was
very much 'up for grabs'. Significantly, most Thai, unless traumatized by specific grievances, preferred to side with the status quo.
In fact, in 1966-67 Saiyud was instrumental in forming the
Volunteer Defence Corps — effectively, village militia. These had
no trouble gaining recruits and grew rapidly. Initially limited to
their local areas, they eventually evolved into more mobile combat
forces. As might be predicted, they were highly effective, because
they knew their areas. Ultimately, they became what in English is
normally rendered as 'Rangers'. The communists would have
called them 'regional forces'. They were to be the units which
broke the military back of the insurgency.

An Alternative Approach

All of this was to come in the future. During the period under consideration here, military action continued to be in the main conducted by regular forces. Nevertheless, military measures were not
the entirety of the government approach. Particularly in the northeast, where the target population, though technically non-Thai was
nonetheless regarded as 'Thai', there were efforts, pushed through
by individuals such as Saiyud, to meet the popular needs through
regional development. Paradoxically, while repression was directed against those perceived as security threats and served to swell
insurgent ranks, simultaneously a 'hearts and minds' campaign was
in effect. Publicly, at least, Bangkok was under no illusions concerning conditions in the countryside and acknowledged that the
rural masses continued to live in poverty.[45] Consequently, even
before the actual outbreak of violence, development programs had
already been begun during the early and mid-1950s. By 1958 this

approach had been broadened and included the first Community Development pilot projects.

In 1960 a National Community Development Program was put into effect, consolidating many of the already existing programs, which were scattered among various departments. According to government literature,[46] the program was designed to bring about the partnership of the Thai government and its people at the local level. Further, it aimed 'to encourage the people to exercise initiative to improve their communities and ways of living through cooperative efforts on the self-help basis' and to 'bring the coordinated support of the various ministries concerned to assist the villagers in carrying out their projects'.[47] By the end of 1961, at least on paper, most northeastern villages were covered by the program — even, it should be noted, as repression sent activists fleeing to the CPT for protection.

Indeed, while National Community Development was directed at villages throughout the kingdom, specific measures to deal with the northeast were also implemented. A Northeastern Committee was created in the National Economic Development Board of the Prime Minister's Office in 1961, and an independent regional development plan was promulgated.[48] Much of the proposed $300 million in plan expenditures was to be provided by the US. These development efforts in the northeast were both reaction to events — calls for redistribution of resources — and an attempt to ward off an even more undesirable event — the outbreak of violence should grievances be left unsatisfied. Some sort of violence was, in any case, expected, since the CPT was known to be working towards that end. In the period prior to the actual outbreak of guerrilla warfare in 1965, the government continued to broaden its rural development programs, proceeding on the theory that advancing the people's economic welfare would gradually eliminate grievances, thereby removing the objective conditions of poverty which could be exploited by the CPT. This effort was facilitated by the US, which had established an economic aid mission to the kingdom in 1950.[49]

The principal vehicle for American assistance in this field was the Accelerated Rural Development (ARD) scheme. Provinces selected for ARD were to be those most in need of immediate developmental help, which, in practice, meant those threatened by communist insurgency as so-designated by the National Security Council (NSC). Once a *changwad* was designated an 'ARD province' by the NSC, the staff and equipment available to the governor were augmented. ARD created, trained, and equipped a local organization with the capability of planning, designing, constructing, and maintaining rural roads and other small village projects. Simultaneously, steps were taken at the national level to give the governor authority to implement village level projects on his own initiative without constant referral to higher authorities in Bangkok for approval.[50]

By 1969 the governors of the 24 ARD-designated provinces, most of them in the northeast, had progressed from a point where they had virtually no resources with which to mount any type of development program to one where they had staffs of some 250, millions of dollars worth of equipment, and a vastly increased budget. The government had committed a cumulative total of $58,824,000 to the program, supplemented by $49,308,000 from the US. The manner in which these funds were expended, it should be noted, reflected economic priorities — road building and maintenance were the dominant categories. Other ARD activities included mobile medical teams, district farmer groups (cooperatives), and youth and potable water programs.

Results of the ARD program as judged in 1969 were mixed. Though physically and statistically there was a great deal of progress to show, the ultimate objective was to 'reduce — or even to eliminate — insurgency through the development effort'.[51] This did not happen. To the contrary, American and Thai evaluations consistently noted that ARD made no meaningful difference in the disposition of the target population,[52] despite the fact that the actual activities involved were generally used and appreciated. Even where there was a demonstrated improvement in the lot of the villagers in an area, as measured by a classic indicator such as increase in per capita income, the rosy statistical picture often did not reflect the poor realities of the security situation. Only certain groups benefited from the increased contacts with market mechanisms; but examination of even those who had actually profited from development showed there was no apparent change in orientation towards the government or the communists. In fact a Cornell University report confirmed a phenomenon which had already been observed by some American officials: namely, that there appeared to be a strong association between rate of structural growth and incidence of insurgent activities.[53]

Thus ARD had failed to achieve a great deal towards realizing its objectives. What did emerge time and again from the official analyses of the program was that northeasterners were loyal Thai in their orientations and were both concerned with the problems of survival and fearful of an abstract menace called 'communism'. They responded well to efforts to integrate them into the processes of decision making and development, but these efforts remained so limited in scope as to have little real impact upon their situation.

That the ARD program did not reach its goals was not surprising. For it was an economic response to a political problem. It was simply one facet of a unidimensional Thai approach to development. That approach attempted to address the grievances which had resulted in political warfare through a strategy emphasizing economic concerns. This was as predictable as it was ineffective. What the communists were after was a restructuring of the existing systems of social stratification through seizure of state power. That violence was their vehicle resulted from their inability to utilize peaceful means to accomplish their ends. This they could not even hope for, because they were frozen out of the political system. So, too, were most others who sought to change the system from within. Unless willing to be co-opted by the government, they had no choice but to sit on the sidelines or to join the insurgents. There were no other viable opposition groups.

The solution to such a structural dilemma, then, should have been political development. Yet this Bangkok could not see. The emphasis upon maximization of economic growth had been inculcated in the Thai elite through a long process of exposure to and assimilation of Western development ideals. Thailand's pre-1932 absolute monarchs, particularly Mongkut and Chulalongkorn, chose to advance the kingdom by methods and in a fashion of their own choosing, but always their conception of 'modern' focused on economic advances. Even after the monarchy became constitutional in form, there was little political development, because power devolved to the authoritarian structures of the bureaucratic polity rather than to any form of constitutive system. Thus Thai development notions continued to maximize economic growth to the virtual exclusion of all other forms, notably and particularly political. This emphasis was widely noted at the time in the appropriate literature.[54]

Under these circumstances, the logical government course of action, when faced with unrest in an underdeveloped region such as the northeast, would be that which was carried out: to attack the economic dimensions of the problem. Examination of ARD objectives shows this to have been the government's course of action. Though political development receives mention, this aspect of the program was completely overshadowed by economic factors, such as infrastructure development. The skewing of goals was reflected in the indecisive ARD results.

The argument is frequently made, and its implications of cultural chauvinism all too often not appreciated, that Thai actions in the post-World War II era were taken solely at the behest or instigation of American containment policy.[55] Such a view is simplistic. Certainly the US presence and influence in Thailand were significant. Yet Thailand's collaboration with the US during the period under examination represented a marriage of convenience, driven by a shared security perspective, whereby both states sought to maximize their gains. When the partnership's drawbacks came to overshadow its advantages, the Thai backed away from the more overt forms of collaboration. In the arena of counterinsurgency, there is no question but that the Thai authorities were influenced by American, and also Western (especially British), concepts, but not in the military tactical aspects so frequently highlighted in the literature (e.g., 'search and destroy'). These were almost incidental to the heart of the problem, which was misguided strategic focus.

The growth of American attitudes towards, and capacity for fighting, limited wars was a prominent feature of the Kennedy presidency.[56] It went hand-in-glove with the foreign aid rationale that 'development' was to be equated with Western-style economic modernization and would result in maximization of national potential and domestic peace.[57] Due to historical circumstances mentioned above, the Thai accepted this orientation. To attribute such acceptance solely, or even mainly, to American insistence is inaccurate. The process was far more unwitting on both sides. There were, after all, alternative counterinsurgency models available at the time, but Bangkok opted for that used by its allies, the West. Western doctrine, though, posited three essential tasks for successful resolution of revolt: (a) military operations against the insurgents; (b) population and resources control; and (c) elimination of grievances.[58] Thus, within an economically dominated 'development' strategy, the elimination of grievances naturally emphasized the provision of resources and resolution of economic complaints, rather than elimination of other forms of dissatisfaction, such as weaknesses of the political system. This accurately describes the role — and fate — of ARD, wherein goals such as 'roads built' and 'wells dug' quickly overshadowed the more abstract objectives, among them fostering popular participation in the political process.

Contending Ideological Visions

Such a misdirected 'development' approach, coupled with the overemphasis upon military operations, allowed the CPT not only to survive but to slowly expand. The party erred initially in emphasizing the military content of Maoism over its political aspects. Thus it attempted to initiate the overt phase of its insurgency in 1965 without sufficient infrastructure development and consequently suffered setbacks. By 1969, however, it had regrouped and begun to implement a slow, deliberate construction of the foundations necessary to support its revolt. Simultaneously, an increase of support from external sources served to boost the flagging momentum of the movement.

The CPT's timing was right. As the decade of the 1970s began, Thailand found itself enmeshed in a multi-faceted structural dilemma not unlike in form that which had confronted Vietnam before the Vietnam War (Second Indochina Conflict). An economy based upon extractive agriculture was ruled by a regime with only tenuous political links to the populace. The government bureaucracy, monopolizing all power, was able to crush efforts seeking formation of a viable constitutive system. Further, while on the one hand the bureaucratic polity remained at odds with the fledging constitutive system, on the other those seeking to frame the particulars of the constitutive system remained at odds with each other. This idelogical conflict revolved principally about the need for a 'democratic' (normally interpreted by its backers as 'parliamentary') or 'socialist' framework.

In contrast to the approach of either the government — or its opponents who favored a parliamentary option — was the Maoist variant espoused by the CPT. Indeed, in its pronouncements the party regularly cited the People's Republic of China (PRC) as the appropriate model to be followed in economic and political development. The CPT's 'Ten Point Program' was little more than a rephrasing of the tenets espoused by Mao during his long campaign for power in China and reflected the Maoist belief that development could take place only when the political structure of society had been altered. As indicated in its major pronouncements, the CPT saw Thailand as a semi-feudal colony of American imperialism and thus not truly independent or free. The Americans were aided within Thailand by a variety of counter-revolutionaries (e.g., fascists, landlords, arch-feudalists [i.e., the royalty]), all of whom maintained a repressive system. To establish freedom and democracy, the government had to be overthrown and in its place a 'people's government' instituted. Land would be redistributed to the peasants, debts cancelled, industry sensibly developed for the benefit of the Thai people rather than of foreign and indigenous capitalists.

Aside from these general notions, however, there was nothing in the 'Ten Point Program' or other available literature which would have allowed the observer to make an accurate list of specific programs which the CPT planned to apply. Reports from 'liberated areas' served to confirm that the CPT proceeded in a fashion to be expected within the parameters specified by the Maoist blueprint: heavy emphasis on political indoctrination accompanied by an effort to raise the standard of living.

Adoption of Maoism had more fundamental pitfalls. Obviously, it had developed as a response to the unique conditions of China. The CPT took the Chinese experience and attempted to interpret Thai realities in the same fashion. Throughout its history, for example, the CPT maintained an active interest in creating various united fronts: the principal contradiction, according to the party — in imitation of the Chinese approach — was American imperialism versus the Thai people. Consequently, the CPT devoted considerable time and effort in its efforts to arouse the Thai people against 'the imperialists'. Ironically, such was to misread Thai reality and to ignore the far more urgent 'contradictions', to use their own term, particularly that between the constitutive system and the bureaucratic polity (i.e., democracy or oligarchy?). This misreading was reflected in the near total lack of success the CPT was to experience in its attempt to build a viable nationwide organization, particularly a united front reflecting the demands of non-elite groups.

Similarly, the emphasis upon the peasantry was an element of Maoism that seemed, on its face, appropriate in a state such as Thailand where 85 per cent of the population was located in rural areas. Yet this orientation neglected the shift that had occurred throughout Southeast Asia, Thailand included, whereby a substantial proportion of the 'rural population' actually resided in local urban centers. Furthermore, the CPT strategy ignored the fact that in Thailand there was only one true power center of consequence, Bangkok, with its four million people (the second urban site, Chiangmai, had but 100,000). Bangkok was the socio-economic-political-cultural locus of the kingdom, and, in many respects, all that went on within the kingdom served to 'feed' the capital. Developments there had a profound impact upon all else which went on, but the CPT chose to eschew urban struggle, even as an adjunct to a rural thrust, on the grounds that it could not be decisive. As events were to demonstrate, though, conditions were ultimately far more ripe for an urban seizure of power *à la* Moscow 1917/18 than for a Maoist people's war.

Nevertheless, despite CPT strategic miscues, as the Vietnam War drew to a close, the insurgent situation in Thailand grew worse.[59] By this time, the Thai government was in trouble. David K. Wyatt has written:

> By the early 1970s, the Thanom-Praphas regime faced a major security crisis. It was not simply that the army was mired in two exhausting conflicts, trying to stem a rising tide of internal insurgency while maintaining forces in Indochina. They also increasingly feared that their closest ally, the United States, was deserting them. When President Nixon moved to Vietnamize the Indochina conflict, to let 'Asians fight their own battles', and to reopen diplomatic relations with the People's Republic of China, a power the Thai believed to be supporting the antigovernment insurgency in Thailand, Field Marshal Thanom's response was to attempt to cash in on a decade of development, to bolster his now-aging regime with a bid for the support of those elements of Thai society that had most benefited from economic, social, and educational change. He was to find — like King Chulalongkorn in 1873–74, or Vajiravudh in 1912, or Prajadhipok in 1932, or even like Phibun in 1957 — that their response lacked both gratitude and respect.[60]

Thailand's commitment to economic development had reaped the whirlwind. Social turmoil itself had many causes, all of which came together in the early 1970s. Among the most salient were: a growing population, cramping lifestyles and straining social services; an accelerating urbanization, which for many meant a serious decline in quality of life; a substantial growth in the number of workers as industry became more export-oriented, but a failure of wages to match inflation or services with demand; a dramatic expansion in the number of students, especially at the university level, even as the ability of the system to absorb them declined (at least in positions commensurate with their qualifications); and growing friction as the bureaucratic polity expanded, bringing to all areas its officials, its innumerable rules, and its corruption. Traditional values showed signs of strain even as the security forces, which normally stifled dissent, fragmented into contending factions divided by strategic differences on how best to deal with the myriad external and internal problems.

Significantly, demands for redress of grievances could not be dealt with in any substantive fashion, because the mechanisms of a constitutive system simply did not exist. The bureaucratic polity thus had reached a point of crisis. A wave of student demonstrations in June 1973 snowballed in October with the arrest of activists demanding greater democracy. As violence erupted, the military regime collapsed with startling rapidity. For the next three years (1973-76), a succession of democratic governments sought to come up with a viable form of popular rule.

Such could not remain the case indefinitely, though. October 1973 marked another benchmark in modern Thai political history, an episode which ranked in importance with the 1932 'revolution' that ended the absolute monarchy. Unable to deal with internal structural contradictions in the face of pressure from abroad, the bureaucratic polity, as represented in the popular mind by the military, found itself unceremoniously ousted. Still, this occurred only because the regime's coercive power, notably the armed forces, was paralyzed by internal factionalism. Divided, the services nonetheless remained intact in terms of actual strength. Given proper circumstances, observers noted, institutional cohesion might easily return — and thus the bureaucratic polity could again rise to threaten the emerging constitutive system.

Such was not long in coming. With the chaos which naturally enough attended the search for representative government once the mechanisms of authoritarianism were displaced, bureaucratic, especially military, cohesion was bound to reappear, particularly given the divided nature of those supporting 'democracy'. Indeed, as forces of the left and right battled to shape the constitutive system to their liking, the kingdom slid towards chaos. Demands by the left for the mobilization of new segments in the process of interest articulation aroused fears of 'mob rule' among traditional segments of the Thai polity. They, in turn, made common cause with factions of the military favoring a return to the previous manner of conducting political affairs. A 6 October 1976 coup brought the bureaucracy again to power through a bloody assault on the perceived center of leftist influence, Thammasat University.

October 1976 was, like its predecessor three years previously, a watershed event. In every sense it was indicative of the national polarization that had resulted from the efforts of the constitutive system to rise from the smothering embrace of the bureaucratic polity. More violence had seemed imminent before a faction of the military, apparently not involved in the actual assault on Thammasat, seized control of the government and declared martial law. Yet it was a military badly divided and strongly influenced by those ideologically committed to a more pluralistic notion of politics — and the more limited role of the military therein.

This was demonstrated in the rush by the armed forces to remove themselves from the actual exercise of governance by appointing as prime minister Thanin Kraiwichian, Chief Justice of the Supreme Court. This move, far from returning affairs to a state of normalcy, further contributed to national polarization. Though Thanin plunged into his work and produced a flurry of legislation, his rigid approach quickly alienated even those rightist elements who should have been his most ardent supporters. The left did not wait to see how things developed. Former officials had already gone overseas in the immediate aftermath of the Thammasat bloodbath. Numerous other individuals, ranging from students to activist workers to politicians, now fled into the jungles or made their way to Indochina. Eventually, they were to number in their thousands. Their bitterness was great, and their estrangement from the establishment total. In the opinion of many, they represented the flower of several generations.

Here at last was the systemic crisis for which the communists had long hoped. After years of laboring in marginalized areas, unable to penetrate the heartland, the CPT finally found itself with the political space that necessarily accompanied a state of polarization. As the acknowledged premier opposition group in the kingdom, the party was ideally situated to become the key actor in shaping and directing the forces demanding change — the first requirement in forming an actual united front. Ideologically, the CPT was prepared, because Maoist doctrine incorporated the strategy of the united front as a vehicle for welding the opposition into a cohesive body. Since the party was the only real group about which anti-government forces could coalesce, the second important task in united front formation, the conversion of partners to the communist mode of thinking, was virtually accomplished by default. Efforts at reform had clearly failed. No longer did the CPT have to deal with organized, vibrant partners who could justly demand an equal voice in policy matters. Instead, it had only to find the means to absorb and utilize the high quality manpower which streamed into its base areas. Ideological unanimity was the price extracted for granting sanctuary to the fugitives, who were, in any case, ripe for fresh approaches to societal revision.

New CPT Strategic Dimensions

Presented thus with new recruits from diverse backgrounds and occupations, many of whom were 'progressive' in their orientation, the CPT saw a chance to replicate the popular front strategy which for Mao had culminated in his anti-Japanese united front. CPT propaganda had for more than two decades identified the American imperialists and their reactionary allies as the great enemies of the Thai people. Though this message had fallen largely on deaf ears, judging from the slow progress made in recruiting ethnic Thai and in organizing the insurgency, the CPT (and many knowledgeable observers) felt the events at Thammasat had finally revealed to all the true fascist character of the military regime and its obedience to the instructions of the Americans. The preliminary human results of the unmasking were already inundating CPT strongholds throughout the country in the form of those fleeing the wrath of the system. Surely, the CPT figured, there would be many more such recruits.

Inspired, the CPT launched an intense campaign to form a viable united front.[61] For its standard bearer the party erected the Committee for Coordinating Patriotic and Democratic Forces, the CCPDF (also translated as the Coordinating Committee for Patriotic and Democracy Loving Forces). The core of its membership and leadership came from the post-October 1976 fugitives. The task at hand was to expand this core so that it could be linked with the already existing infrastructure in the countryside. The CPT, in other words, had an organization of leaders: It needed to mobilize their followers. To do so required that specific strategic decisions be made, decisions that could certainly not occur in a vacuum, because elements supporting reform would be attempting to conduct their own mobilization campaign. Both would contend within the same structural environment; whichever was more successful would emerge with state power.

Initially, the CPT was the force more advantageously situated to take advantage of existing political realities. The state, though still dangerous, was seemingly all but paralyzed, its decisionmaking in chaos. The CPT moved quickly, using the two approaches appropriate for building a front: united front from above and below.[62] In the former, the communist party formally established links with other organizations, thereby gaining the participation and services of those organizations' members. The latter strategy, in contrast, called for appealing to the rank and file of rival organizations in an effort to bring the parent bodies into the front. An examination of CPT united front calls broadcast over 'Voice of the People of Thailand' (VOPT)[63] shows a fair mixing of these two approaches. In the year following the October 1976 coup, not less than 75 VOPT broadcasts called for a united front 'to oppose the fascist warlord clique, the US imperialists' lackeys'.[64] The broadcasts culminated in the 4 October 1977 announcement that the CCPDF had been formed.[65]

The campaign was notable for the degree to which it adhered to Mao's united front instructions. Broadcasts did not focus on the CPT program or its ideology, both of which were scarcely mentioned, but rather on the need of 'the people who love democracy and justice' to unite against 'the common enemy', the government. Emphasis was placed on shared goals and on demonstrating that people from the entire social spectrum had joined in the struggle. A particular attempt was made to appeal to Thai patriotism, and the CPT was portrayed as the defenders of the true Thai culture and of the kingdom against imperialism.[66]

Unlike previous CPT united front efforts, the CCPDF version went to some lengths to create international links. The reasons for this were several. First and foremost was the fact that the 6 October 1976 events, accompanied as they were by grisly photographs of lynched students being battered by enraged right-wing mob members, created a reservoir of sympathy for 'progressive forces' and left the Thai government with an unenviable negative public relations image as a repressive regime. Groups of both overseas Thai and foreigners were quickly formed throughout the world to demand the return of 'democracy and freedom'. Most members of these groups were not professed communists, but the CPT recognized that it could enlist their energies through front mechanisms. A second reason was the lesson learned by the communists during the Vietnam War (recall that while the CPT was 'Maoist', the Vietnamese and their clients, the Pathet Lao, had considerable influence due to their major support and training role): international links could play a decisive role in hampering establishment countermeasures. The Thai government, so the CPT line went, was a lackey of the American imperialists and could not long survive without the support of international capitalism. While the CPT could work to disrupt the internal mechanisms of Thai capitalism, foreign friends could best assault international capitalism's stranglehold on Thailand.

Hence the CPT, working through the CCPDF, created links with overseas elements opposed to both the American economic/military presence abroad and to the Thai government. This was not particularly difficult, for with the end of the war in Indochina, Thailand had replaced Vietnam as the favorite Southeast Asian target of radical organizations throughout the Western world and Japan. Though they were not creatures of the CCPDF, 'solidarity organizations' willingly acted as its agents. Some, such as the European Coordinating Committee for Solidarity with the Thai People (ECCSTP), went through their own processes of front construction, gradually adding members and expanding their activities.[67] The result was a fairly well developed network through which propaganda could be disseminated and whereby the CPT — always acting through the CCPDF — could 'relate its struggle into [sic] a wider international community'.[68] The 'solidarity organizations' acted as the CPT's spokespersons, distributed material such as statements detrimental to the Thai government, and solicited donations of money and medical supplies to support the cause. The criticism of the Thai government in the solidarity press echoed the CPT's current propaganda lines.

An examination of the literature published by the groups reveals several major themes which were pursued: (a) the repressive nature of the Thai government and the widespread nature of the opposition to it; (b) the links between Thai and international capitalism, and the domestic effects in Thailand of these bonds; (c) the actions and statements of the CPT and CCPDF; and (d) actions and statements of various solidarity groups which supported the CCPDF. The publications went to great lengths to emphasize the independence of the CCPDF's partners,[69] while simultaneously voicing support only for the CCPDF, of which the CPT was presented as just one member among equals. The goal, of course, was to portray the communist insurgency in Thailand as but one center of struggle in the worldwide war against international capitalism and American imperialism. Observed the VOPT:

> International organizations and justice-loving groups of people abroad have warmly and sincerely supported the struggle of the Thai people. We have friends everywhere, because we are on the correct side.[70]

Allowing for overstatement, the CPT was not without cause in seeing 'friends everywhere' — or at least potential friends. After all, the insurgency had just received a substantial influx of high quality manpower. Though the formal organizations of which they were members, or which they represented, were not huge, they were by no means insignificant. More importantly, each of the new recruits could reasonably be expected to establish, for the CPT, links with numerous other individuals who had remained behind, either openly or in hiding. The united front had been formed to carry out this task. With its mechanisms in place and structural conditions so propitious, the future of the party looked bright, so bright, in fact, that Morell and Samudavanija, respected analysts of the Thai scene, were moved to write: 'Success for the communist movement was certainly not imminent; but its potential had been enhanced inordinately by the influx of young new leaders. To a great extent, the future of Thailand now rests in their hands.'[71] Inspirational words, they were to find themselves consigned to the dustbin of misjudgement due to CPT strategic error.

For the time being, however, the party felt secure enough to broaden its assault on the old-regime.[72] Throughout the insurgency, the CPT had carefully avoided even the appearance of criticizing the sacrosanct royal family due to its central position in Thai culture and popular esteem. Following the events of Thammasat, however, and the return of the military to a central role in government, albeit a more circumscribed one,[73] the party broke with its cautious attitude and vigorously attacked the monarchy. These attacks were directed against both the institution and the incumbent, Bhumipol Adulyadoj, the ninth king of the Chakri dynasty, and represented a significant change of strategy — virtually all aspects of the 'old feudal order' were now fair game and were denounced in favor of a proposed new society, a communist society.

It was the role of the monarch in support of the status quo — even if it was a status quo then in considerable disarray — that was particularly infuriating to the left. Previously, such a stance by Bhumipol would have been enough to assure all political elements that at least a measure of fair play would prevail. But in the aftermath of 6 October's bloodshed, there was bitterness among some over the failure of the king to intercede to halt the violence, as he had in October 1973. That he could hardly have done so, given the rapidity of events in October 1976 as compared to October 1973, was not deemed relevant. Among the disillusioned new recruits of the CPT, bitterness towards the King was substantial.

Consequently, it came as no surprise that in early 1977 the CPT decided to abandon its hands-off approach to the monarchy. From later broadcasts made on the VOPT, it was clear that the top insurgent leaders believed the time was ripe to attack the royal couple for their links with the traditional, reactionary elements. The intent was to discredit the monarchy and thereby to weaken its position as a rallying point for the government. VOPT was the primary vehicle chosen for the attacks, which proceeded in several distinct phases. These phases, in turn, were not planned but rather responses to perceived tactical openings as events developed within the Thai political sphere.

Initially, until early June 1977, the communists were unsure how to proceed. Most attacks were of an oblique nature, criticizing royal wealth, ceremonies, and habits — and even, on one occasion (12 March 1977), attempting to draw upon the monarchy's prestige to attack the government of Prime Minister Thanin. The only direct attack was a 1 April reference which stated that the monarchy could be done away with as it was 'obsolete and deteriorating' (for complete table see the works cited in note 72 above). In mid-June, though, the strategy changed. By that time the stringent conservatism of the Thanin government had made itself manifest, and popular dissatisfaction with the regime's policies was on the rise. The communists correctly perceived that the monarchy was instrumental in rebuffing impatient calls from within establishment circles, both political and military, that Thanin be sacked. Instead, both the King and Queen urged that Thanin's government be given a chance to establish itself. The CPT, therefore, sought to link the monarchy with the unpopular regime and directly attacked the King and his retinue.

Changes in the International Situation and Strategic Schism

By mid-1978, then, the CPT had two principal lines that it was pursuing: (a) Thai leaders were lackeys of Western imperialism, selling out the nation, and had to be resisted through a united front of all concerned citizens; and (b) the Thai monarchy was collaborating in this effort and in the murder of the Thai people. By the attacks on the monarchy, the CPT made clear that it had irrevocably broken with the past; and by utilizing the Maoist mechanism of the united front, it sought to mobilize the populace against a structure which was deemed both repressive and nonproductive. Though the attacks on the monarchy foundered upon what seemed to be a still-substantial level of support for the institution, the united front campaign seemed hopeful. Conditions in urban and rural areas remained turbulent and, for many, impoverished. Externally, too, the situation seemed good, with support solid from the communist states of Laos, Cambodia, Vietnam, and China.

Suddenly, this fine situation collapsed under the weight of events in Southeast Asia.[74] Any conception of Vietnam as a war-weary nation desiring an interlude of peace was rudely shattered when Hanoi, in November 1978, signed a treaty of friendship and cooperation — which included a military pact — with the Soviet Union, and then the next month invaded Cambodia. The speed with which this *blitzkrieg* routed Pol Pot's forces and installed in power a client regime, the Kampuchean United Front for National Salvation, was stunning to the Thai. It brought to pass Bangkok's ultimate security nightmare: regular Vietnamese divisions on the kingdom's borders. Rekindled thus were the fears of communist expansionism which had driven official Thai foreign policy since 1945. Amidst the populace, too, even amongst prospective communist recruits, the expected onslaught of a foreign army made all but insignificant any purported threat from abstract qualities such as 'capitalism' or 'imperialism', as advanced by the CPT.

China's thrust into Vietnam in February 1979 heightened fears that the kingdom was about to become involved in communist intramural bickering. These doubts and fears extended to within the ranks of the CPT itself. Ironically, perceived expansionism by the communist Vietnamese rather than American imperialism now seemed to pose the greatest threat to the survival of the Thai nation — and thus to the Thai revolution. With its close ties to both China and Vietnam, the CPT leadership was caught in a dilemma of whether to support one side in its dispute with the other, or to attempt to stand aloof and hope that events would sort themselves out. Eventually, the debate involved virtually all echelons of the party.[75]

The discussions were all the more intense, because they occurred even as internal disputes over strategic approach convulsed the CPT leadership. At issue was the Maoist plan of using the countryside to encircle the cities. According to an analysis written later by John McBeth,[76] the CPT leadership claimed that it recognized Maoism was only a guide to action, that there were alternative strategies that could also be used in Thailand as circumstances dictated. In particular, the Vietnamese approach, which called for greater emphasis upon a fusion of military and political, urban and rural, actions, had brought victory in Indochina.[77] Thus it held an attraction for many CPT cadre, especially those who had been trained in Vietnam. It seemed to offer a more clearcut opportunity for success. But while the leadership might profess flexibility in strategy, in reality it proved rigid in its adherence to the Maoist line.

Most fundamentally, it was unwilling to expand its very narrow definition of united front formation. To critics within the party, it seemed incapable of moving beyond form to substance. It was not enough, they argued, to recruit the disenchanted from the urban areas. These urban areas had to be mobilized in the same fashion as the countryside. But this the CPT Politburo saw as falling into the trap which had led to the slaughter of the Chinese Communist Party (CCP) before Mao achieved unquestioned leadership.

What fused the two debates, CPT 'foreign policy' and strategic approach, into an explosive whole was their link to the larger rifts within the international communist camp. Since the CPT itself was tied to both the Chinese and the Vietnamese-Lao, with the latter strongly linked to the Soviets, the Thai could not avoid being forced into a position where backing one strategy or the other, Maoist or Vietnamese, did not have foreign policy repercussions. Similarly, efforts by Thailand, particularly under the Kriangsak administration, to establish better relations with China, Laos, and

Vietnam, advanced at the expense of the CPT. That these countries would court Bangkok at all was a result of their increasing rivalry in the wake of Hanoi's victory in South Vietnam and subsequent efforts to dominate its Indochina partners, Laos and Cambodia. The Pathet Lao had been so thoroughly controlled by the Vietnamese for years that they posed little problem, but the Khmer Rouge were an altogether different story and relied upon Chinese aid to buttress their independence. Caught between the proverbial rock and a hard place, the CPT ran out of room in which to maneuver when Vietnam seized Cambodia.

Apparently, if McBeth's articles are accurate — and they are the best insight we yet have — the invasion was subsequent to several years of Vietnamese attempts to gain greater influence within the CPT at the expense of the pro-Chinese Sino-Thai leadership. This effort took its most prominent form, according to McBeth's CPT sources, in a campaign by Hanoi to deal directly with the CPT's northeast party organ, which contained a good many personnel whom the Vietnamese had trained, together with a 'suggestion' that Pathet Lao personnel operate with CPT guerrillas in the Thai northeast. Further, Hanoi apparently blocked shipments of arms from Peking which had to transit Laos. When the CPT refused to go along with Vietnam's plans, it paid the consequences. In January 1979 the Central Committee of the Lao People's Revolutionary Party (LPRP), which took its directions from Hanoi, ordered the Thai communists to vacate their bases in Laos. Coming as it did hard on the heels of the loss, amidst the turmoil of the continued fighting along the Thai-Cambodian border, of CPT sanctuaries in Cambodia itself — from which, at the time of the Vietnamese invasion, more than half of all CPT operations were originating — this was a substantial blow.

After months of debate, a dramatic VOPT broadcast by Si Inthapanti of the CCPDF announced that the matter had been thrashed out. It offered a united front to the government to fight against 'threats from Vietnam'.[78] In a stinging attack, the broadcast charged that the Vietnamese, under the direction of the Soviets, were attempting to export revolution, and that any encroachment into Thailand would be resisted by the united Thai people. Further, the author continued, given the existence of the greatest threat to the kingdom since World War II, in the form of Vietnamese divisions on the Thai border, it was criminal for the Thai government to devote the overwhelming bulk of its resources to suppressing the revolution when it ought to be safeguarding the kingdom from external foes.

With a change of appropriate labels, this broadcast could have passed for a Maoist proclamation directed at the *Kuomintang* during the anti-Japanese struggle in China. And as the KMT had done, until Chiang Kai-shek was personally pressured to do otherwise, the Thai government rejected the offer out of hand. On 11 July 1979 Yunnan-based VOPT announced that it was temporarily going off the air,[79] apparently a victim of Peking's desire for stronger links with Bangkok in the face of its own deteriorating geostrategic position in Southeast Asia. Sources further revealed that a bitter internal battle, complete with defections of CCPDF members to the Vietnamese side and their formation of a rival communist organization, *Pak Mai*,[80] was wracking the CPT. This became apparent when high-ranking CPT members began to defect to the government, to include, initially, two members of the CCPDF leadership, Bunyen Wothong (vice-chairman) and Thoetphum Chaidi. Others followed, notably Thirayut Boonmee. CPT Politburo member Damri Ruangsutham was captured, though he claimed 'he was on a mission to see former political activist Sang Patthanothai to act as a middleman in truce talks between the CPT and the government in an effort to form a united front against the Vietnamese'.[81] Soon prisoners and defectors spoke of clashes between *Pak Mai* elements and units of the established CPT.

While rival footsoldiers were taking shots at each other in a growing turf war, the nexus of crisis remained in the inner circles of the CPT. The Sino-Vietnamese split had caused dislocation of base areas and disruption of supply lines, but it was the ideological issues that were tearing the party apart. So intense were they that plans for the Fourth Party Congress were repeatedly delayed. Meantime, events in Thai politics continued to unfold at breakneck speed.

Replacement of Kriangsak by army commander General Prem Tinsulanond, a royal intimate, took place in March 1980 when the so-called 'Young Turks' — an influential grouping of troop commanders — withdrew their support for the former's rule. Strongly committed to military professionalism and a limited role for the military in politics, the Young Turks found themselves cast as kingmakers. In the end, 'Papa' Prem, as he was known to the centurions, was to rule Thailand for the next eight years. During that time, he was to oversee a remarkable transition: parliament became a more elected body, the economy boomed, and the Thai revolution crumbled as a proper counterinsurgency strategy was implemented. Initially, though, Prem stumbled. His stand on several important issues raised Young Turk fears of corruption and powermongering. Consequently, they rose against him on 1 April 1981.

There followed a game of political hardball, with Prem demonstrating he was as adroit at his new profession as he was on the battlefield. After initially being captured by 'his children', he was able to escape to the royal palace. It now appears the Young Turks were forced to release him in response to a direct summons from the throne for Prem to appear. Subsequently, the royal family accompanied Prem to a loyal base up-country, from which a counterstroke was prepared. This proved unnecessary, for the mere fact that the monarch had sided with the government doomed the coup to failure. It ignonomously collapsed.[82]

The 'April Fool's Coup', as it came to be known, had an important impact upon the CPT debate over strategic approach. Dissidents within the party argued vigorously that if the CPT had been ready — had it mobilized within the urban areas as the alternative approach advocated — it could have provoked a civil war between the two sides. This, in turn, would have brought foreign intervention, as the protagonists requested assistance. The result would have been chaos, with the CPT there to pick up the pieces. In April, however, the dissidents pointed out, the CPT's 'rural areas surround the cities' doctrine meant it had no forces whatsoever in Bangkok. Consequently, it could only watch from the sidelines.

What the dissidents wanted was to modify the Maoist strategic orientation in favor of one more relevant to Thai conditions. Rather than the simple rural-urban dicotomy, they pushed for 'three strategic zones'. The First Zone was to be Bangkok, the center of capitalist strength in the kingdom. There, the CPT could make use of the growing non-communist but 'progressive' organizations to directly attack the system. The Second Zone was to be the rural areas where the majority of the populace resided. There, the struggle would take the form mainly of covert political organizational work (i.e., the construction of infrastructure). Finally, in the Third Zone, the jungles, the CPT main forces were to remain based and ready for strikes to support the infrastructure in the Second Zone. Within each zone, the dissident analysis continued, there were to be two 'battlefronts', political and military. To arrive at the proper combination of the two, each zone was to have an independent command headquarters for policy and tactical decisionmaking. Each zone would have equal importance in the strategic plan, and their headquarters would not have to refer all questions to the central leadership. Instead, the central organs would issue only overall policy guidance.[83]

For the Politburo this proposal represented a dangerous splintering of authority. Battle was joined at the long delayed Fourth Party Congress, held in regional sessions throughout 1982. The dissidents demanded change, pointing out that the Maoist approach was appropriate for a huge country such as China where the focus of unrest was in the countryside and where space provided ample room for sanctuaries. Such was not the case in Thailand, where growing urbanization had shifted the political center to the cities — Bangkok, in particular — and where there were few places the government could not reach with its forces. Examining the crises that had shaken the system during the 1970s, the dissidents observed, clearly pointed to the need for strategic revision. China was no longer the model. Vietnam, Cuba, and Nicaragua (particularly the latter) were more appropriate to what was going on in the kingdom.

Stunned by the vehemence of the attack, the Politburo countered. At the Party Congress, the old guard was reportedly able to turn back the dissidents by two votes (those casting ballots included Central Committee members and representatives from various districts, provinces, and zones). The vote, however, only made matters worse, because the dissidents protested that it was rigged. Thus the split in the ranks became all the more pronounced. It was the beginning of the end for the CPT. Battered by the hostile turn of external events, as well as the proper government counterinsurgency strategy to be outlined in the next section, the membership's disillusionment was the final straw. The trickle of defections became a hemorrhage.

Government Search for a New Approach[84]

In a sense, the CPT had self-destructed. This, however, is not the complete picture. Individuals were willing to leave the party only because they had somewhere to go. It was changes in the political environment that created such a haven. These were not changes that came about quickly or easily. What is of particular relevance is that they came about from within — in response to deliberate decisions made by individuals who decided that structural change was necessary.

Shortly after the October 1973 events, in November, Prem Tinsulanonda, then still a relatively obscure officer, was made the Deputy Commanding General of Second Army, charged with security in the Thai northeast. Among his many duties was responsibility for directing the northeast region's counterinsurgency program. He took over at a time when the 'COIN [counterinsurgency] effort' was disorganized and less-than-effective. That Prem, as the second-in-command, was placed in charge of his region's most significant operational endeavor spoke worlds as to institutional priorities. The military elite had more important concerns. Yet Prem seized the opportunity. Modifying the original CPM (civil-police-military) approach of Saiyud by enhancing its political aspects, he soon began to see results. Psychological operations, persuasion, and heavy use of the civilian provincial governors and their resources constituted a marked departure from the normal emphasis upon firepower. By 1975–76 Second Army had become a model of sorts in dealing with the insurgency.

That Prem would perform in the manner he did was no surprise to those who knew him well. Observes Saiyud:

> When Prem was in charge of the Cavalry School in Bangkok, I was with army headquarters. Together, with several others, we formed a 'Golf Committee'. We discussed the security situation while playing golf! Prem, especially, had time to ponder the situation. Therefore, we talked a lot about how to deal with the insurgency. Prem was also very influenced by the thinking of the King and Queen, who maintained a keen interest in counterinsurgency and had papers on the subject regularly prepared for them. How precisely all the elements came together, I don't know, but, obviously, a combination of things resulted in a correct approach.[85]

This approach can be characterized as development for security, with 'development' understood as a socio-economic-political process. 'It is the weakness of the system which allows guerrillas to grow', states Saiyud flatly.

The target, therefore, is the population, not areas or enemy forces.

Problems of the system must be addressed. The popular base of the insurgents must be destroyed. Strengthen the villages first, then go into the jungle after the guerrillas.[86]

This Prem did, acting within his own area of control. Eight years had passed, however — from Saiyud's 1965 assignment to CSOC/ISOC until Prem's 1973 assignment to the northeast — before his philosophy could blossom in full force. During the interim, those who did not share the system's view that repression was the answer to its problems had had to be content with doing whatever they could. Once in charge, Prem could do things differently. His methodology was not unlike, in form, that used successfully in numerous other areas around the world by counterinsurgent forces. A target area was first blanketed with troops, who insured that the CPT's armed units were driven off. Then, all particulars of the population were learned and the insurgent infrastructure dismantled through systematic intelligence collection and exploitation. Civic action programs were instituted, militia units formed. Special operations in known insurgent strongholds kept the insurgent main forces at bay.

What gave substance to the form, however, was the growth of the constitutive system. Prem's forces, rather than being the law, became the administrators of the law. They could be, in effect, the embodiment of the Buddhist ideal of how things ought to have been. Democratic political space legitimated traditional demands upon the system for a just order.

Prem's success attracted attention. From then on his rise was rapid. In 1976 he became the commander of the entire Second Army Region. Only two years later, in September 1978, he assumed command of the army as a whole. By February 1980 he was prime minister. His key base of support throughout was the Young Turks, those most influenced by their counterinsurgency experiences and a desire to move the military towards more professional concerns. They were joined, though, by another group, the Democratic Soldiers.[87] They were to be of equal importance. For if the Young Turks provided the brawn, the Democratic Soldiers provided the brains. Their major difference was that while the Young Turks came from the line, the Democratic Soldiers were drawn from staff officers. Further, while the Young Turks sought to impose a knight's code of honor upon their institution and society, the Democratic Soldiers were more intimately involved in the business of counterinsurgency planning.

Learning from communist defectors and their own study, the Democratic Soldiers advanced 'democracy' — which they left quite undefined — as the key weapon against insurgency. Among their major supporters were Major General Chaovalit Yongchaiyut, Prem's aide-de-camp, later to be head of the army and to oversee the destruction of the CPT, and Major General Harn Leenanond, head of army operations (G3), later to command Fourth Army in the south and to destroy the CPT there as he had helped Prem to do in the northeast while a member of the latter's staff. These two individuals were apparently the principal authors of an extraordinary document, Prime Minister (PM) Order No.66/23 (the 66th order in the Buddhist Era Year 2523, or 1980), 'The Policy for the Fight to Defeat the Communists', subsequently augmented by PM Order No.65/25 (1982), 'Plan for the Political Offensive'.[88] What they set forth was a politically-driven strategy to meet the communists. Said 66/23, unequivocally: 'Political factors are crucial [to the success of counterinsurgency], and military operations must be conducted essentially to support and promote political goals.'[89] The follow-up 66/25 left no doubt what Prem had in mind:

> Let the development of democracy be the guiding principle...We estimate that the CPT has slowed our democratic development, using weak points as propaganda subjects to deceive the people.

> Simultaneously, the CPT itself has pretended to give democracy to the people. What the CPT has in mind, however, is tactical democracy...[To meet them] all patterns of dictatorship must be destroyed.[90]

Put in other terms, if lack of 'development' — in an all-encompassing socio-economic-political sense — was the cause of insurgency, then it was the army's task to foster that development. That such a view could come to the fore would have been impossible without the old-regime crisis which erupted with October 1973. Just as certainly, though, the old-regime crisis took the path it did because the military acted in a very particular manner. It retreated from politics, at least from the politics of the bureaucratic polity. Prem's strategy represented a victory for those who had sought to turn the security forces towards a more viable approach for dealing with insurgency. Prem, for instance, did not alter his beliefs in

response to events. He had long held them. Yet they were unable
to have an impact until the political space created by the advent of
the constitutive system provided an opportunity. He seized it.

Sarochna has attempted to further study the precise origins of
Prem's PM Order No.66/23.[91] His findings reinforce those here.
He sees two 'streams' of influence, the first coming from Saiyud's
CPM approach, the second from the operational experience
gained by high ranking officers in Second Army Region. The CPM
experience, in turn, had two facets: (a) the emphasis upon a coordinated, integrated approach combining civil and military techniques, as set forth by Saiyud in numerous speeches and publications;[92] and (b) the emphasis upon political rather than military
aspects, which came later. Saiyud's role in developing CPM has
already been mentioned, as have the contributions of several other
individuals. Sarochna notes additional officers whom he feels were
instrumental in influencing others with the approach. They were
to become familiar as the insurgency was defeated: Lieutenant
General Wasin Isarangkoon, operational assistant to the army chief
of staff; Lieutenant General Rian Disabanjong, deputy army chief
of staff; General Prayoot Charumanee, army chief of staff; and
General Sanha (or Sant) Chitrapatima, deputy army commander
and previously Fourth Army Region commander (the south). To
this I would add what I consider an important omission, General
Pichitr 'Pete' Kullavanijaya, ultimately deputy supreme commander of the Royal Thai Armed Forces (Saiyud, it should be noted,
became the supreme commander under Prem).

As for those important in the second 'stream', the operational
experience gained in the northeast, Sarochna lists Prem and Harn,
whom we have noted, as well as Major General Pathom Sermsin
and Colonel Lert Kanisthanaka (the latter did not achieve the rank
of the others, which he surely would have, because he was killed
in an operational helicopter crash during the conflict). Considered
in sum, this is a good compilation of those whose ideas were
instrumental in framing the '66/23 approach'. They shared a
recognition that the greater the suppression, the greater the
increase in CPT recruits. All were heavily influenced by their contact with villagers themselves and with their grievances. Just as
importantly, their attitudes, as with the Young Turks, had been
shaped by the Thai involvement in Laos and Vietnam.

Neither of these experiences has yet been adequately documented. The crucial impact of Vietnam service upon the Young

Turks has been noted by observers, but I would surmise that equally important was the clandestine effort in Laos. There, in support of the H'mong forces used by the US-led, -trained, and -equipped 'Secret Army', the Thai at one point had 27 light infantry and 3 artillery battalions deployed.[93] What was unique about this force was that while its men were 'mercenaries' — that is, recruited specially for service in the units — its cadre was comprised completely of regular Thai Army officers and noncommissioned officers. Necessarily, the procedures of such an unconventional force would leave an impact upon those who served in it, even though it was not involved in counterinsurgency *per se*. It has already been noted, for example, that Saiyud commanded the force early in its existence, and at least some of those who became Young Turks also had service with it. Additionally, Pichitr, to cite another illustration, after two years in Vietnam, spent three years in Laos. These experiences were certainly crucial in shaping the views of those men towards counterinsurgency. Continued secrecy, though, makes information difficult to come by.

A similar problem attends the influence of the key figure mentioned by Saiyud above, the King. It can scarcely be an accident that many of the individuals who emerged as instrumental in the change of Thai counterinsurgency policy, to include most conspicuously Prem himself, were close to the throne — and were known to be prior to their rise to power. Yet the role the royal couple actually exercised in influencing appointments, if any, cannot be learned.[94] Nevertheless, it is clear, if we can judge by inference from the numerous meetings that important figures held at the palace and from the oblique comments of obligation made by officers, that the King, in particular, was instrumental in encouraging those who sought to replace armed suppression with political action.

More important than such detective work, for our purposes here, is the outcome. Of this there is no doubt: Prem, in concert with like-minded individuals, completely reoriented the Thai counterinsurgency approach. Asked years later what had been the principal factor which brought about change in the campaign, after the years of fruitlessly trying to convert his fellow officers, Saiyud responded simply:

> Prem. What made the difference was having someone who could order support. This made all the difference in the world. We already had the ideas and the concepts. They had been in place for years.[95]

To implement these concepts, Prem took CSOC/ISOC out of its advisory role and placed it again in the operational chain of command. Not only was it given the power to direct CPM Task Forces, as had been the case initially under Saiyud, but the regional army commanders, who had always existed independently, were fully integrated into the structure. Gradually, all regular army and security force units in operational areas were likewise placed under the CPM Task Forces. To ensure correct use of these newly unified forces, greater care was given to their commanders. In short, professional considerations became paramount in determining who would receive operational assignments, a substantial change from the criteria in force under the pre-October 1973 regime.[96]

External influences played a role in strengthening this trend. The communist victory in Indochina in 1975 reinforced traditional Thai security concerns and enhanced the need for military professionalism. Numerous units that previously had had the luxury of political involvement were redeployed to the border area to meet the threat. The necessity for competence became all the more pronounced as Vietnamese and Lao incursions were repelled; additional regular forces were withdrawn from counterinsurgency tasks and placed on a conventional footing. Their place was taken by militia.

Thai 'People's War'

Use of militia was not a new concept in Thailand. It had been an integral part of Saiyud's counterinsurgency plans. Yet Saiyud's response had been premature. His ideas for self-defense forces and local participation were ahead of not only the bureaucracy but even the populace. Tradition-oriented Thai peasants were not yet given to defending themselves. 'The villagers were more afraid of the police than the enemy', Saiyud has noted.[97] This ended with October 1973 and its aftermath. It was democratic political space that thrust popular concerns to the fore — and with them the willingness to defend what was theirs.

What *was* theirs? That which was 'Thai'. In this formulation we begin to pull together the many loose ends which have appeared in the course of this manuscript. Old-regime crisis emerged when the instruments of coercion were paralyzed by internal struggle. They were not, however, destroyed. Instead, through the deliberate acts of numerous individuals, the security forces were reoriented. Not only did they adopt a new, political approach to counterinsurgency, they threw their weight behind the new constitutive system. Their willingness to allow it to grow was crucial, as was the role of the King in refusing to acquiesce in sporadic efforts to change the administration by using the previous mechanism of choice, the coup. The result, regardless of the particulars — and Thai efforts to form a viable parliamentary system went through numerous configurations, with representatives chosen in diverse ways — was a reorientation of concerns away from those of the bureaucracy to those of the people. Politics, in short, came to the populace.

There is no particular point at which we may judge the people came to think of the system as 'theirs'. October 1973 was surely a benchmark. Just as important, though, were the events that followed, when the left and right battled for control of the emerging constitutive system. In every sense this was a campaign of the streets. The CPT, the illegal left, erred in not recognizing the need to get into the battle directly. The legal left, which was on the streets, erred in adopting foreign cultural idioms and forms. In particular, proponents of rapid change made the mistake of interpreting their reality in terms foreign to the bulk of the population. The left saw the military as a creature of the West, rather than recognizing that its structural position was a logical consequence of Thai historical factors; and activists ascribed to it Western motives. The result was that they were quite unprepared for the reaction their actions sparked.

It was no accident that what have normally been termed 'right-wing pressure groups' achieved the strength they did in the post-October 1973 era. They built upon those cultural idioms salient to popular existence — 'Buddhism, Nation, Monarchy'. In a sense, the second of these subsumed the other two: to be a Thai was to be a Buddhist within the hierarchy that culminated in the monarch. To lose one's place in this hierarchy was to lose one's identity as a Thai. That the CPT, as the principal opposition group, could recruit manpower comes as no surprise. Scott's analysis of the two distinct groups present within any insurgent group allows us to explain this: CPT leadership came initially from marginalized elements of the alienated (culturally and, in many cases, racially) urban elite; the manpower came from the abused peasantry. Thai peasants had historically participated in rebellion when they were pushed too far. Yet the CPT leadership, joined by that of the legal left, seems to have little understood just how far it had strayed from Thai cultural idioms. The two groups appear to have assumed that the same conditions which had given them an alternative worldview would automatically be shared by others. They projected their individual cases onto the whole, and by so doing, they distorted Thai reality.

Supporters of the 'status quo' used the years 1973 to 1976 to rally the populace against those who would destroy their world. Though the left prided itself on its mobilization abilities, its forces soon found themselves swamped by mass mobilization carried out by the right. The Village Scouts organization alone, for example, which had a paramilitary component and which drew its membership through appeals to nationalism (defined particularly as loyalty to the monarchy and Buddhism), reached a membership of 2.5 million by mid-1978, or over 5 per cent of the total population.[98] The CPT infrastructure could not begin to match this strength.[99] Neither was the legal left, for all its organizational skills, able to attract such numbers.

What should be noted is that the Village Scouts was but one of several such bodies, with others, such as *Nawaphol* and *Krathing Daeng* ('Red Gaur'), though fewer in numbers, far more militant. When the legal left was perceived to have taken the logical next step in its 'anti-Thai' approach, threatening the monarchy by attacking the Crown Prince, the carnage of October 1976 resulted. Specifics of the episode become, in such a context, virtually incidental. The clash would have occurred eventually, at some place and time, given the shape of the emerging cultural confrontation.

It is interesting to note, in this respect, that a neo-Marxian 'structural violence' analysis, as frequently advanced by some elements of the legal left, would only heighten the tension between the radicals and the masses. Violence committed by members of the bureaucracy may have been, in one sense, common, but it cannot be judged to have been pervasive. Repression threw up the manpower mobilized by the CPT, but most peasants remained outside the theater of conflict. The rhythms of life, in other words, were in no significant manner regulated by considerations of lethal force. Neglect, rather than intrusion, was the norm. The societal fabric was kept intact by the specifics of agricultural and Buddhist practice.

At the apex, the god afar, if we may think of him as such, was the King. Men who perpetrated unjust acts, it was felt, violated his order; they did not perpetuate it. Constitutism, therefore, blessed by the King, could channel nascent nativism, as well as the more immediate demands for social justice. The growth of the constitutive system, therefore, was reinforced by traditional Buddhist concepts of the just order. Leftist appeals for confrontation were foreign to this structure.

This is not an attempt to advance an argument that violence or confrontation were not a part of Thai existence. It is to say that they were not a part of the sanctioned aspect of Thai existence. Buddhism, the Nation, and the Monarchy were cultural idioms tied to the ideal order, however divorced it might have been from specific exceptions. Leftist ideology, on the other hand, built upon nothing. Instead, it was seen to attack the ultimate linchpins of Thai existence. In this sense, it virtually mobilized its own opposition. What emerged was as close to 'holy war' as Buddhism allowed.

It was the CPT attacks upon the monarchy that all but sealed the party's doom. There followed a mushrooming of popular mobilization by 'rightist' groups. When regular forces were withdrawn to meet the external threat, their place could be taken by militia, because there already existed a popular base upon which to build. The population aroused became the population armed. Thus were born the 'Rangers'. Begun while Prem was army commander (1978-80), this militia concept turned the communist methodology of infrastructure development on its head. It used locally-recruited manpower, often drawn from the already existing nationalist organizations such as the Village Scouts, to operate against the insurgents, while in the villages nationalist mass organizations ensured systemic loyalty. Controlled by regular army personnel, the Rangers had by the end of 1981 grown to 160 companies, or about 13,000 men,[100] more than the CPT armed strength of 12,500 at the time. So plentiful were the recruits that they were difficult to absorb properly. Lack of control at times forced the disbandment of units, but others were recruited to take their place. Soon, the militia structure covered all areas of the kingdom.

This development occurred with almost startling rapidity. In a sense it capped another effort, one which had paved the way for its implementation. Again, we confront the ill-understood influence of the Laotian campaign. The 1973-76 democratic interlude coincided with the winding down and, eventually, the end of the Indochina conflict. Though no systematic survey has been done, many of the returning soldiers from Laos, not being regulars who could continue in the army, were apparently absorbed into the growing right-wing response to the challenge of the left. Additionally, as the government pushed to integrate all areas of the kingdom, growing numbers of ex-soldiers were hired as security forces by the construction companies charged with building strategic roads. As such, they engaged in regular combat with the insurgents.[101] Others became members of a growing effort to settle contested areas with ex-soldiers and their families.

All of these measures met with success. That CPT 'people's war' should be buffeted by Bangkok's 'people's war' was irony of the first order. What followed was almost anti-climactic. Because the change in government strategy coincided with the larger changes in the international situation and with the intra-party strategic debate, all elements necessary for the demise of the CPT came together simultaneously. Hard fighting remained, but as the decade of the 1980s wore on, the communists were in increasingly difficult straits. No incident symbolized this more than the fall of their headquarters and principal base area, located in a formidable position in the Khao Khor mountain range along the Petchabun-Phitsanulok provincial border.[102] The operation, led by General Pichitr Kullavanijaya, was complete by early 1982, just in time for the CPT Fourth Party Congress.

Held, as noted previously, in staggered fashion in different regions, the Congress ended acrimoniously. There followed a dramatic increase in defections. What began as a trickle became a hemorrhage. Important to the willingness of the communists to lay down their arms was the element of Prem's political strategy that held the insurgents would not be treated as prisoners but as those returning to the fold. With minimal security precautions, they were allowed to resume normal lives.[103] In all the main operational areas, developments proceeded in similar fashion. Placing hand-picked officers in key positions, Prem kept the campaign going. In the deep south, his success in the northeast, and Pichitr's success in the Tri-Province region, was duplicated by Harn, whose use of 'politics first' was particularly effective.[104] Chaovalit, as army commander, coordinated the whole. By mid-1983, the CPT had, for all practical purposes, become a nuisance rather than a threat.[105]

It was a different Thailand to which the insurgents returned. Not only had the constitutive system created a new political environment, but Prem's administration had paved the way for an economic boom by abandoning statist policies in favor of greater integration within the world economy. This is not the place to consider these changes in detail.[106] What is important is that changes formalized under Prem resulted in a period of significant economic expansion which continues to the present. Rapid industrialization and urbanization spawned a whole host of problems, but ones so different in their immediate concerns to those being discussed by radicals that the CPT appeared, at best, irrelevant.[107]

Too late, the CPT leadership offered a compromise to its own membership. A position paper dated 3 July 1984 was circulated entitled 'Four Strategic Zones and Five Battle Fronts'.[108] It adopted the dissidents' tripartite division of the conflict within Thailand itself, but to it was added a Fourth Zone, the international arena. The crucial role foreign activity and support could have on events within the revolutionary country itself were thereby recognized. Similarly, the five battle fronts built upon the dissident proposal. To political and military spheres of operations were added economic, cultural, and diplomatic. In particular the document recognized the need to pursue non-military approaches, such as subverting newspapers and important social groups. As a first step, a 'Mass Organization Plan'[109] concentrated on establishing links with the three key groups needed for the construction of a new united front: farmers (peasants), labor, and students.

A plan of action was outlined in 'Coordination of Forces to Overthrow the Present Regime',[110] a document which appeared to have drawn upon the Nicaraguan experience, wherein the party ascertained that it needed to bring together a reaction involving four groups: legal political parties, the CPT itself with its own mass organization, the Thai People's Liberation Army (TPLA), and leading 'progressive' elements within the Thai armed forces. By infiltrating legal political parties, the rationale went, the CPT could provoke a conflict between moderates and the 'right wing'. This would necessarily involve the progressive and 'fascist' factions within the military. Hence, either wittingly or unwittingly, the result would be cooperation of the CPT and the progressive military against the ruling class, with the TPLA able to tip the scales in favor of the former.

This new approach, though it contained certain unrealistic elements, was clearly a step in the right direction. At least it sought to deal with Thai realities in a systematic fashion, rather than strategically stuffing Thailand into the Chinese mold. Nevertheless, it was too little, too late. More fundamentally, the moment of old-regime crisis had passed.

Conclusions

Thailand had 'won' its battle with the insurgents of the CPT. Noteworthy as the victory was, however, particularly in light of the results in Cambodia, Laos, and Vietnam, it would be incorrect to see it as a model of a particular combination of tactical or operational techniques. To the contrary, it was a victory for a *strategic* approach which sought ultimately to respond to Thai realities, particularly political realities. Only the change in those realities made effective the techniques chosen. Just as certainly, though, had the techniques not been carried out, the results of the struggle could have been very different. In this sense, the counterinsurgency existed in a symbiotic relationship with its society.

As Saiyud has stated above, it was the weaknesses of the Thai system that provided the opportunity for the CPT. Yet this should not be read to mean a group of conspirators sought to take advantage of societal weakness. The system itself 'threw up' the manpower that became the CPT. Thus my explanation has leaned heavily upon the unique historical particulars of Thailand. The emergence of the bureaucratic polity, the authoritarian focus of which was oriented almost exclusively towards economic development, was bound to produce a reaction. This could take the form of rebellion or insurgency. Use of the strategic model provided by Maoism, combined with the absorption of manpower produced by government abuses, allowed the CPT to grow — and allowed insurgency to win out over peasant rebellion. The insurgency, seeking structural change to pursue socialist development, established itself in remote areas so as to secure the sanctuaries necessary for achievement of critical mass. It then sought to expand to the lowlands. This proved possible in some areas, particularly the northeast. Yet in each of its three main operational areas — the northeast, north, and south — the party was dealing with unique circumstances which favored recruitment among marginalized individuals. Unable to penetrate the central heartland of the kingdom, it had to wait for new developments.

These came with the explosive ouster of the bureaucracy, as exemplified most prominently by the military, from power and subsequent chaotic efforts to fashion a constitutive system through implementation of parliamentary mechanisms and increased local government. Sudden allowance for interest articulation and aggregation naturally enough produced different views of how this should occur and what shape the result should have. To that end, the forces of the left and the right, as they are termed in Western shorthand, locked in conflict. If this democratic political space was midwife to societal conflict, it also produced the salvation for the system. New military leadership emerged that carried with it a vision of counterinsurgency as countermobilization.

As the fate of the absolute monarchy in Thailand makes clear — it was, after all, the monarchy that attempted to 'modernize' the kingdom — political mobilization is a dangerous business in the absence of institutions into which unleashed popular forces can channel their energies. In the counterinsurgency campaign, Thailand's existing cultural practices and idioms provided these. Numerous mass organizations in support of the traditional 'pillars' of society — Buddhism, the Nation, and Monarchy — were formed. Their energy amounted, at times, to millennial fervor, as would be anticipated in a time of profound structural upheaval. In voicing their support of the 'pillars', members could opt for utopia — a perfect Buddhist world — even while remaining firmly fixed in reality — support for the system that protected the pillars. That the security forces were able to mobilize this outpouring while the communists could not resulted, of course, from the fact that the communists never really attempted to do so. Instead, their ideological worldview overpowered their strategies, an error for which Mao would have condemned them. For the essence of the united front strategy passed on by Mao called for exploitation of structural reality as the would-be revolutionaries found it. This, the government, rather than the insurgents, was able to accomplish.

'Government' is a term which must be used with some reservations, though. Prior to October 1973, a fundamental weakness of the Thai counterinsurgency campaign was that it was not a national effort but rather a task assigned to the security forces. It was entirely logical that those who led these forces responded to violence with violence. Some, to be sure, were more enlightened than others and recognized the counterproductive nature of repression, but they were neither in positions of power nor citizens of a system which could behave otherwise. This is not to say that countermobilization against the insurgents could not — and did not —

occur on a tactical scale. It did, particularly while Saiyud was given command authority through the mechanisms of CSOC/ISOC. Yet such could only be a short-term solution given the long term structural dilemma at hand: how to ask the populace to fight for 'their' system when they had little direct stake in it aside from the lifestyle offered by the status quo. This became possible only when a faction of the military, represented most signally by Prem and Saiyud, became the government and could mobilize the populace behind democratic institutions.

This process further highlighted the importance of cultural idioms. The bureaucratic polity was not necessarily predatory. It was kept in check by the same cultural dicta that had in the past checked the absolute power of the monarchy. CPT efforts at mobilization could overcome this worldview and replace it with an alternative construct where the representatives of the bureaucratic polity had crossed the norms of acceptable conduct. That these transgressions never reached the level necessary to negate existing popular conservatism and latent support for the ideal order resulted from specific decisions made by numerous individuals we have encountered above. In a phrase, they rescued 'the system' from itself. Such was not preordained. Prem and Saiyud, for example, wandered in the bureaucratic wilderness for years before their moment came. Yet they were produced by the same structural configuration that 'made' their opposite numbers, whether in the bureaucratic polity (rival officers) or in the developing constitutive system (the insurgents). That they saw reform as the more proper course resulted from individual choice. When the moment came to be heard, they acted. Had they given heed to opposing counsul, the situation could well have been exacerbated to the point that even the CPT's mistakes would not have kept the party from becoming a key player in the drama of the constitutive system.

It follows naturally enough that the precise techniques adopted by Prem and his cohorts, while necessary, were certainly not sufficient to insure the victory of the parliamentary option in the constitutive system. The counterinsurgency methodologies implemented, from militia to special unit operations, had been in existence, but they had never been brought into play in support of a viable political goal. Predictably enough, to do so is the only possible 'approach' to insurgency. This is what the French discovered in Algeria. They perfected superb techniques for decimating the insurgent infrastructure,[111] but in the absence of a genuine strategic cause for which to fight, their concocted alternative — *Algérie française* — proved to be only a stop-gap solution. Unwilling to forever bail even as the boat filled, Charles de Gaulle pulled the plug on the French commitment.[112] No such end was in store in the Thai case, because the growth of constitutism provided the cause, one sanctioned by the 'voices' that carried the most weight in Thai society, the King and Buddhism.[113]

NOTES

1.   Some decades ago the percentage of young men who actually followed this stipulation was estimated at 90 per cent. More recently the figure is reported to have fallen to 55 per cent. Still, the point should not be lost that even today — and certainly during the modern period addressed by this chapter — fully half of the male population of the kingdom yet feels compelled to follow a specifically articulated path of correct conduct. For an interesting examination of young men's motivations for joining the *Sangha* cf. Toshio Yatsushiro, *Village Organization and Leadership to Northeast Thailand* (Bangkok: USOM, 1966).

2.   A partial listing would include such significant works as Herbert Phillips, *Thai Peasant Personality: The Patterning of Interpersonal Behavior in the Village of Bang Chan* (Los Angeles, CA: Univ. of California Press, 1966); Howard K. Kaufman, *Bangkhuad* (Locust Valley, NY: J.J. Agustin, 1960); John DeYoung, *Village Life in Modern Thailand* (Berkeley, CA: Univ. of California Press, 1955); Michael Moerman, *Agricultural Change and Peasant Choice in a Thai Village* (Los Angeles, CA: Univ. of California Press, 1968); Steven Piker, *An Examination of Character and Socialization in a Thai Peasant Community* (Ann Arbor, MI: Univ. Microfilms, 1964); and Yoneo Ishii (ed.), *Thailand: A Rice-Growing Society*, trans. Peter and Stephanie Hawkes, Monograph No.12 (English Lang. Series, Center Press of Hawaii, 1978). For further information on the 'loosely structured' analysis which established the dominant paradigm for studies on Thai society, cf. Hans-Dieter Evers, *Loosely Structured Social Systems: Thailand in Comparative Perspective*, Cultural Report Series No.17, Southeast Asia Studies, (New Haven, CT: Yale Univ., 1969).

3.   Fred W. Riggs (Univ. of Hawaii), who originally set forth the theory of the bureaucratic polity, has conceptualized its opposite, the constitutive system, as those mechanisms allowing realization of the popular will.

4.   Background on the CPT may be found in Virginia Thompson and Richard Adloff, *The Left Wing in Southeast Asia* (NY: William Sloane Assoc., 1950), esp. Ch.3: 'Thailand (Siam)', pp.51–7; David A. Wilson, 'Thailand and Marxism', Ch.3 in Frank N. Trager, *Marxism in Southeast Asia* (Stanford, CA: Stanford UP, 1959), pp.58–101; Justus M. van der Kroef, *Communism in South-east Asia* (Los Angeles: Univ. of California Press, 1980), esp. pp.17–22, 80–6, 155–63, 194–202, 271–3; Patrice de Beer, 'History and Policy of the Communist Party of Thailand', *Journal of Contemporary Asia*, 8/1 (1978), pp.143–58; *The Road to Victory: Documents from the Communist Party of Thailand* (Chicago, IL: Liberator Press, 1978); Ross Prizzia, 'Thailand: New Social Forces and Re-Emerging Socialist Principles', *Asia Quarterly*, 1975/4, pp.343–65; Prizzia, *Thailand in Transition: The Role of Oppositional Forces*, Asian Studies at Hawaii No.32, Center for Asian and Pacific Studies (Honolulu, HI: Univ. of Hawaii Press, 1985); Yuangrat (Pattanapongse) Wedel, *Modern Thai Radical Thought: The*

Siamization of Marxism and its Theoretical Problems (Ann Arbor, MI: Univ. Microfilms Int., 1981), published as *Radical Thought, Thai Mind: The Development of Revolutionary Ideas in Thailand* (Bangkok: Assumption Business Admin. College, 1987); Kanok Wongtrangan, *Communist Revolutionary Process: A Study of the Communist Party of Thailand* (Ann Arbor, MI: Univ. Microfilms Int., 1981); and Thadeus Flood, 'The Thai Left Wing in Historical Context', *Bulletin of Concerned Asian Scholars* (April–June 1975), pp.55–67.

5. For a theoretical discussion of this distinction, cf. Larry E. Cable, *Conflict of Myths: The Development of American Counterinsurgency Doctrine and the Vietnam War* (NY: NY UP, 1986).

6. Map constructed through interviews with Thai and American intelligence personnel, 1970–78; published as p.12 of my *Thailand: The Threatened Kingdom*, Conflict Study No.115 (London: Inst. for the Study of Conflict, Jan./Feb. 1980). For further data on Vietnamese aspects of the support structure, cf. Office of the Deputy Chief of Staff for Intelligence (G2), US Army Pacific (USARPAC)-Intelligence Div., 'The 35th PL/95th NVA Combined Command: External Support to the Thai Insurgency', Confidential doc. No.AB–335–6–1–74, 1 June 1974. This document, now declassified, was apparently used as the basis for most press discussions on the subject of foreign aid to the Thai insurgency. Chinese support has not been examined in as much depth. The memoirs of Allied agents who infiltrated into Thailand from China during World War II are an important source, however. Comparing their recollections with data from sources relevant to the insurgency reveals that the communists used these same, long-established routes. A summary may be found in John B. Haseman, *The Thai Resistance Movement During the Second World War*, Special Report No.17/1978 of the Center for Southeast Asian Studies (DeKalb, IL: Northern Illinois Univ., 1978), esp. pp.71-9, 85–6. A useful map is found on p.79.

7. I have discussed this issue previously, within the overall context of Thai security, in my *Thailand: The Threatened Kingdom* (n.6).

8. James C. Scott, 'Revolution in the Revolution: Peasants and Commissars', *Theory and Society*, 7/1 & 2 (Jan.–March 1979), pp.97–134.

9. A preponderance of the literature on rebellion *per se*, it is worth noting, derives its data and premises from instances of *peasant* rebellion. Discussion centers on two principal questions: (a) Why do peasants actually become involved in rebellion/revolutionary action? and (b) Which particular peasant strata are most prone to participate in such activities? Good overviews are contained in: Bruce Cumings, 'Interest and Ideology in the Study of Agrarian Politics', *Politics and Society*, 10/4 (1981), pp.467–95; J. Craig Jenkins, 'Why Do Peasants Rebel? Structural and Historical Theories of Modern Peasant Rebellions', *American Journal of Sociology*, 88/3 (Nov. 1982), pp.487–514; Theda Skocpol, 'Review Article: What Makes Peasants Revolutionary?', *Comparative Politics*, 14/3 (April 1982), pp.351–75.

    Also useful is the collection of papers presented at a symposium on 'Peasant Strategies in Asian Societies: Moral and Rational Economic Approaches', *Journal of Asian Studies*, 42/4 (Aug.1983), pp.747–865.

10. Though rarely dealt with explicitly, the precise relationship between peasant rebellion and insurgency remains a simmering debate in the literature. While Scott (n.8) has approached the subject theoretically, his important insights have not inspired a body of empirical work. Ben Kerkvliet raises the issue, then quickly abandons it, in his 'Patterns of Philippine Resistance and Rebellion', *Pilipinas*, 6 (Spring 1986), pp.35–52 (see esp. fn. 4). Nevertheless, virtually all works in the field, consciously or otherwise, adopt a position. For the point is crucial: If an insurgency is judged as essentially a coalition of various local rebellions, then examination must focus on the sources of peasant unrest (whether driven by 'moral economy' or 'rational' inspiration). If, however, infrastructure tightly controls and regulates the insurgency, recruiting manpower from a wide variety of strata, then the focus of research shifts to the mechanisms

of organization. It can readily be seen that these two perspectives are hardly value-neutral. In the first case, rebellion can be said to come from 'within'; in the second, from 'without'. The first case inherently presupposes a certain legitimacy in the uprising; the second lends itself to an explanation of 'manipulation by outsiders'. These are, respectively, the basic positions of the left and right wings of the political spectrum. Predictably, a fusion of the two approaches, with special attention paid to the evolution of a movement over time, yields the most satisfactory results.

11. John McBeth, 'Thailand: Seeking a Strong Local Accent', *Far Eastern Economic Review* (hereafter, FEER), 22 Aug. 1980, pp.30–2.

12. 'New Direction, New Blood', FEER, 27 July 1979, p.7.

13. 'CPT Secretary General in Beijing Hospital', *Bangkok Post*, 6 Nov. 1981, p.3.

14. Cf. John McBeth, 'Thailand: In From the Cold (2)', FEER, 17 Sept. 1982, pp.12–15.

15. Flood (n.4).

16. Internal Security Operations Command (ISOC), 'The Development and Organization of the CPT in Trang and Phatthalung Provinces, South Thailand', mimeo doc. dtd 26 Dec. 1976; Ref. No. Z1013.

17. Cf. my 'Government Policy as a Reflection of the Development Model: The Case of Accelerated Rural Development (ARD) in Northeast Thailand', *Journal of East & West Studies* [Seoul], 10/1 (1981), pp.59–95.

18. For details see Jere R. Behrman, 'Significance of Intra-country Variations for Asian Agricultural Prospects: Central and Northeastern Thailand', *Asian Survey*, 8/3 (March 1968), pp.157–73; Ronald C.Y. Ng, 'Some Land Use Problems of Northeast Thailand', *Modern Asian Studies*, 4/1 (1970), pp.23–42; Millard F. Long, 'Economic Development in Northeast Thailand', *Asian Survey*, 6/7 (July 1966), pp.355–61.

19. Even in 1968/69, 97.3 per cent of the farmers in the northeast were owner-operators. Cf. Andrew Turton, 'The Current Situation in the Thai Countryside', *Journal of Contemporary Asia*, 8/1 (1978), p.112.

20. Behrman (n.18) cites a 1966 figure that northeastern incomes were 65 per cent of the national average.

21. Kamol Janlekha, *Saraphi (A Survey of Socio-Economic Conditions in a Rural Community in North-East Thailand* (Zurich: Geographical Publications, 1968).

22. See Charles F. Keyes, *Isan: Regionalism in Northeast Thailand* (Ithaca, NY: Cornell Univ., 1967); for attitude surveys see Somchai Rakwijit, *Village Leadership in Northeast Thailand* and *Study of Youth in Northeast Thailand* (both Bangkok: Joint Thai-US Military Research and Development Center, 1971).

23. Keyes, *Isan*, p.35.

24. Ibid, p.39.

25. These demands called for a short-term development project to deal with urgent problems and a long-term effort which would include establishment of heavy industries in the northeast, together with an increase in educational facilities.

26. For the context of these demands, cf. my 'Sino-Thai Relations', *Asian Affairs* [London], 5/3 (Oct. 1974), pp.296–310.

27. Keyes, *Isan*, p.49.

28. Donald E. Weatherbee, *The United Front in Thailand* (Columbia, SC: Univ. of South Carolina, 1970), p.24.

29. John McBeth, 'Revolution to Evolution', FEER, 12 May 1983, pp.24–5.

30. Cf. Komsan Madukham, *Dong Prachao: Land of the Dead* (Bangkok: Pitakpracha, 1977) [in Thai]. This is a useful volume, one of 18 such works that Somchai Rakwijit, Research Director for CSOC/ISOC, arranged for his personnel to produce using pen names. The authors, such as Komsan, thus had access to all available data, to include classified material.

31. Interview with Somchai Rakwijit, former CSOC/ISOC Research Director, Bangkok, 13 May 1986. See also David Jenkins, 'The Hit-Run "Government"', FEER, 23 July 1973, pp.26–7.

32. Robert F. Zimmerman, 'Insurgency in Thailand', *Problems of Communism* (May-June 1976), p.27. Additional details may be found in Justus M. van der Kroef, 'Guerrilla Communism and Counterinsurgency in Thailand', *Orbis*, 18/1 (Spring 1974), pp. 106-39 (see esp. pp.119–22).

33. Ralph W. McGehee, *Deadly Deceits: My 25 Years in the CIA* (NY: Sheridan Square Publications, 1983), p.109.

34. Zimmerman (n.32), p.21, observes: 'There is sometimes considerable controversy both within and between various government agencies (Thai and foreign) as to where "Communists" are or are not "active".'

35. Portions of this section have appeared in my 'Thailand's Terror Years', *Soldier of Fortune*, 15/8 (Aug. 1990), pp.30–7 (contd.).

36. Interview with Saiyud Kerdphol, former Supreme Commander of the Royal Thai Armed Forces, Payao Province, 31 Aug. 1987.

37. Cf. Saiyud Kerdphol, *Struggle for Thailand, Section II, A Solution for the North* (Bangkok, nfd).

38. Arnold Abrams and Chiang Kham, 'Mountains of Discontent', FEER, 2 July 1970, pp. 20–2.

39. Kerdphol, *Struggle for Thailand* (n.37), pp.7–11.

40. John R. Thomson, 'The Burning Mountain', FEER, 25 April 1968, pp.218-20.

41. James P. Sterba, 'Thais Attack a Rebel Stronghold', *New York Times* (hereafter, NYT), 18 March 1972, p.3; Sterba, 'Thai Drive Snares Few Red Guerrillas', NYT, 26 March 1972, p.1.

42. Interview with Deputy Headman (name indistinct) of Ban Huasan, Payao Province, 31 Aug. 1987.

43. Interview with Nuyua Sayang, farmer, Ban Huasan, Payao Province, 31 Aug. 1987.

44. Interview with Laopao Sasong, farmer, ibid.

45. Community Development Program, *Summary of National Community Development Programme Thailand* (Bangkok: Dept. of Interior, 1961).

46. E.g., Community Development Bureau (n.45); Thanom Kittikachorn, *Trends in Community Development* (Bangkok: Dept. of Interior, 1964); Vichit Sukaviriya (ed.), *Facts About Community Development Programs* (Bangkok: Ministry of Interior, 1966).

47. Community Development Bureau (n.45), p.1.

48. Keyes (n.22), p.56.

49. According to D. Saharuni, 'United States Aid to Thailand', USAID mimeograph, 6 Nov. 1969, early programs, which averaged about $7 million p.a. through FY 1954, consisted almost entirely of technical assistance. These were expanded in 1955, the growth reflecting increased US concern over the security and development of Southeast Asia after the French withdrawal from Indochina. In addition to technical assistance, the program turned to commodity support and major infrastructure development. Grant assistance during FY 1955–62 averaged approximately $27 million p.a. Also during this time, the US initiated its development loan program to Thailand, which totalled $49.6 million through 1962 and which was supplemented by over $26 million in long term loans by the Export-Import Bank.

50. Saharuni, 'US Aid to Thailand', pp.8–9.

51. George K. Tanham, *Trial in Thailand* (NY: Crane, Russak, 1974), p.75.

52. See, e.g., Ralph E. Dakin (ed.), *Security and Development in Northeast Thailand: Problems, Progress and the Roles of Amphoe, Tambol and Muban Government* (Bangkok: USOM/Thailand, 1968); USOM/Thailand, *Impact of USOM Supported Programs in Changwad Sakon Nakorn* (Bangkok: 1967). Further analysis is contained in Peter F. Bell, 'Thailand's Northeast: Regional Underdevelopment, 'Insurgency', and Official Response', *Pacific Affairs*, 42/1 (Spring 1969), pp.47–54.

53. Joyce Nakahara and Ronald A. Witton, *Development and Conflict in Thailand* (Ithaca, NY: Cornell Univ., 1971).

54. Cf. Norman Jacobs, *Modernization Without Development: Thailand as an Asian Case Study* (NY: Praeger, 1971); James C. Ingram, *Economic Change in Thailand 1850-1970*, rev. ed. (Stanford, CA: Stanford UP, 1971); T.H. Silcock, *The Economic Development of Thai Agriculture* (Ithaca, NY: Cornell UP, 1970); Chandra Rabibhadana, *A Proposal for a Five-Year Plan of Social Development in Thailand* (Bangkok: Thai Watana Panich, 1973); Richard L. Hough, 'Development and Security in Thailand: Lessons From Other Asian Countries', *Asian Survey*, 9/3 (March 1969), pp.178–87.

55. This is a central theme, e.g., in Chai-anan Samudavanija, Kusuma Snitwongse, and Suchit Bunbongkarn, *From Armed Suppression to Political Offensive: Attitudinal Transformation of Thai Military Officers Since 1976* (Bangkok: Inst. of Security and Int. Studies, Chulalongkorn Univ., 1990). For an alternative approach, proceeding within a larger framework of reaction to perceived threat, see my 'The Thai Approach to Peacemaking Since World War II', *Journal of East & West Studies* [Seoul], 7/1 (April 1978), pp.133–55; and 'An Eclectic Model of Thailand's Participation in the Vietnam War', *Peace Research* [Ontario], 11/2 (April 1979), pp.71–6.

56. Cf. Michael T. Klare, *War Without End* (NY: Vintage Books, 1972); Frances Fitzgerald, *Fire in the Lake* (Boston: Little, Brown, 1972); David Halberstam, *The Best and the Brightest* (Greenwich, CT: Fawcett Publications, 1972).

57. Agency for International Development, *Introduction to Program Presentation to the Congress/Proposed FY 1971 Program*, nfd.

58. For a representative selection see US Military Academy, *Revolutionary Warfare*, 6 vols. (West Point, NY: Dept. of Military Art and Engineering, 1967); Naval War College, *Selected Readings for Counterinsurgency Course*, 4 vols. (Newport, RI: USNWC, 1968); Sir Robert Thompson, *Defeating Communist Insurgency* (NY: Praeger, 1966).

59. James P. Sterba, 'Thai Insurgents Seen Increasing', NYT, 27 March 1972, p.18.

60. David K. Wyatt, *Thailand: A Short History* (New Haven, CT: Yale UP, 1984), p.290. This analysis culminates Wyatt's discussion on pp.286–90, which (esp. pp.287–8) agrees with my own work, particularly 'Thai Security During the 'American Era', 1960-1976', *Issues & Studies* [Taipei], 15/4 (April 1979), pp.61–88.

61. For a more detailed treatment cf. my *The United Front in Thailand Since October 1976*, No.71 in Courrier de L'Extreme-Orient series, Centre D'Etude du Sud-Est Asiatique et de L'Extreme Orient [Brussels], Oct. 1979; 'The Communist Party and the Strategy of the United Front in Thailand Since October 1976', *Asia Quarterly* [Brussels], 1980/1, pp.3–18; and 'The Maoist Conception of the United Front, With Special Reference to the United Front in Thailand Since October 1976', *Issues & Studies* [Taipei], 16/3 (March 1980), pp.46–69.

62. See Stuart Schram, *The Political Thought of Mao Tse-tung* (NY: Praeger, 1969), pp. 64–5.

63. VOPT broadcasts, as well as those of other Thai radio stations, are translated and made available in the US Foreign Broadcast Information Service (FBIS) *Asia & Pacific Daily Report*. FBIS is an organ of the Central Intelligence Agency (CIA). On 11 July 1979, under circumstances to be discussed in more detail later in the text, VOPT announced that it was temporarily going off the air. Broadcasts were never resumed, though for a time a 'VOPT News Service' distributed printed party pronouncements.

64. VOPT (Clandestine) (hereafter, VOPT [C]) in Thai to Thailand 1000 GMT (1700 Thai) 7 Oct. 1976.

65. VOPT (C) in Thai to Thailand 1000 GMT (1700 Thai) 4 Oct. 1977.

66. A table of the broadcasts used in this analysis is contained in my monograph, *The United Front in Thailand Since October 1976*.

67. European Coordinating Committee for Solidarity With the Thai People (ECCSTP), founded 10–12 March 1978, listed as its members: Ad Hoc Group for Democracy in Thailand (AGDT), Britain; Thailand-Gruppen (TG), Denmark; Thailand Informations- und Solidaritatskomitee (TISK), West Germany; and Comite de

Solidarité avec le Peuple Thai (CSPT), France. Other typical solidarity groups, cited in *TIC News* [Thai Inf. Center] and *Thai Information Bulletin*: Ligue Communiste Revolutionnaire Section Française de la 4e Internationale, France; United Secretariat of the Fourth International, France; Clergy and Laity Concerned, US; Communist Labor Party, US; Communist Party (Marxist-Leninist of the United States); National Lawyers Guild, US; Friends of the Filipino People, US; Support Committee for the Chilean Resistance, US; Action Against Apartheid, National Conference Working Group, US; Socialist Party of Japan; Pacific Asia Resources Center (PAAC), Japan; Japan Afro-Asian Writers Association; and Ad Hoc Committee for the Thai Solidarity Campaign, Japan.

68. *TIC News*, 1/20 (1 May 1978), p.1.
69. See, e.g., Helen R. Chauncey, 'The Growth of the United Front', *Southeast Asia Chronicle*, No.60 (Jan.-Feb. 1978), pp.2–9.
70. VOPT (C) in Thai to Thailand 1000 GMT (1700 Thai) 27 Sept. 1978.
71. David Morell and Chai-anan Samudavanija, 'Thailand's Revolutionary Insurgency: Changes in Leadership Potential', *Asian Survey*, 19/4 (April 1979), p.332.
72. A more detailed treatment may be found in my 'The Thai Monarchy Under Siege', *Asia Quarterly* [Brussels], 1978/2, pp.109–41; and 'The Status of the Monarchy in Thailand', *Issues & Studies* [Taipei], 13/11 (Nov. 1977), pp.51–70.
73. Cf. my 'The Military and Politics in Thailand: An Analysis of the Two October Coups (1976-1977)', *Issues & Studies* [Taipei], 13/11 (Nov. 1977), pp.58–90; and 'October 1976 and the Role of the Military in Thai Politics', *Modern Asian Studies* [Cambridge], 14/3 (1980), pp.399–440.
74. Cf. my *Thailand: The Threatened Kingdom* (n.6), esp.pp.17-18.
75. Cf. John McBeth, 'A Battle for Loyalty in the Jungles', FEER, 8 June 1979, pp.19–21; McBeth, 'Thailand: Communists at the Crossroads', ibid., 27 July 1979, pp.30–1; McBeth, 'Insurgencies: The Ideological Crossroads', ibid., 8 Feb. 1980, pp.32–4. These were supplemented by conversations with McBeth, esp.one in Manila, Philippines, 22 July 1990.
76. John McBeth, 'Communism: Hazards Along the Neutral Path', FEER, 19 Sept. 1980, pp.43-8. See also McBeth's earlier 'In Search of a New Direction', FEER, 10 Aug. 1979, pp.30–1.
77. For a more detailed discussion on the Vietnamese approach to revolutionary warfare, see two works by Chalmers Johnson: *Autopsy on People's War* (Berkeley, CA: Univ. of California Press, 1973); and 'The Third Generation of Guerrilla Warfare', *Asian Survey*, 7/6 (June 1978), pp.435–47.
78. VOPT (C) in Thai to Thailand 1000 GMT (1700 Thai) 7 June 1979. See also the useful article, 'Thailande: Le P.C. Pro-Chinois Propose au Gouvernement "Une Cooperation Temporaire Contre la Menace D'Expansion Vietnamienne",' *Le Monde*, 26 June 1979, nfd.
79. VOPT (C) in Thai to Thailand 1000 GMT (1700 Thai) 11 July 1979. The broadcast the previous day also stated that VOPT would be going off the air temporarily.
80. This rival organization, *Pak Mai* (New Party), was later to be revealed as the Thai *Isan* Liberation Party, founded in Vientiane on 22 Oct. 1979. Cf. 'Northern Separatists', FEER, 4 April 1980, p.7.
81. 'Critical Time for Thai Communists', *Bangkok Post*, 22 Nov. 1981, p.6.
82. Numerous sources exist for coverage of this episode. Among the best are John McBeth, 'The Coup That Never Was', FEER, 10 April 1981, pp.10–15, together with accompanying articles under the general title, 'Thailand's Night of the Generals'. Also valuable, particularly for its discussion of the centers of power in the Thai polity, is Philip Bowring and Paisal Sricharatchanya, 'Shaking the Pillars', FEER, 19 June 1981, pp.38–43, as well as 'The Power Wielded by a Constitutional Monarch', pp.53–5 and McBeth, 'A Profile of the Young Turks' Camp', pp.44–53, both in FEER, 19 June 1981.

83. Interview with Somchai Rakwijit, former CSOC/ISOC Research Director, Bangkok, 13 May 1986.

84. Much of the material in this section, particularly that related to personalities, has been drawn from personal experience. Additionally, I am indebted to discussions, spanning, in certain cases, at least a decade and numerous locations, with: Saiyud Kerdphol, former Supreme Commander of the Royal Thai Armed Forces; Anthony 'Tony' Paul, former Regional Editor (Asia) for *Reader's Digest*; John McBeth, former Thailand correspondent for FEER; Mike Jones, former British Army Lt.-Col., Special Air Service (SAS) and now a security consultant; and John Cole and Denny Lane, both US Army Colonels and former army attachés in Bangkok.

85. Interview with Saiyud Kerdphol, Payao Province, 31 Aug. 1987.

86. Ibid.

87. Cf. Samudavanija *et al.* (n.55).

88. Texts with commentary may be found in Sarochna Robbamrung, 'Internal Security, Kingdom of Thailand', unpub. paper dated 11 Feb. 1987, prepared for US Army War College. Several sources claim that Prem himself wrote 66/23 — it is not a long document. I have been unable to confirm actual authorship, though it is certain the Prime Ministerial Order was the product of much discussion amongst a small circle that included the officers named.

89. Sarochna, 'Internal Security'.

90. Ibid., p.5.

91. Ibid.

92. These have been compiled in edited form in Saiyud Kerdphol, *The Struggle for Thailand: Counterinsurgency 1965–1985* (Bangkok: S. Research Center, 1986). It is significant that Saiyud attributes impetus for the book, at least in part, to the late Gerry Waller. A veteran of the pre-World War II Indian Army, Gerry was later to serve with the Malayan Police Force during the Emergency, 1948–60, and then as a consultant in Thailand for the Stanford Research Inst. (SRI). He met Saiyud in 1970 and became a close confidant, thus contributing his own insights to the evolution of CPM, which itself drew inspiration from the British approach in Malaya. He died of cancer in May 1983 in Bangkok.

93. This figure appears in John D. Blair IV, 'Thailand 1984: A New Generation Prepares to Assume the Reins of Power', unpub. paper prepared for presentation at the US Pacific Command Security Assistance Conference [site not specified], 3–7 Dec. 1984. It agrees with figures provided by Saiyud Kerdphol, former commander of the force, in an interview, Honolulu, 6 Dec. 1987.

94. *Lèse-majesté* remains a serious crime in Thailand. Even the play *The King and I* continues to be banned. Recent convictions have demonstrated the latitude with which the charge may be interpreted. Consequently, research dealing with the royal family's role in society remains a difficult proposition.

95. Interview with Saiyud Kerdphol, Payao Province, 31 Aug. 1987.

96. For these insights I am indebted to John Cole, esp.his 'Professionalism in the Royal Thai Army: National Defense or Political Actor? The Prem-Arthit Era', unpub. MS, 1 Feb. 1984.

97. Interview with Saiyud Kerdphol, Bangkok, 13 May 1986.

98. This is the figure given by Marjorie A. Muecke, 'The Village Scouts of Thailand', *Asian Survey*, 20/4 (April 1980), p.407.

99. Anthony Paul, 'The Jungle War the Communists Lost', *Reader's Digest*, Asian ed. (Oct. 1984), pp.2–6, gives CPT strength as 14,000 armed insurgents, with another 20,000 directly involved in support activities. No estimates ever placed the mass base in the 2.5 million range (the number who went through the Village Scouts Training Program, a one-week course).

100. Paisal Sricharatchanya, 'Security: Playing the Same Game', FEER, 18 Dec. 1981, pp. 15–16.

101. See, e.g., Jim Coyne, 'Thailand's Battle Road', *Soldier of Fortune*, 7/2 (Feb. 1982), pp. 37–43 (cont.).
102. Cf. Paul (n.99); John McBeth, 'Thailand: The Bulldozer Invasion', FEER, 8 May 1981, pp.26–28.
103. Anthony Paul has noted, in a witty piece, 'Insights: Sex and the Single Insurgent', *Asiaweek*, 8 April 1983, p.24:
    As the surrendering insurgents have flooded into the Army's 'open arms' over the past twelve months, the soldiery have been impressed by the defectors' priorities in the first hours of their new coexistence with capitalism. Said a Phitsanulok-based colonel: 'As far as I've been able to establish, a communist is someone with an over-powering interest in sea-food [notably missing from the jungle diet] and sex. Did Marx say anything about this?'
104. Cf. Rodney Tasker, 'Insurgency: A More Peaceful South', FEER, 11 Oct. 1984, pp.28–9.
105. For an excellent overview see Anthony Paul, 'Winding Down a War', *Asiaweek*, 8 April 1983, pp.16-24.
106. Good overviews may be found in the several articles contained in Ho Kwon Ping's cover story, 'Thailand Inc.', FEER, 23 May 1980, pp.40–6; see also National Westminster Bank, 'Thailand: An Economic Report', Jan. 1981. A later analysis of the Thai economy across time, with a discussion of this increasing integration into the world-economy, is Kevin Hewison, *Bankers and Bureaucrats: Capital and the Role of the State in Thailand* Southeast Asia Studies Monograph Series No.34, (New Haven, CT: Yale Univ. 1989).
107. It is useful for my cultural argument that the structural strains created by this eco-nomic boom have resulted not in the growth of radical solutions but of Buddhist reli-gious movements outside the established hierarchy. Though I do not necessarily agree with the conclusions, a limited overview of this phenomenon may be found in Suwanna Satha-Anand, 'Religious Movements in Contemporary Thailand: Buddhist Struggles for Modern Relevance', *Asian Survey*, 30/4 (April 1990), pp.395–408.
108. Original in Thai; examined with the assistance of Somchai Rakwijit, Bangkok, 3 March 1987.
109. Ibid.
110. Ibid.
111. Cf. Peter Paret, *French Revolutionary Warfare From Indochina to Algeria: The Analysis of a Political and Military Doctrine* (NY: Praeger, 1964); see also Roger Trinquier, *Modern Warfare: A French View of Counterinsurgency* (NY: Praeger, 1964).
112. The most compelling account of both the particulars and the emotions of this episode is to be found in Jean Larteguy, *The Centurions* (NY: Avon Book Div., 1961).
113. With the collapse of the CPT, there followed the usual mopping up, which has con-tinued to the present. Counterinsurgency operations, so effective because they had become a *national* as opposed to a strictly *military* endeavor, were multifaceted. In addition to combat, they involved activities ranging from civic action to road building to agricultural advice. Simultaneously, a substantial psychological warfare effort blan-keted the kingdom. As the CPT threat diminished still further, there were those who began to question the threat this all-encompassing CSOC/ISOC effort might pose for the fledgling Thai democracy. Indoctrinated mass organizations answering to the com-mands and agenda of an unelected element of the bureaucracy could, critics charged, easily prove a Frankenstein. Regardless, this military orientation continues to the pre-sent, together with popular fears that the men on horseback may once again attempt to ride into power — as they appear to be doing following the abortive April–May 1992 coup.
    This, of course, would be the ultimate irony. The Thai military spent four decades following 1932 focusing its concern on the maintenance of power and the accumula-tion of wealth. Faced with a growing insurgency and the chaos of the 1973–76 demo-

cratic interlude, key elements of the security forces became increasingly sensitized to the need for systemic reform. This psychological transformation took concrete shape in the Young Turk movement and in the Democratic Soldiers, both of which dramatically altered the military, particularly the army. When the army chief, Prem, also became prime minister, the entire kingdom was mobilized for counterinsurgency behind the 'politics leads' strategy. In short order, a correct strategy combined with those other factors already cited to destroy the CPT, because the heart of the government effort was to foster popular participation in all aspects of the kingdom's affairs — that is, to nurture the constitutive system.

Having done this, however, and having made the transition from authoritarian to democratic rule, Thailand now faces a dilemma. The military has redefined its role as those activities which 'develop' the country. But there are within its ranks those who feel they — the victors in the counterinsurgency — are most qualified to decide the form and priorities of such development. This creates an inherent contradiction within the constitutive system by creating pressures for a return to the mechanisms of the bureaucratic polity. The extent to which such sentiments can be controlled will decide the future of Thai democracy.

2 Maoist Miscue II: The Demise of the Communist Party of the Philippines, 1968–1993

Barring unforseen circumstances, Manila is on the verge of recording the second major victory against a Maoist insurgency in the post-Vietnam War era. The previous win was that of the Thai[1]. Ironically, as was true in Thailand so has it been the case in the Philippines: government-led 'people's war' has mortally wounded the Maoist-inspired effort by the communists to seize state power.

This is a significant development. Western press reports on the Philippines, though, seem dominated by only two subjects — kidnappings of wealthy Chinese-Filipinos and the country's ongoing electrical power crisis — even as the real news continues to be the steady if not dramatic progress of Manila's counterinsurgency against the Communist Party of the Philippines (CPP), its National Democratic Front (NDF), and its armed wing, the New People's Army (NPA). The CPP itself is in a state of complete disarray, wracked by internal factionalism amounting to a virtual schism between elements favoring opposing strategic approaches to the conflict. Consequently, increasing numbers of communist personnel have simply decided to call it quits. While official Philippine government figures place the NPA's armed strength in the neighborhood of 12,000, there may in reality be only half that number in the field. Incidents are down nationwide, and the Philippine National Police (PNP) has been cleared by President Fidel Ramos to assume total counterinsurgency responsibilities in 21 out of the 74 provinces and several other smaller areas nationwide. Plans proceed to turn the entire counterinsurgency mission over to the PNP as called for by law.

Presently, the Armed Forces of the Philippines (AFP) continues to exercise primary counterinsurgency responsibility under a formal extension of authority granted upon PNP request due to the extraordinary circumstances yet prevailing in many areas. Nevertheless, the law which phased out the former Philippine Constabulary (PC) and merged its personnel with either the PNP or armed forces — virtually all personnel in the PC's numerous

companies chose to become policemen rather than servicemen —
stipulated that counterinsurgency would become a PNP task at the
end of 1992. The AFP's continued leading role in the mission
operates under a one-year lease, with the military slated to begin
focusing on the more conventional task of territorial defense.
Indeed, so changed is the overall security environment that some
Philippine congressmen have even begun to call for the abolition
of the as yet indispensable militia, the Citizen Armed Forces
Geographical Units (CAFGU).

It seems unlikely that such a recommendation will be acted
upon, any more than the military will suddenly opt out of the
counterinsurgency picture. True, government figures list the PNP
as responsible for security in 30,000 villages (*barangay*) as opposed
to the 12,000 which remain the AFP's responsibility, but it is the
military's relative honesty and effectiveness which have allowed
the counterinsurgency to progress steadily. In the past, it was
paramilitary abuse which played a key role in convincing many
Filipinos that revolt was preferable to repression. The greatly
improved conduct of security forces since 1986 has been important in convincing many of these same individuals that the establishment offers a viable route for personal betterment. With the
PNP only beginning to coalesce as a force, the military remains
much more capable of continued counterinsurgency missions.

As for the CAFGU themselves, in many areas a substantial proportion of their personnel are made up of former communist cadre
who have defected because they are unwilling to endure the CPP's
own repression any longer. They are unlikely to view with equa-
nimity the notion that the time is ripe for them to go about
unarmed. Regardless, the suggestion that circumstances have
improved so much that even CAFGU can be replaced is indicative
of the strategic sea-change which has occurred.

This sea-change has gone all but unnoticed in the media. On the
one hand, this is understandable, because with the end of the Cold
War and the withdrawal of American forces, the Philippines has in
many respects become superfluous to the international situation.
Deprived of its geostrategic role as a linchpin in the anti-communist defense shield, it possesses neither the economic nor political
weight to remain center stage (Taiwan would be a useful example
to the contrary). On the other hand, it is perplexing, for it was
only recently that the Western press seemed riveted on the state of
Philippine security. 'Guerrillas Now Hold Edge in War', cried a

typical headline. 'In Philippine Communist Camp, Smell of Victory', opined another.

Gradually, though, the battle has returned to the shadows — for all but the Filipinos. Yet violence associated with the insurgency has declined to an acceptable level. More meaningfully, while the CPP bid for power has not ended, strategically the conflict is now only the government's to lose.

Growth of the Communist Opposition to the Old-Regime

Communism, of course, is a political response to societal realities. The Philippines (see Map 2), as is the case with most Third World countries, has long suffered from an array of socio-economic problems: poverty, malnutrition, disparity of wealth, and so forth. These have interacted with the multi-faceted legacy of three and a half centuries of colonial rule (three centuries by the Spanish, the remainder by the Americans). In particular, the country has been cursed with a skewed economic structure centered about subsistence plots and the cash-generating capacities of extractive industries and export agriculture, a structure unable to absorb fully the Philippines' relatively well-educated work force. Though democratic in framework since independence — which was achieved in the immediate aftermath of World War II — the political system has proved incapable of addressing this reality and in assuring social justice for all. Small wonder, then, argue critics, that the country has a history of peasant revolt, the most recent episode being the present insurgency.

Still, the CPP cannot be seen as a necessary outgrowth of Philippine realities. Indeed, it would probably not have become a going concern at all had it not been for the opportunity provided by the political repression of the Ferdinand Marcos regime. First elected president in 1965, again in 1969, Marcos secured his position by declaring martial law in 1972 (he would not be ousted until 1986). At that time, he attributed his drastic action to a variety of circumstances, among them the threat of communist insurgency, economic and social malaise (to include corruption), and escalating civic violence. In return for his being allowed to exercise extraordinary emergency powers, Marcos spoke of a 'democratic revolution' and a resulting 'new society'. Though it was impossible to judge the veracity of his declared motives as opposed to his pos-

MAP 2:
THE PHILIPPINES

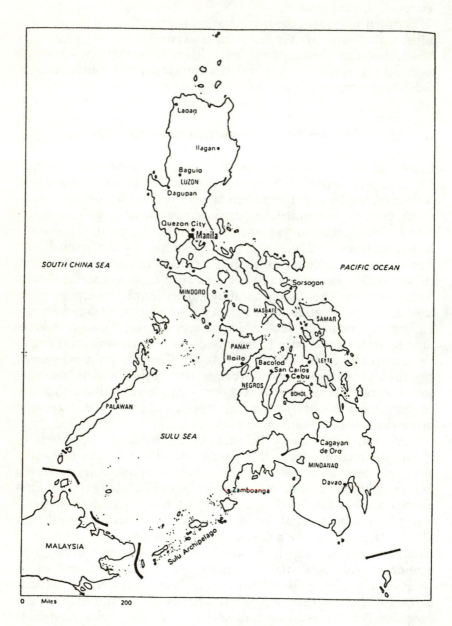

Source: Control Risks Information Service (CRIS), London.

sible personal ambition, Marcos was correct that at that particular juncture the Philippines was facing a difficult period.

The centuries of colonial rule had left the country an Asian hybrid, a mixture of East and West, comfortable with neither. By geography and ethnicity, the Filipinos were Asian; by culture, heritage, and orientation, they were Westerners, 'brown Americans' as the sobriquet went. In an Asian cultural scene nurtured by Eastern traditions, the Filipinos had been formed by a synthesis of local traditions with Catholicism. As a nation which thought of itself as a step further along on the road towards 'civilization', the Philippines experienced discomfort in dealing with other Asian states. The West was the role model; indigenous Philippine ideas, accomplishments, and products were regarded as slightly inferior.

Economically, however, the Philippines had emerged from colonialism in a sorry state. Possessing in any case minimal infrastructure or industry, the islands had during World War II been the scene of heavy fighting and of a harsh Japanese occupation. Shortly thereafter occurred the so-called Huk Rebellion and the dislocation it caused in the 'heartland' of Luzon. The product of these events was a weak free enterprise system heavily dependent upon external sources of capital. Centered about agricultural products and extractive industry, this system benefited a small minority. Foreign capital, especially American, was instrumental in expanding the two sectors just mentioned. The Americans provided 80 per cent of all foreign investment in 1970, and American holdings in that year comprised 19.5 per cent of all Philippine assets in manufacturing, commerce, services, utilities, mining, and agriculture. Particular concentration occurred in certain industries, such as oil, where assets were 80 per cent American-owned.

By the late 1960s even substantial foreign investment could not make up for growing structural problems. Under- and unemployment were widespread, the economy was stagnant, and there was unrest in the countryside, where land distribution was quite skewed, and amongst urban workers. The political process, which would have been expected to meet demands for change, for it was patterned after the American republican and federal system of democracy, was co-opted by the same narrow segment of the population which benefited from the economic arrangements. Corruption was widespread and massive. Notably, even as government bureaucracy, both civil and military, grew, disenchantment with the political process among the politically active sector took the demand-making function out of established channels and onto the streets. Though the precise impetus for and process whereby this occurred have been attributed to a variety of factors, it is clear that the political activism prevalent worldwide — especially in the US — during the 1960s served at a minimum as a catalyst for a resurgence of nationalism with anti-systemic overtones. This movement, while by no means limited to the intelligentsia, had at its heart the universities of the Manila area. Students and instructors were soon joined by others, notably discontented workers.

Simultaneously, the communist opposition, which had been dormant since its decimation in the 1950s by the late President Ramon Magsaysay's counterinsurgency program, experienced a resurgence. Drawing its strength from the same nationalistic organizations of youths, intellectuals, workers, and peasants as were denouncing (and renouncing) the formal political system, a new Communist Party of the Philippines (CPP) in 1968 convened a secret conference and then announced its adherence to the Maoist precept of 'people's war'. The CPP was actually a splinter from the older Philippine Communist Party (*Partido Komunista ng Philipinas*, PKP) but had split with the PKP due to fundamental differences of doctrine and strategy.

As would be expected from a Maoist-oriented party, the CPP was particularly active in united front activities, designed to promote communist goals legally while concealing the actual communist source and direction. Thus the pre-martial law period was marked by the appearance, even prior to the announcement of 'people's war', of several communist front organizations. Central to the orientation of these organizations was the advancement, particularly in the pages of the *Progressive Review*, edited by José Maria Sison, a one-time lecturer at the University of the Philippines, of the concept of 'neo-colonialism'. This approach — which was not an innovation — stated that true national independence from the colonial power, the US, did not exist, because in the neo-colonial arrangement at hand 'the responsibilities for governance of a colony are transferred to the nationalist leaders but only after a process whereby the latter are tamed and integrated into the capitalist system.'[2]

'Neo-colonialism' was to prove a key concept. While it was certainly a part of every Marxist lexicon, it was also a staple of radical, non-communist thought. Hence the CPP could link its aspirations for power with the emerging nationalist sentiments of various aggrieved popular sectors. Furthermore, within this 'neo-colonial' framework of analysis, to be a nationalist was necessarily to be opposed not only to the controlling neo-colonial power (i.e., the US) but also to its domestic 'lackies' (i.e., Marcos and his supporters), who were, according to the line, nothing more than pawns who owed their positions and their wealth to Washington. All components of the existing order, in fact, served to maintain the neo-colonial order and therefore were suspect and subject to attack as the situation dictated. In particular the economic and political structures were interlocking and mutually supportive and could not be considered apart from each other. Bringing down Marcos, in other words, would only lead to a like-minded replacement; the existing socio-economic-political structure required total alteration, a revolution.

Against this background the electoral campaign of 1969 was an important turning point. Though Marcos won re-election, the process was marked by a level of graft and expenditure staggering even by jaded Filipino standards. The embittered legal opposition turned to obstructionism, while among the radicalized elements, disillusionment and discontent gave way to outright opposition. Street demonstrations became commonplace in the capital, particularly as labor elements joined the fray. Far to the south, on and about Mindanao, there was also an upsurge of violence carried out by dissident Muslims dissatisfied with their position within a Christian society. The government responded to these challenges with repression, which further fanned the fires of discontent.

A crucial event in this escalating cycle of violence came in August 1972, when the Philippine Supreme Court ruled that all property in the country which had been purchased by American citizens or corporations since Philippine independence had been acquired illegally. Moreover, the court also ruled in a second case that any corporation which fell within categories limited to majority Filipino participation could not employ foreigners, regardless of the amount of foreign equity involved.[3] Much has been made in some circles of a subsequent meeting by the American Chamber of Commerce in Manila and its further conversations with Marcos, for it was but several days later that martial law was declared. Still, leaving conspiracy theories aside — because there simply is no evidence either one way or the other — it seems likely that the Supreme Court rulings were but the final factor in what Marcos perceived as a rapidly deteriorating domestic situation. In any case, on 22 September 1972 martial law was declared by Presidential Decree 1081.[4]

It is not necessary to review here the progress of martial law or its particular programs. Rather what is of interest is the pattern which emerged, a pattern Bob Stauffer has termed the 'rationalization' of the Philippine polity. 'Rationalization' was an effort to group functionally related bodies into singular, hierarchical, compulsory, non-competitive umbrella groups licensed by the government (e.g., employees' and employers' bodies). Taken as a whole, 'rationalization' amounted to an anti-systemic coup designed to silence populist opposition, whether expressed in governmental institutions such as the Supreme Court or through private channels such as student demonstrations. Coercion was used in a quest for stability.[5]

'Discipline' became a central articulated note of the 'New Society'. In fact such discipline could only be achieved through coercion to eliminate the opposition; a completely controlled press to assure a flow of information determined by the government; the elimination of existing deliberative and judicial institutions from any policy-making inputs into the system; and the establishment of a new constitution that permitted existing power holders to remain in position indefinitely and that legitimized changes in the direction of accommodation of foreign interests, particularly those of the US and Japan.

These moves naturally did not go unchallenged. Initially, opposition was principally an elite phenomenon. Martial law as a formal entity was not the issue amongst the masses that intellectuals and foreigners made of it. To the contrary, for a time there appeared at the village level (*barrio*, which became *barangay* in December 1972) to be widespread support for the new order, because some of its programs effected changes for the better. Rural violence, for example, at first declined substantially; and such programs as land reform, despite their minimal implementation, touched enough people to hold out hope for further positive steps. As time passed, however, opposition spread. Major segments of society, representing all sectors, became disillusioned. By at least the second half of the 1970s, it was clear that martial law was not living up to its 'New Society' billing and that the economy was not functioning well. Furthermore, the increasing integration of the Philippines into the world economy meant there was little immediate prospect for improvements at a time of global recession.[6]

Ultimately, the statistics on 'people's welfare indicators' became a major source of embarassment for the regime. Poverty, rather than declining, seemed to have grown. The gap between the rich and the poor had increased. Official figures listed 58 per cent of all Philippine families as having incomes below the poverty line, of which 80 per cent were rural folk. A 1978 Food and Nutrition Research Institute Survey revealed that nearly 70 per cent of all Philippine children were malnourished and that half of infant deaths were due to malnutrition. Some 38 per cent of Philippine households lacked the minimum energy requirement; 16 per cent were deficient in protein; and 43 per cent suffered Vitamin A deficiency. Millions of persons suffered from disease.

The point was not that these conditions were necessarily new or caused by martial law. Rather, they undermined the justification upon which martial law had been built: that is, it was necessary to curb political liberties if the welfare of the people was to be improved. Such statistics and others were viewed by dissidents within the context of a massive influx of foreign investment capital into the economy,[7] and a relationship between the continued poverty and deprivation, on the one hand, and foreign capital, on the other hand, was widely articulated and accepted. Both foreign government and private aid, loans, and investment were viewed as props for the Marcos regime. Indeed, as time passed, this view espoused the widely believed point that *save for these capital influxes* Marcos could have been toppled. That this was not necessarily or particularly valid was beside the point; it was a critical locus of philosophy about which both outlawed and 'establishment' opponents of martial law could rally.

Drawing upon its Maoist blueprint, the CPP quickly recognized that the declaration of martial law provided it with a golden opportunity to make common cause with dissident non-communist elements. A directive adopted by the CPP Central Committee in October 1972 explicitly recognized the polarization that was bound to result from Marcos' move and stated that the party should capitalize on this by playing down the class basis of the broad resistance movement directed against the regime. Instead, the document summoned 'all those who are interested in achieving national freedom and democracy' to join the CPP in a united front to carry on the struggle. A program for a coalition of anti-Marcos forces centered on: reestablishment of 'democratic rights' for 'anti-fascist forces'; nullification of 'unequal treaties' with the US; bringing Marcos and his 'diehard accomplices' to trial; and strengthening the armed forces of the CPP, the NPA.

Emphasis upon building 'national democracy' (also called 'new democracy' or 'national communism') was borrowed directly from Mao's 'New Democracy' concept — but as articulated publicly by the CPP, it claimed to lean more heavily towards a genuine national coalition under a form of democratic socialism. Subsequent CPP pronouncements seemed to suggest that the party believed there could be considerable latitude for minimizing formal class considerations. Instead, in its public pronouncements, the CPP placed its emphasis upon the importance of certain 'special groups', such as students and the intelligentsia, in the anti-Marcos struggle.

This orientation was formalized in April 1973 when a Preparatory Commission for the National Democratic Front met and issued a 'Ten Point Program' which was to be the keynote document for construction of an anti-Marcos united front. In the explanatory text accompanying the 'Ten Point Program of the National Democratic Front in the Philippines', the pronouncement stated:

> There should be no monopoly of political power by any class, party or group. The degree of participation in the government by any political force should be based on its effective role and record in the revolutionary struggle and on the people's approbation...The coalition government should allow the free interplay of national and democratic forces during and off [sic] elections. Thus, a truly democratic system of representation can develop and operate to the benefit of the people. Such a government should always be subject to the will of the people.[8]

Some analysts viewed this position as a possible departure of great importance from the standard communist strategy for victory through class warfare, that the CPP was actually willing to accept a post-capitalist coalition along the lines of democratic socialism. Supporting evidence for this conclusion, in addition to the CPP's statements, was allegedly provided by observing the priority that the CPP gave to united front construction over armed struggle. Such an analysis, however, was a fundamental misreading of Mao's 'people's war' tenets. In them it was clear that the building of a united front was not an 'optional' tactical expedient. To the contrary, Mao stated that it was a key element *of people's war*.

Of more than academic importance, contained therein lay the shape of a future Philippine society envisaged by the CPP. That shape, contrary to the platitudes contained in the 'Ten Point Program', had no room for democratic pluralism. In fact, the explanatory text of the 'Ten Point Program' specifically denounced 'clerico-fascists', the CPP term for those who espoused social democracy.[9] The same passage made clear that the 'Marcos versus the people' line was for the CPP the Maoist 'primary contradiction', while 'class struggle' was the 'secondary contradiction'. That the 'secondary contradiction' would become 'primary' once Marcos was gone scarcely needed iteration. To hold otherwise would have required that the CPP deny its own Marxist ideals and dialectic brand of reasoning. Hence its own doctrine, its public pronouncements notwithstanding, specifically renounced the sharing of power with non-communist groups unless they were working with the party to construct a communist society.

That those who threw in their lot with the NDF chose to ignore the ultimate political consequences of their collaboration with the CPP — making a pact with the devil, if one will — reflected the increasing polarization within the Philippines and the extent to which the communists were seen as the only credible anti-Marcos force. Thus the NDF grew rapidly, aided by reported human rights violations which served to radicalize even some members of the Catholic clergy. The NPA also expanded substantially. By the early 1980s the communist movement, whether considered in its armed wing or united front, had become a vibrant, growing concern throughout the archipelago.

For his part, Marcos capped the restructuring of the formal political system by a series of maneuvers designed not only to institutionalize his rule but also to provide for a smooth transfer of power. In January 1981 a formal end to martial law was declared by Presidential Proclamation 2045. Subsequently, a plebiscite held on 7 April 1981 was used to change the British-style parliamentary form of government — which had itself been brought in earlier to replace the American-style Presidential form — to a modified French-style system. The resulting powerful presidency was filled, of course, by Marcos in a bitterly-protested 16 June 1981 election. A 14-man Executive Council was created to provide for orderly succession.

Despite the fanfare which accompanied the alleged return to normalcy, all that had actually been done was to put an end to military tribunals and to the use of the term 'martial law'. The powers of the president to legislate and to order the arrest and detention of anyone considered subversive remained unchanged. Edicts issued previously under Presidential Decree 1081 drew their authority, instead, from Amendment Six to the 1973 Constitution as ratified in 1976. All martial law proclamations, orders, decrees, instructions, acts, and organizations remained intact.

These forced political changes served to envigorate the fragmented 'establishment' opposition (i.e., those who prior to martial law had been in the ranks of the opposition or had been disposed towards Marcos' opponents). An attempted boycott of the presidential election drew some support, but not enough to make any difference in the proceedings. Increasingly, therefore, this inability of the 'establishment' opposition to find a viable means to counter Marcos meant that opponents of the regime were forced to turn to those who advocated violence as the only possible counter. The sense of estrangement from all hope of reform often took the form of virulent anti-Americanism. In a growing number of publications, the drift of the opposition towards the left was evident, and increasingly US support was viewed as the linchpin of Marcos' tenure in office. The CPP was able to recruit directly many such disillusioned individuals. Even those not actually co-opted gradually moved to a position where their viewpoints were scarcely distinguishable from those of the CPP. The result was that the party, with growing confidence, was able to assert the rectitude and primacy of its line: only 'people's war' offered a means to end the Marcos dictatorship and its oppression.

In contrast, the moderate opposition consistently had the ground cut out from under it by a relentless combination of Marcos' centralization of power and Washington's consistency of support for him. Caught in this dilemma, a desperate faction flirted with its own violence through the 'Light-a-Fire' and 'April 6 Movement'. These two groups engaged in bombing campaigns which did not seem to have any real objective save to damage Marcos' position by calling into question his capacity to keep matters in hand. The 'establishment' nature of the membership of the groups was exemplified by the arrested leader of 'Light-a-Fire', Ed Olaguer, a former executive of an IBM unit and manager of the country's leading economic daily. The other suspects were businessmen and professionals. Similar in character were the suspects and detainees — as listed by the authorities — after the 'April 6

Movement' bombings which began 22 August 1980 and killed one American and wounded seventy other individuals. Though the organization was quickly decimated, its links apparently extended even to the US West Coast, where the 'Movement for a Free Philippines', a US-based coalition of Marcos opponents, attracted the investigative attention of the FBI.[10]

Unable to make headway by either violent or non-violent means, the moderate opposition faded. Students did return to the streets in October 1981 but were routed. Colleges themselves were forced to crack down on dissidents, expelling them. Many of the disenchanted turned to the NDF, which had room within its structure for a variety of pursuits other than direct participation in armed struggle. Those who were not satisfied with this approach joined the CPP/NPA directly.

Drift towards the violent alternative was of particular concern to the Catholic Church, which nominally embraced 85 per cent of all Filipinos and which acted as a unifying force in Philippine society. Though historically the church could be thought of as a buttress of the status quo, in the Philippines, there was evident the same gradual change evident elsewhere in the world, particularly in Latin America — the continued growth of poverty and repression had split the clergy over the extent to which direct action against the system should be utilized. There were calls by many clergymen for the church to denounce social injustice, and a theology of liberation had developed, attracting church intellectuals and radicals to its ranks.

Thus the church found itself split into three groups: those who favored emphasis upon traditional modes of ministry; those who favored 'critical collaboration', as represented by the Association of Major Religious Superiors in the Philippines (AMRSP);[11] and those of 'the left' who analyzed the situation in neo-Marxist or Marxist terms and favored confrontation. The vast majority of the Philippine clergy fell into the first two groups; even those of a radical stripe did not necessarily suppport communist ideology. Nevertheless, a militant version of the theology of liberation gained strength in some politically sensitive areas, particularly in Mindanao, Samar, and Negros. This led to the arrest of several church persons after 1972 for alleged subversive activities.

Indeed, with the passage of time, the authorities increasingly viewed the church with suspicion, particularly in light of the fact that roughly a sixth of the 99 members of the Catholic Bishops'

Conference of the Philippines (CBCP) were quite vocal in their dissatisfaction with the 'church as institution' approach. They favored, instead, a more activist 'church as people' stance, a strategy which was resisted by the church head, the Archbishop of Manila, Cardinal Jamie Sin. Nevertheless, Sin saw his church being torn apart by the same polarization which had rent society at large, and he increasingly spoke out forcefully against oppression. In late July 1982, three senior government officials publicly denounced Sin as a 'Filipino Khomeini' and claimed that he sought to replace Marcos as president.

Marcos was not oblivious to the danger. Even amidst his suspicion of some church elements, he sought to promote the Catholic faith as an integral part of the Filipino identity. Likewise, he tackled the communists by offering an olive branch of sorts. The PKP, though reduced to but several hundred hardcore members located principally in the Manila area, was allowed a quasi-legality. After its February 1973 national congress, the PKP had indicated its willingness to follow a path of 'peaceful revolutionary transformation'. Thus it was not surprising that Marcos offered in late 1981 to consider legalizing communism.

Construction of the CPP Infrastructure

Foreign communists, to be sure, had been active in the country since the 1920s, but the Philippine Communist Party or PKP was not born until 7 November 1930. Its platform included standard Marxist fare, and its activities soon led to its proscription. So it went underground and operated through labor fronts and the small Socialist Party of the Philippines, with which it merged in 1938 upon orders from the Communist International (Comintern) in Moscow. Such work gained for the PKP a certain semi-acceptability by the close of the initial decade after its formation; and, with the party's participation in the World War II resistance against the Japanese, Philippine communism was able to make significant strides.

The postwar Huk Rebellion, which was viewed by both the government in Manila and the United States as a communist insurrection, seems now, after closer examination, to have been in many respects a peasant uprising of which the PKP was able to take advantage. The rebellion was preceded by a decade of peasant unrest in Luzon, and the *Hukbalahap* (*Hakbong Bayan Laban sa Hapon*, or 'People's Army Against the Japanese') itself drew its initial strength from anti-Japanese sentiment among the abused populace. After the war it was starting to disband when peasant grievances again came to the fore. The government repression which followed allowed the PKP to link up with the movement, offering it leadership and ideological guidance. Yet it does not appear to have controlled it *per se*. While its political brains were PKP, many of its local leaders were not.

Still, the complexity of the 'Huk Rebellion' was not appreciated at the time.[12] But this complexity was significant, because eventually the government's counterinsurgency program was able to succeed, not because of the decimation of the PKP leadership and infrastructure — which did occur to an extent — but instead because certain reforms satisfied peasant grievances and robbed the insurgency of its manpower, the so-called grievance guerrillas. The peasants' grievances were actually quite moderate and consisted essentially of calls for reform of tenancy (lower rents and provision of loans), equal rights under the law, and the right to organize. There was no plan to overturn the system, as was the goal of the PKP. As reforms were achieved in these areas and government repression toned down, particularly under Ramon Magsaysay, the rebellion faded out.

Defeat of the Huks marked the low point of Philippine communist fortunes. The PKP had been decimated, with most of its Politburo captured in October 1952. There followed slow disintegration, and by the early 1960s the movement was moribund. Nevertheless, if the movement had at the time lost its footsoldiers, it had maintained its intellectual base. Hence the party and its efforts to overthrow the system were revived in December 1968/January 1969 when a new 'reconstituted' Communist Party of the Philippines (CPP) convened a secret conference and announced its adherence to the Maoist precept of 'people's war'. Since the CPP was actually a splinter from the older PKP, press materials of the period often referred to the CPP as the 'CPP/Marxist-Leninist' or 'CPP-ML', while calling the PKP itself the CPP. With time this clumsy notation was abandoned, for the PKP faded into relative obscurity, and the CPP became the only standard-bearer for armed Marxist rebellion.

In order to make revolution, of course, there was a pressing need for 'liberation forces'. Even after the Huk Rebellion collapsed, low-level violence had continued as some Huk commanders and their proteges refused to surrender. The young Maoists of the CPP forged tenuous links with these Huk remnants, all of which were active in banditry at the time in the central Luzon area north of Manila,[13] sparking another round in the conflict, but one now consciously modelled after Chinese 'people's war'.[14]

'These people were our best and brightest', theorized Noel Albano during a 1988 interview. Then editor of the Manila daily *Malaya*, once a left-wing standard bearer with close ties to the CPP, Albano continued, 'They were able to revitalize the CPP, which at that point was rather stalled in ideological squabbling'.[15] There followed explosive growth for the movement as the influx of high quality manpower allowed the rapid expansion of infrastructure. Grievances aplenty already existed amongst the masses. The party needed only to tap them.

That they were able to do this was a result in large part of Philippine geography. That is, when the same process occurred in Thailand in the aftermath of the military assault on Thammasat University in October 1976 — the opposition was driven underground into the waiting arms of the communist insurgent movement — the Communist Party of Thailand (CPT) disintegrated in ideological turmoil as the old guard and the newcomers disagreed completely over strategy. In contrast in the Philippine archipelago, each newcomer could find his own niche by achieving organizational success in the 'outer islands'. The decentralized nature of CPP control allowed for experimentation away from the movement's initial center of mass in Luzon. Once they were successful, these individuals could return and reinvigorate the center's strategic thinking.[16]

Such thinking, as already mentioned, was Maoist in strategic design and thoroughly Leninist in operational and tactical flexibility. To grow in a hostile environment, the party adopted Mao's technique of revolutionary warfare, with the rural countryside the principal area of struggle. Using its New People's Army (NPA) as a shield, the CPP painstakingly constructed a political infrastructure — or 'shadow government'. To the task at hand, the party brought an organizational finesse that grew with the years. It was these skills that enabled it to harness peasant dissatisfaction and turn it from rebellion to insurgency. There was never, to my knowledge, an entire area which rose up and subsequently became linked to the CPP, though in some respects the Cordillera Liberation Army in northern Luzon's Igorot areas, a minority upheaval, might be considered in this light.[17] What normally occurred instead was far more painstaking and certainly less dramatic than the romance of the peasant rebellion.[18]

Struggle in the Villages

Contacts were first made with a community by a propaganda team normally working through acquaintances or relatives. This gave the CPP sufficient local presence to make a number of converts, who then formed the basis of sectoral Organizing Groups (OG; all acronyms are those used by the CPP itself in its documents): one each for peasants (i.e., men), women, youth, and children (these are the 'sectors' used in rural OG; in urban areas they often relate to occupations). The OG members were split into cells to compartmentalize the organizations and were indoctrinated by taking designated courses (e.g., 'Special Mass Course').[19]

The best individuals of each OG cell became members of the higher Organizing Committees (OC), which were also sectoral. OC members went through a more advanced series of courses (e.g., 'Five Golden Rays', 'Revolutionary Guide of Land Reform', and 'Lessons for Mass Activists'). Ultimately, the best of these OC members were themselves graduated to become Candidate Party Members (CPM) and, after still further schooling, full-fledged Party Members (PM). By this time, the hamlet (*sitio*) or village (*barangay*) concerned would be co-opted, dominated by a functioning Party Branch (PB). It was the controlling political entity, with its own legal framework and mechanisms for generation of revenue.

As villages were organized in precise sequence, graduating from the OG to OC to PB, they fielded their own armed forces, a 'self-defense corps' at the lower end of the spectrum, a more comprehensively organized *yunit militia* at the upper end. The extent to which these part-time guerrillas were armed depended upon the weaponry available.

If villages and their militias may be considered the base of a pyramid, there remained considerable structure above (for the discussion which follows, refer to Figures 1, 2, and 3). Villages fell under Sections, which corresponded closely to the government's own municipalities (counties). These Sections controlled the village operatives and themselves answered to party Districts, which, in turn, fell under Fighting Fronts (not to be confused with political fronts, the legal or semi-legal organizations infiltrated and partially or completely controlled by the CPP). Fighting Fronts (FF) answered to Island Party Commissions (IPC), these to Regional Commissions (RC), these to the Politburo (PB) and the Central Committee (CC).

While the militia protected the villages in the Sections, each District had its own party chain of command and District Guerrilla Unit, or DGU (approximately platoon size). Likewise, each Front had its own Front Guerrilla Unit, or FGU (approximately company size). Reportedly, at least two Main Guerrilla Units (MGU of approximately battalion size) were also formed — one on Samar, the other on Luzon — but these were not true forces in being.

All of the major levels — District, Front, Island, and Region — had available to them the special *yunit partisano* (partisan units), or 'sparrows', who carried out acts of terror, notably assassinations. Sparrows, together with the soldiers of the DGU, FGU, and MGU (the *yunit gerilya*), comprised the regulars of the movement, those classified as members of the New People's Army, or NPA. It was this division into various categories of forces which accounted over the years for the frequent confusion concerning the number of enemy facing the security forces. Not only did all of the 'soldiers' not carry weapons, there were several different categories of 'soldiers'.[20]

Regardless, the most fundamental point was that in the CPP insurgent hierarchy, everything depended upon the base. The party divided all its manpower into three categories, depending upon the level of individual training: organized masses, mass activists, and party members. An individual working at the OG level was considered a member of the organized masses; those promoted to OC level became mass activists and, in the end, party members. Similarly, the ranks of the NPA were filled by those recruited from militia formations. These individuals themselves were first members of the organized masses and, later, mass activists. Most NPA, therefore, were party members. This was a fairly rigid progression and only broke down when conditions dictated otherwise. Under normal circumstances, manpower for higher formations was never picked up off the streets, so to speak. (See Figure 4 for government conceptualization of this process.)

It was this infrastructure which gave the CPP its staying power.

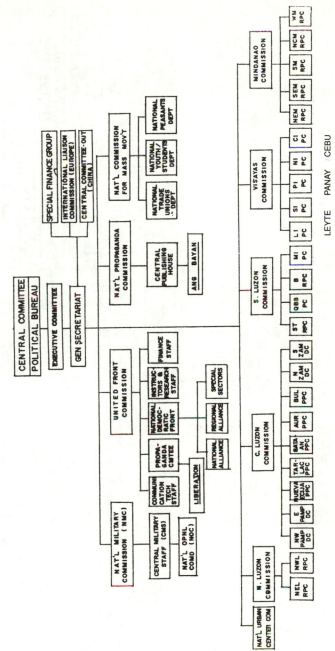

FIGURE 1:
CPP NATIONAL ORGANIZATION
(effective date: 1986)

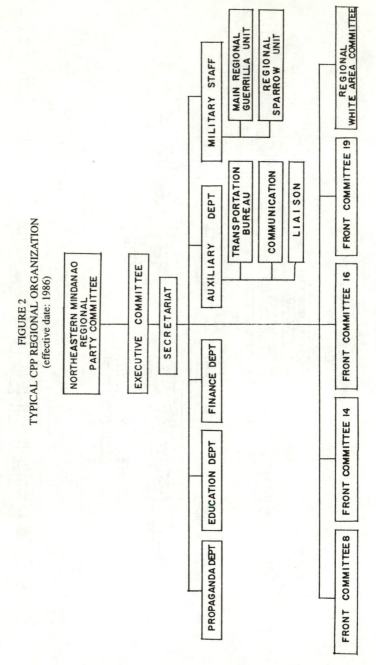

FIGURE 2
TYPICAL CPP REGIONAL ORGANIZATION
(effective date: 1986)

NORTHEASTERN MINDANAO REGIONAL PARTY COMMITTEE

EXECUTIVE COMMITTEE

SECRETARIAT

PROPAGANDA DEPT

EDUCATION DEPT

FINANCE DEPT

AUXILIARY DEPT

TRANSPORTATION BUREAU

COMMUNICATION

LIAISON

MILITARY STAFF

MAIN REGIONAL GUERRILLA UNIT

REGIONAL SPARROW UNIT

FRONT COMMITTEE 8

FRONT COMMITTEE 14

FRONT COMMITTEE 16

FRONT COMMITTEE 19

REGIONAL WHITE AREA COMMITTEE

continue to Figure 3

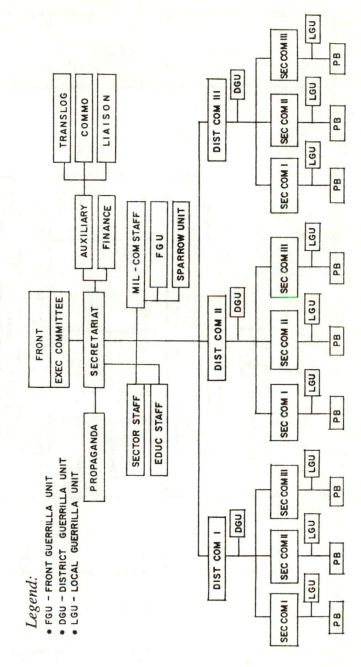

FIGURE 3
TYPICAL CPP FRONT ORGANIZATION
(effective date: 1986)

Legend:
- FGU – FRONT GUERRILLA UNIT
- DGU – DISTRICT GUERRILLA UNIT
- LGU – LOCAL GUERRILLA UNIT

Figure 4:
GOVERNMENT CONCEPTUALIZATION OF ACTIVIST MASS ORGANIZATION AND LEVEL OF AWARENESS
(effective date: 1989)

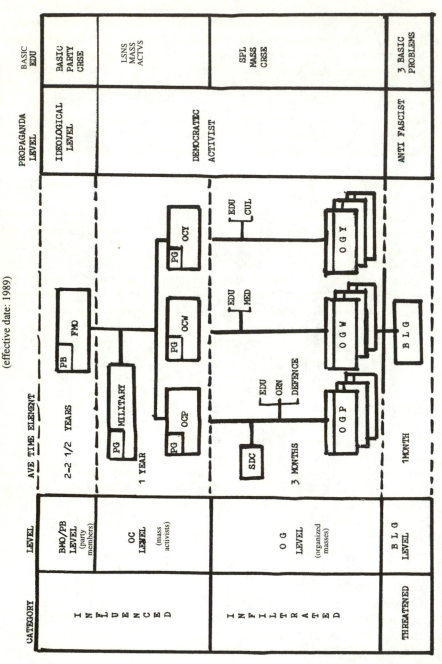

Note: OGY includes OG-Children

Peasant grievances were certainly tapped by the CPP as it gathered momentum. Yet the sheer scope and comprehensive nature of the CPP organization ensured that by the time political events changed dramatically in February 1986, at which time Marcos was ousted, the movement had long since ceased to rely upon those grievances for its survival. It had become an alternative political structure that purported to offer a superior existance for its members — or at least the hope of a superior existence, better than that which they could hope to achieve under the the existing structure of governance. It fulfilled its personnel requirements through internal promotion of individuals who had gone through an extensive socialization process. It met leadership needs through transfers as circumstances dictated. Orders issued from the center were obeyed, with severe sanctions for violations of both general policies and specific instructions. Mechanisms of funding provided sustenance.

Always the goal of the party was to create so-called liberated areas, geographic entities in which life could be ordered as directed by the CPP. The NPA's purpose was to keep the government from interfering with this effort. As the CPP apparatus took hold, terror was used to prevent any dissent or infiltration. Liquidation of enemies was an important feature of the CPP/NDF/NPA campaign.[21]

Struggle in Urban Areas

Creation of its own 'liberated areas' in the government-controlled countryside forced the CPP to grapple with the other half of the equation, the urban areas. In regards to these, it took the party longer to arrive at a correct approach, but eventually it did just that.

Initially, the CPP approached the target only in the most rigid of Maoist frameworks. True, it could see the opportunity presented by the September 1972 declaration of martial law, for it correctly ascertained that this would provide the basis for making common cause with dissident non-communist elements. Hence by October 1972 the CPP Central Committee, in its discussions, had already decided that societal polarization was bound to result from martial law and that the party should capitalize on this by downplaying the class basis of the broad resistance movement directed against Marcos. Subsequently, the party created the National Democratic Front (NDF). When it became an organizational reality, the NDF, far from being an independent umbrella organization of anti-Marcos opponents, as it endeavored to portray itself, was but one of the principal organs of the CPP's United Front Commission, which itself was one of the four main divisions under the CPP's ruling Politburo and Central Committee.

Yet having made this strategic move, the CPP seemed unsure how to derive maximum benefit from the NDF and the subordinate fronts which grew up under it. The answer came with the party's realization that the human geography within which it operated had changed substantially. Analyzed a key CPP document: 'The role of urban centers in advancing the revolutionary struggle increases. If before we concentrated 90 per cent of our efforts in the CS [countryside] and only 10 per cent in the UCs [urban centers], the ratio now should be perhaps 60:40.'[22] From this assessment came a formal policy decision which moved united front activity from a mere strategic orientation to an actual operational measure which created an urban counterpart to the rural infrastructure.

The field for operation was certainly ripe. As corruption and abuses of power by the central government increased in the early 1980s, a host of legal bodies sprang up demanding societal change. The CPP was able to infiltrate a wide variety of these groups and convert them to fronts actually controlled by members of the CPP underground. Church and student bodies were particularly vulnerable because of their extensive involvement in social action.

Infrastructure to support this campaign was every bit as extensive as that in the countryside. Outlined in detail by the CPP's 'Political Program for 1983' and amplifying documents was the necessity of forming highly disciplined, clandestine cells for infiltrating 'cause-oriented groups' — and then using their work to further party goals. Stated the 'Political Program': *'Our key task for 1983 is to develop our ND forces* [National Democratic; i.e., united front; emphasis in original]...Solid and well-oiled UG [underground] machinery activity would make possible the advance of the OMM [open mass movement]...Further, we shall be able to exercise political leadership with a developed UG network.'[23]

Such directions, when they were published in late 1982, did not reflect a new tack by the CPP but rather reemphasized a policy decision made at least the year before. One of the best illustrations of the success of the front mechanisms, in fact, had already come to light that year on Samar, which only a few years before had been the nexus of CPP activity in the archipelago. The case was also indicative of the extent to which infiltration had already progressed in some major Philippine institutions.

When the premier Social Action Center (SAC) of the Catholic Church, Paul VI SAC in Catbolagan, capital of Samar Province itself (see Map 3, in following chapter), was raided in September 1982, documents and interrogations revealed that virtually the entire framework for social work and human rights assistance in the Visayas region — stretching across the central Philippines — had been co-opted. Both the Paul VI SAC and the Visayas Secretariat for Social Action (VISSA) were controlled by priests working for the CPP. In a single year prior to the raid, Father Edgar Kangleon, the SAC's director, had been able, among numerous other support activities, to send 60,000 pesos (then approximately $15,000) to the Financial Department of the CPP's Visayas Commission by using donations intended for the poor. Additionally, by directing Kangleon to give a member of the CPP underground control over the Projects Desk, the party was able to submit and have approved its own development schemes. A significant portion of the funding was obtained through donations sent directly by cause-oriented groups overseas, mainly in Europe.[24]

Materials from the Kangleon case implicated other church groups. Among the most notable, based in the SAC, the Samar office of Task Force Detainees of the Philippines (TFDP, then called simply TFD), the organ which regularly provided documentation on alleged human rights abuses to international cause-oriented groups such as Amnesty International (AI), was headed by a Catholic sister taking CPP orders. TFDP, it was further noted, was an offshoot of the previously mentioned Association of Major Religious Superiors (AMRS), an important church body. Its one-time Executive Secretary, Victor Bulatao, was recruited by the CPP while serving AMRS and was also arrested in 1982 in Samar — while acting in his capacity as head of the CPP's Visayas Regional United Front Group. According to the Kangleon documents, there was even a 'Visayas Church Sector Consultation of the CPP', a 10-member body which included six priests and a nun.[25]

While the church hierarchy initially was extremely vocal in condemning the Paul VI SAC raid, the protests died down after three bishops reportedly were allowed to question Father

Kangleon privately about his activities and his confession. Furthermore, the true scope of the infiltration of the church as revealed by the case was made known to the hierarchy's leading figure in the Philippines, Cardinal Jamie Sin, in a closed session at which the military presented its evidence.[26]

Infiltration was repeated many times in many groups. The League of Filipino Students (LFS), for instance, a nationwide legal body, was used as a front through which CPP underground members could infiltrate normal student activities throughout the country. In one example, a typical LFS operative for the party, Salvador Acebuche, arrested in May 1985 in Samar, was a leading figure in student politics at the University of Eastern Philippines (UEP), editor of the campus newspaper, and a 'documentalist' for TFDP. In regular meetings with CPP cadre, he was given instructions. Besides engaging in CPP-inspired writing and reporting, he was a key figure in the planning and implementation of closely-coordinated demonstrations throughout Samar. These were held in conjunction with other groups being used as fronts in Samar: TFDP; Coalition of Organizations for the Realization of Democracy (CORD); Free Legal Assistance Group (FLAG); SAMADEKKA (a legal student organization favored by LFS activists); Justice, Unity, Sovereignty, and Truth (JUST) Movement; and the Alliance of Concerned Teachers (ACT). Times and dates were scheduled to ensure maximum use of the normally unwitting mass members, as well as maximum media coverage, especially by the foreign press. Local grievances were exploited to draw participants, but the real agenda was decided behind the scenes by the CPP.[27]

By the early 1980s, the party was clearly in the driver's seat in both rural and urban areas. The inefficiency and repression of martial law allowed the CPP to operate strategically virtually at will. Key organizational changes — which I have already reflected in my discussion of CPP structure above — had been made to take better operational advantage of this situation. At meetings of the Politburo and Central Committee, it had been decided to abandon structurally what had remained an approach still oriented towards Luzon, psychologically at least, as well as the continued effort to run operations from the center. Instead, the party leadership decided that it would set strategic policy but would oversee a decentralized movement which would allow each Island Party Committee (IPC) to take operational advantage of local conditions as it saw fit, deploying its tactical forces independently and largely managing its own generation of funds.[28] The motivation for this change appeared to stem as much from social analysis as from strategic considerations. In particular, the party realized that the traditional areas of unrest on Luzon were not suitable for further expansion, because — for a variety of reasons, among them economic progress and simple war-weariness — there was popular reluctance to becoming involved in 'another Huk Rebellion'. The result was the shift in emphasis away from Luzon to the outlying islands, notably, Samar, Negros, and Mindanao.

Samar provides a useful illustration of how the process worked itself out. Party presence apparently had begun in 1970 through the activities of a youth organization, the 'Movement for a Democratic Philippines' (MDP), the followers of which were students at the University of the Eastern Philippines in Catarman (see Map 3, in following chapter). Initial recruits were reacting to the increased authoritarianism of the Marcos administration, but the movement's ranks grew to include local politicians and priests dissatisfied with the government. Many of its leaders were imprisoned when Marcos declared martial law. Subsequently, the dissidents regrouped in the fertile Catubig valley of northern Samar, the so-called food basket of the island. Dissident groups in eastern Samar then crossed the mountain ranges to the north in an effort to control the entire area. Further augmentation of CPP manpower was received from Cebu, which had proved inhospitable for guerrilla action at that time.[29]

By 1972 the CPP had implemented its so-called '*Dulo* Plan', which divided Samar into six districts (*dulo*) targeted for subversion. Author of the plan, according to Philippine government sources, was Jorge Cabardo of Balangiga, Eastern Samar, a dismissed cadet from the Philippine Military Academy (PMA) class of 1971. First penetration was achieved through relatives in the region southwest of Catbalogan, with the primary objective being the central interior. A CPP reorganization in late 1976 divided Samar into northern and southern area commands, both still under direct supervision of the Politburo. This arrangement ended with the 1980 Politburo decision to create Island Party Committees (IPC). The Samar IPC was set up by mid-1981, as was its superior Visayas Commission (with its headquarters in Cebu). These superior organs have run the 'liberation struggle' on Samar ever since.

Initially, CPP expansion forces on Samar were quite small, but they were able to operate in a near-absolute vacuum of government authority. In 1973 the only security force presence on the island was a single Philippine Constabulary (PC) company of 30-40 personnel. They responded to the problem of subversives as one of 'peace and order'. The resulting official misconduct only swelled the ranks of the insurgents. Using as their rallying cry the repression of 'the US-Marcos Dictatorship', the CPP, between 1974 and 1975, was able to penetrate nearly half of Samar. By 1979 Sheilah Ocampo, writing for the *Far Eastern Economic Review*, judged that the CPP controlled 85 per cent of eastern Samar, 40 per cent of northern Samar, and 60 per cent of western Samar. An effective shadow government was in place by 1982, she further claimed, and the island was considered the most solid CPP stronghold.

Though other analysts thought this analysis somewhat overstated the case, it was clear that the situation on Samar was serious by the late 1970s. Manila, faced with what had become the most developed communist infrastructure in the country, deployed no fewer than 12 infantry battalions to the region — a larger maneuver force than had been available to the whole army at the time martial law was declared. Though the number was down to nine battalions by 1981, this was still one of the largest concentrations of military power in any sector. That year, then-Brigadier General Salvador Mison, regarded as one of the top Philippine combat soldiers, took charge of the island (which together with Leyte made up Regional Unified Command 8, or RUC-8).

To complete briefly the story, Mison realized that security force misconduct and misapplication of assets served to drive manpower to the CPP. Consequently, he tightened discipline considerably. A more comprehensive approach was implemented in attacking the CPP effort. In the field, multi-battalion operations were launched to break up the larger guerrilla formations. Simultaneously, to deal with the CPP proselytizing effort, adroit use was made of intelligence assets to uncover and dismantle the main communist political activities. Once key CPP organizational centers, both urban and rural, had been neutralized, the long, tedious task of small unit warfare could begin. By 1985, army strength in RUC-8 was down to five battalions.

Contending Ideological Visions

Even as such military activities sought to grapple with the CPP nationwide, larger developments were afoot. Most significantly, by the early 1980s, the Philippine economy began to experience severe difficulties. Growth of nationalist reaction to real and imagined foreign penetration of the polity has been discussed earlier, to include the integral connections dissidents drew between the political and economic spheres. While the inferences radicals derived from this analysis may be faulted, as may their proposed political solutions, there is no denying the contextual validity of the model which, as the 1980s began, pointed to the Philippines as a 'dependent state' within the overall world market system.

Such a framework was important, because it highlighted the two divergent methods for assessing the state of the economy at the crucial juncture when the CPP was able to achieve 'takeoff'. One method, that utilized by the government and its allies, forcused on internal adjustments which one could reasonably expect Manila to make as the Philippines struggled to maneuver within worldwide recession; the other emphasized the international arena in which the Philippines had to operate and the forces, largely beyond Manila's control, which would shape the economy and the political structure. These, radicals felt, warranted being overthrown in favor of a new order.

In either case, the issue for the Philippines was essentially the same: how to modernize a basically agricultural economy so as to better provide for the growing needs and aspirations of the population. What was at issue was the route by which to do this: either continue in the capitalist mode or adopt a socialist course. The strategy followed by Manila throughout its existence as an independent state, particularly after the declaration of martial law, was that favored by the World Bank, the International Monetary Fund (IMF), and similar bodies, the so-called trickle down theory of capitalism. Under Marcos this involved no major departure from previous approaches, only internal adjustments in the existing structure. It certainly did not call for structural revolution as advocated by the CPP.

Essentially, then, the establishment approach called for the Philippines to develop by exploiting its unique position within the existing international division of labor as it was encapsulated historically by the natural law of 'comparative advantage'. In other words, the Philippines sought to emphasize export-oriented agricultural and primary-extraction development. Simultaneously, import-substitution industries were fostered to a degree compatible with free trade and fiscal prudence. This meant, necessarily, the increasing integration of the Philippines into the world market, a position which left the economy very vulnerable to the vicissitudes of the global economic environment. This vulnerability was compounded by internal economic mistakes and the corruption inherent to 'rationalization'.

Several sources have noted that the very areas of greatest insurgent growth coincided with those regions where the government sought to expand export-oriented agriculture and primary-extraction development. When economic needs were harnessed with the abuse inherent to the mechanisms of an authoritarian state, the result was dispossession for thousands of small landowners. As they fled to the more marginal areas geographically, they were courted by the CPP and often recruited into its infrastructure.[30]

Yet it was primarily the area of internal economic policy and mistakes which preoccupied foreign analysts, a focus which meant attempting to devise approaches and strategies which best 'fit' the Philippine economy to a discernible yet vague role within the global market. Emphasis thus was on 'technical' issues: balance of payments, rationalization of production, vertical integration, and so forth. In contrast, dissidents focused on the other side of the coin: the actual nature and desirability of the Philippine integration into the global market. Among the more extreme elements, such as the CPP, there was little room for compromise.

In their doctrine the current internal and external arrangements created and maintained by the acceptance of the capitalist development model were unacceptable. Instead, the CPP stated, only a communist/socialist approach offered hope for an equitable, prosperous future. Non-communist left-wing elements allowed room for some 'negotiation' with respect to the precise shape a future system would take, but among the Philippine intelligentsia[31] there was widespread acceptance of the radical view that the Philippines was at least a 'new colony' of the capitalist world, especially of the United States. The result was that numerous individuals who did not claim to be communists nevertheless were willing to throw in their lot with the CPP due to the perceived identity of worldviews.

If such shared intellectual visions brought together the upper echelons of the Marxist and non-Marxist opposition, it was more immediate concerns — poverty and its fallout — which actually served to recruit manpower for the CPP. At the end of 1981, Eric W. Hayden, Vice-President for Economics and Strategic Planning in the Bank of America's Asia Division, noted that Philippine economic health in the 1980s would be complicated by several factors: (a) the economy's overall lack of resiliance and quick-response capability; (b) the slower global economic environment; (c) large-scale failures of companies unable to survive the manufacturing rationalization being undertaken; (d) the tremendous financial requirements that would be required to replace much of the existing antiquated capital stock; and (e) the greater role the government would have to assume as an investor in an economy previously driven largely by the private sector.[32]

This analysis remained true throughout the first half of the 1980s. Though the major impetus for economic growth came from the industrial sector, particularly manufacturing, the agricultural bias of the Philippine economy continued. Agriculture accounted for one-quarter of economic output and one-half of total employment; it furnished, together with other primary sector production, the bulk of Philippine exports and, consequently, was the main source of foreign exchange. This reliance upon the primary sector for the generation of foreign exchange meant that, faced with the collapse of the world market for commodities which occurred in the early years of the decade, together with the dramatic increase in oil prices caused by conflict in the Middle East, the Philippines could not generate sufficient funds from exports to fuel development even as import costs skyrocketed. Only attraction of foreign investors kept the economy buoyant.

A suitable illustration of the Philippine economic situation was provided by the important coconut industry. Coconut products were the nation's largest export, and the industry provided employment for more persons than any commodity save rice. The Philippine share of world coconut-oil exports was a whopping 85 per cent, and its coconut-oil alone accounted for 8 per cent of world trade in vegetable oils. In 1980, however, prices collapsed in the wake of higher output and American restriction on food sales to the Soviet Union. Various intra-industry solutions were attempted, such as vertical integration of collection, milling, and exporting assets; diversification of end products; and developing high-yielding hybrids. Yet the real problem was the continuing glut of supply caused by a weakening international market for traditional coconut products, particularly coconut-oil, which had caused a 33 per cent earnings drop during 1979–80 even as volume increased by 15 per cent. The result was widespread unemployment within the industry and the consequent hardship to workers. Matters were exacerbated by corruption and the Marcos government's efforts to ensure that the industry was monopolized by some of the President's closest cronies.[33]

This pattern afflicted all of the primary export sectors. Consequently, the Philippines waged a vigorous campaign to attract international investment capital. In addition Manila resorted heavily to borrowing. Outstanding foreign debt by the end of 1981 had reached nearly US $14 billion and was climbing steadily (it eventually reached some US $26 billion by the time Marcos was ousted). Manila was among the top seven recipients of loans from the World Bank and continually attempted to increase its borrowing from the IMF. The IMF, at least, was reluctant to grant Manila's repeated requests for further standby credits, because it reportedly did not feel that middle-income nations such as the Philippines could continue simply to keep borrowing to meet planned growth targets. That concern was also echoed by commercial banks, which looked askance as the Philippines' recurrent heavy borrowing and its resulting spiraling debt-service ratio, which reached 22.6 per cent in 1981 as judged by the most optimistic figures. The real level was probably even greater but concealed through creative bookkeeping on the part of the Central Bank of the Philippines.

Faced with this situation, the Marcos government focused much of its attention for economic resuscitation in the early years of the decade on the revitalization of the manufacturing industry, which accounted for 25 per cent of Gross Domestic Product (GDP). Annual growth of private capital formation had slowed from the 7–8 per cent level of the early 1970s to the 1 per cent range of the 1980s. The intent in emphasizing the sector was to provide a broader and more competitive export base, as well as increased employment opportunities. To this end, Manila attempted to secure funding for 11 huge industrial projects valued at several billions of US dollars. But possible lenders such as the IMF did not feel the Philippines could afford to accelerate investment in such products, despite the possible relief that growth of export manufactures might promise for the balance of payments situation. Instead, multilateral lending agencies encouraged an end to the protection of import-substitution industries and the adoption of structural adjustments.

These moves, while they would have ensured the Philippines of continued access to loan funds for the short-term, highlighted the dilemma faced by Manila. The short-term results were likely to be an increase in the penetration of the economy by foreign assets and in the difficulties faced by local industry. The troubled economic situation had already forced the government to greatly expand its role in the economy, even as the IMF was urging restraint in public-sector credit. Damage-control action designed to minimize the impact of the Dewey Dee affair pushed public-sector credit in 1981 to an historic high at 52 per cent of domestic liquidity. Government corporations and banks had substantial holdings in six of the twenty largest publicly-traded companies in the country. The end result was inefficiency and stagnation. Rather than diversification and expansion, the government had to fight merely to maintain what was in existence — and what was in existence guaranteed high unemployment, declining real purchasing power, labor unrest, and poverty, all of which fed the CPP challenge.

Hence in many respects Manila was caught in a no-win situation. The obvious connection between grievances and CPP recruitment has already been noted. Yet even the most rational and best-intentioned of efforts taken within the existing ideological framework often had security implications.

To cite but one particularly useful example: if the analysis above may be thought of as the strategic dilemma which faced the economy within the structure of the international economy, then the tactical problem at hand was to contain the growth of the oil import bill. Oil accounted for 88 per cent of all energy expenditures in 1980, down from 92 per cent in 1979, but 93 per cent of the total still had to be imported. This importation comprised fully 44 per cent of total imports-value in 1981. With the total import figure that year put at US $7.134 billion, this amounted to an oil bill of US $3.15 billion. While plans called for the reduction of the oil percentage of energy expenditure to 55 per cent by 1985, this never proved possible. One logical manner in which to reduce the oil import bill, therefore, was to look to alternative energy sources, particularly the vast, largely untapped hydroelectric potential of mountainous northern Luzon.

Studies of the Chico River valley in southern Kalinga, a sub-province of Kalinga-Apayao, had been begun as early as 1962, but it was not until oil prices skyrocketed in the early 1970s that a massive hydroelectric scheme seemed feasible. What was proposed along the Chico River was the largest hydro-electric project in Southeast Asia. While the main purpose was to be power generation, a secondary benefit would be the possible irrigation of some 49,000 hectares of farmland. The basic problem with the scheme was that the four dams would have displaced thousands of people living in six Bontoc and ten Kalinga tribal villages. The tribesmen, who even during the American occupation practiced headhunting, lived a lifestyle which revolved around their labyrinth of mountain rice terraces (a maze so awe-inspiring it was often called the 'eighth wonder of the world'). Their entire way of life was threatened by plans to relocate them. Unsuccessful attempts to reach a peaceful compromise on the dam issue led to increasing violence after February 1974 when Marcos ordered the National Power Corporation (NPC) to begin work on the basin project.

What followed was a textbook case of security forces alienating the population and thereby inspiring the emergence of increasingly radical leadership. Initially, the tribesmen sought to work through government and church-affiliated organizations, but when it seemed that even the government body set up specifically to protect tribal Filipinos, the Presidential Assistant on National Minorities (PANAMIN), was involved in the escalating repression, and that the church groups were unable to halt a campaign of government intimidation and assassination, the tribesmen became more willing to consider offers of aid tendered by the NPA.

In late 1976 the NPA, which hitherto had been shunned by the tribesmen, penetrated the closely-knit Kalinga-Bontoc tribal system. Through a process of persuasion and education, CPP operatives were able to expand their influence. Government units sent into the area, first Philippine Constabulary (PC) battalions, subsequently regular army units, inflamed the situation. By 1981 there had been reported more than 100 dam-related killings, which included the assassination of Macli-ing Dulag, the Kalingan tribal leader who had led his people's struggle against the dams. In the years that followed, the rebellion gained strength and ultimately became the full-fledged thorn in the government's side represented by the tribal forces of Father Conrado Balweg and his associates.

The upshot was that, in the early 1980s, the Philippines found itself with a badly deteriorating economy, a spiraling debt, and worsening security problems integrally linked to the first two problems — for the economic crunch played itself out on the ground in dramatically lower social welfare indicators. The crucial development was that the economic dislocation coincided with the dramatic decline in the efficiency of the Marcos regime brought about by nepotism, corruption, and unbridled avarice.[34] To wit, the depradations of the Marcos clique could no longer be absorbed by the badly limping economy. Since the regime could use repression to ensure that its own resource needs were met, the decline could only be absorbed by the people. This drove many into the arms of the guerrillas.

Government Response to the CPP

Faced with the construction of a covert, alternative political apparatus, Manila's response suffered from that common to governments whose own mistakes and repression have served to spark revolt: it countered with further efforts at repression. Much of this, it is important to note, was carried out by the regional forces which fell midways between the police and the army organizationally, the Philippine Constabulary (PC), as well as by militia which the PC was supposed to be controlling. Essentially a police field force which had grown out of the army itself and its involvement in the Huk Rebellion, the PC in many respects mirrored the army in organization and equipment. Its greatest disadvantage, when viewed from afar, was its regional basing posture which allowed its men to become inefficient militarily and to involve themselves in local politics and corruption. Not all units were second-rate, certainly — a good commander meant a disciplined unit, and there were PC combat battalions which performed military roles with the army and marine corps — but too often problems with the populace stemming from 'military' indiscipline could be traced back to the PC.

At the time martial law was declared, in fact, the army was quite small. It was quickly forced to expand dramatically, a process which spawned its own host of problems. Ironically, the impetus for this expansion was neither martial law itself nor the CPP insurgency. Instead, it was the challenge of Muslim separatism in the form of the Moro National Liberation Front (MNLF). Operating out of the southern Philippines, the MNLF posed a threat of a different sort to Manila than did the CPP. While the CPP sought the overthrow of the existing socio-economic-political system, the MNLF sought autonomy for the country's 2.5–4 million Muslims. The resulting conflict was to prove a significant drain on national resources even as the economy began to decline.

Influence of Muslim Revolt

Armed confrontation between the MNLF's military wing, the *Bangsa Moro Army* (BMA), and the Armed Forces of the Philippines (AFP) erupted after Marcos' 1972 declaration of martial law, peaked during 1973-75, and remained in a state of political and military standoff after a 1977 ceasefire collapsed. Thereafter, the war was smaller than it had been in 1973–75, but it still killed thousands each year. The impact upon the military was enormous, as it expanded substantially. By mid-1982 the combined total of army, marine, and PC combat battalions numbered 70 (later 71). At the height of the fighting, most of which was conventional in nature, a single army brigade commanded by the previously mentioned Salvador Mison on Mindanao had assigned to it 12 maneuver battalions — to highlight the point again, a larger force than had been available to the entire army in 1972. As late as 1978, in fact, nearly 80 per cent of all available government maneuver battalions were committed against a BMA force once estimated at 30,000, later reduced to 10,000–12,000, rather than against the NPA. It was only in 1982 that even half of the military's available maneuver assets were thrown into the counterinsurgency campaign. A comparable amount of assets remained tied up with the MNLF problem.[35]

    That the MNLF revolt erupted after the implementation of martial law was probably due less to any specific incident than to a justifiable belief by the MNLF that secession would be impossible to achieve peacefully through negotiation with an increasingly centralized, Christian polity. Failure to achieve military success led to the revision of the MNLF's original goal in favor of autonomy, but splits within the movement prevented the government from fully exploiting this modification. In January 1976 a truce document between Manila and the MNLF — which proposed autonomy for the Muslims in the south — was signed in Tripoli under the auspices of Libya and the Organisation of the Islamic Conference

(OIC). This autonomy was to be achieved 'within the framework of sovereignty and territorial integrity of the Philippines'.

A fundamental problem with either secession or autonomy for the Philippine Muslim population was that the 'southern problem' was never the clearcut picture of a Muslim south dominated by a Christian north which the MNLF attempted to paint. While Muslim concerns for cultural identity were in a sense justified, as were many of the specific grievances against the government representatives, the Muslim population was not simply a minority — geographically and culturally distinct — amidst the then-49 million population of the Philippines. Muslims actually were a clear minority even amongst the 10–12 million people of Mindanao, known internationally as the 'Muslim heartland', and the Sulu Sea area. They were a majority only in three areas: Lavao del Sur, Maguindanao, and Sultan Kuderat. They were large minorities only in the north and south of Zamboanga and Cotobato Provinces.

These realities led to the emergence of autonomy as the more convincing alternative, but the precise form such autonomy was to take — and the strategy for its achievement — led to the breakup of the MNLF. While defections in a sense hurt the MNLF, they also strengthened it. For the inability to reach an outright military victory led the mainstream MNLF leadership to take greater notice of the polarization of forces in the rest of the country. How best to take advantage of this reality sparked yet another debate, but the view which emerged held that the Muslim cause could not be won without coordination with anti-government, non-Muslim groups which had goals and ideals which were not fundamentally in conflict with those of the MNLF. Hence, from a position of cultural and ethnic chauvinism, the MNLF came to see itself as part of a larger struggle and to accept that a virtual prerequisite for its own long-term plans was the downfall of the authoritarian Marcos government and a return of representative government.

A logical consequence of such reasoning was cooperation with the strongest anti-government force, the CPP, though it could certainly be held that the goals of the communists were in conflict with those of the Muslims. Nonetheless, 'progressive' Muslim elements favored such cooperation. In time, even the more traditional leaders, who saw communism as anathma to all the Muslim religion represented, were willing to sanction some degree of tactical coordination. The general CPP approach to revolt also presented lessons which the MNLF absorbed. Thus the movement began to turn from its narrow focus on religious rebellion to the more complex business of fashioning an insurgency with an infrastructure which could survive even in 'occupied' areas.

Hand-in-glove with the new doctrinal and organizational approach was a more sophisticated evaluation of Manila's vulnerability on the international front — and the important role diplomatic and economic pressure could play in the conflict. Dependent as it was on Middle Eastern Muslim sources for the preponderance of its oil imports, the Philippines had to give particular ear to the advice of and pay heed to the sensitivities of its Arab suppliers.

Simultaneously with this campaign, the MNLF expanded its formal contacts with the 'establishment' opposition. Marcos' greatest rival, Benigno Aquino, met with MNLF head Nur Misuari in July 1981 in the Middle East (the site was variously described as Damascus, Syria or Jedda, Saudi Arabia), where the two signed an agreement of cooperation. Aquino also reportedly was able to offer his good offices in bringing together several of the feuding MNLF factions. For its part, the MNLF reached out even further to Marcos' opposition, reportedly establishing contacts with the Philippine Democratic Socialist Party faction led by Jesuit priest Romeo Intengan (though this faction was decimated by the arrests which followed the 'April 6 Movement' bombings in 1980).

Hence even as the CPP began to expand substantially in the decade of the 1980s — and the economy sputtered — the MNLF revolt remained an ongoing proposition which tied up approximately half of the Philippine armed forces and served as a costly drain on scarce resources. Had the Muslims been willing to effect a joint effort with the communists — an unlikely yet possible proposition — Manila would have faced serious difficulties in responding. As it was, the dramatic expansion of the armed forces which was required to meet the threat of the MNLF revolt actually provided additional forces which were eventually shifted to fight the NPA.

Deterioration of the Security Forces

It would be expected, too, from all that has been said above, that 'the shifting of forces' was indeed how the Marcos regime saw the problem of CPP insurgency. It was not that there were few individuals who appreciated the non-military roots and dimensions of the problem. There were many. Not only had thousands of Filipinos engaged in guerrilla action during World War II and the Huk Rebellion, still others served in Vietnam as part of the Allied effort (some individuals spanned all three conflicts[36]), both in an engineer unit deployed to South Vietnam (commanded at one point by Fidel Ramos, later AFP head and now President) and as civilian advisors in the pacification scheme. These conflicts resulted in a significant reservoir of personnel familiar not only with the mechanics of guerrilla fighting but with the non-military dimensions (e.g., civic action) of unconventional warfare. Yet it was not these individuals who were in power. Indeed, one of Marcos' first actions upon declaring martial law had been to pack off as Ambassador to Thailand the veteran army commander, Major General Raphael 'Rocky' Ileto, who had refused to go along with the President's plans.[37]

Just as Ileto was pushed aside, so during the Marcos years were the upper echelons in uniform increasingly used for the exercise of patronage — irrespective of needs generated by security concerns such as the CPP or MNLF revolts. The number of general officer positions was expanded, and loyal service to the president and his entourage was rewarded by promotion and stars. Professional skills, as demonstrated by command and combat experience, had little to do with the process. Regulations detailing requirements of seniority and schooling were systematically ignored. Eventually, the AFP Chief of Staff position was given to Lieutenant General Fabian Ver, a former Marcos bodyguard who never commanded a troop unit in the field or went through any of the established schooling cycles.

As might be expected, such individuals as Ver often had little concern for execution of the duties accompanying the positions they occupied. Most of them appeared to devote their energies to personal enrichment or miscellaneous chores given them by the palace. Further, once having gained a plum, a loyal senior officer could be fairly assured of retaining it virtually indefinitely. The palace simply extended the man each time his retirement date came due. By 1986 this 'extendee' group alone numbered more than a fifth of the approximately 120 general officers. With promotion to higher ranks increasingly so-monopolized, a growing number of those with field experience were not able to achieve advancement beyond the battalion and brigade levels.

Battalions by 1986 numbered 71 if all units, such as the three air force security units, were included. Most were army and infantry, assigned to 15 brigades under 5 divisions. Operationally, the battalions and brigades were commanded by the 12 Regional Unified Commands (RUC) into which the country was divided. The divisions performed only at a support level. Rank-wise, RUC, division, and brigade commanders were all brigadier generals. Since general officer positions were the main objective of patronage, the brigade level was the firebreak between what, in effect, became two officer corps, a field and a patronage faction. RUC and division commanders were frequently palace favorites; brigade commanders were a mix of combat and patronage appointees. The result was a growing estrangement between combat formations, commanded in the main by those promoted for considerations of seniority and military proficiency, and the upper headquarters, populated through contacts with, and loyalty to, Marcos and Fabian Ver.

The filling of upper-level functional positions by those little capable or inclined to perform necessary military tasks led to a near-complete breakdown in the security force replacement, training, and supply systems:

• In the area of manpower, a typical battalion, which on paper was to have a strength of 630, was frequently able to deploy but 50–70 per cent of that figure. (In the US military 30 per cent losses are judged to render a unit 'combat ineffective'.) Companies which at full strength should have had more than 150 personnel were mentioned in numerous operational reports as putting but 70–80 men into the field. Since there was a high probability that a loss would not be made up, battalions often kept in their ranks those no longer capable of combat duty. One battalion observed in 1986 had 22 such 'P3' personnel, several of them amputees.

• Training, for all practical purposes, vanished. Units were formed, taught basics, then deployed to the field; skills were gained 'on-the-job'. Military schooling was disregarded as a criterion for promotion. Assignment by specialty ('military occupational skill' or MOS) stopped. Neither was there any longer an established connection between position and rank. An individual who could do the job was put into a slot, regardless of formal rank. Promotion to the noncommissioned officer (NCO) level was used to reward superior performance and time-in-grade; it was unrelated to functional position. Ergo, it was not unusual to find senior sergeants who had not even attended their basic NCO course — and privates leading patrols comprised of sergeants. Needless to say, the NCO corps did not serve, as intended, as the backbone of the system. The result was entire battalions operating with *ad hoc* structures.

• In supply, modern infantry arms and ammunition were frequently not available, especially heavy company weapons such as machine-guns and mortars. Technical specifications on indigenously produced weapons were compromised to allow for greater rake-offs, degrading the reliability of the arms used in battle. When units proceeded on operations, there was such a shortage of basic items — boots and uniforms, for instance — that anything was worn. To distinguish between the government and NPA forces, special recognition signals had to be used, such as colored scarves tied around shirt sleeves or on weapons. Organic transport was also woefully inadequate. One brigade examined in 1986 had just two trucks; its battalions had four each, though not all were operational due to lack of spare parts. This lack of transport meant that seriously wounded casualties had minimal chances of survival unless a helicopter was available from higher headquarters, but even a RUC would usually have no more than several aircraft assigned, with these frequently 'down' for maintenance.

That the battalions could continue to function was a direct result of the efforts exerted by the field commanders. With the NCO corps essentially nonexistent in a leadership sense, unit officers shouldered the burden. They were able to do so because of their technical competence, often self-taught, and professional expertise, gained through long tours in combat. Their understanding of revolutionary warfare was often surprisingly sound. This comprehension allowed them to make the most of their limited resources. Of note, too, officers outside Manila normally shared the hardships with their men. The result was generally high troop morale despite the material deprivations.

Still, bitterness towards the regime and its military clients was deep and widespread among that portion of the officer corps — the bulk — consigned to the field. Under the impact of the patronage system, normal career progression was severely disrupted, particularly once the field grades (major through colonel) had been reached. As a result, command tours were all but frozen. Battalion commands of five years in combat became the norm. One individual interviewed in 1986 had a nine-year tenure. Longer tours were on record. Exacerbating the resentment was a near-universal belief that no amount of military proficiency could defeat the insurgency in the absence of reform at the top — which the palace was unwilling to provide. Widespread knowledge of financial wrongdoing only heightened the anger.

A War of Battalions

Ironically, the particulars described above, which could have played themselves out in any number of ways, in the Philippine scenario had the impact of making the situation more difficult for the insurgents — because they strengthened the military as an opponent. While professional dissatisfaction increased as promotion stagnated, for instance, with commanders forced to serve excessive tours in the field, the inevitable result was a military in which more often than not the field units were led by veterans. Likewise, the hardships visited upon the units tended to foster not disintegration but unity. Defection was never viewed as a viable option by more than a few individuals. Consequently, units hung together if for no reason other than the increased prospects of survival which accompanied such a course of action. Even the lack of weapons and equipment had the perverse impact of improving the counterinsurgency, because this ensured that military operations were in the main small unit actions rather than large, costly search and destroy operations. Airmobile assaults and the like were infrequent in a country the size of all Vietnam in which no more than several dozen helicopters were operational at any one time.

Perhaps most important for cohesion, though, was the influence of the professional code maintained by the bulk of the officer corps. Domination of the security forces by graduates of the Philippine Military Academy (PMA), a virtual copy of its colonial parent at West Point, was only the most obvious element in this development. The 'West Point ethos', to be sure, provided an element of institutional glue which had proved lacking in most Third World armies. Just as crucial, however — and still, to my knowledge, an unexplored topic — was the cohesion engendered within the officer corps by the legacy that stemmed from the circumstances surrounding the birth of Philippine nationhood. Not only had Manila been promised independence at the time of the Japanese invasion and conquest, but the Philippine armed forces subsequently played — with much heroism and suffering — a key role in making victory a reality. This, of course, was followed by the successful campaign against the Huks, which, even considering American assistance, was an indigenous effort, particularly under Magsaysay. The result was that the military saw *itself*, as opposed to the left, as the true embodiment of Filipino nationalism. Backed by a large and active cadre of service veterans, many highly decorated, the military as a corporate body was determined to survive Marcos, his cronies, and the CPP.

This determination revealed itself in several ways. On the one hand, there was little open revolt against Manila, because non-patronage officers saw their loyalty not to the person of the commander-in-chief, which Marcos was by law, but to the constitutional reality of the office and to the military (or security forces) as an institution with a code of non-interference in 'civilian' affairs. Commanders in the field continued to function, because they believed their ultimate duty was not to a regime but to a code. On the other hand, such focus upon the code, which was being violated by Marcos and those around him, led many 'younger' non-patronage officers to form the RAM ('Reform AFP Movement'), a secret organization, dominated by PMA graduates, dedicated to reasserting professional ideals. At its forefront were field commanders who believed matters could not continue as they had been for much longer.[38]

Marcos recognized the potential for subversion of an organization such as RAM, but he was too enmeshed in his own world to pay it more than passing notice. Indeed, towards the end of his rule, he seemed all but oblivious to the realities in the countryside which were turning his own officer corps against him.

Thus it developed, as the efficiency and legitimacy of the Marcos regime declined, there was a commensurate increase in the extent to which armed force, as represented by the 70-odd, individual military battalions, became the crucial foundation upon which government survival depended. This proved significant, because in the absence of any other viable government presence, it was the battalions which became, like so many warlords, the rulers of their domains. Consequently, it was the peculiarities — strengths or weaknesses — of any battalion that influenced the situation in its area of operations (AO) nearly as much as the socio-economic-political conditions which had given rise to the revolt. For at no time was the NPA, in any area of the archipelago, able to achieve a concentration of strength such that government forces could not appear at will. The result was that, even in those areas where the CPP had achieved local supremacy through its shadow organization, it could not develop a viable societal alternative to that which had existed previously. This had the effect of keeping the military aspects of the conflict salient, but in these the party simply could not compete with the greater resources of the government, regardless of the substantial disadvantages under which the security forces operated.

Ultimately, the CPP drive, while it grew in numbers, stalled due to its inability to achieve true strategic parity. NPA units could not, even in the favorable strategic conditions provided by the corrupt Marcos regime, protect gains which had been made. The CPP, in other words, could not get the linchpin of the regime, its armed forces, to crack. This placed the strategic campaign in the peculiar position of being heavily dependent upon the most human of qualities, the leadership abilities of individual government commanders. These, by virtue of training and professional orientation, remained generally superior to those of the CPP opposition.

Government Search for a New Approach

Essentially, then, it can be seen, Marcos manufactured the instrument of his own destruction. He had created the proverbial 'two armies' noted by so many writers: a force in the capital for show, which played games unrelated to 'the real world', and a force in the field which was in deadly earnest about its activities, a force which bore the casualties, the frustrations, and the hopes of the military.

With the assassination of Marcos' main rival, Benigno Aquino, in August 1983 when he returned to Manila, events took on a life of their own. Security force elements associated with Ver carried out the assassination; the resulting popular alienation and unrest proved irresistible. As discontent mounted, a snap election held in February 1986, conceived as a means for Marcos to demonstrate his popularity (and to please Washington), instead gave victory to the opposition in the form of Benigno's wife, Cory Aquino. When Marcos tried to reverse the outcome through electoral fraud, millions took to the streets of Manila and elsewhere. Early on, the masses were joined by Defense Minister Juan Ponce Enrile and PC

Commander Fidel Ramos, who had reason to fear for their own personal safety at Marcos' hands. The bulk of the officer corps, in any case, was ripe for defection. In his press conference posturing during the crisis, Marcos could produce an array of patronage senior officers who publicly pronounced their support of the regime. Yet neither the troops nor their real leaders, the field commanders, would follow these cronies.

When the explosion came in Manila, most battalion and brigade commanders had no loyalty to the regime. The crucial decision was that of Enrile and Ramos to back Mrs Aquino. This allowed the alienated, anti-patronage group in the officer corps to support the 'reformists', as the anti-government forces became known, because it allowed them to act within the dictates of their professional code. The military rebels declared not a coup but support for what they claimed was a lawfully elected presidential candidate, Aquino. Hence most commanders were willing to act in their corporate professional interests and did so, disobeying orders from the Marcos camp because they were 'illegal'. In the end, the defection of virtually all maneuver battalion and most brigade commanders to the 'reformist' cause brought the regime down. Marcos' orders to move reinforcements to the capital, while obeyed in some instances, were disregarded in most. Those troops who did arrive eventually defected. This kept the confrontation in Manila a relatively small and bloodless affair which could be settled by the masses in the streets. The 'loyalist' facade crumbled.

For the military, this meant significant changes carried out at a rapid pace. Eventually, 'Rocky' Ileto became Defense Secretary (after an initial tenure by Enrile); Ramos became Chief of Staff of the AFP (for a time the military referred to itself as the 'New AFP' or NAFP); and Mison moved to Vice Chief of Staff. Extendees were retired quickly; leadership positions were given to combat veterans. In the first months after Marcos' ouster, some 80 per cent of all major command positions changed hands. Training and personnel systems were revamped. The supply pipeline, freed in the main from the corrosive influence of corruption, again began to function — with considerable US assistance. Troop deployment posture was examined and modified. Most 'palace guard' units in the capital were deployed to the field. Discipline and control over the militia forces was tightened. Further, the delicate process began of disarming the numerous private armies which had been allowed to flourish under Marcos.

As these military moves were carried out, the nature of the insurgency was transformed fundamentally by the return to democracy. A ceasefire with the CPP was declared by the government effective 10 December 1986 and lasted for 60 days. This was a controversial but necessary move which demonstrated once and for all that the CPP sought not reform but revolution.

Debate on the merits of entering into the ceasefire had dominated the Manila political scene for months prior to its actual implementation. Arrayed on one side within the government had been those in favor of pursuing the peace initiative, a group which included Mrs Aquino and her closest advisors, many of whom had pronounced 'progressive' sympathies after years in opposition to Marcos. In the other corner were the conservative elements, typified by Defense Minister Enrile, soon to leave the administration and become an opposition senator. The conservatives opposed the truce not in principle but as it was implemented. They saw it as little more than a communist tactical ploy designed to allow the CPP to rest and regroup.

In this analysis they were correct. The CPP had never been under any illusions that the ceasefire would provide more than a respite in the conflict. Forced on the defensive by the sudden and unexpected ouster of Marcos, the CPP saw the truce as a means to avoid being isolated from popular sentiment and to regain the initiative. Specifically, the party recognized that it had stumbled badly by refusing to participate in the 1986 election which precipitated the demise of the Marcos regime. Subsequently, after decades of justifying its insurgency in terms of oppposition to the 'US-Marcos Dictatorship', it suddenly found itself having to explain its continued existence in a post-Marcos era dominated center-stage by a tremendously popular, democratically elected leader dedicated to the very causes of social and economic justice the communists claimed for their own.

Disunity appeared in the CPP ranks, with different groups striking out independently in their search for an approach to the Aquino phenomenon. After much discussion, the CPP leadership declared that intra-party unity and future success could best be assured by giving in to the strong public sentiment for a ceasefire and exploration of reconciliation. Such a hiatus would not only avoid the party's being branded as 'anti-peace' but would also allow it to rectify glaring organizational weaknesses which had been revealed in February 1986.

The CPP, the logic went, had been unable to take advantage of the rapid political developments in February 1986 because it had not sufficiently developed its urban components. Extensive though the infrastructure was in built-up areas, it was overwhelmingly a political phenomenon designed to support party activities in the countryside — rather than make an independent contribution of its own. It was particularly weak in the armed force it was able to muster. When the window of opportunity appeared, therefore, it could not put the trained, armed manpower on the streets as needed to assure itself of a center role in developments. This was to be remedied by stepping up as much as possible urban recruitment activities by fronts and by illegal, underground organizations. When a chaotic political situation again developed, as the CPP felt it would due to the left versus right strains present in the Aquino government, the communists would be ready to put their own legions into the forefront of the struggle, allegedly in support of democracy against attempts to restore the dictatorship.

A ceasefire, which necessarily involved freedom of movement and unrestricted political activity, was obviously the best environment in which to carry out such a plan. Hence the communists pragmatically supported the Aquino truce initiative, all the while dickering over technicalities so as to achieve the best terms possible. 'The revolutionary movement is most capable in maximizing its gains in a generally open democratic space', noted the analysis contained in 'Some Notes on the Issue of Ceasefire', the product of a policy review conducted by high ranking CPP cadre on 5 July 1986. 'We are most capable in organizing and mobilizing the people and in taking advantage of the socio-economic programs that may be set [up] by the civilian government [of Mrs Aquino].'[39]

To that end, party political workers were directed to press on with their recruiting and organization efforts. The National Democratic Front (NDF) was given the lead role in this activity. The effort to conceal ultimate CPP authority and intentions meant that the ceasefire negotiations and activities were carried out by, and in the field allegedly implemented on behalf of, the NDF. The NDF even claimed that the CPP was but the leading organization of the NDF's co-equal constituent members and that the NPA was the NDF's armed forces. Such, of course, was far from the case. As already noted earlier, the NDF had been created by the CPP in 1973, as had been the NPA some years earlier. Both took orders directly from the party leadership. But by allowing the NDF heads to appear in public — many NDF leaders were reasonably well-known personalities of various backgrounds who had crossed over to the insurgent camp in opposition to the Marcos regime — the CPP sought to foster the image it wished to project, that of the abused driven to armed revolt by societal injustice and government repression. The real leadership, the CPP hierarchy, was not forced to subject itself to public scrutiny.

As was the case with political operatives, so, too, were combatants told to go about their normal duties but to avoid firefights (called 'encounters' by both sides) which might endanger the ceasefire. 'The struggle will continue', an 18-year old former Political Organizing Team (POT) member observed. Until his capture in early November 1986, he had been charged with recruiting villagers in northern Samar, at that time a point of emphasis in the CPP effort. He went on,

> We were directed to continue politicization even during a ceasefire so as to get a bigger group. We were told not to trust the government about ceasefire talks. Cory Aquino is still the same as Marcos. She is rich. She still belongs to the higher class. So the way she will run the government will be the same.[40]

The other prime actor in carrying out the ceasefire, the military, was aware of this strategy and felt strongly that the ultimate effect of the ceasefire would be to increase CPP capabilities. Stated 'Post-Revolution [February 1986] Communist Strategy in the Philippines: Indicators and Potential', a Ministry of National Defense document distributed to all units in August 1986:

> ... The NDF/CPP/NPA have said and continue to say that although Marcos has been deposed, the warlords and the unjust colonial imperialistic structures still remain, and therefore the parliamentary/armed struggle must continue and even be intensified (in order to attain the NDF/CPP/NPA objective of having a communist government to finally 'liberate' the Filipino people).[41]

In their press conferences held in Manila, NDF representatives were boldly saying as much. 'Now', the document concluded, 'the enemies (NDF/CPP/NPA and affiliates) are waging "total war" [through political and military means] against President Aquino, her government, and the Filipino people.'[42]

Though they could not know it at the time, the military had

been far more accurate than it realized in its assessment. To recap briefly, what ruined the favorable strategic situation for the CPP was the February 1986 overthrow of the corrupt Marcos regime. In a single blow, the party was robbed of its greatest recruiting asset. Additionally, having boycotted the national election which precipitated the 'Edsa Revolution', the CPP was not a player in the mass uprising. Political events were developing at such a rate that they outran the party's ability to react. To get into the game, argued a group within the CPP, required 'rectification' of past errors, specifically the failure to exploit fully the opportunities for mass organizing afforded by 'democratic space'. Thus resulted the 60-day ceasefire which began in December 1986. Able to regroup unhindered as representatives of its leadership, in their NDF guise, met with the government and appeared on TV talk shows, the CPP emerged from the ceasefire greatly strengthened. It was at this point, though, that it misread the situation and blundered into 'total war'.

Recounted Colonel George Vallejera some time later, while serving as a division operations officer on Negros:

What happened was that the communists made a fundamental error. They underestimated the situation. Because they were able to grow 100 per cent in the immediate aftermath of February 1986, they thought their moment had come. They therefore pushed for advantage. They began to experiment with more aggressive tactics, in particular in Bicol [in the extreme south of Luzon Island]. But they hadn't thought the business through thoroughly. What resulted was that they caused all sorts of problems for the people. And the people reacted very negatively. Who gets hurt if infrastructure is destroyed? Who gets hurt if an area is cut off from Manila? The people turned on them [the communists]. We had a dramatic increase in intelligence. It has never stopped.

Now there is an internal struggle in the CPP over what strategy to follow. The 'hardliners', those who favor the more aggressive stance, appear to have the upper hand over the 'moderates', those who want to keep organizing. The hardliners look at the examples of Vietnam and Nicaragua, and they think that they have reached strategic stalemate, the phase of [Maoist] insurgency when the guerrillas can battle the government on its own terms and protect 'liberated' territory. But they're not even close, so their tactics are not appropriate to the strategic situation.[43]

Unintentionally, the 'rectificationists' — the 'moderates' — attempted to make the same argument as Colonel Vallejera. Rather than a heightened military posture, they argued, 'democratic space' provided the ideal medium for continued clandestine organizing and use of fronts. Numerous purges resulted. The grim fall-out was to be found in mass graves discovered in many areas by security forces and villagers. In the end, the hardliners were victorious. Their ascendance brought about a more active CPP military posture. Captured CPP directives called for emphasis upon 'regularization' (i.e., creating standardized units), forming larger formations, upping the tempo of military operations, arming guerrillas with heavy weapons, increased front activity, greater use of mines and booby traps, and greater use of sparrow squads for assassinations. Further, the CPP wanted to hold territory through formation of 'fighting villages'. This last directive was part of a larger CPP campaign to achieve international recognition and belligerent status for its combatants.

Upping the military tempo would have been a mistake on its own terms — the NPA formations were nowhere near the point where they could stand and go toe-to-toe with the Philippine military. More fundamentally, however, the Achilles heel in such an approach was that it pushed to the fore military considerations in what was, after all, a political war.

It was the reintroduction of politics into Philippine life which made this CPP shift such a blunder. In the years following February 1986, elections, so long delayed or rigged by Marcos, were held at all levels, to include municipality (county) and village. The result was that there existed throughout the country mechanisms for the expression of popular will. These, imperfect though they were, began to shape the socio-economic environment by addressing longstanding development concerns and demands for social justice. They could do this due to the federal structure of the country which devolved authority to an extent unusual in a Third World nation.

In Negros Occidental Province, for example, long one of the centers of CPP activity nationwide due to a moribund economy built about a single crop, sugar, Governor Daniel Lacson, Jr. implemented a 15-year development plan centered about economic diversification. In short order, according to published reports, the rapidly growing prawn industry was on the verge of replacing sugar as the province's major dollar earner. Though prawn cultivation itself was not labor intensive, the collateral development in other segments of the economy was substantial. Further, marketing prawns was just one facet of the governor's extensive development schemes.

Similar activity could be found at the local level as elected officials struggled to meet the expectations and demands of their constituents. More important than immediate results was the feeling among the populace that nonviolent avenues were available for interest articulation and realization. Hence the ability of the CPP to appeal to economic and political dissatisfaction was dealt a severe blow. Coming as it did when the party was pushing its hardline strategy — enforced by liquidations of recalcitrant CPP elements throughout the archipelago — this development led to an increased flow of surrenderees. In interviews with them, analysts were often struck by their classic 'grievance guerrilla' profiles. They had given up precisely because the hardline approach contradicted their concern for social justice.[44]

One major labor organizer on Negros, Manuel Jurada Laranero alias 'Bunny', a CPP member with District Secretary rank, put this in perspective when he spoke of direct, face-to-face orders delivered by the ranking CPP men on Negros (one an ex-priest, Francisco Fernandez) to stop engaging in union activities which would better the lot of the workers. 'Bunny' was admonished that sharpening the contradictions was what he was supposed to be about, not helping the system perpetuate itself through reform. Noted 'Bunny', then 39 years of age:

> Whenever there is a problem [between the workers and landlords], we're not supposed to talk but to intensify the struggle through strikes, economic sabotage, and so on. If there is an intensification of mass action, it is complemented by armed struggle. That's what the CPP wants to happen. The higher organ wants people to be engaged in mass action so that attention will be directed from the countryside to the urban areas.[45]

Such a CPP line was hardly new to students of the movement, but for 'Bunny' it was a revelation of gut-wrenching proportions: if social justice was not the issue, what was? The answer, as those who followed the CPP knew, was that the party was after the communist version of social justice. And that involved doing whatever was necessary *tactically* to gain *strategic* victory, defined as communist political power. Old Lenin, to be sure, but new for 'Bunny'. He surrendered.

Philippine 'People's War'

Ironically, the CPP turn towards increased violence came even as the government embraced the primacy of political factors. Beginning in 1988 but adopted formally in 1989 with OPLAN (operations plan) *Lambat Betag* ('Net Trap'), the Philippine military moved from a 'search and destroy'-based philosophy to one dominated by the identification and destruction of the CPP infrastructure. This was a fundamental reorientation of strategy and married a correct military approach with popular support for the revitalized political structure even as the CPP adopted an incorrect military approach amidst a loss of political legitimacy. The results were devastating for the party. As early as 1990, the communists found themselves unable to replace lost manpower or to generate a viable approach capable of dealing with 'democratic space'. In the four-plus years that followed the ouster of Marcos, the party, according to its own count, contracted from 73 to 56 Fighting Fronts. In some areas, such as Negros, CPP documents revealed a 50 per cent loss of 'mass base'. Key CPP/NDF/NPA leaders were captured with such regularity that the Politburo and Central Committee went deep underground, even declining to give their customary briefings to the foreign press.

This switch by the government, of course, had not 'just happened'. Rather it was a direct outgrowth of the wholesale change in personalities which followed Marcos' departure. As field commanders moved into planning positions, they sought a new direction. Crucial to the process were the ideas of Victor Corpus, PMA 1967. In 1970, as a junior officer in an elite PC unit, he had created a sensation by defecting to the CPP. There, he was instrumental in making the fledging NPA a going concern. Six years later, however, disillusioned with the party, he returned to the government fold, only to be imprisoned for ten years. Released when Marcos was ousted from power in February 1986, and later reinstated in the military as a lieutenant colonel, he became the central force in radically reorienting Philippine counterinsurgency away from its fruitless emphasis upon military operations. Instead, the weight of effort went to socio-economic-political development.

Reorientation began with Corpus' assignment, after his release, as a consultant to a Ministry of National Defense counterinsurgency study group which included several key RAM members. Later, in October 1987, with RAM in disarray following its abortive coup efforts — against what it perceived to be a bumbling, hapless Aquino government — he moved to the Combat Research Division of AFP Operations (J3). Working for Colonel Clemente Moriano, Corpus and some other officers, on a team tasked with formulating strategic approaches, went around the country trading ideas with commanders and subordinates. In many areas, such as that of 4th Infantry Division on Mindanao, they found a version of what they had in mind already being used. There, a relatively low-ranking officer, Captain Alex Congman, was credited with implementing a 'Special Operations Team' (SOT) concept which reverse engineered the CPP's infrastructure. That is, government SOTs performed the same function as the CPP's armed propaganda units, followed by the countermobilization of the target area in support of the government. And on Negros, Brigadier General Rene Cardones, who assumed command of that embattled island shortly after Marcos' fall, had by mid-1988 moved this countermobilization approach to perhaps its most developed form of any area in the Philippines.[46]

That the people could be countermobilized, of course, was because the political environment had changed for the better. Thus it was the government which represented social justice rather than the CPP. Congman's simple concept had grown ultimately into a broader 'triad strategy' adopted by the entire army. It gave equal importance to military operations, intelligence, and civic action within an overarching development effort by elected officials. It was this 'triad strategy' which was worked into a final campaign plan — a 'war of quick decision' — that was presented by the Corpus study group in April 1988 to a commanders' conference.[47]

At first the plan, which called for intensive anti-infrastructure operations against a prioritized list of CPP Fighting Fronts — an oil spot technique waged at the operational level — met with a lukewarm response. Rotation to the Chief of Operations (J3) position, however, of Brigadier General Lisandro Abadia tipped the scales in its favor. For it had been under Abadia that the SOT concept had originally been given a chance to prove itself. The result was that the new *Lambat Betag* was completed by late 1988. The following year, 1989, was in effect to be a trial run for the plan, a preparatory phase during which SOTs and other anti-infrastructure personnel, but the AFP decided the situation warrented implementing it immediately. The results, as noted above, were rapid and dramatic, more so because Abadia eventually became army head. 'If we can maintain the democratic system', observed Corpus later, 'the Communist Party of the Philippines is indeed a spent force.'[48]

It is noteworthy that in a sense the Filipinos had reinvented the wheel. Their approach incorporated those elements which other successful counterinsurgencies had found necessary for victory, yet they had been arrived at independent of foreign advice or assistance. American presence, for example, so often portrayed — by both the Western media and the CPP — as crucial to Manila's effort, was actually most important in a material and financial sense. It added very little doctrinally. Intelligence-wise, too, the major American contribution was technical, particularly in interception of CPP signals and the breaking of codes, rather than operational.

Observed Corpus:

> We drew mostly upon my experience. We didn't refer to any books. We had read the US manuals on low intensity conflict, but we blamed those manuals for introducing COIN [counterinsurgency] doctrines that only aggravated the situation. They apply conventional methods to an unconventional situation. In particular, traditional civic action is a mere paliative. It does not go to the root causes of the problem, to the lack of democracy.[49]

Operationally, getting to the 'root causes of the problem' translated into the formula 'clear, hold, consolidate, and develop'. To reclaim an area, the government moved in with its own troops (again, the battalion formed the basic building block) and destroyed or drove out resident NPA units. Overwhelming force was mustered to ensure that this was invariably the case. Once this had been done, the government battalion concerned remained in control of the area while it uncovered and dismantled the communist infrastructure. Simultaneously, a government intelligence net was set up, and citizens were organized into militias to defend the area. Each militia detachment guarded its village and its outlying hamlets and was controlled by several regular government soldiers.

Eventually, when security had been reestablished, government officials could come in to supervise normal functions and development efforts. The militia continued to perform security and patrol duties throughout and day and night, working in shifts. Just in case the communists tried to return in force, part of every battalion was kept at all times in reserve as a strike force. Finally, Special Forces control teams took over handling the militia, and the battalion moved on to the next area to be won back.

Central to the approach was providing the security which allowed elected government to function and to address socio-economic concerns. Most of the infrastructure could be rendered impotent simply by exposure, precisely because 'grievance guerrillas' were at the heart of the CPP movement and responded to decent treatment within the context of the new political and economic environment. The shift in popular attitude was palpable. With it came a decrease in the difficulty government agents had in penetrating the CPP apparatus. The CPP responded with bloody purges to weed out alleged infiltrators. This only drove still more of its members to surrender.

Most important, cutting off the CPP from its mass base was far more than simply a mechanical exercise in neutralizing the movement's infrastructure. In the absence of reform, to eliminate the fundamental grievances which had driven individuals to seek redress through armed struggle, new cells would have constantly sprung up. Traditional 'civic action' — digging wells, providing medical treatment, and so forth — was but a band-aid, as Corpus noted. Root causes had to be attacked. The only way this could occur was if there were mechanisms which allowed the population a role in their own lives. Democracy was one of the best such mechanisms.

The result was that in the closing years of the 1980s it was the government, as represented by the military working with civilian authority, which was moving to 'eliminate the grievances' even as the CPP opted for gunslinging. As a growing number of individuals returned to areas of greater government presence, they flowed into the militia for self-protection. This was a turning point. So often portrayed as little more than thugs and the dregs of society, the militia became the ultimate Maoist nightmare: the people armed and numerous. Evidence of the degree to which the CPP was feeling the bite of this trend could be seen in its stepped up domestic and international campaigns to paint the Philippine government — and especially the militia — as guilty of widespread human rights violations. Extralegal killings were certainly carried out by government supporters, but best evidence showed such activities to pale in numbers *when compared to the institutionalized violence of the CPP* (the left's 'structural violence' argument turned on its head). The government recognized that control over militia activities was critical to prevent the abuses which figured prominently in frequent criticism of the Marcos-era counterinsurgency effort. Obviously, such control was achieved in the main. On the communist side, with its heightened emphasis upon violence, it was not. Everywhere, refugees, asked why they had 'come in', answered with two responses: 'We can no longer take the [CPP's] taxes. We can no longer take the [CPP's] violence.'[50]

There was the CPP's miscalculation in a nutshell. Its strategy of increased exploitation of the people and violence ignored the desire for justice which had been the fundamental driving force at the heart of the Philippine insurgency — the force which had allowed a committed communist leadership to recruit non-ideological peasant manpower. It was the return of the political process to the Philippine people which allowed justice to be pursued and which made the exercise of politics itself the ultimate government weapon.

With hindsight it is possible to recognize the CPP's miscalculation. Less clear, though, is why the situation came to pass. Why, in other words, did the CPP opt for a strategy which seemed sure to backfire on it? Why did the ideologues, those favoring the armed approach, win out? Earlier, Noel Albano observed the manner in which repression drove the 'best and the brightest' of Filipino youth into the arms of the CPP. The importance of Philippine geography was also highlighted, for it allowed a decentralization within which newcomers could each find his own platform by achieving organizational success in the 'outer islands'. These same individuals could then come back and reinvigorate the center's strategic thinking. With the assassination of Benigno Aquino, however, a revitalized 'legal opposition' of sorts developed abroad and in the Philippines. This, combined with the oft-documented change in attitudes upon the part of the students of the 1980s, an emphasis away from activism and towards intra-systemic career concerns (a worldwide phenomenon, just as the student activism of the late 1960s and early 1970s was), meant that the bulk of the politically motivated young people articulated their political demands in forums other than the CPP.

This trend was consummated by the ouster of Marcos and the regeneration of the Philippine political process, flawed though it might appear to many. Further, the removal of the visible 'anti-Marcos' catalyst caused many would-be activists to return to their books and such. This was clearly visible in the leadership ranks of student protests in the late 1980s, where the traditional University of the Philippines (UP) dominance gave way to individuals from smaller campuses, individuals who simply did not have the organizational skills and broad outlook which was developed through activist work on the massive UP campuses. The result was that beginning in 1983 the CPP began to receive little 'new blood' from the most vibrant intellectual sector of Philippine society. Instead, its new leaders came from within the movement itself or from particular sectors, such as the clergy, which had been influenced by unique factors. Predictably, intellectual stagnation set in, the results of which could be seen in the lack of CPP strategic vision.[51]

In contrast, the government leadership ranks were revitalized. The changeover within the civilian administration needs no comment; that within the military has been recognized several times. Thus there developed a situation of 'new blood' facing 'old', if the conflict could be seen, at least in part, from such an angle. What kept the positive trend from becoming more pronounced during the six-year tenure of Mrs Aquino was the lack of government unity of effort. It took the military three years after February 1986 to come to an institutionally agreed upon consensus on the nature of the conflict. Further, impatient at the pace of reform, military elements, led by RAM members, made a half dozen coup attempts. It could be said that the central government in Manila never did reach an understanding of 'counterinsurgency'. Fortunately for Manila, in the provinces the federal nature of the political system allowed the military to work, closely and harmoniously normally, with the civil authorities. This trend was solidified as local pressures upon the center led to a greater devolution of funding prerogatives, thereby making greater resources for the 'develop' phase of *Lambat Betag*.

Unable to deal with the government threat on the ground, the CPP attempted to undermine it through propaganda, particularly emphasis upon alleged human rights violations. Domestically, the party was still able to get help from sympathetic members of cause-oriented groups. Internationally, too, solidarity groups gave not

only moral backing but also financial resources.[52] The NDF located its headquarters in the Netherlands, the better to exploit the
tendency of so many international cause-oriented groups to think
little but ill of a Third World government such as that of the
Philippines. Prime NDF goal, and that of its fellow travellers, was
to get foreign aid to Manila cut off. All that was needed, they analyzed, was enough 'information' that would portray the government in the worst possible light.

Certainly this was not hard to come by. The post-Marcos
Philippine government could not objectively be judged as repressive, but it was terribly inefficient. Consequently, there was no
shortage of heart-rending human 'drama of survival' to stir up con-
demnation. So as to leave nothing to chance, explicit instructions
went out from the CPP Politburo outlining the use of certain
schemes, such as 'the Evacuation', as tactical ploys. In this latter
maneuver, detailed plans were prepared in advance for the 'flight'
of refugees from areas of government operations. Rally points
were designated, demands were rehearsed, and control personnel
were assigned to ensure there were no backsliders. As soon as government troops began a maneuver, an evacuation or another
human rights ploy would be launched, just as would any weapons
system. The point, of course, was to attempt to disrupt government operations, while simultaneously gaining as much propaganda mileage as possible. Unfortunately for the CPP, no combination
of approaches proved able to blunt the government effort. By
1993 its Fighting Fronts had declined to 42. Even the NDF found
itself stymied in its efforts to continue the struggle by co-opting
participants in the open political process.

There has also always been the problem for the CPP that,
despite its acknowledged organizational finesse, it is operating in
the Philippines. Hence, Philippine societal particulars have resulted in a movement at once clandestine yet remarkably open, subject
not only to penetration by government agents but also to the
'retirement' by its members. When a Filipino guerrilla decided he
had had enough, he simply left the fight. Now, increasing pressure
from church and family has caused growing numbers of rebels to
opt out of the struggle — and would-be guerrillas to look elsewhere for redress of grievances. The result has been the virtual
inclusion of the CPP as a legitimate-but-illegitimate element of the
societal calculus, even if a misguided and frowned upon one. CPP
leaders air their views, hopes, and dreams — and even their dirty

laundry — nearly as publicly as any other Philippine politicians.

In the field, of course, people continue to die. Yet 'the war' has long been one of relative scale. In 1990, for instance, the insurgency claimed 3,600 deaths, but this figure was only equal to the number of murders in California, a state with only half the population of the Philippines (some 30 million versus 60 million). In more recent years, with casualties lower still, it is not surprising that there is a quiet optimism surrounding the work of the Ramos-appointed National Unification Commission (NUC). Headed by Professor of Law Haydee Yorac, it is charged with drawing up a comprehensive package for reconciliation with which all can live. A group calling itself 'Warriors for Peace', with members drawn from both former AFP and CPP personnel, even goes about the hinterland preaching harmony and peaceful resolution of conflict.

Attempting to play the spoiler in this rosy situation is CPP founder and current self-proclaimed party head, Jose Maria Sison. Now 53, 'Joma' was imprisoned for a decade during the Marcos regime but freed in the amnesty which accompanied the return to democracy. He quickly resumed his activities, setting up shop with other released CPP personnel in the Netherlands. He did not attempt to reassert control of the party, however, until the 10th Plenum of the Central Committee in July 1992. His move was prompted by what he saw as a dangerous drift from the correct Maoist 'people's war' approach — encircling the cities from the countryside — to a strategy favoring a mix of urban and rural work. This Sison denounced. Another 'rectification' campaign was launched, and 'renegade' regional headquarters were ordered to stand down.

These elements would have none of it. Pointing out that Sison had been elected by a 'quorum' of just 8 of 44 Central Committee members, they deemed his elevation illegitimate and gave their loyalty to the 'Secretary General' on the scene in the Philippines, Ricardo Reyes. The split quickly grew into a breach, with Sison's support centered on Luzon, at least the areas outside of Manila, that of his rivals controlling Mindanao and the Visayas. Significantly, it is these latter areas where the preponderance of CPP strength lies.

As befits the present peculiar position of the CPP within the Philippine political structure, neither side has been reluctant to publicize its side of the issue. Perhaps predictably, the renegades have been the more candid of the two. In a remarkable interview given in January 1993, Reyes observed:

> We had not even reached [strategic] stalemate after 20 years. A whole
> generation has aged...It looks like it is difficult to win. [We must ask
> ourselves] Why don't the people sympathize with us and [why] can't
> we capture the imagination of the younger generation?...There is that
> waning appeal, reflected very clearly in the data. Fewer and fewer are
> joining the New People's Army, fewer and fewer are joining the under-
> ground, especially the best and the brightest of the generations that
> followed in the [19]80s and 90s.. That is fatal for a revolutionary
> movement, if you fail to inspire the young...and so we say, 'Let us
> reexamine the strategy of encircling the cities from the country-
> side'...We even told him [Sison], 'The flaw in your analysis is funda-
> mental.'[53]

Driving the debate, of course, are aspects of Marxist doctrine,
specifically whether to interpret the Philippines as still 'feudal', as
Sison does, using the Maoist blueprint, or as a more developed
form, as the renegades posit. In particular, points out the Reyes
faction, the Philippines is no longer even predominantly rural,
since a majority of the population, in rural areas, lives in urban
areas. And an increasing proportion earns its livelihood through
multiple incomes, negating considerations of class consciousness
and solidarity. In practical terms, the conclusion of the rejection-
ists is that the CPP's proper strategy should be a dual urban-rural
approach closer to that of the Sandinistas in their overthrow of
Somoza than to that of the Maoists in their seizure of China.

Such dispute may soon be a case of little save ideological meta-
physics if present trends continue. Long listed in CPP documents
as 'the banners of the revolution', the most heavily communist-
infiltrated islands, Negros and Samar in the Visayas — those upon
which the CPP once envisaged making a 'last stand' if ever necessary — have witnessed a virtual collapse of the insurgent infrastructure. Indeed, while the improvement of the situation on
Negros has come at the end of the last few years of intense operations, the Samar turnabout has been largely bloodless, fallout from
the continued evolution of the the larger strategic dynamic. The
security forces' greatest weapon has been not the rifle but political
warfare.

Increasingly, therefore, the CPP has been forced to return to its
roots, to covert political organizing. This seemingly would be to its
advantage, given that insurgency is, when reduced to its essence,

but a political campaign of a party seeking to bludgeon its way into power. Yet in a curious way the necessity of becoming increasingly covert has forced a decoupling between the party and its struggle.

That struggle was able to achieve critical mass only because the Marcos dictatorship forced all disagreement underground. There, the CPP armed forces grew in order to protect the rapidly expanding political infrastructure. Today, however, the party must contend with democracy. As its apparatus is dismantled in the countryside, the CPP has been forced to focus on urban centers. But it is in these, as demonstrated repeatedly throughout the history of insurgency, that a rebel movement becomes extremely vulnerable. Not only must it contend with rivals for its political following, but it must justify to prospective recruits why they should risk death when they can change things through the system. The bottom line is that recruitment becomes difficult without the engine of repression to drive the alienated into the fold, and survival becomes problematic as informants turn in those they perceive as armed thugs who make life even tougher than it already is.

Consequently, the party has opted to lash out, seeking to create by increased military action the space it needs to survive. This has proved counterproductive on two counts. First, it has alienated the population; second, it has been foolish militarily, because it does not succeed. In the end, what the CPP has ended up doing is virtually pursuing military action for the sake of action itself. Assassinations, for instance, become nothing more than isolated murders, contributing nothing in a strategic, or even tactical, sense. Politics, in other words, no longer controls the gun. As the CPP has increasingly been perceived as more bandit than rebel, government intelligence has improved dramatically. This, in turn, has led to increased intra-party purges: the beast devours itself. What we now see, then, is a situation where the government holds the strategic initiative.

Conclusions

So it is that we arrive at certain parameters which are essential to an understanding of the insurgency in the Philippines.

● First and foremost, from the analysis above, it will be clear that the insurgency being waged by the Communist Party of the

Philippines (CPP) is a political struggle. It exists to pursue a political end, power. Regardless of historical factors that have contributed to manpower recruitment, at this point in time, the insurgency survives because it is an alternative political movement supported by force. Consequently, as has happened in the Philippines, we see evidenced the principle that political change is as basic to successful resolution of an insurgency as is socio-economic development. Politics, as an independent actor, can shape the environment just as completely as can socio-economic measures.

● Hence the 'causes' of an insurgency must be viewed carefully. Certainly, as in the Philippines, socio-economic-political grievances are at the root of the violence, and they account historically and in the main for the CPP's ability to raise manpower. Yet this insurgency, as with all others, contains tension between the goals of the leadership — in the CPP's case these are generally alienated intellectuals who are strongly committed to Marxist-Leninism — and its foot soldiers — who are primarily estranged peasants committed to armed struggle as the means to obtain a degree of social justice. The point at which organizational mechanisms come to supersede motives of passion is important, as are the mechanisms of control which guarantee that orders from the center will be carried out by the various branches of the movement. Put another way, the Philippine case is part insurgency — here, an ideologically motivated armed effort to make a revolution — and part peasant/worker rebellion. The balance between the two components in any area is fundamental to predicting the impact of government reform efforts.

● With this said, there should be no mistaking the fact that any insurgent movement which has existed as long as the CPP is bound to have highly developed and refined organizational structures and mechanisms of control. Yet there are observers who persist in viewing the conflict as peasant rebellion writ large. This is inaccurate. One does not need to deny the importance of the socio-economic component of the insurgency to recognize that, with the passage of time — nearly 30 years of formal struggle in the case of the CPP — the original grievances, whatever their form, have declined dramatically in salience. I do not find convincing the school of thought which holds that the CPP is the representative of a welling social revolution. I see this argument as inaccurate precisely because it reifies socio-economic disparity (frequently under the guise of 'nationalism') and relegates politics to a secondary role.

Indeed, the argument is neo-Marxian in that it makes politics an outgrowth of socio-economic realities, even while admitting the influence of political factors. To the contrary, 'on the ground', regardless of the relationship between the CPP leadership and its mass base at the operational and tactical levels, the ultimate strategic prize remains political power in Manila. It is towards this end that all communist organizational efforts are directed, not towards social reform within the existing framework of governance.

● In measuring the insurgent movement, therefore, it is a mistake to concentrate on either of two extemes: grievances *per se*, particularly those dictated by structural disparities; or the military component. Concentration on the first, the genesis of the conflict, can lead to tautology: if there is revolt, there must be grievances. Concentration on the second, the most visible aspect of revolt — the use of armed force against the state — can lead to 'bean counting' (how many regulars and so forth). In both cases there is the danger of missing the forest for the trees. The weakness in focusing upon a search for causes is that no amount of empirical analysis, whether quantitative or qualitative, has yet to discern those elements which are both necessary and sufficient to cause revolt. Qualitative structural analysis has proved more enlightening than quantitative multivariate computation only because 'the elegance of the argument' appears more appropriate to the explanation of complex human affairs than does mathematical reductionism. Neither offers definitive solutions. Likewise, focusing upon insurgent armed strength also holds little promise. Armed insurgents are a symptom not an explanation of the problem.

● It is the political organization of the mass base, whether in the rural or urban areas, which is critical. And it is this which makes any assessment of 'who is winning?' so extraordinarily difficult. How do we measure the influence of a political movement which holds no votes? Various means have been devised, from the quantitative to the impressionistic. Early on in the First Indochina War, for example, Bernard B. Fall was able to judge the extent of Vietminh influence by mapping out those areas which no longer paid taxes to the government. Much later, during the Second Indochina War, John Paul Vann adopted a more direct methodology. Even as computers were used to assess pacification, Vann would put his own professed control of an area to the acid test for an observer by the simple expedient of driving about at night in a jeep, headlights blazing, horn blaring. When both emerged unscathed, Vann could claim, without undue fear of contradiction, that he held sway in a region. Methodology notwithstanding, to my knowledge, no comprehensive survey has yet been offered assessing the security situation in the Philippines. I have offered my own partial contribution, blending the impressionistic and the empirical.

NOTES

1. A shortened version of Chapter 1's discussion of the Thai case may be found in my 'Maoist Insurgency: The Rise and Fall of the Communist Party of Thailand', *Issues & Studies* [Taipei], 28/8 (Aug. 1992), pp.73–115. An abbreviated version of this chapter is my 'Maoist Insurgency: The Communist Party of the Philippines, 1968–1993', *Issues & Studies*, 29/11 (Nov. 1993), pp.80–121.

2. 'Theoretical and Practical Problems for Contemporary Radicalism'. *Progressive Review* [Manila], 1/1 (May–June 1963), p.5.

3. For my understanding of this period, I am indebted to Robert B. Stauffer, Univ. of Hawaii (Political Science Dept.). The particular events chronicled here are detailed in his 'The Political Economy of a Coup: Transnational Linkages and Philippine Political Response', *Journal of Peace Research*, 11/3 (Aug. 1974), pp.161–77.

4. This is my own view of events. I feel Stauffer is among those who give too much credence to the possibility of conspiracy.

5. Cf. Robert B. Stauffer, 'Philippine Corporatism: A Note on the "New Society", *Asian Survey*, 17/4 (April 1977), pp.393–407; Stauffer, 'Philippine Authoritarianism: Framework for Peripheral 'Development', *Pacific Affairs*, 50/3 (Fall 1977), pp.365–86; Stauffer, 'The Philippine Development Model: Global Contradictions, Crises, and Costs', *Occasional Papers* (Dept. of Political Science, Univ. of Hawaii), 1/4 (Fall 1982), pp.84–118.

6. For a more detailed discussion of these points, cf. Benedict J. Kerkvliet, 'Martial Law in a Nueva Ecija Village, the Philippines', *Bulletin of Concerned Asian Scholars*, 14 (Oct.–Dec. 1982), pp.2–19. See also Kerkvliet's later work, 'Understanding Politics in a Nueva Ecija Rural Community', in Kerkvliet and Resil Mojares (eds.), *From Marcos to Aquino: Local Perspectives on Political Transition in the Philippines* (Quezon City: Ateneo de Manila UP, 1991).

7. One illustration should suffice here. During the 1946–72 period the World Bank was only minimally involved in the Philippines. It loaned the government a total of some US $300 million. In contrast, once martial law was in place, involvement mushroomed; 1980 loans alone were US $398 million.

8. Cf. Union of Democratic Filipinos (KDP) and the International Association of Filipino Patriots (IAFP), *Ten-Point Program of the National Democratic Front in the Philippines* (Oakland, CA: Int. Assoc. of Filipino Patriots [IAFP], 1978).

9. The passage reads: 'We deplore the attempts of the CIA–directed groups and the clerico–fascists to derail the antifascist movement by pointing to socialism or communism as the main issue now. We state categorically that the main issue now is the question of national independence and genuine democracy'.

10. Cf. Steve Psinakis, *Two Terrorists Meet* (San Francisco, CA: Alchemy Books, 1981).

11. For structure of the Catholic Church at this time, cf. Catholic Bishops' Conference of the Philippines, *Catholic Directory of the Philippines* (Manila, 1983).

12. Acknowledged as the benchmark work on the conflict is Benedict J. Kerkvliet, *The Huk Rebellion: A Study of Peasant Revolt in the Philippines* (Berkeley, CA: Univ. of California Press, 1977). Many other references exist. Particularly useful are Lawrence

M. Greenberg, *The Hukbalahap Insurrection: A Case Study of a Successful Anti–Insurgency Operation in the Philippines, 1946–1955* (Washington, DC: US Army Center of Military History, 1987); and a symposium published as 'The Huks in Retrospect: A Failed Bid for Power', *Solidarity*, No. 102 (1985), pp.64–103.

13. Best work for particulars of this linkup is Eduardo Lachica, *Huk: Philippine Agrarian Society in Revolt* (Manila: Solidaridad, 1971). Reprinted therein (pp.283–301) is the complete text of the important CPP document 'Program for a People's Democratic Revolution'. See also my 'From Huks to the New People's Army', *Soldier of Fortune*, 14/2 (Feb. 1989), pp.26–7 (sidebar).

14. Key theoretical work of the party is Amado Guerrero ('Beloved Warrior'), *Philippine Society and Revolution: Specific Characteristics of Our People's War*. Written under a pseudonym by José Maria Sison, founder and several times head of the CPP, it borrows heavily not only from Mao but also from D.N. Aidit, at that time Chairman of the Indonesian Communist Party.

15. Interview with author, 30 Dec. 1988, Manila.

16. I discuss this issue in greater depth in a sidebar, 'CPP Leadership Problems', to my 'Political Body Count: Philippine Army Tallies Converts, Not Corpses', *Soldier of Fortune*, 14/6 (June 1989), pp.32–9 (contd).

17. This observation touches, albeit briefly, upon the issue noted in the previous chapter: the precise relationship between peasant rebellion and insurgency. Most useful to my own work has been Scott, 'Revolution in the Revolution: Peasants and Commissars'. To reiterate: As he has perceptively noted, all insurgent movements necessarily contain two elements, leadership ranks comprised of members drawn from society's elite, followers taken from the masses. The same 'causes' motivate them but in very different ways. The leadership normally perceives injustice and attempts to deal with it by ideological solution. The followers, in contrast, who historically have been drawn overwhelmingly from the peasantry, attempt to deal with injustice by correcting those immediate wrongs that are identified. This reality leads to a constant tension between the two segments of any insurgency. It also leads me, much like Douglas Pike in his work on the Vietcong, to emphasize the importance of infrastructure and the bureaucratic process within which it naturally enmeshes its adherents (terror is an inherent component of this process). A contrasting view, such as most eloquently advanced by Kerkvliet, would emphasize those perceived injustices which mobilize insurgent manpower — and would see infrastructure and elite control as both contingent and tenuous.

On the Igorot issue specifically cf. my 'The Igorots of the Philippines', Ch.21 in Michael Tobias (ed.), *Mountain People* (Norman, OK: Univ. of Oklahoma Press, 1986), pp.158–63.

18. I have dealt with this subject explicitly in 'Insurgency Redefined', *Far Eastern Economic Review*, 25 Oct. 1990, pp.20–1; and 'Small Victory in a Big War: Philippine Army Routs Communists on Negros', *Soldier of Fortune*, 16/2 (Feb. 1991), pp.30–35 (contd).

19. My understanding of CPP infrastructure has been gained in some six years of regular field work. Greater details concerning sources may be found in the following chapter.

20. E.g., guerrilla strength on Negros in late 1986, just prior to a ceasefire with the government (which later lapsed), was 5,924, of whom only 499 were classified as regulars. For a complete breakdown see Table 1 in the following chapter.

21. Statistics may be found in the following chapter.

22. Notebook of Victor Gerardo Bulatao y Jayme, Secretary of the Regional United Front Group (RUFG), Samar, captured March 1982.

23. Cf. my 'Don't Discount the Philippine Communists', *Asian Wall Street Journal*, 28 April 1986, p.6.

24. Foreign funding, though not large, has been present and important throughout the insurgency. The most comprehensive public effort to examine it took place as part of

the 'Workshop on Philippine Communism', held 2–8 July 1988, Marina Mandarin, Singapore; jointly sponsored by Information & Resource Bureau (Singapore), Strategic Inst. for Southeast Asia (Tokyo), Inst. of Asian Studies, Chulalongkorn Univ. (Bangkok), and Naval War College Foundation (Newport, RI).

25. Numerous documents relating to the Kangleon case are contained in the amnesty file of the principal figures involved. Cf. HQ, Eastern Command, AFP (Camp Lukban, Catbalogan, Samar), 'Amnesty Papers of: Fr. Edgar Kangleon, Antonio Asistio, Juanito Delamida'.

26. A very different view from that I have presented here, one highly critical of the government, may be found in Alfred W. McCoy, *Priests on Trial* (Victoria: Penguin Books Australia, 1984). Discussion of the Kangleon case occurs principally on pp.212–15 and is in my judgement inaccurate. McCoy errs in assuming that the government case and Manila's actions against the social action framework on Samar were based solely on a coerced confession from Fr. Kangleon. In reality, Kangleon's confession, which was not forced, was but one piece of evidence among many.

27. I have discussed this case previously in *The Asian Wall Street Journal* (see n.23 above) and in 'Communist Insurgency in the Philippines: How and Why it Happened', *Gung–Ho*, 7/57 (March 1987), pp.40–5. Cf. MIG 8, RUC-8 file, 'Investigation Report on Salvador P. Acebuche' (numerous docs.).

28. To my knowledge, there is no open source work which attempts to deal in detail with the scope and mechanisms of CPP funding. Obviously, the party must maintain an extensive network for generating the revenue necessary to support its far-flung forces. In fact, 'revolutionary taxation', as will be discussed briefly later in the text, eventually proved to be one issue prompting a popular backlash against the CPP. The 6-month cash-flow for a typical Fighting Front in Panay is contained in 'Six (6) Months Program of the Northern Front Party Committee (NFPC) PIRPC [Panay Island Regional Party Committee] FM: January 87 to June 87':

Income		
DC 1 [District Committee 1]		13,004.65 pesos
DC 2		42,563.05 pesos
DC 3		8,264.00 pesos
EO [Economic Office]		1,817.00 pesos
FWAC [Front White Area Committee]		65,000.00 pesos
FPU [Front Partisan Unit]		4,067.00 pesos
KT–FRENTE [Front Executive Committee]		44,724.00 pesos
		179,440.20 pesos
Expenses	Total	177,865.20 peso
		+ 1,575.00 pesos

If we use a conversion factor of US $1 = 20.5 pesos, the six-month income figure of 179,440.20 is approximately $8,753, or $17,506 p.a., assuming the second half of the year was as profitable as the first. The CPP fielded at least 73 Fighting Fronts at the time, so a straight calculation ($17,506 x 73) would result in a figure of $1,277,964 nationwide for the Fighting Fronts alone. This figure is certainly too low; Panay would hardly seem to be the place to find a particularly wealthy Fighting Front — the resources are not there to support it, especially not in the NFPC area. Another document e.g., 'Summary of Finances NFF [Northern Fighting Front, Samar] For the Period Sept.–Dec. 85 Inclusive', reflects an income of 122,868.52 pesos (versus expenses of 121,683.80 p) for just those three months, or approx. $5,994. Converted to an annual figure: $23,974, substantially higher than the annual figure for the

NFPC/PIRPC. It would be logical to conclude, then, that published estimates which place the CPP's annual budget at anywhere from $2-7 million are well within the realm of possibility. For comparative purposes, it may be noted that the quarterly operating allowance for a government battalion on Samar at the time was 50,000 pesos (or 200,000 p p.a., which is approx. $9,756). Pay and allowances, of course, would be fixed costs not reflected in this figure, which is primarily for food and such. By comparison, a single tire for a *Commando* armored car then cost 40,000 pesos!

29. Cf. my 'Cease–Fire Maneuvers: Staying One Step Ahead of the NPA', *Soldier of Fortune*, 12/5 (May 1987), pp.48–55 (contd.).

30. Cf. Kerkvliet, 'Patterns of Philippine Resistance and Rebellion' (n.10, Ch.1) ; and Gary Hawes, 'Theories of Peasant Revolution: A Critique and Contribution From the Philippines', *World Politics*, 17/2 (Jan. 1990), pp.261–98. This latter source must be used with caution; many of the particulars therein are accurate, yet it reaches conclusions which were demonstrably inaccurate even at the time they were being written.

31. Little commented upon in the literature but significant is the degree to which the shape and spectrum of political views in the Philippines could in many respects pass for a double of that in the United States. The result is that the worldview of the American anti-Vietnam War movement, an elite-dominated phenomenon, may be found in that wing of Filipino politics which sees itself as 'progressive' (hence its profoundly anti-systemic outlook and infatuation with what might be called, to borrow a phrase, 'coercive utopianism').

32. Cf. Eric W. Hayden, 'Manila's Economic Resuscitation Effort', *Asian Wall Street Journal Weekly*, 12 Oct. 1981, p.12.

33. Cf. the series of articles under Guy Sacerdoti and Sheilah Ocampo, 'Cracks in the Coconut Shell', *Far Eastern Economic Review*, 8 Jan. 1982, pp.42–8.

34. Cf. David Wurfel, *Filipino Politics: Development and Decay* (Ithaca, NY: Cornell UP, 1988).

35. Background data on the MNLF conflict may be found in W.K. Che Man, *Muslim Separatism: The Moros of Southern Philippines and the Malays of Southern Thailand* (Manila: Ateneo de Manila UP, 1990); and T.J.S. George, *Revolt in Mindanao: The Rise of Islam in Philippine Politics* (Kuala Lumpur: Oxford UP, 1980).

36. A fascinating biography by one such individual is Edmundo G. Navarro, *Beds of Nails* (Manila: personal imprint, 1988).

37. Interview with author, 13 Aug. 1986, Manila. Ironically, the exile may have been to Ileto's advantage, for in Thailand he became close friends with Saiyud Kerdphol, generally acknowledged as the originator of the successful approach which finally defeated the Maoist strategy of the Communist Party of Thailand (CPT). According to Ileto, they discussed counterinsurgency frequently.

38. No definitive work exists on RAM. Useful background is in Rodney Tasker, 'The Hidden Hand: A Military Reform Movement Takes Hold', *Far Eastern Economic Review*, 1 Aug. 1985, pp.10-13; and Michael Richardson, 'Military Reform in the Philippines?' *Pacific Defence Reporter* [Australia], 12/8 (Feb. 1986), pp.11–12. See also the background chapters in the later work Criselda Yabes, *The Boys From the Barracks: The Philippine Military After EDSA* (Manila: Anvil Publishing, 1991).

39. Joint Meeting–Discussion of [CPP] National Urban Commission and the United Front Commission, 'Some Notes on the Issue of Ceasefire', 5 July 1986.

40. Interview with author, 14 Dec. 1986, Samar.

41. Office of the Assistant Secretary for Plans and Programs, Ministry of National Defense (Camp General Emilio Aguinaldo, Quezon City), 'Post–Revolution Communist Strategy in the Philippines: Indicators and Potentials', 22 Aug. 1986.

42. Ibid.

43. Interview with author, 1 Aug. 1988, Panay. Cf. my 'Victory on Panay: Red Tide Recedes From Philippine Communist Stronghold', *Soldier of Fortune*, 14/2 (Feb. 1989), pp.40–7 (contd.).

44. For additional context see my 'All Eyes on Negros in Philippine Insurgency', paper presented to panel on 'The Militarization of Ethnic Conflict', Int. Studies Assoc. annual mtg., London, 29 March 1989.

45. Interview with author, 4 Aug. 1988, Negros.

46. Cf. my 'Political Body Count..' (see n.16 above); and 'Sea Change in Negros', *East West*, 8/3 (Spring 1989), pp.24–9. Particularly interesting are the several letters to the editor (and my response) of *East West* condemning my analysis of the situation on Negros. See the 'Letters' section of the 8/4 (Summer) number. Subject is discussed further in my 'The NPA Misfires in the Philippines', *Asian Wall Street Journal*, 31 Jan. 1989, p.6; as well as my 'Manila Starts to Win Hearts and Minds', *Christian Science Monitor*, 18 April 1989, p.19.

47. The mechanics of the plan — minus, of course, its operational aspects — may be found in Victor Corpus, *Silent War* (Manila: VNC Enterprises, 1989).

48. Interview with author, 22 July 1990, Manila.

49. Ibid.

50. Though I heard virtually these words from numerous refugees during interviews conducted on Negros, July–Aug. and Dec. 1988, I was most taken with the passion and eloquence of Annalyn Salcedo, age 23, whom I encountered 5 Aug. 1988 on Negros. Former Chairman of the OC Women's Sector in her village, she had eventually reached Party Member status before surrendering to the government in early 1988.

51. Again, I am indebted for my understanding of this subject to a discussion with Noel Albano, 30 Dec. 1988, Manila. Cf. n.15, 16 above.

52. Cf. n.24 above.

53. Interview conducted by Ricardo Reyes, *Manila Chronicle*, 19 Jan. 1993, p.5; cf. my 'Philippine Counterinsurgency Shows Results', *Low Intensity Conflict International*, 1/6 (April 1993), pp.1–3.

3 The Role of Terror: The Case of the Philippines

In the previous chapter, the central role of terror in insurgency was emphasized. Analysts often put themselves into a strategic box by failing to differentiate properly between *terrorism* and *terror*.[1] It is not the means that distinguish the two. Rather, it is the ends for which the acts of violence are undertaken. Terrorism is small-group violence carried out unilaterally by a group in pursuance of self-proclaimed political goals. Terror, on the other hand, though often indistinguishable in form, is undertaken by members of an infrastructure who seek to further the maintenance and expansion of that infrastructure.[2]

Why does such a distinction matter? Because in terrorism the terrorists themselves are the problem. Terror, on the other hand, is symptomatic of larger issues. These larger issues can only be addressed, strategically, by socio-economic-political response. Tactical military measures thus exist to protect such a strategic response. Terrorism, in contrast, must be dealt with by the security forces. Strategic and tactical emphasis lies in the mechanisms of control and repression, with minimal political content.

What we have, then, are two very different phenomena, phenomena which are frequently lumped together and dealt with in similar fashion. Nothing could be more dangerous. While repression may be the main response in dealing with terrorists, it is but one tool, not even the foremost, in responding to the terror of insurgents. It only gives them more recruits.

Means to an End

It is recruits, of course, who are the bottom line for any subversive movement. If terrorists numbered more than a few, they would not be what they are — relatively isolated individuals deliberately targeting property and individuals normally deemed as protected under the 'laws of war.' Instead, they would be insurgents grappling with the intricacies of managing a complex, armed political movement dedicated to the overthrow of the status quo.[3]

Certainly, both terrorists and insurgents look very much alike at genesis. Both start as small groups, normally of intellectuals who see wrong in the existing system and who are determined to do something about it. Yet already at this point they part company: While the insurgent seeks to move forward by rallying others, incorporating them into an infrastructure, the terrorist sets out alone to use violence to strike at the system he deems oppressive. True, he may hope that through the example of the deed he may cause others to rally to his cause; but this remains a secondary consideration. He is, in his mind, a *marquis* operating in occupied territory. All around him are potential or real enemy collaborators. To the insurgent, in contrast, all around is the potential sea in which he, the fish, must swim.

It is not difficult to comprehend why terrorists rarely draw increased support to their side. All societies throw up their marginalized individuals, most thought by the populace to be isolated for good reason. Intellectuals, in particular, are widely distrusted. Nevertheless, violence, if couched in Robin Hood terms, may for a time be tolerated. The system, after all — goes the logic — needs to be reminded that it can push the individual only so far. Eventually, though, patience wears thin, because threat of personal harm is not a comfortable or desirable state to the average citizen. Hence, the populace turns on the terrorist.

This is a strategic milieu unlike that faced by the insurgent. Ironically, the same forces which alienated him do his recruiting work. They throw up a disgruntled mass base which he may organize. This is not, of course, an inevitable process. James Scott has it correct.[4] Insurgent movements involve a continuous process whereby the leadership and followers establish links and interact with each other. Societal causes are a necessary but not sufficient factor for the insurgency.

First, the causes must lead to the alienation of both potential leadership and potential insurgent manpower. Second, the two must establish a relationship. Only when this has been accomplished does a potential insurgency exist. But there is a constant tension present. If the ideological approach of the leadership is able to hold sway, insurgency will result. The movement will go on to pursue ideological goals. If, however, the resolution of immediate grievances wins out, as normally desired by the manpower, then rebellion will result. Both, to be sure, are violent upheavals, but it is insurgency that is of greater concern to the government, because it aims to refashion the political system, 'to make a revolution'.

Terror or guerrilla war or mobile war are only tools to accomplish this end. The precise level of force required depends upon the strength of the system under attack. Terror may suffice in one case; full-fledged conventional action may ultimately prove necessary in another. Likewise, the correct strategy to be followed will depend upon the particulars of the case at hand. Regardless, what links strategy to the tactical use of force is the operational utilization of political infrastructure.

Thus it is that the chief function of insurgent military power, in whatever form, is the projection and protection of this infrastructure. It is easy, therefore, to see the role terror must play in such a movement. The lower classes everywhere are notoriously suspicious of elite causes. Some catalyst must push them into the fold. Frequently, government repression has served this function. So, too, has insurgent terror. But the latter is not aimless killing. Acts of violence are undertaken with a specific desired response in mind, a response that will further the viability of the infrastructure.

What makes such terror so effective is the absence of anywhere to turn for help. 'There has traditionally been no government presence in many areas', says the editor of a leading Peruvian news magazine, commenting on the ability of the brutal *Sendero Luminoso* communist movement to expand its writ. 'Hence, as one source [of ours] puts it, there are no liberated areas, only abandoned areas'.[5]

In such a vacuum it only takes a few armed men to establish an insurgent presence. Their methodology and organization would be familiar to anyone who witnessed the Vietcong at work in South Vietnam — or, for that matter, insurgent groups as diverse as the Communist Party of the Philippines (CPP) or the Liberation Tigers of Tamil Eelam (LTTE) in Sri Lanka. The individual acts of terror would also, on the surface, be indistinguishable from those carried out by terrorists — and would frequently be labelled 'terrorist action'. This would be an error.

Insurgent Infrastructure

Let us take the Communist Party of the Philippines (CPP)[6] and explore this distinction in greater details. The CPP is a good choice, because there is no question but that it is an insurgency. For several decades it has followed a Maoist strategy of 'people's war' in its quest to replace the democratic, market-oriented system of the Philippines with a communist alternative.[7] Further, there is no question but that the CPP regularly commits acts of terror, such as murdering village headmen or gunning down policemen in the streets of the national capital, Manila. Predictably enough, the CPP is often cited as a 'terrorist organization'. But is it? It cannot be, because it has a mass base, and its acts of terror are carried out, at least in its own mind, to protect and expand that mass base. Outrages do not target the 'innocent', only the weak links in the structure of repression. The CPP and typical terrorist groups (e.g., the Japanese Red Army or the Italian Red Brigades) have little in common.

How are we to make such a determination? Proper analytical work holds the answer. Consider, for instance, the infrastructure which the CPP has in place in the Philippines as discussed in the previous chapter. Starting in the 1960s as a small body of less than two dozen disaffected intellectuals, the CPP was able to expand, initially, by linking up with armed remnants of the earlier Huk Rebellion on Luzon, the main Philippine island.[8] Later the insurgents moved on to other islands, particularly those with widespread poverty, such as Samar, Leyte, Panay, Negros, and Mindanao.[9] By 1980 the CPP counted more than 24,000 men in its New People's Army (NPA). Its National Democratic Front (NDF) was an ongoing concern, active both at home and abroad.

Had there not been a receptive environment, the original small body would have remained just that. Terrorism would then have been its logical course of action. The 'demonstration effect' was at work, however, and the would-be insurgents consciously sought to follow the strategic blueprint of Mao. Like true politicians, they searched for a constituency. That there was one waiting resulted from the 1972 imposition of martial law by Ferdinand Marcos.[10]

Socio-economic grievances alone would not have been sufficient to throw up manpower for the would-be insurgents. Poverty and injustice had long been the norm in the Philippines. It was the dismantling of the imperfect yet functioning mechanisms of

Philippine democracy, and the accompanying repression of an authoritarian system run amok ('hacienda government', it was frequently termed), that set the peasant masses looking for a savior. The CPP, already in existence, even if in rudimentary form, was the logical and willing choice.

To the task at hand, the CPP brought an organizational finesse that grew with the years. It was these skills that enabled it to harness peasant dissatisfaction and turn it away from rebellion to insurgency. There is little evidence of spontaneous local uprisings which subsequently became affiliated with the CPP, except the previously mentioned Cordillera Liberation Army in northern Luzon's Igorot areas.[11] What normally occurred instead was the systematic construction of infrastructure already covered in detail.[12] For the sake of clarity, let me outline again the extensive nature of the communist organizational effort. Contacts were first made with a community through acquaintances or relatives. This gave the CPP sufficient local presence to make some converts, who then formed the basis of sectoral Organizing Groups (OG): one each for peasants (i.e., men), women, youth, and children. The OG members were split into cells to compartmentalize the organisations and were indoctrinated by taking designated courses.[13] The best individuals of each OG cell ultimately became members of the higher Organizing Committees (OC), which were also sectoral. OC members went through a more advanced series of courses.[14] Ultimately, the best of these OC members were themselves graduated to become Candidate Party Members (CPM) and, eventually, after finishing the required curriculum,[15] fullfledged Communist Party Members (PM). By this time, the hamlet (*sitio*) or village (*barangay*) concerned would be co-opted, dominated by a fullfledged Party Branch (PB). It was the controlling political entity; and, of course, it had its own 'police force'.

As villages graduated from OG to OC to PB, they fielded their own armed forces. The extent to which these were armed depended upon the weaponry available. In October 1986, for instance, captured CPP documents claimed an 'armed strength' of 5,924 on Negros, one of the movement's linchpins, but its weapons inventory for the same period was less than 900.[16] Organization in other words, was the key. Hardware would be found in due time.

Continuing with the hierarchy: Villages fell under Sections, which corresponded closely to the government's own municipalities (counties). These Sections controlled the village operatives and

	[Key to map opposite]
FNWD	– FAR NORTH WEST DISTRICT
CND	– CENTRAL NORTH DISTRICT
FNED	– FAR NORTH EAST DISTRICT
NWD	– NORTH WEST DISTRICT (Catbalogan)
NED	– NORTH EAST DISTRICT
TWAPB	– TERRITORIAL WHITE AREA PARTY BRANCH (Catbalogan)
IDC	– ISLAND DISTRICT COMMITTEE
CWD	– CENTRAL WEST DISTRICT
CED	– CENTRAL EAST DISTRICT
SWD	– SOUTH WEST DISTRICT
SED	– SOUTH EAST DISTRICT

themselves answered to party Districts, which, in turn, fell under Fighting Fronts (see Map 3 for typical division, in this case, Samar). Fighting Fronts (FF) answered to Island Party Committees (IPC), these to Regional Commissions (RC), these to the Politburo (PB) and the Central Committee (CC).

While the militia protected the villages in the Sections, each District had its own party chain of command and District Guerrilla Unit, or DGU (approximately platoon size). Likewise, each front had its own Front Guerrilla Unit, or FGU (about company size). Reportedly, at least two Regional level units (approximately battalion size) were also formed — one on Samar, the other on Luzon[17] — but these were not true forces in being. Captured CPP documents refer to instances when these regional main forces are reputed to have functioned as tactical entities.[18]

All of the major levels — District, Front and Region — had available to them the special *yunit partisano* (partisan units), or 'sparrows', who carried out acts of terror, notably assassinations. Sparrows, together with the soldiers of the DGU, FGU, and Regional battalions (the *yunit gerilya*), comprised the regulars of the movement, those classified as members of the New People's Army, or NPA.

It is this division into various categories of forces which accounts for the frequent confusion concerning the number of enemy facing the security forces. As the case of *Westmoreland vs. CBS* made clear to the American public,[19] a bean count of the enemy depends completely upon which beans you choose to include in the tally. Hence, guerrilla strength on Negros in late 1986, just prior to a ceasefire with the government (which later collapsed), could legitimately be tallied as anywhere, in round figures, from 500 to 6,000 (see Table 1).[20]

MAP 3:
SAMAR/LEYTE CPP/NPA ORGANIZATION
(effective date: 1986)

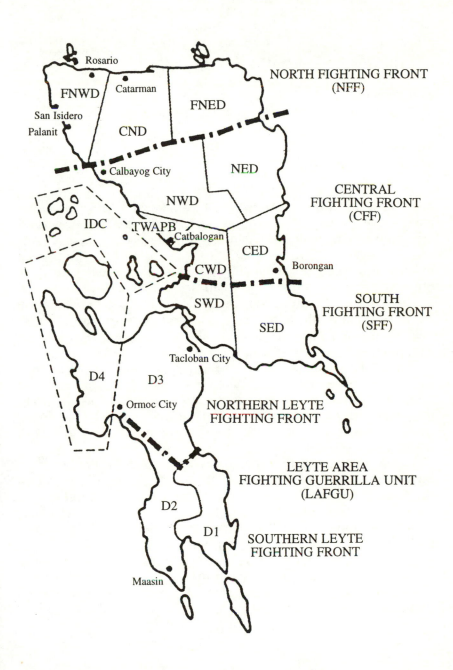

TABLE 1

NEGROS ISLAND REGIONAL PARTY COMMITTEE (NIRPC)
ARMED STRENGTH (OCTOBER 1986)

Formation	Strength	% of Total	% Combined
Yunit Gerilya	394	6.7	
			} 8.5
Yunit Partisano	105	1.8	
Yunit Militia	3,124	52.7	
			} 91.5
Self-Defense Corps	2,301	38.8	
Total	5,924	100.0	100.0

In such an insurgent hierarchy — unlike in a terrorist movement – everything depends upon the base. In the Philippines, all
communist manpower is divided, by the CPP itself, into three categories: organized masses, mass activists, and party members. An
individual working at the OG level is considered a member of the
organized masses; those promoted to OC level become mass
activists and, in the end, party members. Similarly, the ranks of the
NPA are filled by those recruited from militia formations. These
individuals are themselves first members of the organized masses
and, later, mass activists.[21]

Most NPA, therefore, will be party members. This is a fairly
rigid progression and only breaks down when conditions dictate
otherwise. Therefore, to strangle the armed elements and the party
branches, they must be cut off from their mass base, the organized
masses. This is precisely what the Philippine military presently
does.

Rather than going after the guerrilla units themselves, which is
the case in counterterrorism, the Philippine security forces' efforts
are directed towards holding and clearing territory by rooting out
the infrastructure in the villages. This allows elected government
to function and to address socioeconomic concerns Most of what
the US government once termed the VCI (Viet Cong
Infrastructure) — a term whose use has jumped beyond its original
Vietnamese context — is rendered impotent simply by exposure.
The military claims that it actually takes little time 'to break' a
hamlet or village, precisely because 'grievance guerrillas' are at the

heart of the movement and respond to decent treatment within the context of the post-Marcos political and economic environment. One should not push this optimism too far, but the shift in popular attitude since 1986 has been palpable. With it has come a decrease in the difficulty government agents have in penetrating the CPP apparatus. The CPP, consequently, has responded with bloody purges designed to weed out infiltrators. This has only driven still more CPP members to surrender.[22]

Cutting off the CPP from its mass base, to reiterate the point made in the previous chapter, is far more than simply a mechanical exercise in neutralizing the movement's infrastructure. In the absence of reform which eliminates the fundamental grievances which drive individuals to seek redress through armed struggle, new cells will constantly spring up. Traditional 'civic action' — digging wells providing medical treatment, and so forth — is insufficient. Root causes must be attacked. The only way this can occur is if there are mechanisms which allow the population a role in shaping their own lives.

Use of Terror

Ironically, even as the CPP has contracted — its Fighting Fronts, for instance, have apparently declined from more than 70 to less than 50[23] — violence has continued. This is predictable. Two forces are at work: one, bureaucratic process; the other, tactical. Bureaucratically, with the firm establishment of sparrows as regular components of the CPP/NPA's structure, assassinations have become a normal operation. Consequently, numbers of victims have jumped as the units have become better established. Tactically, as the CPP has come under greater government pressure, there has been the need to deal more forcefully with those who would endanger the infrastructure.

These realities highlight the importance of scale and the changing relationship between the elements of terror, recruitment, and infrastructure. The Philippines is sufficiently large and diverse that there are innumerable 'marginal' areas in which subversive political activity can operate with minimal fear of government intervention. In the past, therefore, the CPP was often able to expand its political sway largely through persuasion. The infrastructure was, in a very real sense, the only political game in town: 'political space' complemented physical space; if areas were not already physically isolated from Manila's writ, they were bound to be politically estranged by their hostility to the repression and corruption that flourished during the Marcos martial law period (recall that while martial law was formally lifted prior to the democratic restoration in February 1986, the same statutes continued in effect). The CPP was able to mobilize the peasantry by emphasizing resistance to oppression.

Nevertheless, the very incompetence of the Marcos regime, which made its repression haphazard and not particularly universal, left vulnerable a stance based largely on opposition. Even before the actual reestablishment of democratic process, therefore, political space became far more restricted, as an increasing number of contenders jostled one another in advancing their claims to political support. The moment inevitably came, in area after area, when further expansion, as well as the consolidation of those gains already made, could take place only in the face of opposition. Increasingly, the CPP leadership, once it was no longer the only viable option for those who sought to engage in politics, found itself judged and opposed for the shortcomings of its communist political agenda. Yet as a clandestine, proscribed political body, the CPP could respond in but one fashion to those who questioned it — with violence. This was inevitable, for the infrastructure could not allow resistance or uncertain commitment if it was to survive, much less flourish. Yet in striking out, the party made the fateful transition from messenger to message. The mechanisms of organization — of infrastructure — shifted from being a tool to being an end unto themselves.

Put simply, an alternative body, the CPP, had come into existence. Those who joined it no longer did so purely, or even in the main, in response to grievances, but instead for a more complex mixture of motives. These ranged from desire for advancement to fear.

Terror played an important role in this respect. Those who tried to resist, or were simply unwilling to cooperate, disappeared. How widespread such practices were remains a matter of considerable debate, but it seems clear that the scope of CPP terror was substantial. *Time* magazine correspondent Ross H. Munro threw the issue on the table in 1985 with his 'The New Khmer Rouge' in the December issue of *Commentary*.[24] There, he set forth in some detail the extent to which terror was an integral part of the

CPP/NPA/NDF campaign. This did not surprise security analysts, but the price came as a shock to those accustomed to seeing the NPA as 'Nice People Around', as they were ostensibly called by villagers. The debate that followed was useful, because it stripped away many of the Robin Hood myths that had grown up around the NPA.

Intimidation and coercion are inherent in any armed campaign to seize power. The Philippine communists were, are, no exception. True, CPP terror has always been more discriminating than that of, say, the Vietcong, but it was very real for those who lived under it. Booby traps and bombs, for instance, were rarely used, as in Vietnam, where they were ubiquitous, but liquidation of enemies was a major feature of the communist push.

A CPP document that I examined[25] — shortly after it was captured in February 1986 in Northern Samar Province — serves to illustrate. It included a table listing the number of 'counter-revolutionaries' executed in the Northern Fighting Front in Samar during 1985. They totalled 62, all of them civilians. Another table listed 17 sparrow assassinations, for a total of 79 civilian murders in what was only a lightly populated third of Samar Island. By contrast, government reports for the same period listed only 85 deaths among security force personnel for all of Samar and Leyte (which were under a single military command).[26] Obviously, the CPP was devoting more time to killing civilians than to attacking the military and police.

Even more detailed CPP records had been captured in mid-1985 on Leyte Island.[27] In the first half of the year, 60 Filipinos, mainly suspected informers, were listed by name as having been killed in the Southern Leyte Fighting Front, one of two CPP fronts on the island. Another 129 people were listed as liquidation targets. Most of the condemned were ordinary villagers. In macabre fashion, the operations to kill both these people and suspected spies within the party were codenamed '*Linis*', meaning 'clean' or 'cleanse'.

What is striking in these figures is not the numbers *per se* but rather the comparative scale. The greater number of liquidations than casualties inflicted upon the security forces is typical of an insurgent movement engaged in maintenance of its infrastructure. Also significant is the dominance, in the 1985 figures, of liquidations carried out by regular NPA units as opposed to sparrow squads. For in 1985 sparrows were still a relatively untested innovation. As the sparrows became more established, however, their proportion of liquidations rose.

Statistics to shed more light upon this particular aspect of the struggle are hard to come by, because it is difficult to determine precisely which NPA units are responsible for particular assassinations. It can be established, though, judging by the manner of death, that a high proportion of security force casualties has lately been due to NPA assassination efforts. Nevertheless, no matter how the numbers are crunched, the fact remains that 'counter-revolutionary' civilians continue to be the principal CPP targets. Police records and captured documents I examined in 1988, for example, revealed that 128 persons had been assassinated on Negros during the first half of that year. Only 28 of these were members of the security forces (11 soldiers, 5 policemen, and 12 militiamen). The other hundred were civilians.[28]

It is this reality that has ultimately backfired on the CPP. As its terror reached unbearable proportions, the masses began to turn away from the party, even in some of its previously most solidly held areas. 'We can no longer take the [CPP's] taxes. We can no longer take the [CPP's] violence', was the response.[29] The result was that many, when offered the opportunity, joined the government militia. Terror had clearly overreached itself.

In this respect, it must be emphasized, all things are relative. Terror succeeds not because of the numbers it mows down but because of the fear it engenders. The reverse is also true in causing the populace to feel that enough is enough. For illustration, consider the discussion I had in early December 1988 with Honeylee Pama 'Ibon', age 26, head of the Educational Staff for the CPP's District 2 on Negros (see Map 4). Captured during an 'encounter' with government forces, the unexpected end to her career as a party member came when she was already wavering in her ideological faith. 'It was the killings', she stated, which had shaken her faith in the movement. When I asked how many people she knew about who had been liquidated, she said about ten. I protested that ten people killed in her district — Negros was divided into seven such roughly equivalent CPP areas — hardly seemed like a lot. She responded emphatically, 'That's a lot to me!'[30]

It was an overwhelming point. Several years later, in the newly recaptured CHICKS region of Negros (the name is an acronym formed by the first letters of the major town names in the area; see roughly areas D-1 and D-2 of Map 4), previously the CPP strong-

MAP 4
NEGROS CPP/NPA ORGANIZATION
(effective date: 1989)

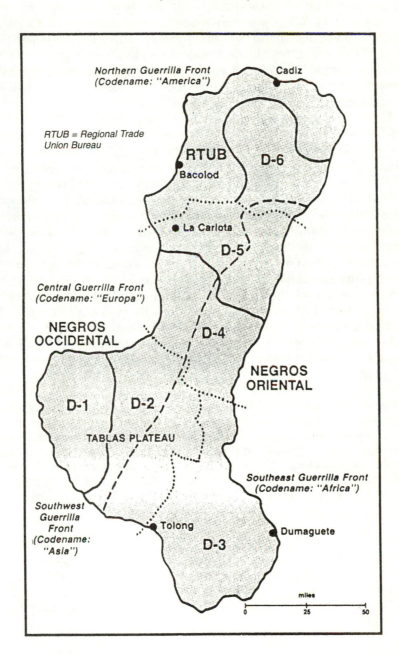

hold on the island, I encountered an even more vivid illustration. I was attempting to ascertain why so many people had joined the government militia (at the time, it outnumbered the regulars by better than 2:1). Whatever the particulars of each individual's tale, the common denominator was the inability to live any longer with the CPP's terror. Of more than a dozen individuals I interviewed in detail, every one could give, by name, at least five personal acquaintances who had been liquidated. A majority had witnessed at least some of the killings they listed.

While questioning individuals and noting the names they gave, I endeavored to cross-check the identities. Elsewise, all I had was a list of unknown validity. Who were these people who were being killed? Why did their deaths have such an impact upon the populace? It soon became clear to me. Asked why he joined the militia, Tachico Tabano, age 19, a peasant who was one of 11 siblings, responded, 'The communists took my father away, claiming he was a counter-revolutionary. I will avenge the death of my father. We were a very close family.'[31] Relatives, friends, acquaintances... at times there seemed no end to such stories. I asked a relatively high-ranking former party official about the coincidence of his surname with that of one of the victims he had named. Did he know him? Yes, he answered. I didn't push the point. Later, a contact pointed out that the executed man was the party official's brother.[32]

As though speaking for the whole community, William Labrador, age 48, a farmer with 'one week of grade one education' and a single child, stated:

> Under the communists, I could not do other work to support my family. I was only a robot. The communists told us what work we could do. If you're not cooperative, they kill you. Also, anyone caught close to the military is suspected of being an agent or a sympathizer of the military [and killed]. There was no court. It was completely arbitrary. I actually saw three people stabbed to death by the [CPP] district leader. I saw this. I pitied them. But we could do nothing, because we had no arms.[33]

Even as we spoke, it was clear that this situation had changed. About us clustered numerous individuals with weapons, each with a similar tale. Labrador's views were doubly potent, because he, as with many others in the militia, was previously a member of the CPP's clandestine apparatus. Obviously, the worst nightmare of the CPP 'people's war' had come to pass. The people had obtained weapons and had risen up — on the government side.

There is considerable irony at work here. Marcos had made the mistake of stifling the political system even as government repression was increased. This produced a popular backlash which the CPP had been able to exploit. Yet for all the talk of Marcos regime 'salvaging' (death squad activity) and filling 'mass graves' (of government opponents) and maintaining a veritable 'gulag' (of anti-government detainees), no startling revelations or discoveries emerged in the years following the restoration of democracy. Indeed, all of the mass graves uncovered turned out to be the work of the CPP purging its own ranks. This is not to say that government repression did not exist. It did. It is to say, however, that it was not of such magnitude in and of itself to stir the masses to action in the absence of political outlets for expression of grievances. Once these outlets were restored and government abuses curtailed, the CPP found that its own terror — which previously could be excused as due to the exigencies of the situation — was intolerable to the populace.

This situation has continued into the present. As Manila's gains have multiplied, so, too, have CPP terror actions. 'It is normal for the enemy to be increasing his use of terror', analyzed Colonel George Vallejera while operations officer for the units of the army's 3rd Infantry Division deployed on Negros.

> He is trying to hit back. He must answer back. Unfortunately, the CPP/NPA goes for our weaker links. We cannot expect normal people, or even the police or CAFGU [the acronym for the militia], to be thinking all the time about guerrilla war. They get sloppy, get killed, and the CPP/NPA appears strong.[34]

Vallejera himself has survived several assassination attempts, including one sparrow effort that turned into an Old West shootout in the street before the house at which he was staying in the provincial capital. The communists, in fact, have specifically sought to hit such leading figures in the campaign against them; but more often they go after the government militia and well known individuals in the countermobilization effort being carried out against them. It is these that most endanger their infrastructure.

Only days before my arrival on Negros in summer 1990, a sparrow squad ambushed and killed Ike Baleseros, an important leader in the 'Sugar Development Foundation' (SDF), a planter-funded self-defense fund with a US $3 million per year budget. SDF had been essential to maintaining a third of the government militia force then in being. After Baleseros' assassination, one of his colleagues noted, his assailants tied his body to his jeep's steering wheel and set the planter ablaze.[35]

A terrorist act? No, an act of terror carried out for a specific purpose, a purpose recognized by all. 'Why would they do that? What was the point?' asked another planter rhetorically. 'Their point is to influence our minds. They are going after those who are active in the SDF, because they need to make it [the SDF] fail. They need people to perceive that it has failed so that they will abandon it.'[36]

'Sparrows' and Beyond

This has not happened. Instead, the government militia has mushroomed. Yet, as mentioned previously, even as its infrastructure has begun to crumble, the CPP has been able to strike out. This it has done through its sparrow units, particularly in Manila. What the sparrows do — assassinate people — is clear enough. Less so is what the CPP sees as the sparrows' actual mission. Are they intended to be the urban equivalent of the DGU and FGU? Are they to function as tactical adjuncts to the more heavily armed 'regular units', as their name, 'partisans', implies? Or is it the party's intention that ultimately they will 'police' its domain? A Panay Island Regional Party Committee (PIRPC) document, to cite but one interesting bit of evidence, calls for 'the armed guerrilla and regional partisans to reach the level of defending the controlling areas of the revolutionary forces and its people'[37] — which would appear to support the latter mission.

In any case, it seems evident that, regardless of precise mission, as they presently operate the sparrows serve principally to facilitate the CPPs political expansion effort. This is done by targeting key figures who impede such progress, either directly or indirectly. Thus a target list contained in a captured NIRPC document cites as appropriate for assassination (order does not indicate priority):

1. key military officials [e.g., Colonel Vallejera];
2. military propagandists;

3. vigilante-building officers [those forming militia units];
4. bureaucratic capitalists [businessmen connected with the government];
5. American and Japanese officials [Manila's two leading aid donors];
6. big and active counter-revolutionary merchants [e.g., Ike Baleseros];
7. key personnel in counter-revolutionary mass media and labor sectors.[38]

In an effort to prevent mistakes with negative political consequences, approval of targets is held at the central organs concerned. There is considerable evidence, too, that at certain times individual targets had to be approved by at least the regional level organ, though considerably more decentralization of authority now appears to be the norm, particularly in Manila.[39] There, the separate Alex Boncayao Brigade (ABB) operates in semi-independent fashion. For the first five months of 1991 alone, a period during which the ABB was particularly active, approximately 60 soldiers, police and civilians were killed by the unit.

While assassinations are normally carried out by gunmen armed with pistols, who operate in pairs (both males and females have been used), there is nothing individual, random, or haphazard about their operations. Targets are carefully selected, planning is meticulous, and operational implementation is labor-intensive. The extensive organization necessary to support small hit teams is illustrated by the manning table for the NIRPC 'Regional Partisan Unit' (RPU) shown in Figure 5.[40]

FIGURE 5
NEGROS ISLAND REGIONAL PARTY COMMAND (NIRPC) REGIONAL
PARTISAN UNIT (RPU)

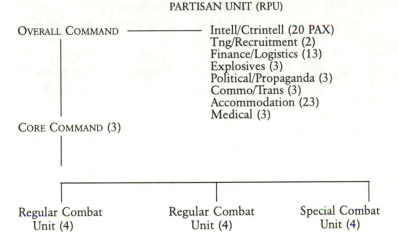

OVERALL COMMAND ——————— Intell/Ctrintell (20 PAX)
Tng/Recruitment (2)
Finance/Logistics (13)
Explosives (3)
Political/Propaganda (3)
Commo/Trans (3)
Accommodation (23)
Medical (3)

CORE COMMAND (3)

Regular Combat
Unit (4)

Regular Combat
Unit (4)

Special Combat
Unit (4)

In such teams we encounter a significant phenomenon: the potential for the transformation of terror to terrorism. An insurgent movement remains viable as long as it can continue to use violence as a tool — as opposed to an end unto itself — to facilitate the functioning and expansion of the infrastructure. Yet in the Philippines there is increasing evidence that CPP terror actions no longer have this essential character, that they are occurring in isolation. Policemen, for example, are being assassinated only because they are policemen, not because they are particularly abusive (or outstanding) policemen whose deaths would be welcomed by the people or useful to the movement. Such uncoordinated tactical actions have not yet become terrorism, because they serve no intended message; but neither do they further any CPP operational design. It is but a small, yet logical, next step to degenerate further into either terrorism (as independent teams strike out on their own) or criminal activity.

Should such a phenomenon become widespread, we would have to look beyond the violence itself and focus upon the more heartening strategic reality: it would indicate the death of the insurgency. At the moment, this point has not been reached. While disintegration of the infrastructure and degeneration of armed action to 'banditry' has advanced in some areas, the realities of the situation dictate that the government will be compelled to continue, for the foreseeable future, to focus its campaign against the CPP's covert apparatus. In doing so, it is important that it recognize acts of terror for what they continue to be in the main, efforts to sustain the infrastructure. This will require that the government response maintain a socio-economic-political orientation.

To this end, it may be noted further that in interpreting the violence which accompanies an insurgency, the English language limits us. The word 'support' implies freely given, as in, 'By winning the hearts and mind we can gain the support of the people'. Correct semantically, this construction has led to an operational fallacy. There are those, ideologues for instance, who give their support because they are committed to ideals. Most people, however, sit on the sidelines until compelled to do otherwise. They give 'support' when it becomes in their *interest* to do so.

Terror is but one tool for creating such an interest. It may show what happens to 'traitors'; it may remove threats quietly from an area of operations. Simply because it is used does not mean the populace is terrorized by the perpetrators. Quite the contrary can also be true. Terror can send a message that is accepted by the population as painful but necessary. The argument for 'necessity' is provided by propaganda. Further, in its most powerful form, terror can serve as the instrument of vengeance for pent-up popular frustrations, as it appears to have done in revolutionary China.[41] 'Collaborators, traitors, exploiters, and criminals' can be dispatched with the approval of the masses. Providing it is not abused, then, terror, while it may alienate some, also fortifies others. At the margins, it can push an undecided group into support it would otherwise not give. Once involved in the actual mechanisms of such support, individuals frequently forget the role terror originally played in the process of recruitment.

On the other side of the coin, the use of terror by the security forces has generally been ineffective or has had disastrous consequences, because the government normally claims to represent a higher standard of conduct and morality. Democratic society, in particular, draws its strength from its ability to deliver justice to a union of voluntary participants. Thus actions which put the lie to that principle may actively serve to undermine the legitimacy of the government.[42]

The insurgents, committed to total war and the need to eliminate certain elements of the foe, are subject to a different set of rules. They, too, must act in the interests of the people, but in the interests of the 'revolutionary people'. The non-revolutionary remainder becomes as much the foe as the security forces and may be dealt with accordingly.

These realities of terror must be understood if the Communist Party of the Philippines (CPP) or any other insurgent group is to be dealt with. The role of terror can never be treated in isolation; that is, mistaken for the terrorism of the ideologically-driven small group. It is the total insurgent movement, particularly its use of political means to achieve political ends, that is the most significant aspect of the revolutionary war being waged by the CPP — with violence available when needed to make a point.

NOTES

1. My original thoughts on this distinction appeared in '"People's War" in Sri Lanka: Insurgency and Counterinsurgency', *Issues & Studies*, 22/8 (Aug. 1986), pp.63–100; see esp. the discussion on pp. 86-7. I have since pursued the subject, most comprehensively in 'Terrorism vs. Terror: The Case of Peru', *Counterterrorism & Security*, 2/2 (May–June 1990), pp. 26-33.

2.   With respect to terrorism, two sources — of the many available — which I have found particularly useful are Richard E. Rubenstein, *Alchemists of Revolution: Terrorism in the Modern World* (NY: Basic Books, 1987) and Conor Gearty, *Terror* (London: Faber, 1991). See also Paul Wilkinson, *Terrorism and the Liberal State* (NY: NY UP, 1979).

3.   Cf. Desai and Eckstein, 'Insurgency: The Transformation of Peasant Rebellion' (n.4, Intro.).

4.   James C. Scott, 'Revolution in the Revolution: Peasants and Commissars' (n.8, Ch.1).

5.   Interview with the author, 15 Aug. 1989, Lima.

6.   No comprehensive work on the CPP has yet appeared. Useful overviews are William Chapman, *Inside the Philippine Revolution* (NY: Norton, 1987); Gregg R. Jones, *Red Revolution: Inside the Philippine Guerrilla Movement* (Boulder: Westview Press, 1989); Richard J. Kessler, *Rebellion and Repression in the Philippines* (New Haven, CT: Yale UP, 1989); and Larry K. Niksch, *Insurgency and Counterinsurgency in the Philippines* (Washington, DC: Library of Congress, Congressional Res. Service, 1985).

7.   Cf. Amado Guerrero, *Philippine Society and Revolution: Specific Characteristics of Our People's War*. Originally published in mimeograph by the 'Revolutionary School of Mao Tsetung Thought', my copy was printed by Ta Kung Pao, Hong Kong. The actual author, as mentioned in the previous chapter (n.14), was José Maria Sison, the CPP's founder and leader until his arrest in 1977. He was released during the amnesty which followed the Marcos ouster and quickly resumed his work for the party. He is presently active in united front operations in Europe.

8.   For the particulars of this linkup, refer to previous chapter.

9.   A useful, unclassified — though limited circulation — reference is Intelligence Service, Armed Forces of the Philippines, *The Reestablished Communist Party of the Philippines*, 4 vols. (Camp Aguinaldo, Quezon City: ISAFP, Dec. 1989).

10. Cf. Raymond Bonner, *Waltzing With a Dictator: The Marcoses and the Making of American Policy* (NY: Times Books/Random House, 1987). More sensational, but useful in parts, is Sterling Seagrave, *The Marcos Dynasty* (NY: Harper & Row, 1988), for which I was research assistant. Seagrave preserves my academic integrity by observing in a note that I 'often disagreed with my [Seagrave's] conclusions'.

11. For background cf. Sheilah Ocampo, 'The Battle for Chico River', *Far Eastern Economic Review*, 20 Oct. 1978, pp.32–4. Also useful is John Lindsey Foggle, 'The Rice Terrace Farmers of the Philippines: A Mountain People's Struggle for Survival in a Developing Nation and World', unpub. MS, 1979.

12. Refer to previous chapter's subsection, 'Construction of the CPP Infrastructure'.

13. Most useful for me in understanding the CPP educational system was a lengthy discussion with 26-year-old Honeylee Pama a.k.a. 'Ibon', 26 Dec. 1988 on Negros. An Education Officer for the CPP's District 2 on the island, she had been captured on 23 Nov. 1988.

14. Course texts, though specific to the Philippine situation, draw heavily upon standard Marxist analysis of society. One useful result is that the ideological terminology is consistent regardless of the Philippine dialect into which instructional material has been translated.

15. E.g., *Silabus Sa BKP* [*Syllabus of the Basic Mass Course*].

16. S-2 (Intelligence), 301st Infantry Brigade, Philippine Army, using captured documents and interrogations, carried the CPP/NPA's weapons inventory on Negros at the time as 621 high-powered firearms (HPF; i.e., assault rifles), 83 long-barrelled weapons (i.e., older rifles), 153 short-barrelled handguns (i.e., pistols), 18 cal. 30.06 (i.e., shotguns), 3 Japanese rifles cal. 27 (from World War II), and 1 machine-pistol, or a total of 879 weapons.

17. Interview with operations personnel, 3rd Infantry Division (Forward), Philippine Army, 11 July 1990, Negros.

18. E.g., CPP document [Tagalog] captured 29 March 1988, 'Visayas Report', report of special meeting of the CPP Politburo (24 Jan. 1988), claimed the Samar battalion had

three companies of 120 men each, equipped with a total of 316 HPR (high-powered rifles; i.e., assault rifles), several machine-guns, and one mortar. Philippine intelligence personnel note that the unit functions in decentralized fashion, with a single account from the field of the battalion's constituent guerrilla units operating together. The 'Visayas Report' itself notes only, 'There are times when the unit is concentrated in a battalion or bigger formation' (*Ngunit may panahong konsentrado laluna sa mga batalyon o malalaking operations*).

19. Cf. Bob Brewin and Sydney Shaw, *Vietnam on Trial: Westmoreland vs. CBS* (NY: Atheneum, 1987); and Don Kowet, *A Matter of Honor: General William C. Westmoreland Versus CBS* (NY: Macmillan, 1984).

20. Figures derived from exploitation of CPP documents and prisoners by 301st Infantry Brigade, Philippine Army, Negros; obtained 3 Aug. 1988 through interview. Apparently, these strength levels were the high water mark for CPP influence on Negros. All subsequent figures have been considerably lower, and CPP documents I have examined lament the party's inability to check its decline. See, e.g., the notebook of Federico Guanzon a.k.a. 'Michael' or 'Pedic', Negros Regional Party Committee (NRPC; also appears as NIRPC [Island]) Secretary, captured with Federico on Cebu in 1989. Therein, in a typical entry, he observes, 'In SWPC [CHICKS area, or the southwest corner of Negros, once a key CPP stronghold] party has lost 48 per cent of its OM [organized masses] due to massive military operations. May not be reorganized. Insufficient forces to protect. Efforts to keep cells intact hampered due to lack of trust between members.'

21. Interview with 27-year-old Panangganan Feliciano a.k.a. 'Katagar', 4 Aug. 1988, Negros. Political Officer of Platoon 'Nissan', one of the four such units comprising the FGU then operating in District 1 of Negros, he surrendered 5 June 1988.

22. Interview with 39-year-old Manuel Jurada y Laranero a.k.a. 'Bunny', 4 Aug. 1988, Negros. Former KBP territorial (also called 'district') secretary under the District Committee Centre (DCC), Negros. Essentially, 'Bunny' was a mid-level operative charged with overseeing a network devoted to front construction within the labor sector. He surrendered 18 June 1988.

23. I explore this subject in greater detail in several works: 'Guerrillas in the Midst of Defeat', *Asian Wall Street Journal*, 26 July 1990, p.6; 'Deadlock in the Philippines', *National Review*, 15 Oct. 1990, pp.30–2; and 'Small Victory in a Big War: Philippine Army Routs Communists on Negros', *Soldier of Fortune*, 16/2 (Feb. 1991), pp.30–5 (contd.).

24. Ross H. Munro, 'The New Khmer Rouge', *Commentary*, 80/6 (Dec. 1985), pp.19–38.

25. Northern Fighting Front [Samar], '*Pagturutimbang san Armado nga Pakig-away sa Probinsiya (1984–1985)*, [Waray: 'Comparison of Relative Strengths of Armed Groups in the Province (1984–1985)'], captured 14 Dec. 1985, captured 17 Feb. 1986 in the CPP's Far North West District, Samar. I discussed the contents at the time in: 'Don't Discount the Philippine Communists', *Asian Wall Street Journal*, 28 April 1986, p.6; 'Island Fighting: 52 IB Tracks Elusive NPA', *Soldier of Fortune*, 11/7 (July 1986), pp.38-45; and 'Communist Insurgency in the Philippines' (n.27, Ch.2).

26. Figure compiled from monthly status reports submitted by units assigned to Regional Unified Command 8 (RUC-8).

27. This document was also discussed in my press articles referred to in n.25 above.

28. Assassinations were tallied for 1 Jan.-30 July 1988 by intelligence personnel of 301st Infantry Brigade, Philippine Army. Accompanying documents indicated that deaths on Negros attributed to combat operations for the same period were: 34 army (1 officer and 33 enlisted personnel), 8 policemen, 53 militia, and 206 civilians versus 218 CPP/NPA. Wounded of all government categories totalled 147 versus 110 CPP/NPA.

29. Interview with 23-year-old Annalyn Salcedo, 5 Aug. 1988, Negros as per n.50 in previous chapter.

30. Interview with Honeylee Pama a.k.a. 'Ibon' (for identification see n.13), 26 Dec. 1988, Negros. Similarly, Political Officer 'Katagar' (refer to n.20) had earlier respond-

ed, on 4 Aug. 1988, when asked what had motivated him to surrender:

> We can no longer keep on killing people whom we don't even know. For what reasons?... We kill *Alsa Masa* [militia], suspected informers, local officials — for example, a mayor who enforces the program of the government — police, soldiers. At first we were told to kill just erring civilians and abusive personalities. Now there is even a CPP/NPA program to hold up commercial vehicles and business establishments. We [my platoon] didn't like this, so we didn't do it.

31. Interview with author, 16 July 1990, Negros.
32. Ibid. This former CPP cadre was clearly troubled by what he had witnessed:

> The communists killed six people I knew. The CPA unit did it; I was not consulted. Out of the six, two were tried by the higher organs. Of these, I was informed. I saw all six killed, shot. One was accused of supporting the military, but I know this was not true. Others were accused of being thieves, robbers, but actually they were not. False accusations were made as a result of quarrels. If you've been accused of *contrarebolution*, they don't check. I wanted these atrocities to end. They had no pity. They were killing us without mercy. The government system is better. I joined CAFGU [the militia] to keep these people from returning. That is their main objective.

33. Interview with author, 16 July 1990, Negros.
34. Ibid., 12 July 1990.
35. Ibid., 19 July 1990.
36. Ibid.
37. CPP document [Ilongot], 'Orientation on Sparrow Operations', Panay Island Regional Party Committee (PIRPC), no date; accompanied by Philippine intelligence exploitation report dated 10 June 1988.
38. Ibid.
39. This decentralization has caused growing problems for the CPP leadership as sparrows turn to crime as a means of improving their circumstances of existence and settling personal, family scores. Some have apparently simply hired themselves out as enforcers and hit-men to the highest bidder.
40. See n.37.
41. See, e.g., *William Hinton, Fanshen: A Documentary of Revolution in a Chinese Village* (NY: Vintage Books/Random House, 1966). It is noteworthy that Hinton consistently avoids discussing precisely what occurs at 'struggle' meetings — frequently death for the 'bad elements'. See also Patricia E. Griffin, *The Chinese Communist Treatment of Counterrevolutionaries: 1924-1949* (Princeton, NJ: Princeton UP, 1976).
42. I have dealt with this issue previously in several articles: 'Perverted Counter-terrorism: The Case of Stalker', *Periscope* [AFIO, Washington, DC], 16/1 (Winter, 1989), p. 11; and (with/Dale Andrade) 'Gibraltar's Lessons for the Democratic State', *Periscope,* 14/3 (Summer 1989), pp.8–9. The widespread infiltration by the CPP of human rights organizations — Task Force Detainees of the Philippines (TFDP) comes immediately to mind — has heightened Philippine security force concern in the area. A battalion commander interviewed on Panay, 1 Aug. 1988, put well what I have found to be a common view among those charged with fighting the CPP:

> Killing an enemy is not an offense. If you hit the infrastructure, it depends how you do it [the killing]. You cannot apprehend someone and kill them. Our system is the same as yours. But if the circumstances are such that we are forced to do that, then we are protected by the law. We are very careful on our legal aspects. Everything has to be in accordance with the law. That is our first consideration.

A brigade commander augmented this in a 3 Aug. 1990 interview on Negros:

> We have to frame our laws to help the government protect itself. It's very obvious that the left has been able to make the government protect it under the guise of things such as human rights.

4 Maoist Miscue III: Disintegration of the Revolution in Sri Lanka

It is now possible to turn to the insurgencies which have wracked Sri Lanka since independence. This case is complicated, because there are several major outbreaks which must be considered: a predominantly Sinhalese, island-wide (Tamil areas excluded) uprising, now crushed, which aimed at toppling the government and instituting a Marxist regime; and the present widespread violence in areas of Tamil settlement which pits Tamils against the majority Sinhalese in a quest for an independent Marxist state. Seemingly dissimilar in character, separated at times temporally and spatially, these episodes are actually connected in a causal sense. They can be considered structurally as facets of a larger old-regime crisis within a revolutionary situation.

A less likely setting for not one but several major outbreaks of rebellion could scarcely be imagined than Sri Lanka (see Map 5 for regional location). Visually stunning and blessed with a temperate climate and a relative abundance of resources, Sri Lanka has the ambience of a South Seas island, this despite its propinquity to the poverty and 'ordered chaos' of India.[1] When independence was granted by Britain in 1948, after four centuries of colonial domination — the Portuguese, 1517–1638, and the Dutch, 1638–1796, had also been overlords — the transfer of power was relatively peaceful. This was in stark contrast to the communal violence which marked the birth of India and Pakistan. Indeed, Sri Lanka's majority Sinhalese, three-quarters of the population (which in the last official census, 1981, numbered 15.2 million), and the principal minority, the Tamils (approximately one-fifth of the total) seemingly had achieved an arrangement of mutual benefit based upon their participation in a secular, democratic state.

Actually, the two populations were divided by a widening rift caused by differences of race, language, culture, and religion.[2] The Sinhalese claimed descent from the Arayans of the Indian north, spoke Sinhala, and were mainly Buddhist. The Tamils were apparently linked to the Dravidian stock of south India, spoke Tamil,

MAP 5
THE INDIAN SUB-CONTINENT

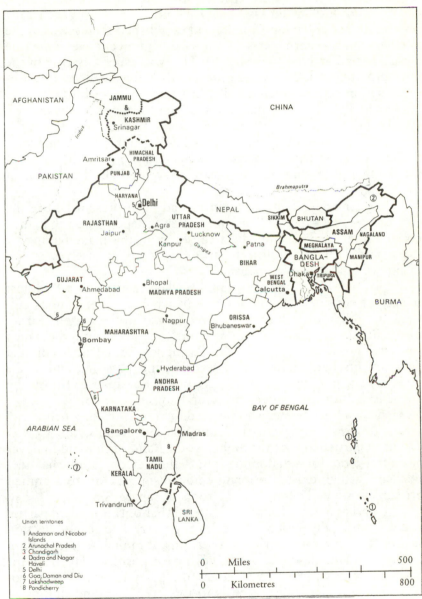

Source: Control Risks Information Service (CRIS), London.

and were primarily Hindu, with some Christian influence.

Tamils themselves were further split into two major groups, Ceylon and Indian Tamils. The Ceylon Tamils (now generally referred to as Sri Lankan Tamils) had established themselves in the northern and eastern parts of the island just centuries after the Sinhalese had arrived (see Map 6). This was especially true in the northern area of Jaffna, where the Tamils had a small yet flourishing kingdom. The Indian Tamils, in contrast, were brought over during the British era by plantation owners to work on the estates, mainly those producing (from 1867) some of the finest tea in the world. Differences between the two Tamil groups, combined with the fact that the new immigrants were settled in the hill areas of the south rather than in the north, prevented the formation of close links.

While Sinhalese-Tamil differences had been present before the end of colonial rule,[3] it was only after independence that they became intense. The immediate cause lay in the maneuvering by the major Sinhalese political parties to wrap themselves in the mantle of Sinhalese nationalism.

Pre-colonial Sri Lanka, its Tamil pockets aside, was a Buddhist society of considerable vitality, one which had an enormous cultural and religious influence on several areas in the region, particularly Southeast Asia.[4] There was little contact with the much smaller Tamil areas. Though the Portuguese and Dutch colonial governments had succeeded in securing the coastline and a few inland areas, not until the British seizure of Kandy in 1816 was the entire island unified under one central administration.

Hence, when the British departed, a return to 'independence' meant different things to the Sinhalese and Tamils, the Ceylon Tamils in particular. For the Sinhalese the 'land of the Buddha' was again free from foreign domination; to the Ceylon Tamils the independence which existed prior to colonialism was lost to a unified Sri Lankan state. Therein lay the roots of separatism.

The parliamentary framework meant that only Sinhalese parties could realistically hope to achieve power, and each election seemed to bring more strident assertions of Sinhalese nationalism by the rival Sinhalese factions jockeying for position. The need for a salient issue with which to attack the party in power was pronounced, and chauvinist appeals to race, religion, and destiny (a chosen people guarding the true faith in its island citadel) served the purpose well.[5] The electorate regularly turned the incumbent

MAP 6
SRI LANKA

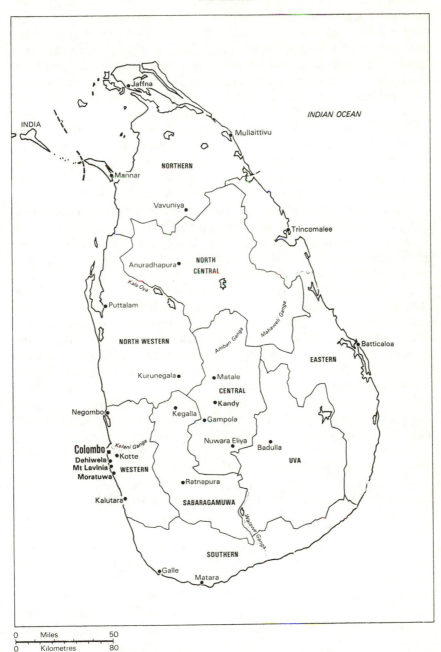

Source: Control Risks Information Service (CRIS), London.

party out of office in every election beginning with 1956.

The Tamils, who under the British had taken full advantage of the opportunities for advancement afforded minorities by colonial rule and favoritism — and thus had gained dominance in the professions and commerce — increasingly found themselves the victims of discriminatory affirmative action schemes designed to favor the long-abused Sinhalese majority. A key juncture in this process was the designation of Buddhism and Sinhala as the official state religion and language, respectively, in 1956. There followed the nationalization of all schools in December 1960, which deprived the Tamils of free access to one of their majority means of social mobility. Instruction in Sinhala became mandatory, and in March 1964 compulsory retirement began of all civil servants unable to work in that medium.

It is important to highlight that the growth of Sinhalese chauvinism was a socio-cultural phenomenon which utilized race as a vehicle but actually transcended it. Appeals to Sinhalese Buddhist sentiments were inextricably enmeshed with promises of material and symbolic gains for the underprivileged classes, Sinhalese rural masses who comprised some three-fourths of the population if the Tamils were excluded. Thus, two major political tendencies of considerable continuing force developed: 'the drive for recognition and recompense by the Sinhalese Buddhist majority, and the egalitarian demands of the economically underprivileged strata of society'.[6] These egalitarian demands were represented principally by the non-Marxist socialism of the Sri Lanka Freedom Party (SLFP), which during the pre-1971 time period dethroned the more free market-oriented United National Party (UNP) in the elections of 1956, July 1960, and 1970 (the UNP was victorious in 1947, March 1960, and 1965).

Growth of Communist Opposition to the Old-Regime

The Sinhalese Insurrection of 1971

Such regular substitution of ideologically-opposed major parties would seemingly provide ample opportunity for the expression of growing egalitarian demands. That such did not prove to be the case was a result of the essential unity within the Sri Lankan elite. The UNP and SLFP, despite their professed dissimilarity, were inextricably linked structurally by bonds of family, caste, and Westernized culture and education.[7] This was also the case with the logical standard bearers for the underprivileged masses, the avowedly revolutionary parties of Marxist persuasion. They were further neutralized by their incessant intramural battles over doctrinal matters (e.g., Leninism versus Trotskyism) and world communist orientation (e.g., pro-Moscow versus pro-Peking).[8]

A period of intense schism during 1963–64 resulted in the formation of several ultra-left parties, among which was the Communist Party (pro-Peking), or CP(P). Even these, though, were not radical enough for some. An internal crisis and split in the CP(P) during 1964 led to the May 1965 formation of an internal CP(P) revitalization movement. At first this group was not constituted as an actual party, but it became an independent body towards the end of 1969 under the name *Janatha Vimukthi Peramuna* (JVP, 'People's Liberation Front').[9] After its formal organizational birth, the JVP adopted a Leninist structure, using a cellular base upon which to pyramid local, regional, and district committees, together with a 25-member Central Committee and a 12-man Politburo.[10] It claimed to be Maoist.

Under the leadership of youthful Rohana Wijeweera, the professed JVP goal was 'to make a revolution'. To this end an elaborate ideology was developed and incorporated into 'five lessons' which were used at indoctrination sessions.[11] Most such work, in keeping with the JVP's Maoist inspiration, was conducted in the rural areas. The formal decision to emphasize the peasantry was reportedly made as early as 1966, while the area of emphasis was broadened to all classes in the rural areas in 1968. A particularly fertile group for recruitment proved to be rural youth. Rapid population growth, an expansion of education which far outstripped employment opportunities, and an inability to influence or participate in the mechanisms of power, all served to alienate and marginalize many young people. Given Sri Lanka's demographics and the particulars of political life as previously noted, this set of circumstances, while island-wide, was felt particularly keenly by Sinhalese youth. Thus it was they who were the prime JVP converts.

There remains near-complete uncertainty as to Wijeweera's precise intentions and plans. In any case, the JVP, a child itself of leftist schism, was hardly a monolithic body. The leadership around Wijeweera was comprised of multiple factions. Bodies of new recruits, after splitting off from one of the older Marxist parties or its youth organizations, would normally, upon joining the JVP, keep their individual identities and leadership hierarchy. To make direction still more complex, even the JVP's elite echelon was divided by personality clashes, with the attendant disruptive impact upon the unity of the membership. The result has been a very incomplete picture of what actually occurred in the crucial period from late 1969 to the outbreak of insurrection in April 1971.

In the most common view of the 1971 events,[12] the JVP was forced to take precipitous action, thereby blunting the effectiveness of its campaign. When the authorities learned in February of the plans for revolt, the JVP leadership made the decision 'to arm the masses'. This prompted increased police countermeasures. Government action prompted pressure from the JVP rank and file for dramatic and audacious action. On 6 March the US Embassy was bombed during a demonstration.[13] The armed forces were deployed throughout the island the next day, and on 13 March Wijeweera was arrested. The following week brought discoveries of hidden arms and explosives. Finally, a declaration of emergency was put into effect. Arrests of JVP members began in earnest.

A small group of JVP leaders reportedly met on 2 April to analyze the situation. They resolved to carry through with their plans by rising up on 5 April. Many felt the time was not right for such action, but once the insurrection exploded, they, too, joined in. Violence was general throughout much of the Sinhalese-majority areas of Sri Lanka (see Map 7). Halliday[14] provides a detailed narrative, the major points of which have been gathered together by Alexander as follows:[15]

> On the night of 5–6 April, three weeks after the declaration of the State of Emergency, police stations in different parts of the island were assaulted by JVP cadres in groups of 25 to 30... The aim of this first attack seems to have been to capture a stock of modern arms, and to consolidate in a liberated region of the interior, blocking communication across the island and providing a base for a second offensive.

> On the first night several police stations fell, and the government soon evacuated several more: at the height of the insurrection some 90 and 100 police stations had been abandoned or had fallen to the JVP (pp. 196–7)... the bulk of the fighting was performed by units of armed youth, often including many members in their teens (p. 198)... By the

MAP 7
THE SINHALESE INSURRECTION OF 1971

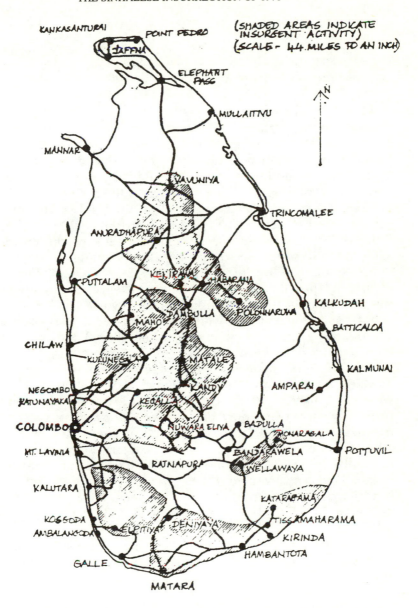

(SHADED AREAS INDICATE
INSURGENT ACTIVITY)
(SCALE - 44 MILES TO AN INCH)

KANKASANTURAI
POINT PEDRO
JAFFNA
ELEPHANT PASS
MULLAITIVU
MANNAR
VAVUNIYA
TRINCOMALEE
ANURADHAPURA
PUTTALAM
KEKIRAWA
HABARANA
KALKUDAH
DAMBULLA
POLONNARUWA
BATTICALOA
MAHO
CHILAW
KURUNEGALA
MATALE
KALMUNAI
NEGOMBO
KANDY
AMPARAI
KATUNAYAKA
KEGALLE
COLOMBO
NUWARA ELIYA
BADULLA
MONARAGALA
MT. LAVINIA
BANDARAWELA
POTTUVIL
RAJNAPURA
WELLAWAYA
KALUTARA
KATARAGAMA
KOSGODA
TISSAMAHARAMA
AMBALANGODA
ELPITIYA
DENIYAYA
KIRINDA
HAMBANTOTA
GALLE
MATARA

Source: A. C. Alles, *Insurgency – 1971* (Colombo: Mervyn Mendis at the Columbo
Apothecaries' Cp., Ltd., revised 3rd ed., 1976), p.148.

end of May, after extremely fierce fighting and continual deployments by the JVP, the government had temporarily driven the insurgent groups back into the upland forests and re-established its control of the rural interior (p. 200)... A few small groups continued to survive in the remoter jungles, but they posed no threat to the regime (p. 207)... The insurrection was an ambitious and highly organized attempt to seize State power (p. 214).

In putting down the insurrection, the SLFP government was able to turn to an array of international sources for arms and material, which were crucial given the ill-prepared state of the security forces at the onset of fighting. Colombo's nonaligned foreign policy resulted in shipments being received from donors in both the East and West blocs. While major fighting ended after several months, it remained dangerous until the end of 1971 for individuals to travel in certain areas, particularly in the North Central Province.[16] Nevertheless, the tactical ineptitude of the insurgents allowed the security forces to gain the upper hand in a suppression campaign marked by a high degree of brutality and extensive loss of life and property. Government competence in this operation was minimal, but the opposition was even worse.

Data gathered on those detained has provided statistics on some 12,000 insurgents or sympathizers of the 18,000 persons who are estimated to have been held at one time or another. Analysis reveals that the detainees were overwhelmingly rural, male, Sinhalese youth less than 30 years of age (more than three-quarters were in the narrow 16–25 age bracket). Most were educated (less than 20 per cent had only primary or no schooling); most held irregular, poorly paid, or low status jobs in the rural sector. Caste affiliation was mixed, though there was strong caste representation in particular areas. Many rank-and-file members apparently came from a 'land army' formed in 1967 to provide employment in conservation and reclamation activities for unemployed youths (it was disbanded in 1970), but overall there was no common group-of-origin.[17]

These characteristics and related data have been summarized by Alles in a set of conclusions with which most sources are in general agreement:[18]

(a) That the movement had its origins in the rural sector particularly among the educated unemployed youth;

(b) That the system of education imparted in the rural schools pro-

vided a preponderance of students prepared for courses in the arts;
(c) That a class distinction has been created as a result of the educational system, between the English-educated students from the urban schools, who predominated in the courses in science, medicine, engineering, agriculture and veterinary science and the students from the rural schools who followed courses in the social sciences and the humanities;
(d) That as a result of this indiscriminate system of education the job opportunities for the educated youth of the rural sector were scarce and unemployment and under-employment predominated in this sector;
(e) That the JVP leadership made use of the educated youth of the rural sector, who constituted the majority of the insurgents, to alter the structure of society and establish a truly socialist society; and
(f) That caste considerations were not a determining factor in the insurgency.

Tamil Insurgency[19]

Hence, an apparent purposive effort by an avowed Maoist revolutionary party 'to make revolution' was crushed. As the situation in Sri Lanka returned to normal, the government continued its appeals to Sinhalese chauvinism as a means to mollify the discontented rural areas. This completely alienated the Ceylon Tamils, who began to seek means to resist. The Indian Tamils, not technically citizens of Sri Lanka, even after independence, remained more concerned with issues of citizenship, minimum wages, and improvement of basic education and health facilities on the plantations. (See Map 8 for population distribution.)

Increasingly, among the Ceylon Tamils, there was a reassertion of cultural identity and growing acceptance of radical solutions. The principal Tamil political party, the Tamil United Liberation Front (TULF), first demanded an independent state, or 'Tamil Eelam', in 1976 and subsequently won 16 seats on the platform in the 1977 national elections. This made it the largest opposition party. Nevertheless, TULF rejected violence to achieve 'Eelam'. (See Map 8 for boundaries.)

Such a position became increasingly difficult to hold in the face of widespread communal violence instigated by Sinhalese mobs fired by chauvinist appeals and enraged at Tamil separatist demands. Splinter groups of radical Tamil youth thus set up a body

MAP 8
SRI LANKA: DISTRIBUTION OF POPULATION (1981 CENSUS)

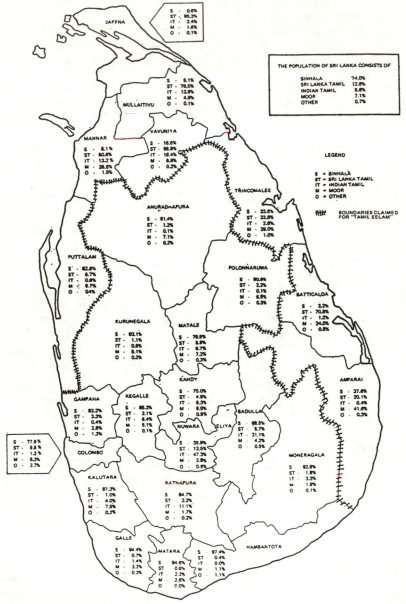

Note: 'Sri Lanka Tamil' is the term now used in government documents for 'Ceylon Tamil'. The latter term remains in use in much of the literature.

committed to liberation through the power of the gun, the 'Liberation Tigers'. Its formal initiation of insurgency began with a 7 April 1978 ambush in Jaffna which left four policemen dead. Sporadic fighting and additional anti-Tamil rioting continued in the years which followed.

The spiral culminated in July 1983. An insurgent ambush left 13 soldiers dead, the worst single loss ever suffered up to that point by the Sri Lankan military in its short history. The subsequent mass funeral of the soldiers in Colombo exploded into nationwide anti-Tamil rioting and looting. At least 400 persons were killed and 100,000 left homeless; another 60,000 fled to India. Police stood by, and in many cases members of the armed forces were reported to have participated in the violence.

This spasm of communal bloodletting served to traumatize the Tamil community and to provide the insurgents, who at the time probably numbered no more than 200 hardcore members, with an influx of new manpower. Thereafter, their strength grew quickly, reaching ultimately an estimated 10,000. In the combat which followed July 1983, Sri Lanka's small, lightly armed, and poorly trained security forces proved woefully inadequate for grappling with the complexities of stability operations. Brutalization of the populace only created further insurgent recruits. The situation soon was out of control. Government writ was effectively lost in the area of most dense Tamil settlement, Jaffna. In other areas of heavy Tamil concentration, the Northern and Eastern Provinces, the security forces barely held their own. The conflict even touched Sinhalese majority areas, a development which was starkly illustrated in a May 1985 insurgent attack on the Buddhist holy city of Anuradhapura in the North Central Province that left nearly 180 civilians massacred.

India, under pressure from its 50 million-strong Tamil electoral bloc in the south, fearful lest it be forced to bear the burden of masses of refugees, and already unhappy at what it perceived to be the pro-Western foreign policy orientation of Sri Lankan President Junius R. Jayewardene's government, began a program of covert assistance to the insurgents and turned a blind eye to their growing presence in its own state of Tamil Nadu. This all but destroyed relations between Colombo and New Delhi.

The assassination of Indian Prime Minister Indira Gandhi in October 1984 at the hands of Sikh separatists brought to power her surviving son, Rajiv. He promptly carried out a sea-change in policy. Lengthy discussions were held with Sri Lankan policy makers to arrive at an approach to the 'Tamil problem' acceptable to both Colombo and New Delhi; the insurgents were informed that India would not accept an independent Tamil state at its back door; and the most active insurgent base camps in India were closed down. On 18 June 1985 it was announced that Colombo and the insurgents, bowing to pressure from New Delhi, had agreed to a 'cessation of hostilities' and their first face-to-face discussions in an effort to frame a political solution to the conflict.

Rajiv Gandhi's reversal of his mother's stance toward the insurgents was prompted by the obvious contradiction contained in supporting separatism within a democratic neighbor even while attempting to combat various domestic separatist movements. Tamil separatism was viewed as especially dangerous, because it had remained a problem in the Indian south ever since the peak of anti-Hindi sentiments in 1964–65. Tamil Nadu itself was a result of the *Dravida Munnetra Kazhagham* (DMK)-led campaign for a separate Tamil entity. When he took office, Rajiv found that the presence in Tamil Nadu of the Sri Lankan insurgents had served to revive anti-Hindi sentiments and latent Tamil chauvinism. The DMK, which had become the state assembly opposition to the ruling '*Anna* DMK' (AIADMK), an offshoot of the old movement, was waging a vigorous campaign to arouse such sentiments and to derive political advantage from them. Thus Rajiv moved vigorously and forcefully to foster a solution.

Despite his efforts, however, five months of desultory talks in Thimpu, the capital of Bhutan, and a truce which never really took hold led to little of substance. That such was the result seemed never in doubt to informed observers. For there was another side to the situation which is most germane to the issues under consideration here. That is, while the conflict certainly revolved around Tamil attempts to redress their perceived and real wrongs suffered at the hands of the Sinhalese, all major insurgent groups — the 'Tigers' having early on split into numerous factions — were Marxist-Leninist, claimed to be inspired by the Maoist approach, and were pressing for goals which extended beyond mere 'liberation' in a racial sense. This aspect of the insurgency received little attention, despite the fact that access to insurgent groups and their literature was fairly easy. Its significance was made plain in discussions with insurgent leadership figures:[20] even a government offer of a considerable amount of autonomy would in the end not have been enough to induce the insurgents to give up their struggle. The fact was that the insurgent groups were committed to a purposive effort to make a revolution. This they stated explicitly — privately, publicly, and in their literature. Wrote Anton Stanislav Balasingham, leading theoretician for LTTE: 'The political objective of our movement is to advance the national struggle along with the class struggle, or rather, our fundamental objective is national emancipation and socialist transformation of our social formation.'[21]

Examining the insurgent movement in detail revealed an alphabet soup of initials. There may at one point have been as many as 42 different groups active. These, however, were dominated by the 'big five': Liberation Tigers of Tamil Eelam (LTTE); People's Liberation Organisation of Thamileelam (PLOT, also frequently rendered as PLOTE in the Western press, a variance caused by use of 'Tamil Eelam' rather than 'Thamileelam' as adopted by the group itself for its formal communications); Tamil Eelam Liberation Organisation (TELO); Eelam People's Revolutionary Liberation Front (EPRLF); and Eelam Revolutionary Organisation (EROS). PLOT aside, these groups agreed in April 1985 to end their constant bickering and ambushes of each other in order to form an Eelam National Liberation Front (ENLF). Subsequently, they sought international recognition along the lines pioneered by the Palestine Liberation Organisation (PLO). PLOT remained allied with several smaller Marxist groups — Tamil Eelam Liberation Army (TELA), the Senthil faction of the Tamil Eelam Liberation Front (TELF), Tamil Eelam Republican Army (TERA), and National Liberation Front of Tamileelam (NLFT).

Looking at the premier insurgent bodies in more detail revealed the following:

Eelam National Liberation Front (ENLF)

● Liberation Tigers of Tamil Eelam (LTTE), or the 'Tamil Tigers'. Led by Velupillai Prabhakaran, probably 32 years of age in 1986, LTTE was the oldest of the Tamil insurgent groups and the most active and powerful. Its radicalism had been reinforced over the years through links with the Palestine Liberation Organisation (PLO — which, it should be noted, maintained a mission in Colombo), and other international terrorist organizations. LTTE's

Marxism, originally thought to be much an ideology of convenience, had grown in intensity as the years have passed. The group had long been noted as the most ruthless of the insurgent bodies and at one time had on its 'hit list' virtually the entire leaderships of all other rebel groups.

• Tamil Eelam Liberation Organisation (TELO). Long one of the least well-known groups, TELO achieved unasked-for prominence during the July 1983 riots when most of its leadership was massacred in attacks by Sinhalese prisoners on their Tamil counterparts being held at Vellikapai Prison. The loss proved to be to TELO's long-term benefit, as its new leader, Sri Sabaratnam, proved energetic and capable. He masterminded major assaults on isolated government positions and expanded TELO's area of operations and influence substantially. An elusive figure for the press, he remained something of an enigma. His nickname, 'Tall Sri', came not from his height, which was quite ordinary, but from the fact that between 1972 and 1975 he was the taller of two 'Sri's' in government custody and was termed 'tall' by the head of his detainment facility to differentiate him from his shorter counterpart. TELO was increasingly favored by New Delhi despite its widespread use of terror. Sri Sabaratnam himself was reported killed in late April or early May 1986 fighting with LTTE.

• Eelam People's Revolutionary Liberation Front (EPRLF). Another of the more active insurgent groups, particularly in the east, EPRLF vaulted into the limelight in July 1984 when it kidnapped an American couple, Stanley and Mary Elizabeth Allen, who were working in Jaffna on a water project for the US Agency for International Development. Subsequently the group, led by tall, bearded, broad-shouldered K. Padmanabhana, grew in strength and capabilities. It regularly executed ambushes and worked actively through front organizations abroad such as the General Union of Eelam Students (GUES) to promote the insurgent cause. Foreign observers who engaged in discussions with its leadership noted the dogmatism of their Marxism.

• Eelam Revolutionary Organisation (EROS). While all other major insurgent leaders were moving about Madras in cars with bodyguards, Balakumar of EROS used a bicycle. This fact was indicative of his group's quiet, purposeful growth from what apparently was a mere band of like-minded radical students to its stature as an active component in the insurgent campaign. Balakumar continued to claim that he was but one member of a collective leadership. Even the initials EROS were egalitarian, for they applied not only to the parent body but also to its numerous offspring, branches, or front organizations, which all took the label EROS. At various times, for example, both the Eelam Revolutionary Organisation of Students (EROS) and the Eelam Research Organisation (EROS) were thought to be the premier body, with all others, such as the Eelam Refugees Organisation (EROS), subordinate.

PLOT Grouping

• People's Liberation Organisation of Thamileelam (PLOT). Bitter rival of LTTE's Prabhakaran, PLOT's head, Uma Maheswaran, broke away as early as 1978 to form his own group. Sri Lankan intelligence sources claimed the original cause of the split had more to do with a woman than ideological differences, but these subsequently became substantial. Despite his close relations with various international terrorist groups, particularly Dr George Habash's Marxist group, the Popular Front for the Liberation of Palestine (PFLP), which trained PLOT personnel at its camps in the Middle East, Maheswaran was vocal in condemning terror actions which led to reprisals against Tamil civilians. He attempted to place emphasis instead on the development of an insurgent infrastructure. To reach more people, PLOT made increasing use of a covert, portable radio transmitter.

• Tamil Eelam Liberation Army (TELA). Apparently, TELA was originally the armed component of TELO. It split with it in the wake of the prison massacre of TELO's leadership. The new TELA boss, Kulasegaram Devasegaram, 'Oberoi Davan', so-called because he was once a waiter at the Lanka Oberoi Hotel in Colombo, was dead not long after his TELO predecessors, killed in August 1983. His assassins were acting at the behest of a rival insurgent group rather than the declared foe. Blame was placed on LTTE. Thus it was not surprising that TELA allied itself with LTTE's most bitter foe, PLOT.

• Tamil Eelam Liberation Front (TELF). In April 1982 disagreement amongst the members of TULF's leadership over its continuing moderate approach to separatism led S. A. Tharmalingham to create TELF, dedicated to more radical solutions but still a public organization. Tharmalingham and other TELF leaders were detained by the authorities in mid-1983. Subsequently, a leadership struggle led to the alignment of the most active faction, under one 'Senthil', with PLOT.

● Tamil Eelam Republican Army (TERA). Also frequently identified as the Tamil Eelam Army (TEA), TERA was headed by Thambipillai Maheswaran, a former engineering student in Britain. He was regarded with considerable suspicion by other groups, which suspected him of using his insurgent status to further a criminal career. Nevertheless, T. Maheswaran remained on good terms with PLOT. Twice held by the government, he escaped each time, even surviving the 1983 Vellikapai Prison massacre. He later masterminded a mass escape and bank robbery in Batticaloa, eastern Sri Lanka's major city.

● National Liberation Front of Tamileelam (NLFT). A then-growing body about which little was known, NLFT supported PLOT and increasingly played a role in operations conducted with that group in Sri Lanka.

As normally the case with clandestine bodies, it was difficult to come up with meaningful strength figures for the insurgent groups. It has already been noted that the guerrillas were unable to increase their numbers substantially until after the July 1983 riots radicalized large sectors of the Tamil community, especially the youth, and provided abundant, motivated manpower. Sri Lankan military intelligence sources, in fact, noted that in 1975 they carried the number of hardcore insurgents as 25. One year after July 1983, this figure had mushroomed to 5,000 and was subsequently put as high as 10,000 — although most of the latter figure were not armed.

The significance of the number, whether 5,000 or 10,000, lay in the fact that, until Sri Lanka could mobilize its manpower pool, the combined insurgents very nearly matched the strength of the army. Thus they stood a chance — if properly armed, trained, and coordinated — of putting the security forces on the ropes. That they were unable to do so owed far more to their own internal problems than it did to government efficiency.

Until the formation of the ENLF, the insurgents engaged in little cooperation and coordination. LTTE's Prabakaran and PLOT's Maheswaran, for example, were themselves arrested in May 1982, together with several followers, after trading shots on a crowded Madras street. Faced with such animosity between the main flag-bearers of the Tamil cause, other groups attempted to proceed alone with plans to create links. A series of meetings held in November 1983 in Madras to discuss the unification was well-attended, and in April 1984 TELO, EROS, and EPRLF, the most dogmatic Marxist groups, announced the formation of their own unified command.

Further unity meetings in December 1984 appeared to bear little fruit. At one, in March 1985, LTTE and PLOT representatives resorted to gunplay to make their points. Yet a series of events in early 1985, when it appeared that external support for the cause might be waning, brought home to the feuding parties the critical role a unified effort would play in the liberation movement's chances not only of success but of survival. Hence, in April 1985, LTTE, TELO, EPRLF, and EROS announced the formation of the ENLF. PLOT remained outside the Front, though its representatives continued to discuss possible participation.

The inability of the two major blocks to unite, whatever the original causes of their estrangement, stemmed not from differences of ideology or goal but rather disagreements over strategy and tactics. All of the groups remained Marxist-Leninist in organization and political persuasion, with a vague conception of Maoist 'people's war' as their model for making revolution. Likewise, they all were firmly committed to 'Tamil Eelam' in the belief that true liberation could come only through both an independent Tamil state and use of Marxist ideology to transform the relations of production. 'Our total strategy', noted A. S. Balasingham, 'integrates both the national struggle and class struggle, interlinks both nationalism and socialism into a revolutionary project aimed at liberating our people both from national oppression and from the exploitation of man by man.'[22]

Organizationally, insurgent groups utilized the standard Leninist constructs, with Politburos, Central Committees, and the like, but they did not always establish a party element separate from the guerrilla forces themselves. This stemmed from their Guevarist rather than truly Maoist approach: As articulated by the Cuban revolutionary Che Guevara through his mouthpiece Regis Debray in the celebrated *foco* theory, the party was to grow out of the revolt by a small, determined band of insurgents (the *foco*) — as opposed to the Leninist approach where the party established its armed wing, then used it to build power.

The primacy of Guevarism was a direct reflection of the ethnic roots of the struggle. The insurgency should not be viewed as simply a case of a small band of dedicated 'revolutionists' taking advantage of a welcome opportunity for subversion. Instead, it seems clear that the dimension of ethnic turmoil, encompassing as it does deeper socio-economic contradictions, spawned the original discontent, or 'alienation', to use the Marxist term. The guerrillas' ideological framework was created as they groped for explanations of the repression they felt was bent on the annihilation of their people. The result was quite an eclectic body of thought, with desires for justice paramount for many of the rank and file but decidedly secondary amongst the leadership to 'deeper' considerations of the necessity for liberation from Sri Lankan capitalism and global imperialism.[23]

Since most insurgent supporters were not even necessarily in favor of 'Tamil Eelam' in the separatist sense, much less the Marxist connotations held by the guerrilla leadership, the insurgent bodies did not make a point of publicizing their ideological views. EPRLF leader K. Padmanabha was uncharacteristically open when he told a Sri Lankan journalist in 1985, 'When Eelam is set up there will be no democracy there. The choice is between fascism or communism. I think the people will opt for the latter'.

More illustrative of the insurgent stance was the explanation offered by a PLOT Politburo member in an August 1984 interview, during which he repeatedly made the point that the insurgents were 'Marxist thinkers' as opposed to 'Marxists'. That is, he explained, he and his comrades attempted to use Marxist principles and methodologies of all varieties — Marx, Lenin, Mao, and the Sandinistas were mentioned — to arrive at an analytical framework appropriate for the Tamil situation. As such, the insurgents were inspired by, trained with, and were willing to fight for other radical causes — again, Nicaragua was mentioned — especially against 'American imperialism'. All this was a learning experience as the particulars of a unique Tamil communism evolved.[24]

PLOT, as evident from the interview above, displayed considerable flexibility in its evolution of 'Tamil communism'. The members of ENLF were more limited in the scope and depth of their analysis. Be this as it may, principal causes of disagreement did not arise from theoretical debates *per se* but from the process of application.

Specifically, PLOT's analysis of the situation held that the key ally of the government was Sinhalese anti-Tamil sentiment, or chauvinism. Indiscriminate attacks which served to fan such sentiments were ultimately counterproductive, PLOT maintained, because they turned what was fundamentally an ideological conflict, being waged against world imperialism (i.e., international capitalism) and its Colombo offshoot, into an ethnic battle. This was disastrous, the analysis continued, as there was little chance of an independent Tamil state emerging in the face of an omnipresent Sinhalese hostility. Common cause must be made, the reasoning concluded, with the radical Sinhalese left to overthrow the Colombo government through joint revolutionary action. Under a Marxist regime the communal problem could be solved in a fashion mutually agreeable to both races.

ENLF, on the other hand, was more colored in its approach by its ethnic roots. This was particularly so as concerned LTTE, which remained the paramount insurgent body. LTTE and its partners were more oriented toward the military elements of the struggle, the effort to drive the Sinhalese — blinded as they were by their bourgeois leadership — from the 'traditional Tamil homelands', and not nearly as concerned with the purported overall niche the fight occupied in the global struggle for liberation of the oppressed. The crucial element, ENLF believed, before all others, was to carry the fight to the enemy through combat operations, thereby liberating 'Tamil Eelam' from Sinhalese fascism. Ideological development and organizational particulars of the future Marxist state would follow.

Tactically, this difference of orientation resulted in the ENLF being the far more active of the two groupings in actual fighting in Sri Lanka. Even when truces were declared during efforts at negotiation, ENLF participants, especially LTTE, were the major source of violations. They also perpetrated the massacres of Sinhalese civilians which were carried out in retaliation for alleged atrocities committed against Tamils.

It is not surprising, then, that ENLF made extensive use of terror, especially the killing, often after torture, of those denounced as informants, traitors, and such. Those so executed were frequently left tied or hanging from lamp posts, spawning the common use of the term 'lamp post killings' or 'lamp post victim' to describe such episodes. Like 'lamp post killings', bombings also increased in frequency as the conflict dragged on, as did attempts to damage physical infrastructure, such as the rail system, which necessarily produced civilian casualties. Far from any attempt to avoid such casualties, there was an apparent increase in effort to

maximize those affected. PLOT also used terror — and comprehensive internal purges were a staple of all groups — but PLOT's
killings were far more selective and designed to attack the 'enemy
within'. There was an effort to avoid actions which would likely
result in reprisals against Tamil civilians, and Sinhalese civilians
were generally not attacked.

Initially, following July 1983, the rebel response to the situation
had the character of the French World War II *maquis*: that is, guerrillas operating with popular support against an enemy force occupying their homeland. The goal was simply to strike back.
Gradually, though, especially as ideological concerns began to play
a greater role in day-to-day decisionmaking, the construction of
infrastructure became salient. This was an important indicator of
the shading of separatist rebellion into insurgency — that is, an
attempt by an ideologically inspired revolt to supplant the existing
system of governance with an alternative structure. The goal had
become 'people's war' in the Maoist sense of the word, for the
purpose of 'liberation'. 'Tamil Eelam' had thus become far more
than a call for a piece of territory. It was a plan for Marxist transformation.

Government Response to the Tamil Insurgency

Needless to say, while an insurgency is far more dangerous to a
government than separatism or peasant rebellion, the immediate
problems for the authorities are much the same: successfully cop-
ing with the military attacks of an armed uprising. By early 1984
the Sri Lankan military, which previously had been able to avoid
all but minimal involvement in the 'counterterrorist' campaign in
the north, found itself faced with the prospect of engaging in protracted stability operations. These, it was ill-prepared to carry out.

Sri Lanka's defense establishment was one befitting the island's
small size: a 14,000-man army (12,000 regulars and 2,000
reserves, or 'volunteers', on active duty); a 3,500-man air force flying a motley collection of small, fixed-wing aircraft and helicopters; a navy of 3,500 men scattered about 32 small patrol craft;
and a police force of roughly 10,000 assigned to small stations
throughout the country. Personnel in all services were poorly
trained. To gain flying time, for instance, the air force used its
planes to run a charter service for tourists. The only reservoir of

combat experience lay in those older personnel who had participated in the suppression of the revolt in 1971.

Army combat power originally was centered on a mere five
infantry battalions, all of which were under their designated 730-
man strengths and stationed in company-size cantonments
throughout the country. Each line battalion was theoretically the
first of three in a regiment, with the other two battalions comprised of 'volunteers'. In reality only one regiment had its two 'volunteer' battalions. None of the reserve component units were on
active duty; all were understrength and armed with outdated
weapons. Single armor, artillery, signal, and combat engineer regiments were also only understrength battalions. At one time
approximately a third of the 'volunteer' personnel themselves, as
opposed to their units, were on active duty to make up manpower
shortages in regular units. Communal disturbances had already
stretched the available units so tightly that air force and navy men
regularly performed as foot soldiers.

Weaponry was likewise woefully inadequate. There was no single infantry rifle. Even the venerable Lee-Enfield was in use in
some units. Heavier backup was a mix of British, Chinese, Soviet,
and Yugoslav arms. Machine-guns were the old British Vickers
medium and general purpose models. Mortars were 82mm from
the Soviet Union, as well as 2- and 3-inch versions from Britain.
There were even some 120mm variants from Yugoslavia. The
armored forces drove vintage Daimler *Ferret* scout cars (15 in
number), supported by turreted *Ferret* (12) and *Saladin* (6)
armored cars. Artillery was limited to a dozen 85mm guns from
the Soviet Union and four 76mm mountain guns from Yugoslavia.
Less than a hundred trucks were available for transportation.

There was no close air support. Fourteen aircraft — 5 HC-1
'Chipmunks', 6 Cessna 150 Skymasters, and 3 Devon Doves —
were based in a 'flying wing' which spent most of its time training
new pilots. A 'transport squadron' had 11 heavier aircraft ranging
from the DH-114 ('Heron' and 'Riley' versions) to the Dakota
DC-3 to the Cessna 337 (utility version). The 'helicopter
squadron' had 13 choppers (2 were later lost in training accidents),
the bulk Bell 206A. Six MiG-17s, given by Moscow during the
1971 troubles when Sri Lanka had a socialist government, were
written off as completely unserviceable in June 1984.

Ten fast attack craft (PCF) with guns were the heart of the Sri
Lankan Navy, though at any one time several were laid up for

repairs. The two newest vessels were indigenously-produced 40-meter craft built at Colombo Dockyards and launched in mid-1983. The remaining eight craft consisted of seven *Sooraya*-class (ex-Chinese *Shanghai II*) and one ex-Soviet *Mol*-class gunboats. Armament was unimpressive, as illustrated by that of the former Chinese boats: 4 x 37mm (2 twins) guns and 4 x 24mm (2 twins). Aside from a single lighthouse support vessel, the remaining members of the naval inventory, some 21 vessels, were little more the coastal patrol craft of diminutive size and capability.

These, then, were the forces which were called upon to grapple with the complexities of guerrilla war in an island the size of Ireland. They were small, lightly armed and equipped, and minimally trained. Prior to July 1983, when the insurgent movement had not yet taken on new life, a few units were posted to affected areas of the north. They kept occupied running in convoy up and down the main roads, the troops amusing themselves by using long poles to knock civilians off their bicycles. It was all great sport; and while the local populace protested vigorously against the unseemly conduct of the 'occupying army' in their midst, casualties normally were few on both sides.

Still, there were excesses, especially in the first half of 1983 as the tension mounted and the guerrillas became more active. The government was forced to move vigorously just before the nationwide riots to punish abuses. In the most serious episode, members of the 1st Battalion, Rajarata Rifles Regiment, were disciplined after taking retaliatory actions against civilians. In protest against the measures, however, nearly 100 other soldiers went on strike and deserted. The entire battalion was consequently disbanded; the deserters, once rounded up, were cashiered out of the service, as were key members of the chain of command. The remaining unit members were combined with another understrength regular battalion to form the first unit of an entirely new regiment. This left just four infantry battalions on the eve of what was to quickly become a war.

The military's 'easy days' ended as insurgent strength increased dramatically. Soon the army, deployed in the north in reinforced battalion strength (roughly four companies), found itself subjected to a series of bloody episodes. Landmines caused casualties four or six at a time, and ambushes added to the toll. The security forces rarely saw their assailants. Unable to close with their opponents, the troops responded in predictable fashion — they all too often gunned down the civilians whom they deemed to be implicated. Though the government was probably truthful when it denied that retaliation was official policy, there was a definite callousness toward the population whose 'hearts and minds' it purportedly sought to win.

This was hardly surprising. Less than five per cent of the soldiers were Tamil, less than three per cent of the officers. Government forces, therefore, saw themselves as cast adrift in a sea of 'hostiles' whose language they could not speak and whose customs they did not share — and who, they were convinced, knew precisely where mines were buried and ambushes planned.

This was a dangerously simplistic view, for the average Tamil wanted only to be left alone by all concerned. Yet as the Sinhalese armed host began to retaliate for its own losses, often burning whole villages (and in one instance in Mannar District, gunning down nearly 100 individuals after a particularly costly ambush), the Tamil masses turned sullenly to the only salvation they saw, the insurgents. Ironically, most Tamils were neither communists nor supporters of 'Eelam'.

By the end of 1984, insurgent activity had grown to the point that it threatened government control of Tamil majority areas in northern Sri Lanka. The security forces had increased in size and quality of weaponry, but a national concept of operations was lacking. There was serious doubt, in fact, that some elements of the armed forces in the north, if pressed closely by an insurgent onslaught, would be able to make an orderly withdrawal. Reports forwarded to higher authorities were routinely falsified to put the best possible face on the situation.

The extent to which the insurgent capabilities had developed was amply demonstrated in a well-coordinated and executed attack on 20 November 1984 in which a Tamil force of company size used overwhelming firepower and explosives to demolish the Chavakachcheri Police Station on the Jaffna peninsula and to kill at least 27 policemen defending it. There followed continued ambushes of security forces, as well as several large massacres of Sinhalese civilians living in areas deemed by the insurgents to be 'traditional Tamil homelands'. Use of automatic weapons, mortars, and RPG-7 rocket launchers was reported.

Even as these developments took place, it became clear to the authorities that a drastic upgrading of security force capabilities was needed, a task which was beyond their immediate capabilities.

For this Sri Lanka hence turned to two sources, Britain and Israel. Former British Special Air Service (SAS) personnel in the employ of KMS Ltd.,[25] which had seen service around the world both independently and as a quasi-official London surrogate, were retained to train a completely new police Special Task Force (STF). These troops took over primary responsibility for security in the Eastern Province in late 1984, effectively freeing the army to concentrate on areas in the Northern Province (which included Jaffna). If effective, it was planned that the strength of the force would be increased and its units deployed further to take over general counterinsurgency duty from the army. Army units would then have been used as the quick reaction element and general reserve. This 'second phase' did not come to pass. On the official level, Britain stepped up its military training assistance and advice.

Israel was approached on the basis of its demonstrated expertise in counterterrorist operations. In the face of much criticism and amidst fears that the lucrative Middle East market for Sri Lankan expatriate labor might be jeopardized, Colombo allowed the establishment of an Israeli Special Interests Section in May 1984, with the United States as the protecting power. Small teams from Israel's internal security service, *Shin Bet*, shortly thereafter began to train Sri Lankan personnel in intelligence gathering and internal security techniques.

Special Task Force (STF) proved reasonably successful, despite its not being able to replace totally the army in counterinsurgency operations.[26] The relationship with Israel was not nearly as smooth, particularly given the political complications it caused, not only in Sri Lanka's foreign affairs but also in Colombo's relations with its large Muslim community. Aside from the fact that Israel was essentially looking for a route to renew the diplomatic relations which had been suspended during the Bandaranaike administration (1970–77) and had no desire to become enmeshed in Sri Lanka's internal fighting, the limited value of Israel's advice probably stemmed from its focus on counterterrorism rather than counterinsurgency.

Who said what and to whom may never be made public, but there is a basic similarity between the unsuccessful Israeli approach to pacification of the occupied Arab territories and that practiced in the early stage of the fighting in Sri Lanka. The 'population-as-the-enemy' philosophy, harsh reprisals, and the emphasis on the military to maintain order rather than to function within a political framework directed toward a solution were common components of Israeli and Sri Lankan strategies.

So, too, were the results identical. With their position in Jaffna consolidated, the insurgents moved in force into areas of the east, which was also claimed as part of 'Eelam', despite the fact that a majority of its population was not Tamil. Additionally, they began to operate in Sinhalese-majority areas. With its forces deployed in 'hot' areas — and having violated the dictum to first secure its own base areas before moving out to engage the enemy — the government was unprepared to meet this new threat. Efforts to increase force strengths further and to purchase new equipment (e.g., a dozen Bell 212 helicopters) did little to improve the serious shortcomings of the security apparatus.

Starting in early April 1985, Sri Lanka entered its most difficult period of the insurgency up to that time. The terror killing by the insurgents of three Muslims, reportedly at prayer in a mosque, led to widespread Muslim-Tamil riots in the east which by the end of the month had left scores dead and more than 33,000 in refugee camps. Insurgent-initiated contacts increased in frequency, killing as many as half a dozen security personnel per contact. Bombs were discovered in the capital city itself, Colombo, and one powerful device, estimated at 35 kilograms of explosive, ripped through a train waiting near the international airport to take hundreds of workers back to their homes.

On 26 April simultaneous attacks occurred at various locations throughout insurgent-affected areas. Ambushes decimated security force patrols at Komai near Pottuvil, 55 miles south of Batticaloa; at Mutur, near Trincomalee; and near Point Pedro in Jaffna. Most spectacularly, apparent PLOT cadre robbed the bank and destroyed the police station at Kikaweratiya in the heartland of the Sinhalese-populated area between Kururnegala and Puttalam. Two days later six more soldiers were lost to another landmine explosion, this time near Pohkandi in Jaffna. On the 29th a parcel bomb damaged several buildings in the Army Headquarters complex at Colombo.

May began with the situation obviously serious. May Day 1985 was celebrated with the discovery of a bomb in the main Colombo railway terminal. On the 3rd apparent EPRLF insurgents simultaneously attacked major naval, air, and police positions in the north but were beaten back amidst conflicting reports on the nature of the weapons used by both sides and the extent, if any, of civilian casualties. Other assaults followed, including a dawn attack on the Mannar Police Station on 10 May which killed two constables and left the building heavily damaged.

Such actions were to pale in significance compared to what occurred on the 14th. That day, a busload of insurgents, disguised as soldiers, rolled into Anuradhapura, the site of Sri Lanka's capital for 1,400 years (fourth century BC to tenth century AD). Amidst the ruins, Anuradhapura was, as it normally is, filled with pilgrims flocking to pay homage to one of the country's most sacred shrines, the *Sri Maha Bodhi*, a *bo* tree grown from a sapling of the tree under which Buddha attained enlightenment. After first attacking the bus station, the insurgents assaulted worshippers at the shrine itself. Ultimately, the dead numbered about 180. All too predictably, massacres of Tamil civilians followed at the hands of enraged Sinhalese mobs.

Rebellion and Revolutionary Process

From the foregoing sections it should be clear that there is a unity of historical causation linking the 1971 insurrection and the present Tamil insurgency. An essential starting point was the nature of the Sri Lankan state at independence in 1948. Despite the fact that its political form was that of Westminster parliamentary democracy, the state was in a structural sense largely autonomous of the society over which it ruled. It was not the representative of any particular dominant or subordinate class; and, as will be explained, the estate sector gave it an independent resource base where the main crop, tea, was grown primarily by what amounted to indentured labor, the Indian Tamils. The symbolic importance attached to participation in the electoral process was high, a reflection of anti-colonial nationalism, but the 'choice' afforded the voters was unidimensional.

The place of the departed British rulers had merely been taken by an indigenous, Western-educated, English-speaking elite with tenuous ties to the countryside. Regardless of the ideological persuasions of particular factions, this elite was structurally one ruling class, the national component of the original landed aristocracy (*pelantiya*),[27] which had utilized its former position to withdraw from direct involvement in agricultural production and to enter a variety of other areas, most importantly colonial government service.

The *pelantiya* solidified its position through marriage, kin, and school ties, thereby achieving almost complete control of goods and services provided by the central government. Since recruitment to the *pelantiya* through land acquisition had essentially ceased by 1920, when most areas of lowland Sri Lanka were occupied by ricelands and plantations (tea, rubber, and coconut),[28] elite regeneration was accomplished through participation in the administration and the mechanisms of exclusive Western education. This autonomous position was further solidified by the dependence of state finances principally upon the three major plantation export crops already mentioned. Of these tea was paramount, contributing more than half of all foreign exchange earnings. Tea, of course, was cultivated almost totally by Indian Tamils, who were denied citizenship and effectively prevented from leaving the plantations.[29]

With its own regenerative mechanisms, interests, and financial base, the autonomous state existed atop a weak class structure which had not developed substantially under colonialism. Nearly all relations of production remained within traditional village confines. Initially, the key psychological preoccupation of all classes was attainment of independence. Once the initial glow had worn off, however, other concerns became salient. These were primarily symbolic — the return of the Sinhalese people and Buddhism to their 'rightful place' — and economic. In particular the growth of capitalist relations of production, a process which had accelerated after 1945, led to the substantial strengthening of the Sinhala-speaking rural capitalist class (*mudalali*).[30] This class, however, found its livelihoods increasingly threatened by a variety of state policies aimed at either nationalizing or exercising control over the activities characteristic of *mudalai* involvement. Concurrently, there was accelerating marginalization of rural cultivators as smallholders were forced into sharecropping by escalating costs of production, and sharecroppers themselves were replaced by the employment of wage labor to faciliate large scale commercial production.[31] Already by the late 1960s at least a third of the peasantry had become landless, working either as sharecroppers or wage labor. Additionally, roughly half of the rural population did not participate directly in agricultural production but was involved in handicraft and other activities. Unemployment and underemployment were rampant. In the decade after 1960, official employment figures, which were a low reflection of the actual situation, more than doubled. This trend was given impetus by a mushrooming population. The country's inhabitants increased by 20.5 per cent, or 2.3 per cent annually, in the same decade just mentioned.[32]

Structurally, then, Sri Lanka in the years after independence was characterized by an autonomous state controlled by *pelantiya* members who had moved into administration and were no longer dependent upon landed wealth extracted from indigenous subordinate classes. They had access instead to a surplus which comprised the majority of foreign exchange earned and which further was generated primarily by a class of non-indigenous virtual serfs, the Indian Tamils. Local *pelantiya* members who were not able to move into the ranks of the autonomous ruling class continued to be directly involved in surplus extraction in the countryside but retained links with national *pelantiya* members through ties of caste, kin, and education. Arrayed as possible opposition was a growing *mudalali* class, which saw its position threatened by state policies, and an increasingly marginalized peasantry/rural population which was dramatically increasing in numbers. There was also a small urban proletariat, many members of which retained links with their old villages.

A crisis in the Sri Lankan old-regime was brought about by several factors. Politically, the mechanisms of electoral politics required that national *pelantiya* factions reach out for allies to ensure their control over the power structure and national resources. In the years immediately following independence, elite parties built the needed alliances through their appeals to Sinhalese chauvinism. This development, however, as noted previously, had the effect of arousing the antagonism of the Ceylon Tamils, for whom 'independence' had meant essentially no more than a change of masters. Nevertheless, the Tamil reaction was initially comparatively minor in terms of the problems it posed for the state, certainly of less moment than the possible consequences of ignoring the aroused chauvinist sentiments of the Sinhalese majority.

Thus, all major Sinhalese parties to some extent sought to play chauvinist cards. The SLFP was first off the mark and was able to parlay its advocacy of the Sinhala language and paramount position of Buddhism into victory in the 1956 election. But the UNP was not to be outdone and added its own chauvinist appeals.

With all elite factions adopting a chauvinist approach, distinguished only in degree, the need for additional discriminators became pronounced. The result was increased ideological differentiation of the elite, with the SLFP emphasizing socialism, the UNP the free market. To an outsider these positions were relative, as both parties at this time were quite similar in their objective approaches to society and the economy. Considerable antagonism developed between them, though. Fiery rhetoric, filled with promises of sweeping structural changes to benefit the masses, became the order of the day. Despite the essential structural unity of the national *pelantiya*, then, the doors had been opened for the ideological split of the ruling class into a mutually antagonistic left and right. The Marxist parties and their successive splits were illustrative of the consequences attendant to the process, as extreme grew from extreme, the JVP being the final product.

This development of ideological positions — and particularly of a major party, the SLFP, publicly and stridently advocating redistributive policies — became of even greater significance due to the economic facet of old-regime crisis. Economic difficulties were brought about by several developments, one a result of Colombo's position in the world-economy, the other internally generated.

Hit by declining prices for its agricultural exports in the decade prior to 1971, especially those for tea, Colombo saw its foreign exchange earnings fall sharply and its foreign borrowings consequently rise dramatically to maintain 'development' and imports, notably rice. That the island was no longer self-sufficient in so basic a staple was due to the colonial-dictated emphasis on monoculture.[33] Economic difficulties reached crisis proportions due to Sri Lanka's inability to absorb productively its rapidly expanding population. Programs derived from the Western development model, such as the expansion of schooling, only exacerbated matters, because these newly-educated and more politically aware individuals found their expected avenues to advancement all but nonexistent.

The combination of political and economic factors placed the state under severe structural strain. Arousal of Sinhalese chauvinism had alienated an important sector of the population, the Tamils, and simultaneously unleashed ideological forces which served to split elite ranks. From this weakened position the state was called upon to cope with a resource crisis at precisely the interval during which the effects of capitalist/'development' intrusion were becoming pronounced. The state made matters worse by attempting to further its extraction of surplus through increased nationalization and economic controls, a trend which involved both SLFP and UNP governments and which particularly affected those activities pursued by the *mudalali*. The elimination of the *mudalali*, in fact, was a major goal of successive governments in their efforts to increase resource exploitation and to exert more direct political control over the countryside. As Alexander has observed:

> In such circumstances it is not surprising that most *mudalali* saw their businesses as intensely personal enterprises which would cease with their death and tried to insure that their children took up other occupations. But the avenues of social mobility which served previous entrepreneurs had now been blocked. Large investments in their children's education only added to the ranks of the unemployed. The cultural connotations of caste and class prevented marriage with all but the poorest families among the *pelantiya*, even where the proposal was sweetened by a large dowry. ... While many had bought land and established elaborate residences, few had become large landholders because extensive areas of rural land seldom entered the market.[34]

Mudalali dissatisfaction increasingly was directed at the most available target, the local representatives of the *pelantiya*. They were joined in their hostility by other marginalized elements of the countryside. Though half the land remained in the hands of smallholders, the largest single group in the rural areas was comprised of wage laborers, a 'rural proletariat'. Another large and rapidly growing group was the unemployed, or those JVP leader Wijeweera characterized as 'waiting to enter the rural proletariat'.[35]

It should be emphasized again that distinguishing characteristics of the *pelantiya* were their Western-style education and ability to utilize English. Dissimilarly, the marginalized classes just mentioned were overwhelmingly educated in rural, Sinhala language schools and fluent in that tongue alone. Class considerations, therefore, were inevitably and inadvertently mobilized in the nationalist response to the elite's chauvinist exhortations. Once mobilized, such passions were difficult to control. Demands for increased Sinhalese participation (i.e., that of Sinhala-speaking, rural-educated, Buddhist rural classes, the majority of the population) in the socio-economic-political life of the country necessarily involved an attack upon the existing structural arrangements which guaranteed national *pelantiya* hegemony. Increased consciousness fostered by education and the ideological appeals of elite factions led to a growing awareness of the structural constraints on individual and group mobility, hence to mounting demands for change.

By 1971 the old-regime had reached a state of crisis due to internal and external pressures. The forces of Sinhalese chauvinism coinciding with class demands had aroused fear in the *pelantiya* that its position was in jeopardy. Reforms designed to relieve the pressure had taken largely symbolic form and had catered to the psychological elements of rural Sinhalese estrangement. Such reforms only led to further demands — and further alienated the Tamils. Yet there was little with which the elite could respond save token concessions, chauvinist appeals at Tamil expense, for to do elsewise would have been to endanger its position.

Significantly, the coercive structure, based as it was principally on a traditional system of values which was also falling victim to evolving internal socio-economic developments, was quite weak. For a population of more than 12.5 million,[36] there were about 10,605 policemen assigned to 41 small offices and 266 police stations, of which 172 were staffed by 20 or fewer officers. Armament was inadequate and antiquated, ammunition was in short supply. The military was in a similar state: small, poorly armed and trained, and without combat experience. Authorized strength for the army was only 6,578; of the navy, 1,718; and of the air force, 1,397.[37] Fiscal constraints did not allow any substantial augmentation of these numbers. Further, the elite was wary lest too strong a security establishment turn on its masters. True, the officer corps was in its upper ranks drawn largely from the *pelantiya*; but lower officer grades and the 'other ranks' (enlisted personnel) were principally from the rural classes. With the national *pelantiya* itself split ideologically, loyalty and control of the entire apparatus could not be guaranteed. An abortive coup in 1960 had made this point clear and had led to institution of a system of vouchers whereby potential officers had to obtain the recommendation of a serving Member of Parliament. Predictably, such a system had only further degraded the capabilities of the security forces.

As outlined already, the scenario which has been generally accepted holds that at this point in time the JVP, which already had plans to engage in purposive revolutionary action to overthrow the existing system, was pushed into hasty action by the exposure of its plans and consequent government repression. Hampered by tactical errors and inadequate armament, the effort failed. It would seem to follow that what occurred was an isolated instance of rebellion rather than a true revolutionary conjuncture. Work by Alexander,[38] however, parts of which have already been used to inform this analysis, casts doubt on the commonly held view of the 1971 insurrection.

Alexander, whose explanation is framed in terms of sociological considerations of class formation and not within revolutionary theory *per se*, demonstrates convincingly that the role of the JVP has been greatly overestimated. This state of affairs has come to pass due to the reliance of virtually all accounts on the same sources: government releases or news reports, especially those of the Western media, all frequently inaccurate and misleading. From his reconstruction of events, Alexander writes that what actually occurred was widespread rural class upheaval resulting from the processes and developments previously discussed here.

Disorganized due to the state of crisis in which it found itself, and incapable of deploying effective coercion, the old-regime was wracked by rural, local uprisings on a national scale, with the areas of heavy Tamil populations not participating for obvious reasons. The JVP was involved in these uprisings and even provided much of the leadership once they got underway, but the actual occurrences were apparently largely spontaneous responses to the perceived destruction of the already strained security apparatus. That is, as reports of the initial attacks by JVP members on police stations spread, the marginalized groups rose up, excited further by local grievances, and launched new assaults. The framework of coercion was in such disarray that what apparently were attacks on just five police stations — not the nationwide, coordinated assault on 74 widely scattered outposts as reported, a figure which was later raised to 93 — prompted the hasty evacuation of an additional 43 posts 'for strategic purposes'.

'It was this action, not the success of insurgent attacks, that deprived the government of control of much of the Sinhalese countryside', claims Alexander.[39] In other words, the coercive apparatus was in such a weak condition that widespread yet unsophisticated military action caused roughly a third of the state's outposts in rural areas to fall or be abandoned outright. From available data and comments of Alexander, it appears that representatives of the *mudalali* assumed leadership roles or even did much of the fighting, perhaps more in the south but apparently in the other areas, as well. Additional groups rallied to them, most importantly the rural proletariat and the 'potential rural proletariat'. A plurality of the upper insurgent leadership brought before the Criminal Justice Commission for trial after the insurrection (41 persons total) were identified as of the *karava* caste (traditionally associated with fishing but no longer so restricted) from the southern coastal regions. *Karava* areas were longstanding strongholds of the radical left in Sri Lankan politics; further, the south in general was a prime source of *mudalali* activity due to early exposure to capitalism. The sketchy biographical data on the 41 leaders which has been published does not allow actual comparison of class and caste, but it would appear that what might pass for a caste dimension in the insurrection is actually one tied up with class. This is certainly the case for data on the rank and file. There, as might be expected, more than half of those detained identified themselves as *goyiyama*, the majority Sri Lankan caste, with a traditional occupation of farming.

Why did the uprising fail? A key factor was weaknesses in revolutionary party ideology and, consequently, strategy and organization. Ideologically, the Maoist doctrinal roots of the JVP led to its focus upon the countryside and failure to cultivate links with possible urban allies. Furthermore, the JVP's conception of the capitalist foe was strongly colored by Sri Lanka's colonial experience and its continuing neo-colonial relationship with the world economy. Hence, the issue was seen as one largely of the Sinhalese masses rising up against exploitation. The result was that JVP dogma took on a strong flavor of Sinhalese chauvinism in the rural areas themselves, even if national insurgent leaders did not specifically advocate such an orientation. This immediately eliminated a further source of possible support, an ethnic united front of sorts.

Just as damaging as the restrictions upon its possible mass base was JVP leader Wijeweera's conception of the revolution as a massive, one-day uprising which would sweep away the old-regime. Thus, while the JVP was organized along Leninist lines, there was no well thought out plan of action. Neither was there a concerted effort to enforce discipline in what remained far more a movement than a party. The administrative and organizational details for a protracted insurgency were simply not carried out, because it was believed, based on analysis of the Sri Lankan case, that such an approach was not needed. Even tactical battle drill was rudimentary.

Inevitably, when the structural opportunity for revolution presented itself, neither the JVP nor any other group had the requisite organization or resources to seize the moment. Certainly no revolutionary body was thrown up by the rural explosions themselves. The JVP was clearly in a crucial position to dominate widespread rebellion as it developed, even with the fundamental ideological and organizational flaws which rendered it both strategically and tactically weakened. The moment was right — the government staggered badly in absorbing what has since been shown to have been, in objective terms, a rather lightweight punch. The resources which would have been needed to topple the state appear minimal. Lightly armed, poorly organized, and barely tactically competent, the rebels nonetheless rocked the nation. Indeed, only after the widespread rebellion sputtered — in the absence of a purposive body willing and able to take advantage of the situation — was the state able to recover, seek external assistance, and finally crush the uprising, Yet the need for external assistance is itself further evidence that a serious situation beyond elite control had developed. The state was able to weather the storm with assistance from the very world system which had generated the economic crisis that played such a pronounced role in weakening the established order. It provided such assistance for ideological reasons — the need for both East and West blocs to woo an important nonaligned actor.

Turning now to the events in the Tamil areas which occurred after 1971, it has been described earlier that the suppression of the JVP insurrection did not end elite efforts to forge alliances with the rural classes for electoral gain. To the contrary, the 1971 experience appears to have so frightened the state that it subsequently went out of its way to appease the subordinate classes. This was done by continuing appeals to Sinhalese chauvinism which structurally disadvantaged the Tamils. Persecuted by policies and laws which discriminated against it, the Tamil community faced its own crisis which in many respects paralleled earlier Sinhalese experiences. Such coincidence stemmed from the fact that, race aside, Tamil society mirrored its Sinhalese counterpart in its essential structural features.

At the apex of the Tamil order was a national elite set off by its Western-style education, ability to speak English, and participation in the administration and the professions. Even amidst the Sinhalese chauvinist appeals, it remained closely linked with the Sinhalese elite. Too, it was culturally distant from the Tamil masses, who were rural cultivators. In the principal Tamil center, Jaffna District of the Northern Province, were 792,246 Ceylon Tamils; the largest town, Jaffna City, Sri Lanka's fourth largest, had a population of but 118,215. Such a distribution obtained elsewhere, as well. A rural elite occupied a position analogous to the Sinhalese local *pelantiya*. The Tamil equivalent of the *mudalali* was present not only in these Tamil rural areas but also in Sinhalese-majority areas. In fact, more than a quarter of the total 1,871,535 Tamil population was located outside 'Tamil areas'. These individuals were often strategically placed in middleman roles or in small entrepreneurial activities.

Though virtually no research appears to have been done on the subject, the same forces at work in Sinhalese society, especially alienation from the land and overpopulation, were also present in Tamil areas. That they did not result immediately in similar class pressures for structural change as characterized the Sinhalese rural areas was initially due to historical circumstance. Traditionally, movement to Sinhalese-majority areas and participation in market, professional, or administrative activities had served as an escape valve. Free access to education, therefore, was especially prized and utilized to ensure such mobility.

Rising Sinhalese chauvinism severely restricted this escape mechanism. Especially damaging were quotas instituted to ensure representation in the universities in proportion to national fraction. The initial Tamil response was to work for compromise with the Sinhalese elite, with which the Tamil elite retained close ties. 'Understandings' and 'agreements' were reached, but these were never observed. Each time the Sinhalese elite faction which was out of power would appeal to Sinhalese chauvinist forces in an effort to gain political advantage by frustrating the government's designs. Tamil, for instance, was made a 'national language' in 1978, even as Sinhala remained the only 'official language'. Theoretically, some administrative and educational transactions could be carried out in either tongue. In actual practice only members of the elite could speak each other's language, and Tamil was thus rarely used, even in official functions in the capital. Likewise, a framework for local autonomy legislated under the District Development Council (DDC) concept, which in theory would have established institutions with powers capable of safeguarding parochial interests, was never fully implemented.

The result of this continuing frustration and the inability to gain viable guarantees of protection for Tamil position and culture was a tightening of Tamil solidarity and the ascendance of separatist political solutions. Still, initially, these were reminiscent of the irony in Sinhalese Marxism: radical though separatist demands might be, they were espoused by an elite which remained closely linked to the state power structure. Politicians of the Tamil United Liberation Front (TULF), for example, which demanded an independent state, nevertheless sat in Parliament and were on reasonable, even good, terms with their Sinhalese elite counterparts. Their position in favor of 'Eelam' was used far more as a bargaining chip than as an actual goal for action.

Yet once Tamil solidarity was raised as a response to Sinhalese chauvinism, Tamil chauvinism proved as difficult to control as its counterpart, particularly as it tapped the latent structural contradictions of Tamil society. In particular there was a growing body of Tamil-speaking, marginalized rural persons of some educational attainment who resented the dominant position of the English-speaking Tamil elite and saw its tactical moderation as playing into the hands of the Sinhalese state. Where the JVP was the Sinhalese radical response to marginalization, the 'Liberation Tigers' were the Tamil answer. Splinter groups of radical youth formed this body and committed themselves to Marxist revolution directed at both the Sinhalese and the existing class structure. The paramount role of Sinhalese chauvinism in sharpening Tamil structural problems by choking off traditional escape mechanisms was reflected in intense Tamil chauvinist sentiments (characteristic of the insurgent mainstream to this day).

Initially, recruitment was difficult, even amidst favorable structural conditions, because of the tremendous reservoir of conservatism in Tamil society. Cultural attributes which bolstered such an outlook were reinforced by pragmatism. As long as there was apparent communication between the Tamil and Sinhalese factions of the elite, the overwhelming majority of the Tamil community was unwilling to support with violence the goal of 'Eelam'. Such was the strength of hierarchy and deference within tradition-oriented Tamil culture that even while in armed revolt, 'the boys', as the 'young hotheads' were affectionately called, strove not to alienate their elite elders. 'The boys' made the most of their Robin Hood image and spoke of revolution; but in matters of ultimate importance, the TULF elite spoke for the Tamil community. Neither did this elite fear disruption or terror at the hands of the youthful radicals.

July 1983 changed this relationship. The sheer magnitude of the violence traumatized the Tamil community and put the lie to the elite policy of accommodation. For the first time physical survival of the entire Tamil community was perceived at risk; the state at best as either unwilling or unable to offer protection, at worst a participant in a plan for genocide. Actually, as should be clear at this point, the state was caught up in the contradictions of its 'alliance policy' and could not carry through with its promises to ensure Tamil safety precisely because of the salient role the mobilized forces of Sinhalese chauvinism had come to play in draining off revolutionary pressures. In such an environment it was predictable that a revolutionary body such as the 'Liberation Tigers' should gain ascendancy. It offered not only the organization necessary to strike out against the enemy but also the ideological framework for the explanation of the Tamil situation and a course of action to rectify the problem.

That the Sinhalese masses turned on the Tamils in July 1983 had as its proximate cause the costly ambush of the Sri Lankan Army patrol. In a larger sense, though, the explosion of nationwide anti-Tamil violence had many of the same features as the 1971 insurrection. The difference was that by 1983 Sinhalese chauvinism had directed the pent-up frustrations and passions of the masses towards the Tamils rather than against the state elite as called for by earlier leftist ideological appeals. A promised government analysis of the July 1983 events has never been completed, so conclusions must necessarily remain rather impressionistic rather than empirically grounded. Be this as it may, from eyewitness accounts of mob leadership, it can be ascertained that at least some of the same groups which supported the JVP or were allied with it in 1971 were active in anti-Tamil actions. Similarly, a trip through many damaged areas revealed that numerous spots where attacks against Tamils had been widespread had also been sources of JVP activity in 1971.[40] In Colombo known JVP members were recognized by observers at the scenes of at least several incidents.[41] Additionally, it appears that the urban counterpart of the 'proletariat in waiting' was prominent in the violence. This may be judged from those areas where Tamils were particularly subject to abuse and their property to destruction; eyewitnesses frequently reported mobs streaming out of Sinhalese slum areas.

Amidst the upheaval, the security forces were conspicuous in their absence. In some cases police and military members actually participated in the violence and looting. The elite responded to the crisis by all but vanishing. President Jayewardene was not even seen in public for nearly a week, and loyal units ringed the presidential residence. More so than was the case in 1971, the widespread unrest ended not so much due to state strength or coercion but because it was inherently limited without the presence of an ideologically-motivated, purposive body with the organization capable of seeking advantage from the chaos. The JVP had not yet been able to reconstitute itself as a viable force; and the only other well-organized revolutionary body, the 'Liberation Tigers', was neutralized by its adherence to a Tamil chauvinist orientation.

Echoes of 1971 appeared in another form. While state finances were relatively healthy at mid-year, the damage wrought to the economy in July 1983 was tremendous[42] and per chance coincided with the beginning of what has proved to be a severe drop in demand for export crops. Tea prices ultimately declined by 50 per cent; rubber and coconut remained depressed. What would have been a difficult period anyhow became a crisis as the state attempted to mobilize the resources necessary for repression of the Tamil rebellion. This at first was simply not possible, but as the situation worsened, enormous budget deficits were accepted as the price necessary for systemic survival.[43] Efforts to generate additional revenue locally led ultimately to stringent austerity measures and sharply increased prices for many staples. Most of the deficit, however, had to be financed through loans and grants from members of the world economy.

Driving the enormous increase in expenditures was the need to fashion virtually from scratch a viable force capable of conducting 'stability operations'. Suppression of the 1971 insurrection had been quite *ad hoc*; and upon completion of operations, the military was kept at a small size. The key service, the army, for example, to repeat the figures, had just 12,000 men, of whom only some 3,000 were in the five infantry battalions, the critical components for actual combat operations. Armed forces effectiveness was limited and reliability suspect, a judgement which seems to have been valid in light of military performance during July 1983. This past notwithstanding, change was required in the face of the Tamil rebellion. For drawing its strength from the unleashing of the latent forces pent up in Tamil society, the revolutionary movement proved more than a match for the armed forces and the police.

The insurgents quickly came to effectively control the north and large portions of the east.

The government was crippled in its counterinsurgency program by its inability to set forth a viable socio-economic-political solution within which stability operations could proceed. This stemmed from the fundamental structural contradictions outlined in this section. To address the insurgency adequately would have required articulation and implementation of a solution which would have eliminated Tamil grievances. These grievances, however, were a direct result of the Sinhalese chauvinism which the state had unleashed through its efforts, first, to gain allies, and, subsequently, to deflect hostility from itself. Even the smallest UNP attempts at reform were met with determined resistance from the rival SLFP, which continued to work actively to tap ubiquitous Sinhalese fears and passions. To offer statesmanlike solutions would risk redirecting class frustrations from Sinhalese chauvinism into anti-state action such as occurred in 1971.

Memories of previous insurrection and turmoil led the government to exacerbate its own defensive posture by moving gingerly in its organization of the 'loyal areas' of the country to ensure their security. This left them open to insurgent attacks. Though these were primarily Sinhalese areas racially, the government was understandably wary of providing many modern firearms to a majority community already quite split ideologically. Far greater than the risk of loss was the chance that the weapons could be ultimately turned against the security forces themselves.

The result was that the government was trapped in a situation which, in the absence of an unlikely dramatic influx of external assistance, could only deteriorate over time. This, in fact, could be seen as a logical and necessary culmination of the old-regime crisis which began after independence and steadily intensified.

Government Search for a Counterinsurgency Strategy

By mid-1985, when the Thimpu talks began, the island was in a state of serious disorder, which the security forces proved unable to alleviate. It is appropriate at such a juncture, therefore, to examine in some detail precisely what counterinsurgency strategy the government was attempting to pursue and why it was unsuccessful. Most fundamentally, the government was crippled by its inability to set forth a viable sociopolitical solution within which stability operations could proceed. Military success, therefore, even when gained, was little more than momentary tactical advantage. Hence, regardless of efforts to improve the military posture *per se*, there was little impact upon the overall poor security climate.

At first, in the months after July 1983, there were the expected thrashing about and striking out blindly by Colombo's forces as the insurgents became more active. In March 1984, though, it appeared a new approach was at hand. Oxford-educated Lalith Athulathmudali, a possible successor to President Jayewardene, was named head of the newly-created Ministry of National Security and Deputy Minister of Defense (Jayewardene himself was Defense Minister). This effectively placed control of the armed forces and counterinsurgency operations under one man. Intra-service coordination improved under a Joint Operations Center (JOC), as did military discipline and employment. Still, it was not long before it became evident that the government effort would continue to be plagued by inefficient planning, unimaginative leadership, and continuing instances of 'indiscipline'.

As the military and insurgents blooded each other, delegates from various sectors of Sri Lankan society continued talks with the relative moderates of the Tamil United Liberation Front (TULF) at an All-Party Congress (called, in the Sri Lankan predilection for initials, 'the APC') designed to seek solutions to the ethnic impasse. There were times when the antagonists appeared near agreement on some form of local autonomy which would satisfy moderate Tamil demands for 'independence' yet retain the essential national unity demanded by the Sinhalese. None of these schemes panned out, falling victim to the increasingly narrow room for maneuver which hemmed in moderates of both sides. As a unitary state, with provinces and districts run by centrally-appointed officials, Sri Lanka was unable to view even limited scenarios for the devolution of power as anything other than steps toward separatism. And any partition of 'Lanka' was out of the question.

In its particulars there was much in the mindset of the majority Sinhalese which was akin to Zionism, with all its characteristic pugnacity — and rigidity. The Buddha himself, it was taught, had chosen the island as his bastion for the survival of the faith. His religion vanished from India, the land of its birth, but in 'Lanka' it was to remain protected and nurtured. Sinhalese legendary heroes aplenty held Tamil invaders at bay that it might remain so. Thus the Sinhalese came to see themselves as a chosen people, living in a chosen land, and following the one true faith. Their missionaries revitalized decaying Buddhism near and far. By historical circumstances, the Sinhalese view went, other races and religions, notably the Hindu Tamils, had come to be incorporated into the independent state of Sri Lanka, but there was no question in the majority mind as to whose land the island truly was. Those who were not Sinhalese and Buddhist were welcome as privileged guests of sorts, fortunate enough to have been washed up on the shores of paradise and valued for their contributions; but any assault on the essential parameters of the system meant an end to the welcome. The resulting misbehavior of the armed forces, comprised of young, ill-educated, rural, Sinhalese-speaking males, was predictable.

In the absence of a well-defined socio-political approach to the Tamil problem — a strategy which would cut popular support out from under the Marxists — the government's counterinsurgency program rapidly became little more than an attempted exercise in human and organizational architecture. Lalith stated in an August 1984 interview[44] that improvement in the tactical situation was to take place within a strategic framework which had as its objective the isolation of the insurgents in Jaffna through Sinhalese settlement in the non-Jaffna areas of the insurgents' claimed 'Eelam'. This would be carried out using existing government resettlement schemes, a part of the massive Mahaweli Development Programme, to create an equal mixture of ethnic groups — Tamil, Muslim, and Sinhalese — in areas such as Trincomalee and Batticaloa Districts, then with Tamil-Muslim majorities. The stated rationale was that in areas of mixed population there would be a minimum of ethnic conflict and radicalization, because the people would tend 'to get along'. The likelihood that such a scheme would almost certainly be the subject of attack necessitated some form of 'home guard', but that was to be left until later.

Completion of such settlement was envisaged for 1986–88, at which time the insurgents would be effectively isolated demographically in Jaffna. They would have no appeal elsewhere. In Jaffna, Lalith noted, a 'heats and minds' approach was futile, as the cancer had already taken root. A solution could only come when a new generation of Tamil leaders emerged within an environment where it had been clearly demonstrated that the government could not be beaten. This might, he concluded, necessitate a willingness to accept a 'Northern Ireland' for the following 15–20 years. It was the Minister's expectation that Tamils of talent and ability who did not sympathize with the insurgents would leave the Jaffna area.

In some respects this approach was sound. It was based on a correct realization that the problem had two dimensions: legitimate Tamil demands for redress of their grievances, on the one hand, and utilization of those grievances as a vehicle for an illegitimate assault upon the integrity of the state by communist insurgents, on the other. Through the events of July 1983 and the abuse of civilians which had transpired since, a large proportion of the Tamil population had become insurgent sympathizers, particularly in Jaffna. Unable to make headway in impeding the growth of insurgent influence there, and faced with insurgent attempts to expand into marginally-affected, Tamil-populated areas elsewhere, the logical course of action was to isolate the rebels.

This attempt at human engineering, of course, was doomed to failure, because it turned reality on its head. It was based on the premise that if only the insurgents themselves could be controlled, isolated, and eliminated, the majority of the Tamil people would be freed from the grip of fear and free to negotiate with the government in good faith. Yet the Tamil people, speaking generally while allowing for individual exceptions, had not become supporters of the insurgents through guerrilla terror. Rather, they had been driven to the rebels by the government's failure to reach an equitable political solution and by its failure to protect them from the abuse of both some elements of the security forces and unruly Sinhalese mobs.

Within such a mindframe, the means soon became the ends. Increasingly, the Sri Lankan effort focused on the mechanical aspects of small unit warfare. Even these were carried out badly. Factions within the government, as well as key military officers, were aware of this critical shortfall but seemed unable to influence policy decisions. It was as though paralysis had set in at every level of Sri Lankan decision making, beginning with President Jayewardene. The most commonly offered rationale for the lack of movement toward a political solution, fear of a Sinhalese backlash, while not a straw man by any means, eventually became an excuse for inaction and reflected the general institutional paralysis.

As the insurgent threat spilled out of Jaffna, the government met it with *ad hoc*, haphazard schemes. Both privately and publicly, Colombo's spokesmen talked not of the need to solve the various dimensions of the ethnic problem, but of their 'fight against *terrorism*'. This shift in perspective was to be of fundamental import.

Focused on *terrorism* rather than *insurgency*, Colombo ordered its military leaders to go after the guerrillas and to stamp out the rebellion. But there was little movement toward a political accommodation which would have isolated the guerrilla hardcore and the insurgent leadership. Hence, while the security forces were battling the insurgents themselves, there was essentially no effort being put into the critical task of cutting them off from their support and infrastructure. Indeed, as the insurgents *mobilized* the target population, the government could not engage in *countermobilization*, because it had no theme or plan about which such action could be based.

In the absence of sociopolitical guidance, the counterinsurgency effort had by mid-1985 degenerated into a series of ill-planned uncoordinated efforts. Principal areas of weakness were:
● Unity of effort had not been established, despite the creation of the Ministry of National Security headed by Lalith. There was no effective use of the Cabinet itself for planning. In the Joint Operations Center (which had under it District Coordinating Officers) management by exception appeared to be the rule. Even in the absence of an overall policy, which was certainly cause enough for a lack of coordination, misguided policies continually split the counterinsurgency effort still further. An excellent illustration was provided by a May 1985 plan to place all Members of Parliament (MPs) in charge of the counterinsurgency campaigns in their electoral districts by giving them 'Presidential Powers'. As electoral districts did not coincide with administrative districts, this would have created some 168 separate counterinsurgency campaigns. Later modification of the proposal in late May — so that the District Development Council Executive Committees, which included the MPs, would perform the appropriate tasks — reduced substantially the fragmentation (Sri Lankan government publications listed the number of administrative districts as either 24 or 25). Yet the problem of disunity of effort remained.
● The loyal areas of the country had not been organized to ensure their security. The few steps taken had been insufficient and ineffective, leaving the Sinhalese heartland open to guerrilla raids, as well as to leftist Sinhalese subversion. Once a Home Guard was

formed, its structure, supervision, and training were inadequate. The reported practice of authorizing each MP to recruit 1,000 armed personnel was a further fragmentation of effort and risked the establishment of semiofficial vigilante groups and private armies.

● Colombo had attempted to hold the entire country, rather than securing its own 'base areas' in the Sinhalese areas and then moving out in a territorial offense to regain contested areas (the 'oil spot' strategy). Police and troop strengths were inadequate for such an 'all or nothing' approach. The result had been the effective neutralization of the security forces in defensive cantonments. Police huddled in their stations; the military could move about only in strength.

● The demoralizing and debilitating effects of this malemployment could have been minimized — and perhaps turned to some value — if the security forces had utilized mobile operations as necessary for the successful prosecution of counterguerrilla warfare. This was not done. Operations took the principal form of daylight, motorized road patrols or raids rather than small unit, round-the-clock, off-road patrols and ambushes conducted for the purpose of dominating and securing target areas. The consequent fragmented deployment posture produced minimal results, with security force casualties relatively high due to attended and unattended mine ambushes.

● Civic action or other work with the populace had played no role in the campaign, as the security forces had been preoccupied with purely military countermeasures. This shortcoming showed itself in more than the failure to administer to the needs and latent loyalties of the people. It raised its head in the basic operating assumption that the human environment was hostile and to be treated as such. This missed the point that the population in the insurgent environment — and the Tamils were no exception in Sri Lanka — was essentially neutral. It sought, above all, security. Protection from both troop indiscipline and mob attacks would have guaranteed the tacit loyalty of most. Safeguarding them from insurgent reprisals would have led to their nonparticipation in guerrilla support mechanisms. That the security forces were unable to adopt such a methodology had much to do with their orientation toward personal survival rather than on service and mission.

● In a further failing which greatly affected the populace, no regroupment program had been instituted. Instead, many villagers

had been summarily ordered or driven out of declared and undeclared 'no go' areas with little or no provision for alternate livelihood or habitat. Many such persons entered refugee camps, but many others fled to India or elsewhere. An unknown number joined the guerrillas.
• Related to this factor, forbidden zones had been declared and peoples' lives had been disrupted without the employment of adequate human or material resources needed to make such measures effective. Thus the government had been left with the negative consequences of such actions while it reaped few, if any, of the intended benefits. No systematic effort had been used actually to clear and hold the zones. Population and resources control
measures had been haphazardly and irregularly enforced, creating considerable hardship without an accompanying campaign to ameliorate the pain and to insure fairness of burden. Neither had an effective psychological warfare campaign pointed out clearly the ultimate responsibility of the insurgents for the deprivation. Consequently, more often than not, the security forces themselves were seen as the source of dislocation, rather than the insurgency or the guerrillas.
• Finally, the security forces were frequently ineffective, because they did not move, even after the initiation of widespread hostilities, to bring Tamils and other non-Sinhalese into their ranks. The police were in better shape in this respect than the military, but both were essentially attempting to fight in an alien environment. The most common reason given in interviews (for the few Tamils in the military) was that they were incapable of passing the entrance examinations — which, it should be noted, were in Sinhalese! Such a mindframe extended to the failure to utilize pseudogangs ('turning' surrendered or captured guerrillas back against their former comrades) or even local guides during operations. Inevitably, the security forces remained completely cut off from the human environment in which they operated.

The International Situation and the Role of India[45]

Still, the government position was made immeasurably more difficult by the ability of the insurgents to operate from base areas located in the sanctuary of India's southern state of Tamil Nadu. That democractic India should be involved with Marxist insurgents attempting to overthrow a democratic neighbor was on the surface a paradox but not altogether unexpected given the regional imperialism which had been an essential driving force of New Delhi's foreign policy since independence. The close ties India enjoyed with the Soviet Union were well known, even while the nation looked to the West for cultural approval. Ironically, it was Sri Lanka's pro-Western orientation which played a crucial role in the development of India's succor for the insurgents.

Sitting astride key sea routes, Sri Lanka's geostrategic position had long been recognized. Britain used it as a locus for domination of the Indian Ocean. The port which was the headquarters of this effort, Trincomalee on the eastern coast, was one of the finest natural harbors in the world (and had an oil storage area of some 100 finely preserved tanks left by the British). There was also a functioning airfield.

Of primary attraction to the West, though, had been Sri Lanka's democratic institutions and its eventual commitment to market mechanisms — despite the formal title 'Socialist State of Sri Lanka' adopted by an SLFP government. After President Jayewardene's United National Party (UNP) assumed office in 1977 following a landslide victory, the country was regarded as something of a showcase of Third World self-development. Western aid donors became actively involved in major infrastructure projects. Not surprisingly, in its foreign policies Colombo was supportive of Western interests, and in the Non-Aligned Movement (NAM) it was consistently a voice of moderation.

Such a posture did not sit well with New Delhi, which prided itself on its own 'nonaligned' position even while maintaining extensive military, economic, and diplomatic links with Moscow. Highly classified Indian documents — which surfaced after a group of clerks at the very center of the Indian government decided to up their salaries by selling photostat copies to all takers — revealed an inordinate fear among India's top policymakers at 'encirclement' by the United States. As reflected in the thinking of the late Indian Prime Minister Indira Gandhi, Washington was judged to be engaged in a strategic design to sandwich India between China, one the one hand, and the smaller pro-Western states of Pakistan, Sri Lanka, and Bangladesh, on the other. Most alarming to the Indians was their conviction that Jayewardene planned to grant American military forces base rights in Trincomalee. This, New Delhi stated publicly and privately, would pose an unacceptable threat to Indian national security.

In reality neither Washington nor Colombo appears to have ever discussed a military base in Trincomalee, though the Sri Lankans were keenly interested in the commercial development of the port's oil tank farm and, in fact, called for joint venture bids to accomplish this. That American firms were favored by Sri Lanka was held up by India as further proof of menacing US intentions. Placed within the context of bitterly resented American ties with Pakistan and Washington's warming relations with Bangladesh, New Delhi was sure it had spied out a looming threat. Sri Lanka was to pay the price.

To gain better intelligence on developments concerning Trincomalee, Indira Gandhi agreed to a plan by the Indian equivalent of the CIA, the Research and Analysis Wing (RAW), to establish links with some of the then-small Tamil guerrilla groups operating in the Sri Lankan north. Communal strife had been a growing problem to the Colombo government, and RAW chose to portray the groups it contacted as but manifestations of the Tamil reaction to such conflict. Hence as early as May 1982, interrogations of the captured guerrillas involved demonstrated, RAW became involved in a program of training Tamil guerrillas in sabotage and intelligence gathering, especially techniques for reporting back on ship movements and Western port calls at Trincomalee.

Two of the small Marxist 'liberation movements' were the initial recipients of Indian largess: PLOT and TELO. Breakaway groups from the 'Liberation Tigers', both were at the time in contact with the remnants of the *Janata Vimukthi Peramuna* (JVP). When the Indians arrived with their offer of training and assistance, the Tamil groups and the JVP remnants were actively attempting to organize their 'people's war' to bring down the Colombo government to install allied Tamil and Sinhalese communist governments.

This orientation was shared by all of the major Tamil insurgent groups, though only PLOT and TELO seem to have maintained extensive links with Sinhalese insurgents at so early a date. World public opinion subsequently was led by insurgent calls for an independent Tamil state, 'Tamil Eelam', to think of the guerrillas as ethnic separatists. Separatists did indeed, as noted above, come to provide a large proportion of guerrilla manpower, but the Marxist-Leninist orientation and goals of the insurgent groups had never wavered.

The Research and Analysis Wing (RAW) ignored this reality to the detriment of its original aims. RAW's training, in any case, judging by the descriptions given by captured guerrillas who went through it, was by the book and more appropriate to commandos of the Indian services than to active insurgents. There was, for instance, heavy attention paid to the sabotage of bridges and fixed-point targets.

Rather than using their newly-acquired skills to ascertain ship movements or watch Sri Lankan troop dispositions — this information to be sent to India using invisible writing — the guerrillas moved back into their insurgent groups. There, they became instructors. They were joined by compatriots who had received similar training from international terrorists, initially the Palestine Liberation Organisation (PLO), later from a whole array of groups, to include, they claimed, the Irish Republican Army (IRA) and African National Congress (ANC). Libya also appears to have become involved, as judged by the story of at least one insurgent later taken prisoner.

Not all the major Tamil insurgent groups had relations with Indian intelligence at this time, but the situation changed following the July 1983 communal rioting. As the only organized Tamil armed force available, the guerrillas were able to assume the role of 'protectors' of the Tamil community. Dozens of non-Marxist, loosely organized separatist groups were brought into the communist fold through persuasion or coercion. Guided by a new set of instructions, RAW became involved with the other groups not already under its tutelage. So, too, did the other major Indian intelligence agency, the Intelligence Bureau (IB, also called the NIB, or National Intelligence Bureau), together with several of the many Indian paramilitary forces. The Indo-Tibetan Border Force, for example, conducted guerrilla training in the Indian north.

New Delhi's logic was again remarkably flawed. Faced with an anticipated tough parliamentary election in December 1983, Indira Gandhi badly needed the support of Tamil Nadu's 50 million Tamils, one of the country's largest electoral blocs. Tamil Nadu itself had been formed earlier to defuse growing Tamil nationalism in India. Thus Indira acceded to demands that she give the Sri Lankan Tamils a 'self-defense' capability and ordered the dramatic expansion of Indian covert involvement with them. Additionally, she hoped thereby to stem a growing tide of Tamil refugees, already numbering 100,000, which was streaming across the narrow Palk Strait, the 20 miles which separated the two countries.

More fundamental to her calculations, though, were the same geopolitical considerations which had prompted the original involvement with the guerrillas. That is, Indira was piqued at President Junius R. Jayewardene's abandonment of the 'non-aligned' stance of his predecessor — Mrs Sirimavo Bandaranaike, a close personal friend of the Indian leader — in favor of his more pro-Western posture. Seeing a chance to resolve the problem under the guise of humanitarian concerns, and reap domestic political benefit in the bargain, Gandhi ordered a separate program quite apart from the training of the Tamil guerrillas being conducted in Tamil Nadu. This was nothing less than the formation of an invasion force for a 'Bengali solution', the use — as had been done in the creation of Bangladesh — of Indian-trained indigenous personnel for an invasion which would be accompanied by Indian forces posing as guerrillas themselves. The training for these guerrillas was conducted in northern India, especially at Indian Army camps located in the state of Uttar Pradesh and along the Indo-Pakistani border, and was supervised by regular Indian military personnel. In contrast, guerrilla training at the Tamil Nadu camps, besides being much more politically oriented, was supervised by RAW operatives and active and retired soldiers seconded to the intelligence services.

Diplomatic pressures from the US and Britain combined with what seemed to be a less pressing situation in Sri Lanka during early 1984 to cause a postponement of Indian invasion plans. Yet by this stage the Indian training effort had taken on a life of its own and continued to operate based upon the domestic reasons cited above. At first limited to instruction, this continuing program in Tamil Nadu eventually included provision of weapons and equipment. With such assistance the guerrillas were soon able to gain the upper hand in some areas of the country over the security forces. As the inexperienced troops reacted with brutality, throwing up still more recruits to the guerrillas, the latter skillfully stage-managed their campaigns as ones for Tamil independence rather than for a Marxist-Leninist state — an aim they continued to espouse in their own documents, in the political classes given to all new recruits, and even in interviews with anyone who took the trouble to meet with them in their Tamil Nadu headquarters.

As the conflict grew in scope and intensity, Colombo turned to foreign sources as mentioned previously. Israel and Britain were not the only places Sri Lanka sought assistance. America, for instance, provided important foreign aid and increasingly was drawn, with Britain, into active diplomatic support for Sri Lanka in its often bitter exchanges with India. Pakistan and Saudi Arabia helped to obtain arms, with Islamabad becoming involved in training Sri Lankan security personnel and home guards at sites in Pakistan itself. China became a prime source of small arms and equipment, as did Singapore and Belgium. South African armored vehicles were obtained.

Thus in the end, India's encouragement and succor of the insurgents led to precisely the result it so feared — a Sri Lanka heavily involved not only with extra-regional forces but also with New Delhi's chief regional rivals, Pakistan and China. For their part, the other states of South Asia saw India's role in the Sri Lankan affair as but further evidence of New Delhi's hypocritical regional imperialism and so gave what assistance they could.

Rajiv Gandhi, once in power following the assassination of his mother in October 1984, at first moved rapidly to right the situation. His own burgeoning Sikh problem, similar in many ways to the Tamil disquiet in Sri Lanka, gave added impetus to his initial decision to distance New Delhi from its erstwhile guerrilla friends. Indian covert assistance was scaled back; arms shipments were seized (one PLOT container intercepted in Madras contained arms and munitions valued at US $4 million); and naval patrols began to intercept guerrilla boats attempting to cross the Palk Strait. Finally, after a series of Jayewardene-Gandhi meetings, New Delhi forced the insurgents to enter into the 'cessation of hostilities', announced 18 June 1985, and to appear at the face-to-face talks with the Sri Lankans held in Thimpu. When the insurgents balked, India closed down the ENLF's major base areas and forced their temporary relocation to Sri Lanka itself. PLOT saw the sea-change coming and was able to save its camps by cooperating.

Five months later, however, the Indian government had again changed its tune. The ceasefire had never really taken hold, and violence was again general. The Thimpu talks had collapsed in the face of irreconcilable positions, the guerrillas sticking to their demand for 'Eelam', the government opting for increased local autonomy. Though New Delhi had upped its profile and finally become a direct participant in the discussions, it was unable to influence the outcome. For its troubles, it paid a high domestic price, as an upsurge of Dravidian nationalism led to massive protests in Tamil Nadu and challenges to 'Hindi authority'.

When President Jayewardene told the influential *India Today* in November 1985 that he saw no option to 'decisive military action', Rajiv decided to cut his losses. While continuing to express his desire for a diplomatic solution and to send representatives to Colombo for talks, the Indian leader apparently turned the actual handling of the situation back to the same subordinates who had been active throughout the conflict. They proceeded to harangue Colombo at every turn on the need to negotiate with the guerrillas. That there realistically could be no middle ground between the positions of Sri Lanka, as a sovereign state, and the insurgents, as communist rebels demanding not only independence but delivery from the evils of capitalism, was ignored. In actions and words, New Delhi's stance moved back toward the unproductive policy of Indira Gandhi. The guerrillas were again allowed to operate virtually unhindered. Indian customs officers even checked them in and out of the country. If heavy weapons were needed for special operations, they were obtained on hand receipt from the Indian military.

The results were the same: strained relations with Colombo and greater Sri Lankan determination to avail themselves of all possible sources of aid. Israel, for example, even began to fit Sri Lankan security force amputees with artificial limbs. When New Delhi learned of Colombo's use of foreign pilots for training and administrative flights, it warned again against external involvement in the conflict. From Colombo's perspective, a more disingenuous position would have been hard to imagine.

Continuing Developments

Violence was again general by December 1985. Indeed, from the standpoint of the government position, the hiatus had been disastrous. While major government and insurgent military formations for the most part avoided attacking each other, even as both went about their normal activities, troops in key areas such as Jaffna were confined to their cantonments. This allowed the guerrillas to make major shifts in their deployment, especially to move men and material from the north to the east of Sri Lanka, as well as to ferry resupplies across the Palk Strait from India.

In such an environment the insurgents were able to use their clandestine infrastructure effectively to coerce obedience from the passive Jaffna majority. Continued terror killings and assassinations in broad daylight brought home to the populace that there was little hope in resisting the new insurgent regime. Any signs by Tamil moderates of accommodation with the government were met with violence. Among those struck down were prominent TULF politicians.

For its part the government was willing to accede to the temporary loss of Jaffna for two reasons. Foremost was the need to placate the Indians, who, regardless of the situation on the ground, insisted that maintaining the ceasefire was of paramount importance. This continued to be New Delhi's position, for minimal activity by the Sri Lankan security forces served the larger purpose of keeping the lid on political tempers in the Indian south. Alleged incidents of murder and destruction were crucial in whipping up Tamil Nadu support for the insurgents and thereby creating pressures on New Delhi for a harsh line against Colombo. This occurred even as the military operations concerned were ineffective in reestablishing government control. Though Colombo doubtless did not agree with the Indian logic that no operations were at that point better than those which were being carried out, it bowed to the paramount need of maintaining at least a modicum of official Indian support. Such 'support', of course, was rapidly becoming of dubious value.

The bitter pill of territorial alienation was made easier to swallow because a holding action in Jaffna was in Sri Lanka's military interests. Increasingly, security forces in the north had become isolated and ineffective for conducting viable stability operations. Additionally, as the locus of conflict had spread elsewhere to more important regions, especially the Eastern Province, the continued attempt to garrison Jaffna tied down valuable men and resources in an ineffective strategic posture.

Had the government used these reasons as motivation for staying put in Jaffna while turning its focus elsewhere to more vital areas, there would have been some benefit derived from adversity. Instead, a lack of strategic vision led to the squandering of scarce resources in an uncoordinated response to widely dispersed guerrilla attacks. New personalities were brought into play — such as the appointment as Joint Operations Commander of Lieutenant General Cyril Ranatunga — but these had no impact upon the conduct of the counterinsurgency campaign. Troops were scattered in defensive positions, generally of such limited strength as to make only the holding of their own fortifications possible. There was little attempt at the conduct of stability operations and no use of the classic 'oil spot' technique for the systematic seizure and domination of target areas.

In particular the government effort was hamstrung by the failure of political leaders to set forth clearly a proposed political solution — a goal toward which military operations could be directed. Success in the field, therefore, while not altogether uncommon, was not directed toward the accomplishment of any strategic purpose and thus was largely meaningless. It remained the case that in any given encounter the security forces, if able to effect reinforcement, could still concentrate superior combat power and use it competently enough to deal the insurgents a setback. This became even more the case as weapons and material purchases continued to augment the force structure. The increased presence and use of helicopters and fixed wing support aircraft, for example, made an impact upon the tactical situation. Regardless, such military improvements were only temporary and were not accompanied by enhancement of the general security climate. In fact, as 1986 progressed, the government lost ground in the principal areas of conflict.[46]

Jaffna was completely under the control of the insurgents, who reorganized it into a large base area from which to strike elsewhere; while the situation in other Tamil areas such as Mannar, Vavuniya, Mullaittivu, and Trincomalee was rapidly becoming as bad. Large stretches of these latter districts were under insurgent sway. The once placid Hill Country, where the Indian Tamils were concentrated, was the target of insurgent infiltration and was hit by widespread violence. Elsewhere in the south, evidence was uncovered of revitalized links between the guerrillas and Sinhalese radical elements. Several instances of joint operations came to light, as did the sharing of arms and intelligence.

These insurgent gains occurred even as the divisions within the guerrilla movement and the Tamil community itself became more apparent. In particular, it was clear that the Jaffna Tamils (i.e., those Ceylon Tamils who originated in Jaffna) were the driving force of the insurgency and were in many respects resented by other Tamil communities. In areas of the Eastern Province, for instance, Tamils cooperated with the security forces as soon as troop indiscipline was brought under control and a modicum of personal security guaranteed. Similarly, regardless of the troubles, the majority of the Indian Tamils remained loyal, an orientation further solidified by the granting of citizenship to all who had chosen to remain on the island rather than be repatriated to India (which most pointedly declined). Perhaps most significantly, the Muslims, Moors who linguistically would have been classified as Tamil, were firmly in the government camp, with increasing numbers enrolled in the Home Guard and some specialized branches of the security forces.

Divisions also became more apparent in the habitually divided guerrilla movement. During April and May 1986 LTTE turned on TELO and slaughtered an estimated several hundred of its combatants in Jaffna. Some were burnt alive after surrendering. Subsequently, LTTE announced that it was pulling out of the ENLF 'temporarily' — and simultaneously sent several of its members to 'surrender' and provide the security forces with the locations of its rivals' camps in Sri Lanka.

That such disunity of both guerrilla forces and the Tamil community did not result in government gains was ample testimony to the ineffectual nature of Colombo's approach. Its failure to adopt a strategy for victory appeared to stem in the main from its preoccupation with Sinhalese sentiment. This was understandable given the threads of continuity which had ran through Sri Lankan politics since independence, especially the rising tide of Sinhalese chauvinism that all major Sinhalese political parties attempted to channel to their electoral benefit. And despite its overwhelming parliamentary majority, the ruling United National Party (UNP) was keenly aware that its dominant position was largely due to electoral mechanics (i.e., winner-take-all voting districts) rather than actual popular dominance. In the most recent national elections (1982 and 1983), the electorate, in fact, had been fairly evenly split.

Faced with such a situation, where a strong opposition was working actively to tap ubiquitous Sinhalese fears and passions, the UNP opted for a path of short-term political expediency and seeming safety. It sought to wear down the insurgents militarily while placing its faith in the ability of Indian pressure — to be exerted sometime in the future, when it is assumed that New Delhi would realize the self-destructive folly of backing the insurgents, whether one saw them as separatists or communist guerrillas — to force insurgent acceptance of a modified status quo short of their goals.

While possible in the short-term, such a strategy had little chance of long-term success, for it guaranteed that the conflict would remain open-ended, a posture Colombo could not sustain economically or politically. Economically, the 1986 budget contained an estimated deficit of Rs. 26,986 million (US $983.1 million) against expenditures of Rs. 67,800 million (US $2.47 billion). The Ministry of Defence alone was slated to spend 70 per cent over its 1985 *budgeted* amount, or Rs. 562.6 million (US $212.8 million). These massive outlays, which were beyond the capacity of the economy to endure for long, were heavily dependent upon foreign grants and loans. Politically, an effective insurgent international propaganda apparatus had so impainted the image of the struggle as one for communal justice that Sri Lanka found itself diplomatically on the defensive. Colombo became increasingly isolated from possible sources of material and diplomatic assistance. Major friendly powers, such as the US and Britain, declined to become more committed to a situation which could only result in a worsening of their relations with India. Neither had they or other nations shown any willingness to move against the expatriate funding which had been the major source of insurgent finances. The result was that Sri Lanka had to proceed alone.

By any measure the situation in the country was serious. Plagued by its own lack of coordination and its inefficiency, the effort to restore stability had ceded the initiative to the insurgents. World opinion remained focused on the communal aspects of the struggle. The more fundamental aspects of their conflict — the Marxist-Leninist ideology of the insurgents and their ability to utilize perceived and real Tamil grievances to further their own cause for 'liberation'; the growing brutality of the guerrillas against not only Sinhalese but also all Tamils who opposed them; and the role of India in the development of the conflict — were largely overlooked. It seemed inevitable, then, that in the immediate future the conflict would continue to escalate. Whether it would reach a crisis stage depended upon reform in the government counterinsurgency program. The situation was by no means irretrievable, but bad could only become worse the longer the government failed to arrive at a political strategy for dealing with the roots of insurgency. Without such a framework, military measures could have little positive impact toward the restoration of stability.

From Bad to Worse: India Intervenes[47]

Government response during 1983–86, then, did not address the problem as one of insurgency. Security forces were committed to crushing the 'rebellion' without an overall plan for their employment having ever been formulated. Such a plan, of necessity, should have been socio-economic-political in nature and designed to address the grievances of the insurgent mass base. This would have driven a wedge between the leadership, the real militants, and their followers. The major focus of security force measures should have been to further the implementation/realization of such a plan. Military measures, in other words, could only have been viable if used to further a political solution.

India's analysis of the situation was correct in one sense — it recognized the need for a 'political solution' — but, more seriously, incorrect — in that it was predicated upon an inaccurate determination of what constituted 'Eelam' for the terrorist-cum-insurgent movements. India's actions did not 'cause' the troubles but did make them far worse than they would have been had the two parties involved, the government and the insurgents, been forced to deal with each other in relative isolation.

In the main, New Delhi seemed at a loss as to how to control the creature it had nurtured. The guerrillas, after all, were only of value in the geopolitical chess game if they could be used to pressure the Sri Lankan government into a recognition of India's paramount position in the region. If they refused to play their role, they were expendable. Likewise, the geopolitical effort would come to naught if, as appeared increasingly likely in the early months of 1987, Sri Lanka proved capable of taking the match by a knockout. A victorious Sri Lanka, particularly one which had achieved the win despite the extensive Indian covert operation, would be in no mood to pay homage to New Delhi's concerns.

Even as Indian diplomats deprecated the capabilities of the Sri Lankan military — and the situation seemed bleak — that force rebuilt and moved to wreck the Indian geopolitical framework. Though they did not put together the necessary campaign plan for ending the insurgency, the Sri Lankans did finally come up with an approach for the *military* domination of insurgent-affected areas. After first securing the lower half of the Eastern Province in early 1986, the security forces next drove the guerrillas from the strategic Tincomalee port vicinity by the end of the year. In February

1987 the Mannar area, on Sri Lanka's north-western coast, was tackled. The critical action involved the seizure of the principal insurgent base camp by forces under the command of Major Gabriel Mohan Rockwood, an officer of mixed Sinhalese and Tamil descent, fluent in both languages.

Recapturing the Mannar region allowed a vise to be applied to the central districts between it and Trincomalee. These were pacified, leaving only the Jaffna peninsula itself as a location of major insurgent concentrations. As a built-up area, its seizure was bound to be costly. The green light came when a rash of insurgent outrages occurred in April 1987, including bombings in Colombo and the massacre of Buddhist monks in the east. President Jayewardene responded by ordering the all-out 'Liberation I' offensive in May. By this time internecine fighting within the guerrilla movement had left the LTTE as the dominant group. As noted previously, they were more militarily oriented than their rivals and drew inspiration from the suicide tactics of the Middle Eastern terrorists. Thus they wore cyanide capsules around their necks and fought tenaciously in defense of what they termed their 'sacred soil'. Security force casualties were heavy, with nearly 100 men falling in the first day alone.

Nevertheless, the plan of attack was well thought out. A feint convinced the insurgents that a *coup de main* would be attempted against Jaffna City itself, so the Tigers concentrated their forces there. They were unprepared for the two-brigade thrust which went instead to secure the remainder of the Jaffna peninsula. The security force offensive was successful, and Jaffna City dangled like a ripe fruit. 'Liberation II' was set to follow in June. Its goal was to surround the city, placing the guerrillas in a stranglehold.

At this point India could take no more. New Delhi first threatened Colombo in an effort to curtail security force operations, then took the dramatic step of airdropping 'relief supplies' to the purportedly beleaguered population of Jaffna. That Sri Lanka could mount no effective response to a direct Indian intervention seems to have brought home to Colombo its difficult position. When Western diplomats informed the Sri Lankan government that no direct help would be forthcoming, the pro-Western group in Colombo was overshadowed by the position of a pro-Indian cabal. In the weeks that followed, intensive discussions were held with the Indian High Commission in the Sri Lankan capital; and, for the first time, Indian observers were allowed to venture into the Tamil regions to ascertain the situation for themselves.

Ultimately, a bargain was struck and signed on 29 July 1987. To defuse Tamil demands for 'Eelam', Colombo agreed to grant autonomy to a de facto Tamil state created by linking the Northern and Eastern Provinces. In return, the Indians agreed to end their support for the insurgents and to police the accord. Most important to India, though, as spelled out explicitly in the annex and exchange of letters accompanying the main body of the treaty, was Colombo's agreement to recognize that on certain actions it must consult with New Delhi. Among these were the use of Trincomalee by foreign warships and the construction of a 'Voice of America' station north of Colombo (which New Delhi feared would be a signals intelligence site).

Consequently, India's own version of the American 'Monroe Doctrine', referred to by area scholars as the 'Indira Doctrine', after the late Indian prime minister, seemingly had a victory. Within hours Indian troops began to land in Jaffna on 30 July 1987 as Sri Lankan forces were confined to barracks. Around the world the accord was hailed as a bold move by two statesmen bent on bringing peace to their region.

Many motives may have been involved, but a desire for 'peace' was certainly not a premier one. The accord grew out of power politics. Hence, from the beginning, its implementation was troubled. There were simply too many conflicts regarding the meaning of the treaty's provisions.

For the Indian military, the ambiguity extended to its role. The 52nd Infantry Division deployed its three brigades in combat array, complete with Soviet-made BMP-1 armored fighting vehicles. Yet after a few tense confrontations, positions were taken up uneventfully and bivouacs reverted to a virtual peacetime posture. Most of the action was confined to closed-door meetings between Indian liaison officers and insurgent leaders. Reporters who had flown in specially for the anticipated show were able to get some good photographs, then drifted back to their regular beats. They missed an interesting episode.

Indian arrogance at first was overwhelming. When not strutting, they were obsessed with fears that they might look incompetent. With several notable exceptions, the Indian officer corps simply did not appreciate the realities of the conflict. The universal attitude was one of contempt for the Sri Lankan security forces, which came from the fact that the struggle had dragged on as long as it had against 'lightweight' guerrilla opposition. More observant commanders demurred, though always privately. They had noted, they said, the fitness of the Sri Lankan troops, their excellent equipment and good training. Clearly, they had become — were — a capable force. It followed that their opponents must be substantial fighters. More ominous, they observed, was the obvious extent of the insurgent arsenal.

As the Indians struggled to come to grips with the situation, the Sri Lankans promptly kept up their end of the deal by releasing the first batches of prisoners they held and by returning to their cantonments. Soon they were deploying to the south, where opposition to the accord erupted into widespread violence. Yet the insurgents were unwilling to comply with the treaty provision that stipulated that all their weapons were to be surrendered within 72 hours. The insurgent leaders had acquiesced in the agreement only under duress and the certainty that the Indians would move against them if they did not. Still, they did not trust the Sri Lankans, and they certainly did not trust each other. LTTE, in particular, had ample grounds to fear for its physical security once disarmed, since its combatants had regularly slaughtered their rivals throughout the conflict.

The days wore on, and several much-publicized 'handovers' from 4 August produced only a fraction of the known arsenals of the various groups. Heated discussions occurred. LTTE, as the dominant group, was the key, but it was the least willing to compromise. It behaved as though it had won a victory of sorts and daily increased its demands. Yet the linchpin of the accord, if it were to work at all, was compromise. Everyone had to give up something he could not: The Tamils had to opt for 'autonomy' rather than independence, for participation in parliamentary democracy rather than a 'socialist' state; the government had to accept the same autonomy it had often sworn never to allow and to face the wrath of its own people for its alleged 'sellout'; and the Indians had to accept that they could not gain their geopolitical goals in the face of determined Sri Lankan opposition. New Delhi recognized that while it could surely seize Sri Lanka, it could not hold it, any more than the British had been able to hold an India determined to see them go.

Groups other than the LTTE proved more prepared to adjust to these new circumstances. This was because, though all were Marxist and had developed Leninist infrastructures of sorts, the

Tiger organization remained the most militarily oriented. That is, since the other groups had ultimately followed the doctrinal approach of forming political movements which commanded armed forces, shelving military plans did not rob their liberation campaigns of their vitality. They merely prepared to revert to political organizing. The Tigers, in contrast, saw all things as coming from their fighters. Their political movement was decidedly secondary to armed struggle — and their manpower showed it. Drawn principally from young, low caste youths of limited education, the Tiger formations reveled in machismo. Video-cassette recorders showed 'Rambo' non-stop, and eager youths talked endlessly of guns. For them, weapons had become their route to upward social mobility. They were hesitant to give them up, for they stood to lose the most from peace and a return to the normal selection procedures of Sri Lankan society.

While the Tigers sought to circumvent the agreement, the other insurgent groups watched uneasily. Allied with LTTE in wary partnership was EROS. Opposed to this alliance was the 'Three Star Group' of PLOT, EPRLF, and TELO. The concern of this latter alliance, and even of EROS, was that it would be tarred by whatever fallout was sure to follow from LTTE intransigence. Like true Marxists, they saw opportunity in what one insurgent leader called 'the new realities of our situation'. In the Tiger approach, they sensed disaster.

Finally, the chickens came home to roost when the Tigers decided to force the issue. A group of detained LTTE members, led by the Jaffna commander, Kumarappa, swallowed their suicide capsules as they were being prepared for transport to Colombo, where they were to stand trial for violating the agreement. Their deaths prompted an orgy of bloodletting. As Indian peacekeeping forces stood by, the Tigers massacred more than 200 Sinhalese villagers in the east.

An outraged Jayewardene penned off a quick note which instructed the Indians either to serve in their role as peacekeepers or depart the country. To ensure that the point was made, the order was leaked to the Sri Lankan press, which had been heavily censored since the accord to ensure that nothing 'disruptive' was said.[48] Visits by the Indian defense minister and chief of army staff quickly followed, as did subsequent orders to take whatever actions were necessary to carry out the provisions of the accord.

When the Tigers refused to give up their arms, the Indians

attacked on 10 October 1987. They quickly learned what their more observant officers and the Sri Lankan security forces had already noted — the insurgents were a tough lot. Faced with determined resistance, New Delhi was forced rapidly to increase its on-island strength from an estimated 10,000 to close to 30,000. Elite units such as the Gurkhas and the Parachute Regiment were thrown into the battle. In bloody fighting through October, it was tough going. At one point the Indians attempted a flanking movement using a paratroop drop in the vicinity of Jaffna University near LTTE headquarters, only to have their men cut to ribbons. An entire platoon was wiped out before urgently requested assistance from the Sri Lankan air force allowed survivors to fight their way to a linkup force. Other engagements were equally intense.

By the time November began, the Indians claimed they had secured all of Jaffna. By their own admission, their casualties numbered more than 200 killed, though it was difficult to ascertain the true situation. So absurd were the daily briefings at the Indian High Commission that reporters took to calling them 'The Five O'Clock Follies', in remembrance of the same dog and pony show conducted in South Vietnam by the American command. Reporters who did manage to get to the vicinity of the battlefield on brief, staged tours stated afterward that talk of victory was 'premature'. Not only did the insurgents still control large areas of the city, but their key formations had faded into the countryside.

Obviously, what had not been anticipated was that no tactical concessions would prove capable of satisfying the insurgents' strategic demands. Still, in not making greater use of the 'political space' afforded them by the Indian presence, they blundered badly. Their foot soldiers certainly paid the price.

This was true on the other side of the trenches, as well. The violence had been far more destructive than would have been the case had the Sri Lankans been allowed to carry out 'Liberation II'. After long years of fighting, Colombo's security forces had adjusted to the realities of combat and had proved able to keep civilian casualties within acceptable limits in their Jaffna push. In contrast, the Indians were new at the game. As a result, Jaffna became a virtual ghost town, a status never achieved during the previous four years of conflict.

Still, whatever might be thought of the tactics used, a push against the LTTE, whether by the Sri Lankans or the Indians, was necessary if only because their movement had gone so far astray.

Rather than following any Maoist strategy, it had become enmeshed in a cult of violence, violence divorced from its political goal — the 'liberation' of the Tamil people. In the months that immediately preceded the 29 July 1987 accord, ominous events demonstrated that the Tigers were about to move wholesale into imitation of the suicide tactics favored by radical Islamic movements. A 'land torpedo', for instance, a truck packed with explosives, had been used to demolish the main Jaffna telecommunications center. Its atomized driver, 'Commander Miller', had joined the growing pantheon of immortals, those who were deemed martyrs for the cause. Posters of Miller's bearded likeness, beret previously etched onto the negative, were everywhere in Jaffna, exhorting the people to greater sacrifice. A 'Black Tigers' suicide commando had even been formed to carry out one-way attacks.

In the end, like Hitler, Tiger logic claimed that it was better to perish in a great *Gotterdamerung* than to compromise. Tragically, the Tamil people had little say in framing this nihilistic strategy. They were taken along strictly for the ride, so to speak.

Renewed 'People's War' in the South[49]

The Indian presence, while having some tactical advantages, was strategically disastrous, because it not only reinforced the nationalist aspects of the 'Eelam' appeal amongst the Tamil mass base but also provoked a Sinhalese nationalist reaction that was tapped by the dormant JVP. The causes which threw up the JVP manpower were the same as had produced the 1971 explosion. The fire had been doused, but the kindling had remained. The new conditions provided the spark.

As the Indians attempted to deal with the Tamil insurgents, the Sri Lankans were forced to move troops south. There the agreement, with its accompanying deployment of Indian forces to Sri Lankan soil, had prompted rioting and violence. These culminated in the attempted assassination on 18 August 1987 of President Jayewardene (a later move was made against Rajiv Gandhi, as well, when he arrived in Colombo for discussions). Hailed by the world for his bold stroke in signing the peace accord, the Sri Lankan leader found himself fighting for his political life.

The assassination attempt was only the tip of what appeared to be a very large iceberg of discontent and anger directed at the ruling UNP for its perceived authoritarian drift and abuse of power. The presence of Indian troops had served as a rallying point for the otherwise fragmented and lackluster opposition. Even Buddhist monks joined in anti-government riots; some clergymen were arrested with stolen semiautomatic weapons in their possession.

Exploding nationalist passions once again exposed the dark side of Sri Lanka. Power grows from the barrel of a gun, opined Mao (originally in 1938). And in the absence of functioning politics, he might have added, there is no recourse save the gun. That much should have been clear to Sri Lankan decisionmakers in light of the origins of the Tamil insurgency. In the absence of political process — the resolving of grievances through political decision-making — there is nowhere else for popular discontent to go save the streets or the ranks of the insurgents. Yet Colombo had not understood it with the Tamils; it did not understand it with the Sinhalese.

As mentioned earlier in this chapter, that politics could be assessed as dead in Sri Lanka seemed a contradiction in a nation which since its independence in 1948 had maintained a functioning parliamentary democracy. But if politics may be further defined as shaping the human environment, Sri Lanka's system had become a failure. Behind the facade of democracy, successive governments had taken procedural steps that had severely restricted representation of the popular will. Electoral mechanics saw the nearly 50:50 split in the popular vote in the 1970 and 1977 elections reflected in lopsided parliamentary majorities for either of Sri Lanka's major political parties, the UNP, in power since 1977, or the SLFP, which ruled with an enormous MP (Member of Parliament) margin during 1970–77, despite losing the popular vote! Both parties used this statistical gift to centralize decisionmaking and authority, roundly abuse opposition voices, curb individual freedoms, and censor the media. Rules were even pushed through allowing the replacement by party officials of any MP who had the courage to criticize his own party — this for MPs who, in any case, were not required to reside in the districts they represented.

Some two decades of such actions resulted, predictably, in a political system manned by individuals owing their allegiance not to their constituencies or to higher principles but to their parties. Electoral corruption, intimidation, and manipulation of voting rules prevented popular discontent from fielding alternate representatives. Rather than see its four-fifths majority endangered in

1982 — a crucial level because it allowed the amending of the constitution at will — the UNP simply held a referendum to extend the life of the parliament another term. Though the UNP won the vote, the narrow margin of victory reflected the true polarization of the electorate.

Fueling popular resentment was the increasing isolation of the government bureaucracy from the population. Without the political system acting as overseer (it was too busy looking after its members' needs), the permanent cadre in official positions turned to its own concerns. Corruption reached monumental proportions even as basic services deteriorated island-wide.

The worsening lives of the people escaped notice in many quarters, foreign and domestic. Progress in economic macroindicators served to conceal serious problems in the microworld of Sri Lanka's majority, problems of health, nutrition, livelihood, and opportunities for advancement. Large segments of the population had limited access to health care, malnutrition was widespread, un- and underemployment were rampant. Educational attainment frequently proved a dead end due to the unavailability of suitable employment.

Discriminatory legislation and regular episodes of anti-Tamil rioting, which culminated in the nationwide explosion of July 1983, were passed off by the world as communal conflict. Actually, as noted earlier, they reflected attempts by the Sinhalese majority to claim from the successful Tamils their slice of what increasingly was viewed as a zero-sum distribution of rights, resources, and privileges. Faced with a system unwilling to provide for their well-being or even to protect them, the conservative Tamil populace turned to the only available option championing their interests, the Marxist insurgent movements.

The steadily escalating fiscal and manpower demands of the campaign to fight Tamil separatism, in turn, further curtailed Colombo's human and economic development efforts. Yet in another of Sri Lanka's many ironies, the Tamils earlier had become prominent in business and government service precisely because of their need to escape the structural conditions which were different only in degree from those afflicting the Sinhalese majority. Tamil areas were the poorest of the island, with limited carrying capacity. Hence migration to and employment in the larger Sri Lankan community were imperative. Driven back into itself, Tamil society had little choice but self-defense.

Similarly, the factors discussed above drove the Sinhalese community to self-defense. Contrary to a view fashionable in many circles of the Colombo elite, the JVP had not caused the insurgency. Neither could it even be said to be leading it. It was racing to keep up with it! What the JVP *had* demonstrated was a tactical sophistication which allowed it to ride each wave of discontent as it surfaced. In this sense the movement had learned a great deal from its earlier lack of success in 1971, when the insurgency briefly threatened the survival of the government only to collapse under crushing blows as the insurgent cause moved far ahead of its popular base. The JVP worked harder to avoid repeating its earlier error. Previously sympathetic to the Tamil cause, for instance, it flip-flopped and adopted a hardline pro-Sinhalese stand when it became clear that such was to its advantage.

This served it in good stead when the Indians entered the picture, because it allowed the party to wrap itself in the mantle of nationalism. Indeed, JVP documents said virtually nothing of party ideological stance, concentrating instead on the betrayal of the country by its rulers. It was but a logical next step to advance a simple connection: 'the same people who sold you out are responsible for the poor conditions of life in which you find yourselves.' Yet this linkage was normally reserved, in its most explicit forms, for instructions to JVP cadres. It was to be introduced to the masses only when the party felt conditions were safe to do so.

Predictably, a government which had steadily isolated itself from the people was not likely to recognize the root of its problems. As violence steadily escalated, the administration reacted in fumbling fashion. Security forces were deployed, but because their presence did not protect socio-economic-political measures designed to deal with the structural basis for the problem, their activities could only place a temporary damper on the violence. In their rear the insurgency gained strength. Whole areas of the country effectively became 'no go' areas after dark, and urban unrest grew dramatically. Anonymous 'struggle committees' functioned in virtually all businesses and closed them down at will simply by posting notices instructing work to cease lest reprisals be taken.

By murdering prominent examples of those who did not comply with their demands, the insurgents gained authority far beyond their numbers. Consequently, sources stated, the industrial sector was functioning at what appeared to be merely 20 per cent capacity. Such economic paralysis, in turn, fed the JVP cause. Many busi-

nesses reported they were unable to meet their loan and tax obligations. They concentrated only on at least paying their workers. As
this, too, became impossible, the ranks of the unemployed provided fertile ground for JVP recruiters.

There was a recognition of these realities in some quarters,
though in not nearly enough. For most it was business as usual.
Throughout the entire conflict — both against the Tamil and
Sinhalese insurgents — there appeared no comprehensive strategic
plan. Neither did there seem to be an appreciation of the imperative to move the counterinsurgency out of the realm of the *ad hoc*.
Even a change in leadership, with Ranasinghe Premadasa replacing
the retiring Junius R. Jayewardene, brought only more of the
same. Instead, the government again called for the security forces
to beat back the revolt. This they did.

Revamped Security Apparatus[50]

As in any rebellion, it was the army which was the linchpin of the
effort. Growing from its mere four infantry battalions (recall that
a fifth battalion was disbanded for indiscipline), it went to 24 battalions that were nearly twice the size of their predecessors. They
had grown not only numerically, but in effectiveness and equipment as well. Essential to this expansion process was the use of the
regimental system. Each of the country's five regiments — Gajaba,
Gemunu Watch, Vijayabahu Infantry (all of these first three named
after great kings), Sri Lanka Light Infantry (which traced its ances-
try to the colonial Ceylon Light Infantry), and Singha ('Lion') —
had five component battalions, numbered one through five (with
one regiment having not yet produced its fifth battalion). Each
infantry battalion, in turn, was given seven companies: five line, a
headquarters, and one with support weapons. This 1,200-man
body allowed the most experienced officers to maneuver their
fledging charges, a necessary adaptation to rapid expansion and its
consequent influx of green recruits, both officers and men.

It was a difficult unit to control, though, given the dispersed
deployment requirements of guerrilla war. As soon as adequate
numbers of junior officers became available to allow for promo-
tions throughout the system, the size of a battalion was cut back by
one line company, bringing strength down to about 900. Further
pruning of the structure progressed as officer resources allowed.

All battalions save two were armed with the Chinese-manufactured T-56 (the familiar AK-47 produced in three models) and its variant, the T-81, which could launch rifle grenades; their light machine-gun was the standard Chinese export version of the RPD. The two non-standard battalions carried the FNC (Fabrique Nationale Carbine) manufactured in Belgium, together with the FN Minimi SAW (squad automatic weapon). Also present, in addition to the T-81, were numerous German Heckler & Koch *Granatpistolen* (grenade-launchers), which was much like the US M79, and fewer Armscor (South Africa) 40mm six-shot grenade launchers. These were augmented by RPG-7 rocket launchers and 60mm mortars in each platoon headquarters. Battalion support weapons were predicated upon the mission and availability. Typical was a heavy machine-gun section with two .50 Brownings, a mortar section with ten 81mm mortars, and an anti-tank section with four 106mm recoilless rifles.

To teach employment of these weapons, both individually and in coordinated units, required the creation of a schooling infrastructure which a half dozen years before had not even existed. Courses ranging from 'Junior Leadership' (for noncommissioned officers) to 'Combat in Built-up Areas' had to be designed and implemented. Although the demands were staggering, they were met surprisingly quickly and professionally.

It took longer to evolve a tactical command structure. Only as the conflict reached its peak did the army place its battalions under permanent, numbered brigades — though those remained continually changing in composition — and its brigades under divisions. In theory, there was a brigade for each of Sri Lanka's nine provinces. These were grouped into three division headquarters, only two of which were operational, the third being designated for the area under Indian occupation.

When a battalion was assigned to a brigade, of course, it responded to the orders of the latter's commander. The regimental commander handled recruit training and personnel assignments (officer assignments were formally done by army headquarters but with the advice of the regimental commander). The regimental commander also maintained the battalion equipment stores. Supplies were ordered through cantonments (since the war was internal, units revolved around more-or-less permanent installations). Ammunition was drawn directly from army headquarters. Such were the demands of manpower that the regimental output

was further augmented by three national training centers. In time
it was hoped to standardize procedures; for the moment, the pressing requirements of continual operations led to *ad hoc* solutions.

Superimposed upon the tactical organization of the army was
another makeshift solution, the counterinsurgency structure itself.
Administratively, Sri Lanka's nine provinces were already divided
into districts, 22 in all (refer again to Map 8), each headed by a
Government Agent (GA) who saw to it that government services
and programs were carried out. To deal with the insurgency, these
GAs were paired with a Coordinating Officer, whose responsibility it became to handle the security effort in the district. Often, to
simplify the chain of command, the Coordinating Officer would be
the commander of the battalion in the district. The brigade commanders, in turn, acted as Chief Coordinating Officers for their
provinces and reported to Area Commanders. Areas 1 and 2 divided the Sinhalese heartland into southern and northern sectors,
respectively; Area 3 was the Tamil-populated zone under Indian
occupation.

Used historically with considerable effect by the British and
French, this system had the advantage of setting in place security
personnel whose mission was to win back their areas. They could
be assigned assets, military and civil, as circumstances dictated.
Coordinating Officers controlled all security forces deployed in
their districts; they were to work closely with the GAs to develop
a plan for the protection of normal civilian administrative and area
development functions. For this work they were aided by a permanent
staff whose job it was to know intimately the area. In particular,
intelligence assets remained assigned to the 'Coord' headquarters
and guided the employment of operational personnel.

The framework culminated in a Joint Operations Center (JOC),
headed by the country's only four-star general, Cyril Ranatunga.
But the JOC never really hit its stride as a coordinating body.
Instead, manned by senior serving officers, it usurped actual command functions to such an extent that it *became* the military. The
service headquarters, in particular the army, were reduced to little
more than administrative centers. Attempts to rectify the shortcomings resulted only in a JOC which functioned as a weak
supreme command, with the service chiefs rotating as its head at
three-month intervals. This clumsy arrangement eventually, too,
fell by the wayside as operational requirements became more
pressing, but the essential confusion of roles remained.

Tactically, then, the Sri Lankan security forces had demonstrated a knowledge of counterinsurgency techniques and theory surprisingly advanced for so young a force. Strategically, however, they felt that the national leadership had failed them. That there were no moves to rectify the situation through overt pressure or coups, as happened in other cases we have considered in this work, was a credit to the professional ethos. For there was no shortage of individuals, both civil and military, who recognized that there had to be a political strategy for dealing with the issues which were allowing the insurgents to gain strength.

'These politicians are always making things a shambles', a second lieutenant observed from the base where he commanded a two-platoon force. 'They go for short-term popularity. In a few years, they can leave office. But the army and the police don't get to leave. We have to deal with the problems they have left behind. What we need is honesty and a plan.'

Indeed, it was these two issues — corruption and the lack of a plan — which cropped up over and over again.

'It is the children of our battered peasantry who are joining the JVP', analyzed a GA as his Coordinating Officer partner nodded in agreement. 'The root cause of these troubles is landlessness.'

'We are in a race for the minds of our children', added the Coordinating Officer. 'I don't believe in body count, but the politicians do. How are we going to resolve this problem? We have been at this for 18–19 years [he was a veteran of the 1971 insurrection]. These people aren't thinking. We need a solution!'

Opined a brigade commander in another area, 'The army can only do so much. It can restore the situation to a point. But if there is no effort to address the socio-economic causes, all this will come back. We have to have some sort of plan to guide us. But I doubt if we'll get it. The politicians have made a real mess of things. We can't expect people who are a part of the problem to recognize it.'

One of his battalion commanders noted, 'Our corrupt power-holders are the major reason we have this situation. If you take the sympathizers, they're not really JVP. They're just anti-government.'

A company commander of the battalion observed, 'The mechanisms for hearing people are not very effective. There are real reasons why people are on the road. But there are no real solutions being offered.'

As on a ship at sea without a compass, each 'captain' made do as best he could. Unlike in Colombo, the situation in the rural areas, though very unsettled, was gradually brought under control. This was so because the Coordinating Officers and tactical commanders, older and wiser after their careers in the Tamil areas, were more than capable of planning their own mini-campaigns. The Achilles heel of their efforts, of course, was that in the absence of coordination and guidance, each commander had constantly to reinvent the wheel and to deal with problems the ultimate cause of which was beyond his control. He could only ameliorate their local impact.

'Look at this map,' said a Coordinating Officer, pointing to the wall:

> The green areas are small river valleys where the people are clustered. They were driven from their land when the British took it over for the estates [tea and rubber in this particular area]. Now, with population growth, there are too many people for the land. And where can the people go? See these villages here? They can't even be reached by road. It takes five hours to get to the nearest school. So the children grow up without an education and no hope for meaningful employment. So they're stuck in their poverty. But all around they see what was once their land, and they see the people living on it getting rich. And those people are Indians [i.e., Indian Tamil estate workers]. Now the Indian laborers are followed by Indian troops. Then along comes someone who tells them he'll set all this right, that he'll get rid of the government that sold out the country and made everyone poor. Is it any wonder people join the JVP? I do what I can but...

Thus daily the commanders sent their troops out on operations, primarily cordon and searches, as well as night ambushes, generated by intelligence leads. Units appeared to have little trouble getting information once they established their presence in an area. One commander in an area I visited in 1989 was deluged by a hundred letters a day, 80–90 per cent of which he estimated contained accurate information.

Why such a response? Paradoxically, the army's presence eliminated the worst abuses of the system. It did this by enforcing a standard of conduct the system itself was unwilling to provide. Most people, to be clear, did not want to become insurgents. Rather, when the immediate abuses of the system were halted, they were only too willing to go back to figuring out how they were going to put bread on the table. And, because most retained faith that ultimately the democratic system would respond to them, they were only too willing to inform on the JVP once they saw that there was a viable hope for functioning democracy. The JVP added to this trend by its widespread and grisly resort to terror.

The danger inherent to such a posture, though, was that it could not go on forever. 'The situation requires a political solution', observed a Coordinating Officer.

> The security forces are only suppressing what the problems throw up. My troops are tired. We have been at this for six straight years, first in the north, now here. The boys cannot go home on leave [due to the JVP terror campaign]; their families are not safe. We are still holding up, but everyone has his breaking point.

Similarly, the constant strain of operations could lead to abuses. Ultimately, these two forces did come together in a terrible end to the JVP problem. As we have noted, the need to combat the JVP insurrection had the effect of drawing off Sri Lankan security force resources and attention during the Indian Peacekeeping Force (IPKF) presence, which at its peak was reported to have reached 80,000, to include more than 40 infantry battalions. Further, the Indian use of the non-LTTE 'Eelam' groups to form the so-called 'Tamil National Army' (TNA) compromised them as quislings, thereby contributing still further to LTTE dominance. Tactical errors of force employment ensured that the IPKF would be ineffective in combating LTTE guerrilla tactics. Consequently, by the time of IPKF withdrawal, in January–March 1990, almost three years and several thousand IPKF casualties later, the LTTE was more firmly established than upon the Indian arrival. This was compounded by further LTTE entrenchment during a subsequent Colombo-LTTE negotiation period (which it also used to decimate the Tamil 'national forces' left behind by the IPKF). When hostilities again broke out, the security forces found themselves faced with the task of waging not counterinsurgency but conventional war (with an active guerrilla force component) for the purpose of regaining alienated territory.

The result was that the country faced a vastly more complicated situation, a war on two fronts. This it could not handle. Increasingly, shortcuts were taken. Political leadership, even while instituting some very necessary socio-economic measures in the south, turned to what has come to be termed 'the Argentinian solution', so-called after the 'Dirty War' strategy used in that country in the 1970s to end its own challenge from radical guerrillas. Put simply, the niceties of reform, targeted response, and legal process were dispensed with; anyone suspected of subversion fell to paramilitary, vigilante, or death squad activity. In the process, old and new scores on both sides were settled in abundance, though alleged JVP sympathizers certainly comprised the bulk of the victims. As in Argentina, the dead in the Sri Lankan south apparently numbered some 20,000, to include the key members of the JVP leadership. A Sri Lankan general's analysis of the 'campaign' was on the mark: 'We have done terrible things, terrible things.'

In ending the JVP threat, though, the security forces were able to turn their attention to the Tamil insurgency. In a virtual re-run of its earlier actions, the Sri Lankan military slowly retook those areas it had captured years before, pinning the main LTTE combat power again in Jaffna. It was a different kind of war: deaths numbered in the thousands, reaching a peak in July–August 1991 in a series of set-piece battles around Jaffna. The 25 days of fighting at Elephant Pass, the land bridge which connected the Jaffna peninsula with the rest of Sri Lanka, saw the first insurgent use of armor, stopped with 106mm recoilless rifle fire and hand-to-hand fighting, and insurgent dead alone numbering more than a thousand. Elsewhere, terror bombings and assassinations became almost routine. Even national leaders, such as Rajiv Gandhi of India and President Ranasinghe Premadasa, fell to apparent LTTE bomb attacks (on 21 May 1991 and 1 May 1993, respectively), as did numerous other important figures.

Conclusions[51]

This has remained the nature of the struggle to the present. Heavy fighting in Jaffna in early 1994, as the security forces attempted to tighten their grip around Jaffna City, resulted in government casualties approaching those suffered by the LTTE in the Elephant Pass action. Guerrilla action had become but a sideshow to a South Asian playing out of the Battle of Stalingrad. Maoist insurgency, too, had long since fallen by the wayside.

Despite the transformation of the conflict in its military sense, though, the essence of the struggle remains the same: it is a political conflict that demands a political solution.

Security forces are capable of retaking the 'far north' (Jaffna), though casualties will be heavy. Effective control exists already in the 'near north' (the Tamil areas below Elephant Pass) and the east, with local elections successfully held in March 1994. Retaking the final areas held by the insurgents, however — which are substantially fortified — has no meaning unless carried out within a political solution designed to address those grievances that have allowed the insurgents to recruit their manpower.

Such is not to deny the role terror has played in guaranteeing LTTE insurgent control, but it must be recognized that LTTE repression today is only a tactical aspect of a much larger strategic process which has involved substantial popular support for the insurgency, support that has gone on for more than a decade. While the LTTE has squandered much of this capital by using its mass base as a human shield, the LTTE's rivals — who have of late shown a willingness to settle for autonomy within the existing political system — are not positioned to take advantage of the situation. They may not even be willing to participate substantively in the struggle against the Tigers, because they are alienated from them by circumstances not by fundamentals. The March election results demonstrated continued support amongst Tamils for parties comprised of 'their own'.

Still, in the present circumstances there is promise. The very length of the struggle has interacted with the personal characteristics of the LTTE leadership, particularly Prabhakaran himself, to produce an LTTE overemphasis on the military aspects of the struggle at the expense of the political. Organization for political struggle, always underdeveloped in the LTTE, especially when compared to the other Tamil insurgent groups, has deteriorated still further. Political structure has been weakened, too, by internal purges which have killed off key figures in the LTTE leadership.

This has left the LTTE with little option but to continue fighting, for it would find itself at a disadvantage in any political campaign. The bloody 1991 clash at Elephant Pass highlighted this militaristic orientation. Nonetheless, it also highlighted the degree to which the present situation is, for all practical purposes, a military stalemate, one demanding a political solution.

Stalemate should not be construed to mean government defeat. Security force performance during the Elephant Pass operation was commendable, as was the courage displayed. Morale remains high.

Yet, while insurgent areas can be retaken, this will be exceptionally difficult, both financially and militarily. Jaffna, to cite the immediate objective at hand, has been turned into a truly formidable defensive position. In addition to anticipated high security force casualties, civilian loss of life is bound to be politically unacceptable. (It may be noted that even the 'soft' option of blockade carries with it the certainty of significant civilian casualties.)

Fortunately, intervention by New Delhi is no longer a major concern. The LTTE's assassination of former Indian Prime Minister Rajiv Gandhi — apparently in retaliation for his ordering the IPKF into action, as well as the fear that he was on the verge of returning to power — has caused a crackdown upon insurgent base areas in Tamil Nadu and closer operational cooperation between Colombo and New Delhi.

Nevertheless, even assuming a victory in Jaffna, achieved regardless of costs, no force can fight indefinitely without a clear goal in hand. Retaking territory is not a goal, because the territory was only physically lost (thus making necessary the military fight) after the populace was politically lost. Hence there must be in place a plan for recouping the political situation. Unwittingly, the LTTE, by abandoning Maoist insurgency, has provided the government with the opening.

The LTTE has consistently locked itself into a rigid bargaining position which refuses to accept 'Eelam' *de facto* (i.e., local control, autonomy) rather than *de jure* (i.e., independence). This fact has been realized by LTTE's Tamil rivals, who can now be brought into the political solution, together with the war-weary Tamil masses, through institution of a viable system of regional and local government. Such political decentralization must be accompanied by devolution of decisionmaking authority such that socio-economic issues can be addressed by the newly formed political institutions. Colombo has taken steps in these areas. Ironically, it could be argued that it has been the agony of the IPKF interlude and their ultimate slaughter at the hands of the LTTE that has brought home to the non-LTTE groups and the residents of the Tamil insurgent areas the necessity of autonomy as opposed to independence. Still, autonomy implies local decisionmaking authority, not meaningless trappings of power and prestige.

Tactically, it must be borne in mind that previous efforts to implement a solution have foundered on the time element. In dealing with an insurgency, speed in implementing a solution — even if it is only a perceived solution — is necessary. Dithering is interpreted as double-dealing. A 'political solution' of necessity contains not only 'political' components but also 'social' and 'economic' facets. Alleviating linguistic and educational grievances, for instance, would fall under the term 'political solution' as I am using it. The ultimate goal, of course, is that something must be in place for which people are willing to fight. The insurgents are waging a political campaign, albeit one in which violence plays a large role in maintaining their support. The government can deal with such a campaign only by waging an effective countercampaign for public support. What politician can run for office offering nothing? Such is precisely what Colombo has been doing.

All else follows from this. How precisely to go about implementing the mechanics of security force employment and information gathering are concerns best left to professionals. The keys, certainly, are unity of effort and adequate intelligence. Yet any politician who has been in a hard-fought campaign, particularly one in which the other side has employed 'bully boys', will know instinctively what is involved. That is why a synonym for insurgency — first advanced by insurgents themselves — is political warfare. For as Clauswitz once wrote — and Mao, who studied his works closely, reiterated — war is but politics by 'other means'.

NOTES

1. For a dated but still fairly comprehensive treatment of various aspects of Sri Lanka see K.M. de Silva (ed.), *Sri Lanka – A Survey* (Honolulu, HI: UP of Hawaii, 1977).

2. Information on the subject of Sinhalese–Tamil relations has been gathered generally from several sources and augmented by fieldwork conducted over the last decade. Excellent discussions are contained in A. Jeyaratnam Wilson and Dennis Dalton, (eds.), *The States of South Asia – Problems of National Integration* (Honolulu, HI: UP of Hawaii, 1982); see esp.C.R. de Silva, 'The Sinhalese–Tamil Rift in Sri Lanka', pp.155–74; and A. Jeyaratnam Wilson, 'Sri Lanka and Its Future: Sinhalese versus Tamils', pp.295–312.

3. Cf. Jane Russell, *Communal Politics Under the Donoughmore Constitution 1931–1947* (Dehiwala, Sri Lanka: Tisara Prakasakayo, 1982).

4. An excellent source is K.M. de Silva, *A History of Sri Lanka* (London: C. Hurst, 1981); also valuable for its discussion of Sri Lanka's cultural influence upon the region is Jean Boisselier, 'South–east Asia: Sri Lanka', in Jeannine Auboyer *et al.*, *Oriental Art – A Handbook of Styles and Forms*, trans. Elizabeth and Richard Bartlett (NY: Int. Publications, 1980), pp.97–130. For details on a majority of the British period see Lennox A. Mills, *Ceylon Under British Rule 1795–1932* (NY: Barnes & Noble, 1965).

5. Detailed discussions are contained in S. Arasaratnam, 'Nationalism, Communalism, and National Unity in Ceylon', Ch.12 in Philip Mason (ed.), *India and Ceylon: Unity and Diversity* (London: Oxford UP, 1967); B.H. Farmer, 'The Social Basis of Nationalism in Ceylon', *Journal of Asian Studies,* 24/3 (May 1965), pp.441–39; and Robert N. Kearney, 'Sinhalese Nationalism and Social Conflict in Ceylon', *Pacific*

Affairs, 37/2 (Summer 1964), pp.125–36. See also Michael Roberts (ed.), *Collective Identities, Nationalisms, and Protest in Modern Sri Lanka* (Colombo: Marga Inst., 1979); Social Scientists' Assoc. *Ethnicity and Social Change in Sri Lanka* (Colombo: Karunaratne & Sons, 1984).

6.   Robert N. Kearney and Janice Jiggins, 'The Ceylon Insurrection of 1971', *Journal of Commonwealth & Comparative Politics,* 13/1 (March 1975), p.49.

7.   Cf. Janice Jiggins, *Caste and Family in the Politics of the Sinhalese 1974–1976* (Colombo: K.V.G. de Silva & Sons, 1979); Tissa Fernando, 'Elite Politics in the New States: The Case of Post–Independence Sri Lanka', *Pacific Affairs,* 46/3 (Fall 1973), pp.361–83; and Robert Oberst, 'Democracy and the Persistence of Westernized Elite Dominance in Sri Lanka', *Asian Survey,* 25/7 (July 1985), pp.760–72.

8.   Cf. Robert N. Kearney, 'The Marxist Parties of Ceylon', Ch.7 in Paul R. Bass and Marcus F. Franda (eds.), *Radical Politics in South Asia* (Cambridge, MA: MIT Press, 1973), pp.400–39; Charles S. Blackton, 'Sri Lanka's Marxists', *Problems of Communism,* 22/1 (Jan.–Feb. 1973), pp.28–43; and George J. Lerski, 'The Twilight of Ceylonese Trotskyism', *Pacific Affairs,* 43/3 (Fall 1970), pp.384–93.

9.   The name JVP was adopted shortly before the 1970 elections in May.

10.   Precise structure of the JVP remains a matter of dispute; cf. Kearney and Jiggins (n.6), p.52.

11.   A useful summary is found in Kearney and Jiggins (n.6), pp.54–5; cf. A.C. Alles, *Insurgency – 1971,* rev. 3rd ed. (Colombo: Mervyn Mendis at the Colombo Apothecaries' Co., 1976), pp.42–6; and Fred Halliday, 'The Ceylonese Insurrection', *New Left Review,* No.69 (Sept.–Oct 1971), pp.75–8.

12.   Principal sources on the 1971 insurrection are: Paul Alexander, 'Shared Fantasies and Elite Politics: The Sri Lankan "Insurrection" of 1971', *Mankind,* 13/2 (Dec. 1981), pp.113–32; Alles (n.11), S. Arasaratnam, 'The Ceylonese Insurrection of April 1971: Some Causes and Consequences', *Pacific Affairs,* 45/3 (Fall 1972), pp.356–71; Blackton (n.8); Halliday (n.7); Janice Jiggins, 'Caste and the Insurgency of 1971', in Jiggins (n.7); Robert N. Kearney, 36/1 'A Note on the Fate of the 1971 Insurgents in Sri Lanka', *Journal of Asian Studies,* 36/3 (May 1977), pp.515–19; Kearney, 'Educational Expansion and Political Volatility in Sri Lanka: The 1971 Insurrection', *Asian Survey,* 15/9 (Sept. 1975), pp.727–44; Kearney and Jiggins (n.6); Gananath Obeyesekere, 'Some Comments on the Social Backgrounds of the April 1971 Insurgency in Sri Lanka (Ceylon)', *Journal of Asian Studies,* 33/3 (May 1974), 376–84; W. A. Siswa Warnapala (pseudonym, 'Politicus'), 'The April Revolt in Ceylon,' *Asian Survey,* 12/3 (March 1972), pp.259–74; Warnapala, 'The Marxist Parties of Sri Lanka and the 1971 Insurrection', *Asian Survey,* 15/9 (Sept. 1975), pp.745–57; and A. Jeyaratnam Wilson, 'Ceylon: A Time of Troubles', *Asian Survey* 12/2 (Feb. 1972), pp.109–15.

13.   Halliday (n.11), p.80, claims the JVP was not involved in this attack. Other sources consulted disagree, claiming the attack was the work of JVP militants.

14.   Halliday (n.11).

15.   Alexander (n.12), p.124.

16.   Alles (n.11), p.137.

17.   Cf. Obeyesekere, Kearney and Jiggins (n.6), esp. p.44; and Alles (n.11), Ch.22 (pp. 256–67) and Ch.23 (pp.268–81).

18.   Alles (n.11), pp.280–1.

19.   Information in this section has been developed through analysis of a variety of primary sources during the course of ongoing violence, as well as by fieldwork involving discussions with both insurgent and government figures. Cf. my "People's War" in Sri Lanka: Insurgency and Counterinsurgency', *Issues & Studies,* 22/8 (Aug. 1986), pp.63–100; and 'Counter–Insurgency in Sri Lanka: Asia's Dirty Little War', *Soldier of Fortune* [hereafter *SOF*], 12/2 (Feb. 1987), pp.38–47.

20.   Interviews by the author, Sri Lanka and India, summer 1984.

21. A.S. Balasingham, *Liberation Tigers and Tamil Eelam Freedom Struggle* (Madras: Political Committee, LTTE, 1983), p.42.
22. Balasingham (n.21).
23. I discuss the points raised above in more detail in 'Marxist Tamils Won't Stop at Separatism', *Asian Wall Street Journal* [hereafter AWSJ], 8 May 1986, p.6 [repr. as 'Tamil Rebels Aim Beyond Autonomy', *The Asian Wall Street Journal Weekly* (hereafter, AWSJW), 26 May 1986, p.12]; 'The Ethnic Roots of Sri Lanka's Ideological Struggle,' AWSJ, 12 Aug. 1987, p. 8 [abridged version under the same title in AWSJW, 31 Aug. 1987, p.12]; and 'Book Review – Stanley Tambiah, *Sri Lanka: Ethnic Fratricide and the Dismantling of Democracy, Issues & Studies*, 23/9 (Sept. 1987), pp.135–40.
24. Interview conducted by author in Tamil Nadu, Aug. 1984.
25. KMS = 'Keeny Meeny Services'. It has been claimed that the name is taken from the Swahili words used to describe the movement of a snake through long grass and came into the SAS vocabulary during the Mau Mau Rebellion in Kenya. SAS sources who served in Kenya and are fluent in Swahili, however, have cast doubt on the veracity of this information.
26. Cf. my 'Sri Lanka's Special Force: Professionalism in a Dirty War', SOF, 13/7 (July 1988), pp.32–39.
27. The term *pelantiya* is not the precise equivalent of 'landed aristocracy', but the structural position of the *pelantiya* appears to justify equating the two in this discussion. Alexander (n.12), p.120, has defined *pelantiya* as 'a putatively endogamous group of landlords, living a common lifestyle modelled on a vision of the feudal past, and controlling all local government offices'. It is important to bear in mind that in the argument being advanced here, the 'national *pelantiya*' has ceased altogether functioning as an actual landed aristocracy.
28. Cf. Gananath Obeyesekere, *Land Tenure in Village Ceylon* (London: Cambridge UP, 1974).
29. Historically, regardless of identity of ownership, the dominant form of land organization in the tea sector has been the 'estate', where 80 per cent of the labor force was comprised of Indian Tamils.
30. Alexander (n.12), p.121: 'The economic activities of the *mudalali* were concentrated in four main areas: transport (trucks, buses and hire cars); rice milling and rice purchasing; fish and vegetable wholesaling; and retailing through village shops and market stalls'.
31. This latter development is detailed for Anuradhapura District in James Brow, 'Class Formation and Ideological Practice: A Case From Sri Lanka', *Journal of Asian Studies*, 40/4 (Aug. 1981), pp.703–18. The author, though, is concerned principally with aspects of the process itself as sharecroppers are replaced by wage labor and does not consider causes for the transition. See also Barrie M. Morrison, M.P. Moore, and M.U. Ishak (eds.), *The Disintegrating Village – Social Change in Rural Sri Lanka* (Colombo: Lake House Investments, 1979). For historical background consult Tilak Hettiarachchy, *The Sinhala Peasant in a Changing Society* (Colombo: Lake House, 1982).
32. Wilson (n.12), p.111.
33. Cf. Alexander (n.12), p.122: 'The colonial policy of financing food imports (distributed as free or subsidized rations) with the earnings from plantation agriculture, provided no incentives for the development of peasant agriculture. By 1970, irrigation systems had broken down, crop increasing techniques such as transplanting and careful weeding were not widely used, and the condition of the fields seemed pitiful in comparison with Java or South India. Although the increasing cost of food imports and the technical developments of the Green Revolution, [sic] led to changes in government policies in the late sixties, for the most part the policies were mere paper plans.'

34. Alexander (n.12), pp.121–2.

35. Jiggins (n.7), p.125.

36. As measured in the Oct. 1971 census, the population was 12,747,755.

37. Kearney and Jiggins (n.6), p.41.

38. Alexander (n.12).

39. Ibid., p.127.

40. Fieldwork conducted Summer 1983.

41. Interviews conducted by author, Summer 1983. There are few academic works which seek to discuss the events of July 1983. See, e.g., James Manor, 'Sri Lanka: Explaining the Disaster', *World Today*, 39/11 (Nov. 1983), pp.450–9.

42. Cf. 'Summary of Economic Impact', US Embassy (Colombo) mimeo, undated; also William Claiborne, 'Rioting Shatters Sri Lanka's Hopes for Economic Development', *Washington Post*, 2 Aug. 1983, p.A10.

43. Latest available information, e.g., indicates that total expenditures for 1985 were Rs. 65,821 million (US $2.398 billion), for a deficit of Rs. 29,496 million (US $1.075 billion). The projected deficit for 1986 was Rs. 26,986 million (US $983.1 million) on a budget of Rs. 67,800 million (US $2.47 billion). The official exchange rate for Nov. 1985, when the figures became available, was Rs. 27.45 = US $1.00.

44. Interview with author, Colombo, Aug. 1984.

45. Portions of this section have appeared in my 'India is the Key to Peace in Sri Lanka', AWSJ, 19–20 Sept. 1986, p.8 [repr. under the same title in *The Island* (Colombo), 5 Oct. 1986, p.8; abridged version under the same title in AWSJW, 22 Sept. 1986, p.25]; and 'Peace in Sri Lanka,' *Daily News* [Colombo], 3 parts, 6–7–8 July 1987: 'I. India Acts in its Own Interests', 6 July, p.6; 'II. Bengali Solution: India Trained Personnel for Invasion of Sri Lanka,' 7 July, p.8; 'III. India's Political Solution Narrow and Impossible', 8 July, p.6. Published under the same titles in *Sri Lanka News*, 15 July 1987 (contd.), pp.6–7; in *The Island* as 'India's Covert Involvements', 28 June 1987, pp.8 and 10.

46. Cf. my 'Winning the War in Sri Lanka,' AWSJ, 30 April–1 May 1986, p.8 [repr. under same title in *The Island*, 2 June 1986, p.6].

47. Portions of this section, to include details on sources, have appeared in my 'Sri Lankan Minefield: Gandhi's Troops Fail to Keep the Peace', SOF, 13/3 (March 1988), 36–45 (cont.); and 'Handling Snakes and Unfriendly Troops in Sri Lanka', *Honolulu Star–Bulletin*, 22 Sept. 1987, p.A–17.

48. Cf. my 'The Indian Factor', *The Island*, 20 Sept. 1987, p.8. This article had been submitted to the censor on 22 Aug. by *The Island* for publication the next day, but it was refused release *in toto*. It was finally cleared in Sept. and published with editorial changes by *The Island* for timeliness. What the censors wanted to object to, in particular, was my assessment that peace was not at hand: 'Rather, as Tamil insurgent leaders have made clear during interviews, "the presence of the representatives of the Indian bourgeoisie" will only change for a time the parameters of the fight.' The piece also predicted, based on further interviews, a virtual three-front war in the Tamil areas, the Sinhalese south, and India itself.

49. Portions of this section, to include details on sources, have appeared in my 'In Sri Lanka, Despair Explodes Into Violence', AWSJ, 16 Aug. 1989, p.6 [abridged version as 'Sri Lanka's Despair Breeds Violence,' AWSJW, 21 Aug. 1989, p.15]; and 'Chaos in Colombo: Sri Lanka's Army Awaits its Marching Orders While Politicians Dither', SOF, 15/2 (Feb. 1990), pp.48–55 (contd.).

50. Data and quotations appear in my 'Professionals in Paradise: Sri Lanka's Army Gears up for "Tiger" Hunt', SOF, 15/1 (Jan. 1990), pp.52–9 (contd.). All sources were quoted anonymously under agreement with them at the time; the result is the candor evident in the text.

51. Cf. my 'Sri Lanka: The Dynamics of Terror', *Counterterrorism and Security*, New Series 1/1 (Spring 1994), pp.19–23.

5 Making Revolution: *Sendero Luminoso* in Peru as Maoist Conclusion, 1980–

Finally we come to the case of Peru, where Maoist insurgency is allegedly yet alive and well, having moved into a form appropriate to the modern world. In reality, what is at hand is a Maoist conclusion, the logical bankruptcy of a concept no longer viable.

This may seem a strange judgement. Recent reports from Peru make clear, after all, that the insurgency there continues, the efforts of the Alberto Fujimori government and a positive strategic trend notwithstanding. Though there are several rival insurgent movements, it is one in particular, *Sendero Luminoso* ('Shining Path', also known simply as *Sendero*), with which we are concerned.[1] Brutal and secretive, it has impressed all over the years with its relative effectiveness as it has pursued the self-professed goal of making a 'true' Maoist revolution. Even so, it has remained much a mystery in all but its general outlines.

Perhaps most vexing to many analysts in this respect is accounting for the apparent support *Sendero* appears to have mobilized. It is, after all, a Maoist insurgency; yet it engages in practices which would seemingly alienate potential followers. For it remains virtually an article of faith, both in official and popular literature, that to achieve success an insurgent movement must win the 'hearts and minds' of the people. The clandestine mechanisms of rebellion, continues the argument, are so dependent upon popular support that they cannot possible survive in an environment where the populace is controlled mainly through repression.

There lies the problem in Peru. *Sendero* engages in the widespread use of terror; but all indications were that, until the capture of its leadership in September 1992, it was expanding. Indeed, there were those who judged it was but a matter of time before the government in Lima collapsed. What can explain this waxing and waning? Could a movement have been thriving if brutality was its main tool? Or has our befuddlement simply a product of our lack of data? Was *Sendero*'s terror just a smokescreen behind which something more substantive was going on?

As I have endeavored to show in this work, the answer must be 'yes and no'. Reality, especially as concerns Maoist insurgency, lies in the relationship between the mechanisms of grievance-driven recruitment, infrastructure, and terror — and the manner in which these change over time in their relative importance in the maintenance of the insurgent movement. Grown accustomed to viewing insurgencies in almost static perspective, we must recognize, finally, that the passage of time profoundly affects the components just noted and hence the nature of the movement concerned.

This is true for individual insurgencies; it is also true for the genre. Maoist insurgency has become increasingly divorced from the masses it purports to serve. Few cases illustrate this as well as does *Sendero Luminoso*, and it is for this reason that I close with it. It will show the depths to which the concept has sunk, the triumph of form over any purported democratic substance.

Maoist Opposition to the Old-Regime

Sendero has always stated that its inspiration is Maoist. Precise implementation varies in particulars from the Chinese model. *Sendero*, for instance, does not appear to accept the necessity for a united front strategy and, further, is more dogmatic concerning self-reliance than Mao appears to advocate — but faithfully reproduces its form: people's war is to be used to gain control of the countryside for the purpose of encircling the cities. Hazleton and Hazleton have described this strategy thus:

> Sendero has made very few public statements about its agenda and strategy, but [*Sendero* leader] Guzman's plans for a protracted armed struggle have Sendero's activities evolving through several stages. The first stage was one of 'agitation and propaganda', in which Guzman and his followers recruited, trained, and organized cadres in the isolated Andean highlands. In 1980, when democracy was being restored in Peru, Sendero initiated its second stage of creating the social and material bases of a people's army. It also made its presence known through attacks on public buildings and other symbols of authority. Liberated zones were created in which Sendero imposed its antitechnological, subsistence peasant model by brutal methods, destroying farm equipment and crops, closing regional markets, and killing informers and reluctant supporters. In 1982, Sendero launched its so-called third stage, which was to initiate an armed struggle in the rural

areas and gradually move into urban areas to create the conditions for the fourth stage — a people's war.[2]

Though the Hazeltons later judged that *Sendero* altered this strategy in favor of 'a quicker, urban-based revolution',[3] this is doubtful. It may well be the case, as with other Maoist-inspired movements (e.g., that in the Philippines) that the *Senderistas* have chosen to emphasize both urban and rural components of people's war. But to claim that the original strategic blueprint has been abandoned is, I would argue, a misreading of the evidence.

Regardless, when analyzing the manner in which *Sendero* has implemented its strategy, analysts tend to emphasize its unique trajectory.[4] This, too, is a misplacement of emphasis, since, allowing for the differences already noted, there is little in *Sendero*'s growth or methodology that would set it apart from other Maoist movements, unless we wish to interpret extreme voluntarism and self-reliance, as well as improper interpretation of the united front framework, as negating Peruvian Maoism as a strategic variant (i.e., we would be left to argue that whatever *Sendero* is doing, it is not 'really' Maoism). Nonetheless, *Sendero* itself claims to be Maoist. And while it may depart quite radically from the *foco*-style insurrections frequently attempted by Latin American rebels, including Peruvians in the past, its tactical, operational, and strategic aspects are not particularly unique when viewed in international perspective.

Further, in analyzing the movement and attempting to pass judgement upon its approach, one cannot allow its opportunism to pass automatically for ideological intent. It seems clear that military strategy has played as prominent a role as political in the actual selection of target areas. This has resulted in a pattern of activity which is predictable. A foreign military observer stationed in Lima stated some years ago:

> The *Sendero* plan is to split the country along the *sierra* [mountains], then cut off Lima from its main food supplies (which are mainly to the north; in the south the road net is not nearly as well developed). *Sendero* has spread all along the spine and continues to grow. Nineteen eighty-nine was to have been the 'year of decision', but it will probably take one and a half years before anything major occurs. But it's coming. This country is in serious shape.[5]

Few would dispute that final line. Peru (see Map 9) would

MAP 9
PERU'S DEPARTMENTS

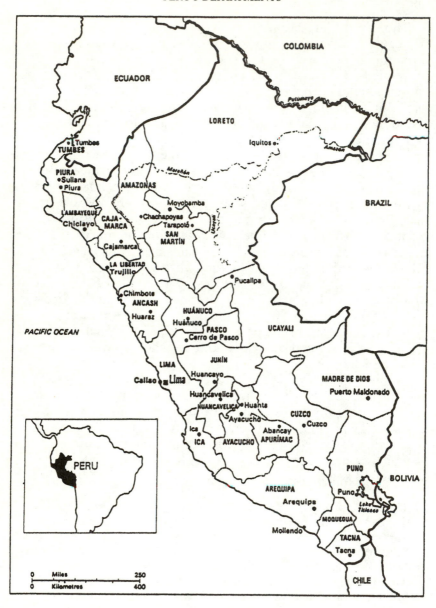

Source: Control Risks Information Service (CRIS), London.

appear an insurgent's dream. An enormous expanse the size and population of Texas, New Mexico, and Arizona put together (almost half a million square miles with 23 million people), the country is divided into three main ecological zones: a desert coastal strip, a mountainous interior, and a jungle-covered eastern portion. Topography alone would make national integration difficult. Colonial Spain added to the problem by tying its communications and transport network to the extraction of the country's vast mineral resources. The two major rail systems, for instance, built in the nineteenth and early twentieth centuries and stretching inland from the coast to mining centers, were never linked. The result of this pattern was the development of a few areas, the marginalization of most others.

Towering over all regional competitors in the development race is the capital, Lima, now swollen to some six million inhabitants (30 per cent of the national population). Here, wealth and power have historically been concentrated. While independence from Madrid came in 1824, little changed for the Indian majority. Reduced to the status of second-class citizens when Francisco Pizarro and 180 conquistadors deposed (and murdered) the last Inca king in 1533, they continued to labor after 'liberation' under the auspices of Spanish-blood and *mestizo* (mixed blood) overseers. Land ownership and political power were concentrated in the hands of the few.

Predictably, Peru, as with so many other Latin American nations, was hit by a Marxist-led insurgency in the early 1960s. This was defeated, but in the process the military became radicalized. It recognized that there was considerable merit to the critique of Peruvian society's inequities. A coup in 1968 brought the men in uniform into power. From the center, they set out to reshape the country, nationalizing foreign concerns and carrying out a radical, sweeping land reform. Ultimately, economic reality caught up with them, and in 1980 the military returned to the barracks, leaving behind a mixed legacy.

It was that same year, 1980, that a splinter of the original Peruvian Communist Party, the so-called 'Communist Party of Peru in the Shining Path of Mariategui' (Mariategui is the father of Peruvian Marxism), or 'Shining Path' (*Sendero Luminoso*), launched a new insurgency in the remote, mountainous wasteland department of Ayacucho (see Map 9 for this and other locations).

'Corner of the Dead', as the name translated in the Quechua

Indian language spoken by 90 per cent of the population, Ayacucho was the fringe of the fringe. An impoverished area twice the size of El Salvador, it had missed out or been only marginally affected by the reforms implemented under military rule. Life for the Indian majority was horrific, so it made, on the surface, sense that insurgency would blossom there. Nonetheless, as sources have pointed out, there were areas even worse off than Ayacucho, and they had no insurgency. Clearly, other forces were at work.

Questioned about this reality, a well-versed foreign observer in Lima observed in 1989:

> There is no peasant revolt in this country in the traditional agrarian revolt pattern. Land reform has long since been carried out. Since bodies like cooperatives already exist, there is no one to rebel against. There is only an extraordinarily ineffective system. The focus of resentment is corruption and arbitrary authority, not land or the causes you see in a traditional peasant uprising. Peasant organizations built up by the traditional left are very anti-*Sendero*. Indeed, extreme elements of the legal left wage pitched battles against *Sendero*. The societal problems here are necessary but not sufficient to explain *Sendero*. Looking at the movement reveals a host of puzzles. Some will argue that *Sendero* has been able to exploit changes, others see them as a product of them. We know the leadership is not peasant. Yet no one seems to have been very systematic about analyzing it. *Sendero* has been successful primarily due to the isolation of the areas in which it has operated — but it also has been able to operate well in areas where a greater degree of organization is required. Hence, we're left with a riddle: have societal causes produced activism, or has activism taken advantage of societal causes?[6]

We may take exception to certain parts of this analysis — land reform, for instance, did not reach a majority of the peasantry. Yet, in a sense, the final riddle is irrelevant, and the distinction in causation need not be made. In the *Sendero* movement, it is the ideologically-motivated leadership with a Maoist blueprint which has prevailed over membership and whatever more immediate concerns it might have; and it is insurgency that we find ourselves examining. The reasons certainly lie in the manner the movement established itself. In particular, one thing is clear: *Sendero Luminoso* is not a peasant rebellion that has been 'captured'.

Initially, Sendero seemed to be following in every respect the footsteps of Mao. A radical hardcore at the National University of

San Cristóbal de Huamanga (founded 1677, reopened 1959), located in Ayacucho city itself, was able to gain control of the rapidly-expanding university administration in the late 1960s and retain it until 1978. Breaking away from the Marxist mainstream, it formed — under the leadership of a philosophy professor appointed to the Education Program in 1962, Abimael Guzman Reynoso — *Sendero Luminoso*. Using the university as its base area, it systematically established links with the countryside, reaching out to the peasants and purportedly seeking to learn from them. *Sendero*'s leaders even studied Quechua and married into the community. They used their classroom converts to provide entrée and to further spread their message, which was that life would be better under a communist state modelled after the China of the 'Great Proletarian Cultural Revolution'. This vision they had fleshed out — at least key individuals, such as Guzman — through several stays in China (1969–74) where they received ideological and military instruction. Guzman went three times.

When the time was deemed right, in May 1980, after over a decade of patient work, *Sendero* moved from the underground organizational phase to a campaign of violence. The principal target was Ayacucho's infrastructure, from power lines and clinics to community leaders and teachers, the glue which held society together. '*Sendero* has an ideology', observed an analyst, 'to destroy society in order to build a new society. They don't want to modify. It's easier to build anew than to change the existing thing'.[7]

However, the armed columns which sought to implement this vision were not comprised wholly of the peasantry they claimed to represent. An official of an embassy in Lima noted in 1989:

> *Sendero* has sympathizers in most areas, as well as armed individuals in towns. But the heart and soul of the movement remains youth from the disenfranchised, landless, former middle class. Frequently, the youth who joins *Sendero* will have university training, be 20–25 years old; his father held land. All the modalities are present in Peru for a popular uprising, but one has not happened. This [*Sendero*] is not a *campesino* [peasant] movement. True, it can recruit from disenfranchised peasants, but at least 50 per cent of *Sendero Luminoso* columns comes from the middle class whose parents were small landowners. Almost all are Spanish speakers. It is not a European movement, however; neither is it pure Indian. It is *mestizo*. Indeed, it is not certain there was ever a real link between *Sendero* and the landless, illiterate peasants of the mountains. The cadre came out among political and intellectual leaders in the countryside. These political and social lead-

ers *were* the movement. Most areas where *Sendero* has been most successful have had no government presence at all. Isolation, therefore, had a great deal to do with their success. Our sources tell us that most *campesinos* look at *Sendero* with the same suspicion with which they view the government: 'they are foreigners telling us what do'. Some of their own young are drawn to the movement but not the population in general.[8]

Adds another, Peruvian analyst:

The full-time *Sendero* elite is very small and has a college education. But the typical *Senderista* is an 18-year-old Indian with only a grade school education, if any. He will have an agricultural background. Yet *Sendero* is not an Indian movement. How can *Sendero* be an Indian uprising? Its main targets have been Indians, more than the white population. If it was an Indian uprising, it would strike against the white minority. Its support group is among the Indians. But the basic question is what the hell are they after? A lot support *Sendero* because they are young kids who have been trained. *Sendero* takes them and puts the fear of God into them.[9]

The pattern revealed by these two observations is consistent with that seen in the other insurgent movements we have examined: leadership ranks comprised of members drawn from society's elite, followers taken from the masses. There is a subtle difference, however. All sources I questioned agree that *Sendero*'s columns, while certainly drawing upon peasants (*campesinos*) for manpower, field a large proportion of elite membership. I know of no available evidence that would allow us to quantify this relationship, or even to discern the extent to which it has been altered over time as peasant recruitment has increased, but it is an important element. It implies a movement which, at least in its crucial formative stages, is (or was) more 'activist taking advantage of social causes' than 'societal causes producing activists'. In short, we are not looking at peasant rebellion, because the wrong folks are doing the rebelling. It is not the poor and dispossessed who are fighting for a better life of their own volition. It is their social betters fighting, they claim, on their behalf. At the start of 'people's war' *Sendero* numbered at most 180 militants trained by Guzman, latterly as the university personnel director (1971–74).

Construction of Insurgent Infrastructure

It is not difficult, therefore, to see the role terror must play in the movement. Earlier we have observed that the lower classes everywhere are notoriously suspicious of elite causes. Some catalyst must push them into the fold. In Peru, terror has served that purpose. It is not aimless killing. *Sendero* is brutal but not indiscriminate. The embassy official cautioned:

> It is not committing genocide. We are not witnessing pent-up rage exploding. Rather, we are seeing carefully designed and calculated terror. They target individuals in advance, then execute them in ways which have symbolic meaning. *Sendero*'s most recent tactic is the 'armed strike'. Cadre pass out leaflets that in 72 hours there will be a strike. Subsequently, *Sendero* will kill several who violate the strike, bomb several businesses. and burn some transport. Horrible methods of execution will be used, ways which are symbolic in a mythological sense. For example, one of the most common is to slice the throat of the victim, because then the soul cannot escape from the mouth.[10]

It is the absence of anywhere to turn for help which gives such terror its effect. Recall the analysis noted in Chapter 3: 'There has traditionally been no government presence in many areas', says the editor of the Peruvian news magazine. 'Hence, as one source puts it, there are no liberated areas, only abandoned areas'.[11]

Thus it only takes a few armed men to establish *Sendero*'s writ. Their methodology and organization should come as no surprise given our previous discussion.[12] Contacts are first made with a community through acquaintances or relatives.[13] This gives *Sendero* sufficient local presence to make some converts, who then form the nucleus of a 'Popular Committee'. The Committee's leadership normally consists of five individuals. At the head is a political commissar (*Comisario Secretario*). He is assisted by individuals charged with: (a) security — organizes mechanisms of control and defense; all travel, in particular, is controlled; (b) production — determines matters of provision and logistics; in particular, which crops will be grown; (c) communal matters — administers normal societal functions such as justice, marriage, and burials; and (d) organization — classifies the population by sectoral group: children, juveniles, women, peasants, or intellectuals; these divisions are then used for study sessions and other activities.

This political organization exists in the open and maintains influence in part through its ability to call upon a *Sendero* armed column for support. It is the columns which normally carry out acts of terror. Such actions are particularly intimidating, because the local communist party organization of *Sendero* remains underground in clandestine three-man cells (each has a secretary, subsecretary, and an information specialist). The result is that no one knows for sure who is informing on them. This paralyzes attempts to fight back. Given the virtual absence or intermittent nature of the government's presence, there simply is no one to whom villagers can have recourse.

These details illustrate the importance of scale and the changing relationship, as stated earlier, between the elements of terror, recruitment, and infrastructure. Peru is sufficiently large and diverse that there are innumerable marginal areas in which subversive political activity can operate with minimal fear of government intervention. Ayacucho was just such an area during *Sendero*'s many years of organizing before the outbreak of armed action. Throughout those preparatory years, the movement expanded its political sway largely through persuasion. In the process, it benefited from the 'political space' provided by the military government's (1968–80) efforts to mobilize the peasantry behind its reform measures, efforts taken without the concomitant capacity to implement them effectively in a region Lima did not consider important.[14] *Sendero* hence garnered considerable sympathy and support among the Ayacucho population by addressing grievances initially raised by the military itself.

Nevertheless, popular sympathy could carry the movement only so far. Eventually, the moment came — precisely at what point is yet unknown to us as outsiders — when *Sendero*'s leadership felt that it must resort to force to consolidate the gains made and to expand further. The infrastructure already in place was the vehicle for expansion. Terror and guerrilla action served to protect it and to give it power.

It is at this point that the crossover occurs in an insurgency: the impetus behind the movement is no longer grievances as such but the mechanisms of organization themselves. These manifest themselves, in particular, in recruiting. Because an alternative political body has come into existence, with all the coercive mechanisms that adhere to such status, it need no longer rely only upon those with grievances derived from structural injustice to fill its ranks. Instead, it can appeal to a more complex mixture of motives.

'Human factor considerations', in other words, come to the fore.[15]

The advance and consolidation of *Sendero* in this respect has been very methodical. When a region targeted is deemed to have sufficient popular committees, a 'Support Base' can be declared (see Map 10).[16] According to several sources in Peruvian intelligence, the annual production in such areas is divided in half, with 50 per cent going to the people, the other 50 per cent going to the *Sendero* apparatus for stockpiling and use during operations.[17] Examining the map reveals 20 such bases known to be in existence in 1989, with an additional 80 popular committees. These are healthy figures even if not particularly large.

Hence there exists an extensive dual web enmeshing the people: the overt system of sectoral organizations, coordinated by the 'Revolutionary Front for the Defense of the Village' (*Frente Revolucionario de Defensa del Pueblo*), and the covert system of the party, with its cells. These party cells, in turn, are coordinated by 'Local Committees' (*Comites Locales* or CL), which themselves fall under 'Sub-Zones' (*Sub Zonales* or SZ). The Sub-Zones belong to 'Zones' (normally referred to as CZ after the Spanish *Comite Zonal*), the Zones to 'Regional Commands'.

It should be borne in mind that in each case what is being described is a *level of organization* working in an area of operation. What I am rendering as 'Zone', for example, is actually a 'Zone Committee' (CZ), in the Spanish, exercising a span of influence and control over a physical area and human population. There is no rigid system for the assignment of territory. Sub-Zones (SZ) generally correspond to government provinces, the components of the larger departments, but this is not always the case and may be modified at will.

Apparently, boundary changes are the responsibility of the Regional Commands, each headed by a secretary and sub-secretary, working with five other staff members responsible for military operations, logistics, security, agitation and propaganda, and administrative organization. Peru's size makes these Regional Commands quite independent. Yet they do not appear to have the degree of autonomy enjoyed by, say, a Communist Party of the Philippines regional body.

To illustrate how this system works in practice, we need only consider Ayacucho. The central organs of *Sendero Luminoso* are of standard Leninist form. A Politburo and Central Committee, together with a 'Permanent Committee', or Secretariat, oversee

MAP 10
SUPPORT BASES AND POPULAR COMMITTEES WITHIN THE AYACUCHO
REGIONAL COMMITTEE (effective date 1989)

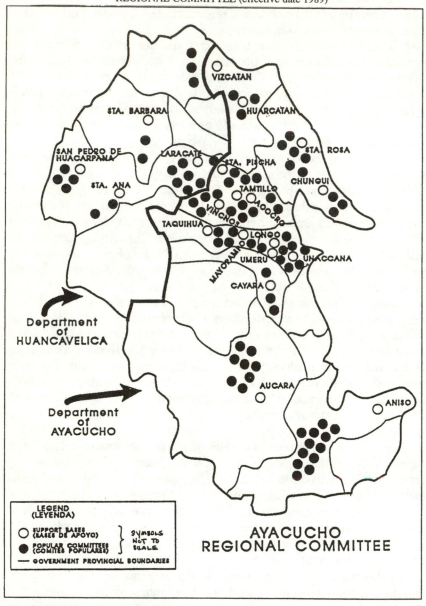

Graphics: Soldier of Fortune magazine.

party operations. These party operations are conducted in six regions nationwide, each headed by a party Regional Committee: south, central, north, northeast, the metropolitan area (Lima), and 'the principal area' (Ayacucho). That Ayacucho rates its own Regional Committee stems from its being the birthplace of *Sendero*. Actually, as the communists expanded, the Ayacucho Regional Committee came to embrace more territory than the department of Ayacucho alone. Ayacucho Department thus comprises four of the Regional Committee's five Zones. The other Zone, however, is to the west in the neighboring department of Huancavelica. Regardless, all five Zones are further divided into a varying number of Sub-Zones, normally three or four (see Map 11).[18]

There is one anomaly (shown on Map 11) that I have as yet been unable to work out. Each of the Ayacucho Zones appears to have under it, on an equal status, not only its Sub-Zones (SZ) but also a certain number of Local Committees (CL). The operational reason for this remains to be determined, but it seems the few CL in question have progressed to the point that they may eventually be given SZ status.

Just as the role of these particular CL is unclear, so, too, are the lines of command vague between the political infrastructure just outlined and *Sendero*'s military component. In a normal communist guerrilla movement, the primacy of politics dictates a chain of command that is quite standard — all military formations are controlled by party organizations. A district guerrilla unit, to cite a hypothetical illustration, would report to and take orders from the district party apparatus. Not so, it would seem, for *Sendero*, where 'Guerrilla Zones' (ZG is the Spanish acronym) are defined by operational necessity and may straddle any number of SZ (see Map 12 for ZG in Ayacucho).[19] Principal authority is supposed to lie with the Political Commissar of the ZG, but there have been increasing reports of military commanders taking charge. Since the latter, like the commissar and the three other ZG staff members (logistics, information, and organization), is a party member, the division may not be serious. Nonetheless, it is unorthodox and certainly merits further examination as data becomes available. For the moment, we may note that, like the tension between the leadership and the followers, all insurgent movements also must grapple with the issue of who wields the power: those who 'talk' or those who 'fight'? Invariably, military ascendance results in a

MAP 11
SUB-ZONES AND LOCAL COMMITTEES WITHIN THE AYACUCHO
REGIONAL COMMITTEE (effective date: 1989)

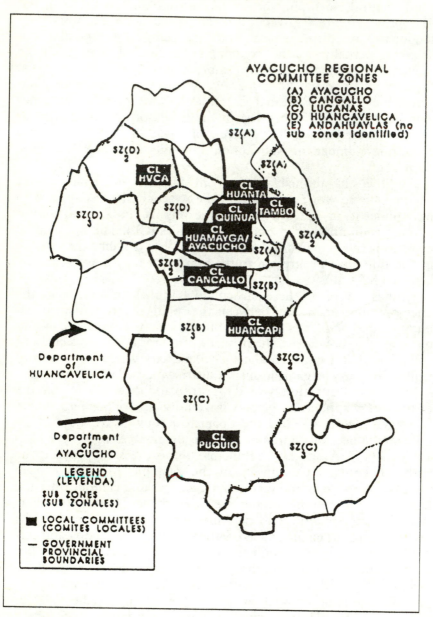

Graphics: Soldier of Fortune magazine.

MAP 12
GUERRILLA ZONES WITHIN THE AYACUCHO REGIONAL COMMITTEE
(effective date: 1989)

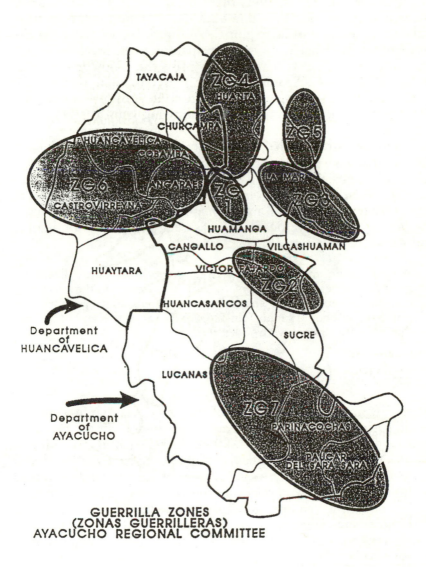

GUERRILLA ZONES
(ZONAS GUERRILLERAS)
AYACUCHO REGIONAL COMMITTEE

Graphics: Soldier of Fortune magazine.

bloodier conflict, because decisions begin to be driven by considerations of force.

More to our expectations than the apparent politico-military command arrangements, within each ZG is found the classic guerrilla tripartition of main, regional, and local forces, called in the *Sendero* setup, respectively, the principal force, the local force, and the base force. Together, these comprise the 'Popular Guerrilla Army' (EGP is the Spanish acronym). Recruitment is standard, with local forces gaining manpower from the most promising base force personnel, the principal force drawing from the best local force men.

'Men', it may be added, is certainly a misnomer, since as much as half of any *Sendero* unit is comprised of women. This high percentage of female combatants has prompted any number of explanations. Some note that women join as a route to freedom from the horrible conditions of marriage most must endure in the highlands.[20] An alternative possibility has been offered by a longtime aid worker:

> Women are not mistreated *per se* in the *sierra* [mountains]. There is a great deal of beating both ways. In truth, it is women in the *sierra* who control the purse strings. They function as equals, so it's perfectly logical that they should simply join *Sendero* like anyone else, not because they're particularly downtrodden.[21]

Insurgent Strategic Dimensions

Men or women, the numbers involved are not very large. Peruvian intelligence estimates that in Ayacucho in mid-1989 the principal and local forces fielded about 250 personnel each, the base force, 750.[22] Only the principal force there appears to have high-powered firearms (HPF), normally AK-47s captured from the police, mixed with some RPG-7s from the same source. The essential formation is the column, which operates with no fixed table of organization and equipment. Groups of 10–15 personnel are the norm, with larger units formed by consolidation. All of these combatants must be party members.

Constantly moving, the columns go from village to village. That such small numbers are able to have the impact they do amidst a population, in Ayacucho alone, of more than half a million, stems from their ability to project their presence and to deal with those who defy the *Sendero* political apparatus. With combat power serving as a shield, the communist political organization has the capacity to organize the communities which the government often lacks. 'There is at least one instance', relates a journalist of long experience in Latin America and Peru, 'where 2,000 villagers were brought together by three columns of 40 armed men, then given various courses of instruction. It's unclear as to what precisely course content was, but plays and so forth were held. Several *Sendero* cadre reportedly got drunk and were strongly disciplined.'[23]

If they were only 'strongly disciplined', they were lucky. *Sendero*'s puritanical regulations are more often enforced with savage discipline. It is this same mode of behavior which has ultimately proved the movement's undoing in many areas of Ayacucho. In at least several recorded instances, whole villages have risen up and, using homemade weapons, often no more than sharpened stakes, wiped out or chased away the *Sendero* cadre. They have then appealed to the security forces for assistance in meeting *Sendero*'s inevitable attempt to exact retribution. Such help has often been slow in coming, but co-ordination and use of militias is improving.

Faced with this situation, *Sendero* has had to expand its efforts into areas other than the Ayacucho heartland. One of Peru's top military leaders offered this mid-1989 analysis:

> The Upper Huallaga is the key area right now, although Ayacucho is the heart and soul of the movement. The Upper Huallaga is being used as *Sendero*'s training camp and source of major financing. They are putting together their armed forces there. Providing security for the drug lords is good training.[24]

The dilemma the government faced at this time was substantial. Peru was the source of perhaps 65 per cent of the world's coca, from which cocaine was extracted, and the 3,000 square-mile Upper Huallaga Valley was the major production area. In an economy which until recently was effectively bankrupt, coca planting remained virtually the only growth industry, and, certainly, the only livelihood for tens of thousands of peasants. Capitalizing on the ill-will aroused by government eradication efforts, *Sendero* was able to establish a mass base. Unlike the 10–15-man columns of

Ayacucho, actual companies (60–120 men) were formed in the Upper Huallaga, and deals with drug lords reportedly provided M-60 medium machine-guns, 81mm mortars, and grenade-launchers, a considerable upgrading of armament.

America's complete preoccupation with the drug war did not make the situation any easier for the Peruvians. Wedded to a strategy of plant eradication, Washington financed an anti-drug firebase at Santa Lucia, north of Tingo Maria in Huanuco Department (population, 609,200), from which Drug Enforcement Agency (DEA) personnel operated with Peruvian forces. Lima was constantly pressed to go after growers and refineries more aggressively. Yet, said the high-ranking military officer cited above:

> The US has its own priorities and strategy. We fit in only because of the drugs. Our attitude is simple. Coca is just raw material. It is the refining which gives it astronomical value. It is the people on the distribution end who have the power and influence. The growers are small fish. Still, in the States there is no serious campaign to fight drugs. Down here we have 150,000 *campesinos* who earn their living off the stuff. To go after them is a mistake. It is the drug lords who are the real threat. We help the US right now, because as far as our security is concerned, there is no distinction between the drug lords and *Sendero*. [But] our policy is to solve the security problems first, to get rid of *Sendero* and then the drugs. Our first priority must be attacks on the system.[25]

It was a dilemma. Buoyed by its successes in the Upper Huallaga, *Sendero* pressed its organizational efforts in other parts of Peru, especially in the critical breadbasket of the Mantaro Valley, located to the east of Lima in Junin Department (population, 542,900). Additionally, it tried hard to work in the teeming slums of Lima. There, paradoxically, where conditions seemed most ripe for revolt, *Sendero* had uneven success.

Failure in Lima's slums was but one of the many problems which afflicted the movement. Though expansion in the Upper Huallaga was easy early on, against the command of Brigadier General Alberto Arciniega, late in the decade, progress became more difficult. For Arciniega flatly stated that security concerns had to take precedence over the drug war. He allowed the peasants to cultivate their coca, as long as they did not throw in their lot with *Sendero*. In pursuing such a risky strategy, Arciniega faced a host of obstacles, not the least of which was the staggering amount of money available to drug traders. To keep his units clean was a virtually impossible task but one he handled in such a manner as to earn praise from many sources. In response, *Sendero* turned to a more military-oriented approach. Observed one interviewee, 'There are strong indications that in the Huallaga Valley the military component of *Sendero* has been overshadowing the political, and that the columns themselves are not very well coordinated.'[26]

Regardless of problems, it is clear that *Sendero* has been able to maintain its presence and infrastructure. It has done so with very little external assistance. Though it has cautiously modified its strategy of total self-reliance and now apparently works for some forms of outside support, especially in Europe from the 'solidarity groups' that have consistently been a source of funds for Latin American and Asian communist insurgencies,[27] the campaign remains essentially an internal phenomenon. A Peruvian analyst explains:

> There is no groundswell of support [for *Sendero*]. 'The Inca's Last Rebellion' explanation is bullshit. Many people attempt to vote with their feet, to flee areas under *Sendero* control. But the *Senderistas* do have a sizable level of support, though all of this base is not necessarily active. If you put them as a political party, they would be, for sure, a minority party, a tiny party even, but in some areas of the country they might be as much as 20–30 per cent of the people there. These, to be sure, are not the most populated areas (e.g., Ayacucho, the Upper Huallaga Valley). In other words, 'Shining Path' is an armed party. They are not a tiny band of conspirators. They do have a social base.[28]

This social base allows *Sendero* to survive. As it presses to incorporate others into its mass base, violence assumes greater proportions. The analyst continues:

> *Sendero* is very consistent in its approach to popular war, though it may be noted it is using much more the Vietcong methods than the methods of early Mao. Terror and coercion are for it very important ways to gain support, going hand in hand with propaganda and agitprop. Persuasion versus terror is an incorrect dichotomy in analyzing their methods. Indoctrination holds the key. The 'propaganda of the deed' is very important. The perception of strength goes a long way to being a magnet. True, there are cases of sheer coercion. Yet, generally, there is a good balance between indoctrination and coercion.[29]

Again, we take exception to some specifics. The view that the Vietcong use of violence was a more integral part of their approach than of its Maoist predecessor would appear in many respects to be more a creation of analytical oversight than reality. The general thrust of the analysis above, though, is accurate: balance between persuasion and coercion held the key. As long as *Sendero* could continue — as Mao would advise — to use violence as a tool, as opposed to an end unto itself, to facilitate the functioning and expansion of the infrastructure, the movement could remain viable. Similarly, on the government side, it was critical not to focus on *Sendero*'s brutality and thus miss the forest for the trees. The movement did have a mass base, even if it was a small mass base when considered on a national, or even regional, scale. Yet it was precisely upon this reality that the communists did stumble: they used their Maoist approach, their tools, in a purposive effort to force a solution for society's ills upon a populace not ready to accept their answer.

We can appreciate this flaw by returning to the case of Ayacucho, where *Sendero* was born. The 'Corner of the Dead' sobriquet came not from the miserable environment but from the fierce Indian battles which bloodied the soil even before the Spanish arrived. With the coming of the communists, however, the term became something of a self-fulfilling prophecy. As outlined above, *Sendero* initially focused upon organizational work and reaching out to the people. Once the 'revolutionary struggle' was inaugurated, however, the death rate rapidly soared to 500 per year, with 2,000-plus dead in 1983 alone. This translated to about 100 deaths per 100,000 population per annum, far ahead of the murder rates in such US crime centers as Washington DC or Detroit.

Further, it was not just the numbers but the *way* those 500 were usually killed — butchered would have been a more appropriate term. As the American official noted earlier, inherent in every insurgent murder was a message, often associated with Indian myths since the target population was Indian. Thus feet would be cut off and sewed on backwards to prevent the walk to heaven; or the mouth would be stitched shut to prevent the soul from properly escaping; or an entire community would be forced to inflict a knife wound on a writhing victim, so that all would be implicated, hence involved. In return, the authorities frequently inflicted their own retribution. Peru came to rank high on Amnesty

International's watch list. Although not always a reliable source, the rating was worth sober evaluation.

And it was killing which had an increased impact due to the very lay of the land. Though virtually the entire department was mountains, with peaks rising as high as 5,453 meters (17,890 feet), the jumble of crags was cut by innumerable river valleys. A patrol might require equipment suitable to a Himalayan climbing expedition one moment, a group of Arizona rattlesnake hunters the next. Snow-capped peaks torn by fierce winds overlooked cactus-filled desert. A journey which might have taken less than half an hour by helicopter would require days on foot. To make the Alice-in-Wonderland geographical transition complete, in the northeastern reaches, high jungle brought to mind stretches of Southeast Asia. Lush vegetation embraced strategic hamlets guarded by militias and marines. Society, in other words, was atomized, so a brutal action in a small community had a disproportionate impact.

There was no particular will to resist. Life, to borrow a phrase, was already nasty, short, and brutish. The land was poor and so, therefore, were the people. Poverty was absolute; average life expectancy barely passed 50 years. Malnutrition was the norm; the infant mortality rate was double that of the rest of Latin America. Most of the people, the Indians, had been frozen out of the national mainstream for centuries. As Lima had become a passable copy of any Western metropolis, the small villages, or *pueblos*, in the Andes had languished in a virtual caste system.

'This is one of the most racist societies on earth', commented a source, a former general officer and government official.

> I have a theory. Our Indians, which are a majority, have been mistreated since Inca times. The Incas were tyrants. They treated their subject peoples like slaves. They were the first imperialists. When the Spanish came, it was the same. Then, when we became independent, the rich also mistreated them...so the Indians became like animals. *Sendero Luminoso* is the answer to that.[30]

That, at least, is how *Sendero* looked at the situation: a harsh life in a harsh land coupled with centuries of harsh oppression. They were the liberators promising a way out. It should have been instant rebellion. Huancavelica Department, next door, for example, was even poorer. It had an infant mortality rate double that of Ayacucho! Yet, as noted, reality did not fall in line with ideology,

and the populace refused to rise. Following its early organizational successes, *Sendero* found that it could not expand its mass base
through persuasion alone but had to turn instead to terror.

For what could it offer? As was the case in northeast Thailand,
the carrying capacity of the land and its integration into the
national polity were the heart of the problem. It was for this very
reason that *Sendero* all along intended Ayacucho to be but a spring-
board to the seizure of state-power. It was this role that the populace refused to assume. Unwilling to accept the role of democratic
alternative, the communists had no choice but to move beyond
persuasion and feedback mechanisms (the mass line) to coercion.
This was possible, of course, because the mechanics of Maoist
organization were powerful enough, in the societal vacuum which
passed as the Peruvian state, to hold sway. Indeed, once its initial
welcome had worn thin, *Sendero* expanded due only to the mis-
steps of the government.

Government Search for an Approach

Lima's repression, in particular, played a major role in insurgent
growth by forcing the populace to opt for self-defense under communist guidance. Initially, Lima was slow to react to the communist challenge at all. The newly installed civilian government of
President Fernando Balaunde Terry was sure that the military
demands for commitment of forces, made as early as 1980, were
but a screen for their renewed involvement in politics. So he sent
instead the Civil Guard, which, through its brutality, promptly created *Senderistas* out of previously uncommitted *campesinos*.
Finally, as 1982 ended, Lima relented and deployed army units. An
Emergency Zone was declared in Ayacucho and neighboring areas.
Battle was joined. By this time, of course, *Sendero* was deeply
entrenched. Those who did not go along willingly were forced by
terror to toe the line. Army atrocities made the situation worse.

There matters remained, as under Balaunde's uninspired
administration, the country drifted. In particular, the economy, for
all practical purposes, collapsed. Great hopes were raised when
April 1985 brought to office Alan Garcia Perez, a 35-year-old
social democrat who represented the centrist-leftist *Alianza
Popular Revolucionaria Americana* (APRA, or the American
Popular Revolutionary Alliance). He seemed a breath of fresh air.

He proved, instead, something of a cyclone run amok. Unilateral decisions, such as declaring that Peru would no longer fully service its substantial foreign debt, led to a cutoff in much foreign aid and to the flight of capital. There followed economic chaos.

To make matters worse, Garcia refused to take remedial action, relying instead upon the printing of money to meet Peru's financial obligations. In one illustrative move in the summer of 1989, he ordered the governing board of directors of the National Bank to print more money — equivalent to one-fourth of all notes then in circulation. When the board balked, he simply stacked it with compliant directors. The crisp, new bills earned him a temporary reprieve, as he was able to pay government salaries (the government was, and remains, Peru's largest employer); but the influx of worthless paper set the *Inti* on a tailspin which saw it eventually soar from 3,000 per US $1 to a million to one. Small wonder, given the scope of such difficulties, that regional development and integration languished.

Still, it should not have been surprising that there were individuals who could see their way clear to solutions. Though a deeply flawed state, Peru was nevertheless a democratic system, even if a struggling one. Remarkably astute, for instance, was the analysis of a government adviser connected with a leading official think tank, himself a former high-ranking general officer and government official:

An oligarchy rules this country. The military knew this when it took power in 1968. Then, we had a social pyramid where one per cent had everything. The military [1968–80] set out to change this. It was very difficult, but it was necessary. Our problem was strategic — how to do that. Various ways with which you're familiar were tried, including widespread land reform. The purpose of the military was right, but it is possible that in the execution we were in error. We have a version of the same problem now. It's logical that the oligarchy doesn't want to lose its privileges. That is the principal conflict [in Peru]. They don't put their profits back into development of the infrastructure and [thereby] increase employment. Velasco [General Juan Velasco Alvarado led the 3 October 1968 coup and what came to be called 'the Peruvian Experiment'] tried to impose his will on these people. We should have avoided confrontation by relying more on persuasion. You can't turn the country against foreign investment, as we inadvertently succeeded in doing. We also forgot the attitude of the revolutionary populace. We thought because we were a popular government, there would be no space for a subversive recruitment. In this we were incorrect. *Sendero* ideology is very complicated, a hybrid of all manner of doctrines. But they found the proper space for development of their forces. We weren't taking decisive action to develop areas such as Ayacucho, and they sought out those areas. The problem was compounded after the military left power. The Balaunde government failed to move vigorously against the guerrillas, because he was too afraid the military would use its strength to get back into power... Now we are caught in our current dilemma. When Garcia got into power, he was very popular. Yet he has exacerbated the very conditions which created the opening for the subversives. Mass communications has made the situation even more unsettled, because publicity strengthens the terrorist image. ... We need to revive our earlier plans and be very self-critical. We must look for the enemy within, not as a manifestation of outside forces. Special operations must be used against revolutionary operations. You have to look at the problem with a strategic vision. You must support economic and social actions of the government, because it is these contradictions which produce the conflict. In the mountains the government must take actions to lift the level of life. Further, we have not yet integrated the regions of insurgency — as well as many others — into the national life. Our country is so large and so diverse. It is not integrated. We don't have a nation-state. We have a meeting of regions. The real problem of Peru is integration.[31]

Such analysis was not an exception. Obviously, the crucial question was whether these sentiments, expressed in Lima, could be translated into action on the ground in places such as Ayacucho. Increasingly, even while Garcia remained president — he was to be replaced in June 1990 by Alberto Fujimori — they were. Ironically, as in the other cases we have examined, it was military officers, rather than their civilian superiors, who took the lead in this effort. In the forefront, of course, was the army.

Peru's army just prior to Fujimori's election on 10 June 1990 was fairly large, with some 50 infantry battalions. It was organized in a standard format: divisions, which were in reality brigade-size, headed by a brigadier general; battalions — the term really meant nothing in a formal organizational sense since *ad hoc* arrangements predominated — were three per division; three to four companies per battalion; three platoons per company; three 10-man squads per platoon. Personnel arrangements were weak. Too many officers were kept occupied with 'other duties'. The noncommissioned officer (NCO) corps was not a viable entity. MOS (military occupational specialty) training existed only for the officers, leaving troops to learn what they could on-the-job. Further, units were not deployed as such. Groups of individuals were simply put together. Most tellingly, for what it said about the lack priority the insurgency held in the upper echelons, the heaviest concentrations of forces — complete with armor, mechanized artillery, and air support — were along the borders with Ecuador and Chile, countries with which Peru had fought wars in the past.[32]

In such a framework, the character of individual commanders assumed salience. The controversial success of Brigadier General Arciniega has been mentioned. Likewise, good commanders rotated with bad in other areas. It was indicative of just how weak the *Sendero* position was that whenever a competent commander was present, the communists experienced difficulties.

An illustration was provided in 1989 when Brigadier General Howard Rodriguez was given command of 2nd Division in Ayacucho. He sought to use his four battalions in the most efficient manner. The area of operations was divided into nine zones, each with a variable number of BCGs (*Base Contra Guerrilla*), which were sited in key locations where they could protect population concentrations and civic action projects. Altogether, the BCGs numbered around 50. Each, in turn, was manned by 50 men broken down into three officer-led patrols of 15 each. The extra men comprised the headquarters element. (It may be noted that the 50 BCG x 50 men comes to 2,500, which would appear a near-total deployment of four battalions.) There was no long logistical tail. Two helicopters serviced the entire enormous area that was Ayacucho. At any one time, one of the 15-man patrols was out on long range operations (defined as 3–5 km of straight-line distance, which would normally be much more when terrain was considered); the second was closer in, on local operations; and the third was present in the BCG for security and training.

In addition to the officer commanding the patrol, each included an NCO, an RTO (i.e., the radio operator), and a 'sanitation man'. Normal patrols lasted anywhere from 15–20 days. Rations of corn, rice, and sugar were carried in field packs. The universal garb was a black pullover sweater with fatigue trousers and a black ski cap (most equipped with pulldown masks to conceal the face during operations in areas where anonymity was important). Standard battle rifle was the Belgian-made 7.62x51mm FN FAL, though in every patrol at least one soldier carried a shotgun.

Belgian 7.62mmx51mm FN MAG 58 machine-guns were in the inventory but were in my experience not often taken on patrols. A wide variety of other weapons were present. Patrol leaders often favored the German Heckler & Koch 9mm MP5 submachine gun. For communication the US-made A/N-PRC-77 and the French TRC 372 were used, but the rugged terrain played havoc with radio effectiveness.

Though the top priority for patrols was to seek out the enemy, civic action was also a normal part of the routine. That the troops were at times faced by profound decisions caused by the nature of the war was obvious from the number of orphans who had been 'adopted' by the division and who lived at the headquarters. Naturally, there were other, more ambitious projects at hand. One major effort was to punch through the eight kilometers of road from Huancayo to Ayacucho. The intent was to cut substantially the days required to make that tortuous journey. It was a trek regularly undertaken by the populace due to traditional linkages between the towns. A road would immeasurably lighten the burden. Other projects which were being undertaken by the two engineer battalions at hand had similar goals: to improve the quality of life.

That the 'hearts and minds' approach was making headway was obvious from the numbers enlisting in the *rondas campesinos*, or self-defense forces. Frequently maligned by the Peruvian left, the militia — as was the case, for example, in Thailand, the Philippines, and Sri Lanka's south — were seen as the linchpin of the counterinsurgency effort. In the late 1980s, they were still spread unevenly and in various states of organization. In Ayacucho, they frightened many urban bureaucrats, because they had sprung up autonomously in widespread areas. Frequently they were armed only with sharpened stakes and knives. Yet they had attacked *Sendero* cadre, even units, and begged the authorities for arms. In Ayacucho, they were frequently given old shotguns. In Lima at the time, a fierce debate continued concerning the wisdom of passing out weapons on a more widespread basis.

In time, this was done nationwide. Pending the formal decision to arm wholesale the militia, which would follow Fujimori's election, the principal military aim was to link the units, whatever their weapons, to the BCGs with effective communications. Troops could thus respond to calls for assistance. Backing up both the troops and the militia were 'special companies' and a strike force kept at divisional headquarters (a strike force, of course, would be comprised of one or more 'special companies', but a special company would not necessarily be on duty in the strike force at any one time). The BCGs and the militias secured their area by establishing a government presence and by taking the countryside away from the insurgents. They were, in effect, an anvil. The hammer was provided by the 'special companies' and strike forces.[33]

Even before the change in governments, the combination set forth above — regular patrolling by the BCG units, militia static defense, and strike force reaction by the special companies — appeared to be having an effect upon Shining Path operations. In Ayacucho itself, the situation had stabilized. Yet the focus of insurgent action simply shifted elsewhere, in particular to a renewed effort to isolate Lima.[34]

The New Hiatus: Peruvian 'People's War'?

Lima, of course, did not fall, but the government of Alan Garcia did. The state of despair to which he had reduced the country has been brilliantly captured by Alma Guillermoprieto, a staff writer for *The New Yorker*, in discussing the candidacy of Fujimori's ultimate rival for the presidency, the renowned novelist Mario Vargas Llosa:

> Mario Vargas Llosa debated whether to run for president in 1987, arguably the worst year Peruvians had endured in this century. Drought parched the land. Whatever can be described as the industrial sector (a handful of manufacturers of cement, hairpins, and Inca Kola, more or less) was decrepit and near extinction. Unemployment was well over 50 per cent. Inflation would soon reach the breathtaking high of 7,600 per cent a year. A huge and inept bureaucracy gobbled up whatever small proportion of the government budget was not devoured by graft and interest payments on a foreign debt equivalent to 45 per cent of the GNP. Shining Path, the guerrilla movement led by Abimael Guzman — a stolid former small-town college professor otherwise known as President Gonzalo — rampaged through the countryside, bringing the art of murder to new levels of senselessness and gore. Presiding over this mess was Alan Garcia, a toothy opportunist of some charm and no scruple, who was about to seal his country's financial disaster by declaring a moratorium on all payments on the foreign debt. By the end of Garcia's term, Peru had been declared

ineligible for foreign loans, its per capita gross national product had shrunk by 13.7 per cent, and net government reserves were $142 million in the red. 'The Peru of my childhood', the author [Vargas Llosa] writes, 'was a poor and backward country; in the last decades mainly since the beginning of [General Juan Velasco Alvarado's] dictatorship and in particular during Alan Garcia's presidency, it had become poorer still and in many regions wretchedly poverty-stricken, a country that was going back to inhuman patterns of existence.' It was clear to everyone that the 1990 presidential elections would be decided on economic issues, even more than on the urgent question of dealing with the Shining Path.[35]

Though his analysis of the situation was correct, Vargas Llosa was unable to inspire the masses. Instead, they elected a virtual unknown, Fujimori, Rector of the Agrarian University of Peru, with no prior political experience, to the presidency by a margin of 57 to 34 per cent. 'El Chinito', as Fujimori was nicknamed during the campaign, promptly instituted a draconian economic solution and various reforms, all of which culminated in his 5 April 1992 *autogolpe*, or coup against his own government. Congress was disbanded, though subsequently elections for a replacement body were held under a new constitution, approved narrowly by plebiscite. These actions cost Peru dearly in international alienation and cutoffs of foreign aid, particularly from the US. Such factors did not prove crucial, because on 12 September 1992 Guzman was captured.[36]

Found in Lima through old-fashioned detective work, Guzman was detained together with, ultimately, much of his Politburo, as well as members of the Central Committee and hundreds of other cadre of various degrees of importance. So centralized had *Sendero* become that cutting off the head dealt the movement a body blow. Hundreds of guerrillas surrendered, and insurgent incidents nationwide dropped markedly, even as Fujimori's economic reforms — notably his privatization efforts — caused the economy to grow at roughly 7 per cent per annum. Most crucially, the specter of demoralization which had set in was lifted. The populace abandoned its defeatist mindset. Simultaneously, Fujimori expanded considerably the arming of militia formations nationwide and the tempo of counterinsurgency operations by regular forces.

Here the situation has remained. *Sendero* has rapidly reconstituted its infrastructure; insurgent attacks have again begun to climb, as has inflation, though not substantially in either case. Fujimori remains exceptionally popular, despite his rubber-stamp parliament and disapproval abroad at the apparent upswing of human rights violations as the security forces have gone on the offensive. Yet matters have not returned to anything approximating their previous abysmal state. Nor are they likely to do so.

The reasons are apparent: Fujimori's 'anti-democratic' moves, in fact, have been grounded in popular desires to a greater extent than was the case with the actions of the corrupt system he displaced. What remains to be seen is whether his attempts to institutionalize this grounding prove viable. Regardless, his foe is no longer the same. For all its 'Maoist' form, *Sendero* has proved to have little substance. Furthermore, it has been outmobilized for the moment by a government which, even if imperfect, is an improvement, not only upon that which it replaced, but upon any conceivable alternative Shining Path could offer. Despite its imperfection, the system nonetheless offers mechanisms for peaceful change. Had Peru the more vibrant federalism possessed by the Philippines, this might allow for the decentralization of decision-making and thus the growth of enhanced democracy; the insurgency would consequently find itself completely marginalized. As matters now stand, there is a hiatus of sorts in the struggle, with the government having a temporary advantage in the effort to provide a viable solution to the popular demand for lives of dignity.

Therein lies the answer to the riddle of a movement such as *Sendero Luminoso*. To wit, how could a group which in 1980 numbered in the neighborhood of 180 people have brought a system the size of Peru to its knees, whatever its shortcomings? Misguided analysts were sure the answer had to lie in some form of popular appeal, but reality was more stark: It was the sheer magnitude of the violence which the insurgents inflicted. Over ten years (1980–90) they caused economic destruction estimated at a figure equivalent to one-third to one-half of the GNP; they killed some 30,000 people. They were able to grow because the system was so incredibly weak, systemic response so inappropriate.[37] When the momentum of their original appeal to grievances had run its course, however, terror was all that was left to the movement to consolidate its gains and expand further. There never were put in place by Guzman democratic mechanisms for involving the population in decisionmaking. With the wholesale adoption of terror, even feedback as a tool for organizational behavior modification was abandoned. Thus we see the logical conclusion to Maoist insurgency.

NOTES

1. Primary material for this chapter was collected during fieldwork in Peru in Aug. 1989 and has been supplemented since by correspondence with sources as well as additional research. Peruvian realities necessitate that no person quoted be identified by name. I have earlier drawn upon my research for the following publications: 'Corner of the Dead', *Soldier of Fortune* [hereafter SOF], 15/3 (March 1990), pp.44–51 (contd.); 'The Guerrilla Myth', SOF, 15/5 (May 1990), pp.56–9, 65–8; 'Peru's Fatal Distraction', SOF, 15/7 (July 1990), pp.30–3; 'Terrorism vs. Terror: The Case of Peru', *Counterterrorism & Security*, 2/2 (May–June 1990), pp.26–33; 'Making Revolution With Shining Path', Ch.10 in David Scott Palmer (ed.), *The Shining Path of Peru* (NY: St. Martin's Press, 1992), 2nd ed. forthcoming; and 'Making Revolution: *Sendero Luminoso* in Peru', *Small Wars and Insurgencies*, 3/1 (Spring 1992), pp.22–46.
    No definitive treatment of *Sendero Luminoso* exists, though there is a substantial body of English-language material. Best known work is probably that of David Scott Palmer, as well as of Cynthia McClintock. Representative works by Palmer, who at one time shared an office with *Sendero* leader Abimael Guzman Reynoso, include: 'Expulsion From a Peruvian University', Ch.14 in Robert Textor (ed.), *Cultural Frontiers of the Peace Corps* (Cambridge, MA: Harvard UP, 1966), pp.243–70; 'The Sendero Luminoso Rebellion in Rural Peru', in Georges Fauriol (ed.), *Latin American Insurgencies* (Washington, DC: Georgetown Univ. Center for Strategic and Int. Studies/National Defense Univ., 1985), pp.67–96; 'Rebellion in Rural Peru: The Origins and Evolution of Sendero Luminoso', *Comparative Politics*, 18/2 (Jan. 1986), pp.127–46; 'Terrorism as a Revolutionary Strategy: Peru's *Sendero Luminoso*', Ch.5 in Barry Rubin (ed.), *The Politics of Terrorism: Terror as a State and Revolutionary Strategy* (Washington, DC: Johns Hopkins UP, 1989), pp.129–52; and (certainly his most comprehensive work) 'The Revolutionary Terrorism of Peru's Shining Path', Ch.12 in Martha Crenshaw (ed.), *Terrorism in Context* (College Station: Pennsylvania State UP, forthcoming). Palmer, of course, is the editor of *The Shining Path of Peru* (see above).
    Illustrative works by Cynthia McClintock are: 'Why Peasants Rebel: The Case of Sendero Luminoso', *World Politics*, 37/1 (Oct. 1984), pp.48–84; and 'Peru's Sendero Luminoso Rebellion: Origins and Trajectory', Ch.2 in Susan Eckstein (ed.), *Power and Popular Protest: Latin American Social Movements* (Berkeley, CA: Univ. of California Press, 1989), pp.61–101.
    Considerable exception to Palmer's work, as well as that of McClintock, is taken by Deborah Poole and Gerardo Renique in their horatory piece, 'The New Chroniclers of Peru: US Scholars and Their "Shining Path" of Peasant Rebellion', *Bulletin of Latin American Research*, 10/2 (1991), pp.133–91. More balanced and useful is their *Peru: Time of Fear* (London: Latin America Bureau [Research and Action], 1992. Another new contribution of note is Simon Strong, *Shining Path: The World's Deadliest Revolutionary Force* (London: HarperCollins, 1992).
    For the structural origins of agrarian activism in Peru, cf. Jeffery M. Paige's Ch.3 (pp.124–210), 'Peru: Hacienda and Plantation', in his *Agrarian Revolution: Social Movements and Export Agriculture in the Underdeveloped World* (NY: The Free Press, 1975), as well as his conclusions, pp.334–76.
    On the origins of *Sendero*'s worldview: Colin Harding, 'Antonio Diaz Martinez and the Ideology of Sendero Luminoso', *Bulletin of Latin American Research*, 7/1 (1988), pp.65–73. On Guzman: Nicholas Shakespeare, 'In Pursuit of Guzman', *Granta*,

No.23 (Spring 1988), pp.150–95. The best primary material on Guzman's philosophy is a Spanish–language interview he gave in July 1988 to *El Diario* [Lima]. It is available in an English translation done by the Committee to Support the Revolution in Peru, *Interview With Chairman Gonzalo* (Berkeley, CA: 1991).

A lengthy overview of the insurgency prior to the 1990 elections is Raymond Bonner, 'A Reporter at Large: Peru's War', *The New Yorker*, 4 Jan. 1988, pp.31–58. Efforts to explore recent trends in *Sendero* funding through involvement in the narcotics trade include: Arnaldo Claudio and Stephan K. Stewman, 'Peru, *Sendero Luminoso* and the Narcotrafficking Alliance', *Low Intensity Conflict and Law Enforcement* [London], 1/3 (Winter 1992), pp.279–92; and William Rosenau, 'Poor Peru', *The American Spectator*, 23/12 (Dec. 1990), pp.16–18.

There are numerous Peruvian works in Spanish dealing wholly or in part with *Sendero*. Among the best are those by Gustavo Gorriti, esp.his *Sendero Luminoso: historia de la guerra milenaria en el Peru* (Lima: Apoyo, 1990), the first of several projected volumes; and the prolific Carlos Ivan Degregori, esp. *Ayacucho 1969–1979: el surgimiento de Sendero Luminoso* (Lima: IEP, 1990).

2. William A. Hazleton and Sandra Woy–Hazleton, 'Terrorism and the Marxist Left: Peru's Struggle Against Sendero Luminoso', *Terrorism*, 11/4 (1988), p.481.

3. Idem, 'The Influence of Sendero Luminoso After One Decade of Insurgency', paper presented to Int. Studies Assoc., London, 1 April 1989.

4. See, e.g., James Anderson, *Sendero Luminoso: A New Revolutionary Model?* (London: Inst. for the Study of Terrorism, 1987). The title is suggestive: 'A New Revolutionary Model'. In the first two pages of the introduction (pp.11–12), he thrice calls attention to *Sendero* as 'a unique variety of guerrilla movement' expanding in unique fashion with hitherto unseen speed.

5. Interview by the author in Lima, 18 Aug. 1989.

6. Ibid., 15 Aug. 1989.

7. Ibid.

8. Ibid.

9. Ibid.

10. Ibid.

11. Interview by the author in Lima, 17 Aug. 1989.

12. By now it should be clear that the organizational framework here is, in a sense, generic to communist insurgencies. A readily available comparison may be made with the organizational structures of the Communist Party of the Philippines (CPP). See, e.g., my work (esp.maps) covering the Philippine islands of Samar, Panay, and Negros, respectively: 'Cease–Fire Maneuvers', SOF, 12/5 (May 1987), pp.49–55 (contd.); 'Victory on Panay', SOF, 13/2 (Feb. 1989), pp.40–7 (contd.); 'Political Body Count', SOF, 14/6 (June 1989), pp.32–9 (contd.). Consult also Michael C. Conley, *The Communist Insurgent Infrastructure in South Vietnam: A Study of Organization and Strategy* (Washington, DC: American Univ., 1966).

13. At the time I carried out my research, I had not yet examined what is certainly the most cited work on *Sendero* infrastructure, that of James Anderson (see n.4 above). Consequently, it is useful to compare the findings of Anderson with my own. We appear to agree on most particulars.

14. Cf. McClintock, 'Peru's *Sendero Luminoso* Rebellion: Origins and Trajectory' (n.1).

15. Cf. Andrew R. Molnar *et al.*, *Human Factors Considerations of Undergrounds in Insurgencies* (Washington, DC: American Univ., 1965).

16. Original map constructed from data gathered in Ayacucho, Aug. 1989. Graphics by SOF.

17. Interviews by the author in Ayacucho, 23–25 Aug. 1989.

18. As per n.16 above.

19. See, e.g., my discussion of this problem in the Philippines; cf. sources listed in n.12 above. Map particulars as per n.16.

20. Interview by the author in Lima, 17 Aug. 1989.
21. Ibid., 20 Aug. 1989.
22. Interviews by the author in Ayacucho, 23–25 Aug. 1989.
23. Interview by the author in Lima, 20 Aug. 1989.
24. Ibid., 26 Aug. 1989.
25. Ibid.
26. Interview by the author in Lima, 18 Aug. 1989.
27. Interviews by the author in Ayacucho, 23–25 Aug. 1989.
28. Interview by the author in Lima, 18 Aug. 1989.
29. Ibid.
30. Ibid., 14 Aug. 1989.
31. Ibid., 19 Aug. 1989.
32. As one wag pointed out to me in 1989, in explaining this seeming anomaly of military deployment, 'All Peruvian heroes are men who died fighting Chile in hopeless situations. They haven't gotten over that.' Chile, for that matter, won the War of the Pacific in question (1879–84) and captured Lima, an episode which apparently remains a searing memory for many military Peruvians, together with the subsequent seizure by the Chileans of a portion of Peru. A border war with Ecuador in 1941 has sputtered to life periodically since then with less sensational results.
33. In Ayacucho in 1989 the strike force was comprised of *Compania Lince* (*CIA Lince*), or 'Company Lynx'. Though it had some special equipment, its strength came principally from its rigorous training in the Ranger/commando tradition.
34. A good overview of this campaign may be found in Gordon H. McCormick, *From the Sierra to the Cities: The Urban Campaign of the Shining Path*, RAND Paper R–4150–USDP (Santa Monica: RAND, 1992). McCormick had earlier authored several works on Shining Path, to include another RAND study, *The Shining Path and the Future of Peru* (1990), and 'The Shining Path and Peruvian Terrorism', in David C. Rapoport, *Inside Terrorist Organizations* (NY: Columbia UP, 1988). He has been taken to task at times for the nature of his data, as well as his interpretations; e.g., John T. Fishel's review (untitled) in *Small Wars and Insurgencies*, 3/3 (Winter 1992), pp.319–21. Yet his material can be useful.
35. Cf. Alma Guillermoprieto, 'The Bitter Education of Vargas Llosa', *New York Review of Books*, 41/10 (26 May 1994), pp.19–27.
36. Alma Guillermoprieto is again a good source for specifics; cf. her 'Letter From Lima: Down the Shining Path', *The New Yorker*, 8 Feb. 1993, pp.64–75.
37. My phraseology here comes from the insights offered by David Scott Palmer during a discussion on 30 Nov. 1993.

6 Remarks

In the chapters of this work we have seen a progression of sorts, a progression in which Maoist insurgency has become increasingly divorced from the masses it purports to serve. The militaristic components, those associated with 'people's war', have come to overshadow those embodied in the 'united front' and the 'mass line'. Thus the crucial role terror has played in the campaign of the last movement examined, *Sendero Luminoso*, is both predictable and logical. I have called 'Shining Path' a Maoist conclusion, because it represents the state to which the approach leads, *must* lead. This results from the profoundly undemocratic basis of the form.

In making such a statement, one can only read in dismay certain past scholarly efforts to analyze Maoism and the violence which is an integral part of it. A representative offering is that articulated by Mark Selden:

> The thesis of this essay is as follows: Out of the ashes of military strife which enveloped China and Vietnam in protracted wars of liberation emerged a radically new vision of man and society and a concrete approach to development. Built on foundations of participation and community action which challenge elite domination, this approach offers hope of more *humane* forms of development and of effectively overcoming the formidable barriers to the transformation of peasant societies.[1]

What has been demonstrated in the case studies is that such a view is fatally flawed. Far from providing a new vision for participation and community action, Maoist insurgency is a means for popular mobilization to support military action. That Mao addressed the masses is beyond question — that he may have been sincere in the process can be allowed without detracting from the argument — but in this he was only being logical. His problem was to gain manpower, first, for his armed forces, second, in support of those armed forces. This was essential to carry out the revolution. The people were indeed the water in which the guerrilla fish were to swim. Yet what the 'mass line' and the 'united front' were concerned with was ensuring the proper temperature of the water, not in letting its currents sweep the fish where they might.

Mao had no intention of responding to the needs of the people as a matter of principle; he needed their support for the revolutionary endeavor, and he would use those issues inherent to world capitalism and imperialist action — as set forth in communist theory — to gain it. Marxism provided the strategic template; Leninism provided the operational component, the lessons in the development of infrastructure. Mao's synthesis of both, mixed with his own analysis of the Chinese situation and tactical experiences in guerrilla warfare, resulted in a viable technique for action. The sheer scale of the project was immense. Where Lenin needed but a few battalions to bring down a tottering old-regime, however, Mao needed a myriad.

Always, in pursuing this point, we come back to the essence: 'Mao' needed. In other words, 'the revolutionary leadership' needed — not 'the people needed'. It is the contribution of Scott to have recognized the Janus–like nature of insurgency, with the leadership and the membership pursuing different ends, and the qualitative nature of the movement depending upon the terms of their relationship. Where the immediate concerns of the mass base have won out, revolt has resulted. Where the leadership has gained control, insurgency has been the outcome, pursuing the ideological goals of the cadre. That revolutionary elites have proved adroit at addressing the actual contradictions in various systems has been held up by analysts such as Selden as proof of a leadership committed to the masses and social justice. I argue, to the contrary, that this is a misreading of the evidence.

Ironically, this same evidence comes closer to supporting the conventional view, that of activists exploiting grievances, than to the alternative, that which sees the revolutionary elite as springing from the masses. Indeed, as we now know from a wide body of evidence cited earlier, the initial recruits of the Maoist revolutionary endeavor in China itself were not drawn from the masses *per se* but from fringe elements of the populace. Only when the revolutionary movement became a going concern was it able to exploit the mechanisms of and contradictions in the old-regime, as it did in Jiangxi. This certainly eliminates a necessary cause–effect, ecological relationship.[2] And it means the revolutionary conjuncture has as much to do with purposive (deliberate) action as with structure.

It is their emphasis upon structure which affords common ground in the conventional and alternative views of insurgency. Mao's strategic contribution was in his insistence upon grounding the revolutionary endeavor in reality. Time and again he emphasized that the Marxist–Leninist approach was only viable if it addressed concrete circumstances. In this determination we see the essence of a mind which stands among the ranks of the so-called 'great commanders'. He knew that what he was about was rooted in violence; he said so repeatedly in his works. Only the transformation of society through revolutionary action could bring about the desired result. Proper leadership, then, was indispensable: Purposive action had to be cognizant, always, of structure.

Where the conventional approach went astray, as illustrated well by the US intervention in Vietnam, was in its overemphasis upon the purposive exploitation of structural contradictions. If the insurgents were taking advantage of grievances, went the logic, then the 'fix' was 'to eliminate the grievances'. Correct as far as it went, this approach foundered on a simple reality: it was elite driven. So, too, was the alternative view: The revolutionary elite must recognize the grievances and lead the people to eliminate them through systemic revision. Both mistook elite action for democratic process. At the analytical level, this mistake resulted in quotations such as that above from Selden, wherein a bloody dictatorship as was Mao's China became transformed into a '*humane*' development model (the emphasis upon the word is in his original).

On the ground, we saw, to offer an illustration, the suspicion with which Christian 'base communities' were viewed by Philippine patrols I accompanied. For democratic though they were in impulse, the base communities too often were formed at the behest of CPP cadre whose elite goals, whatever their words, were at variance with the quest for justice that inspired the membership. What should have been a foundation for democratic construction was used instead as a facade for subversive mobilization. Such could hardly be otherwise, given the Leninist roots of Maoist action.

It was the recognition of this necessary connection between Leninist mobilization and violence which gave the works of Alexander Solzhenitsyn their power.[3] He saw the unholy combination of Leninist dictatorial form with Marxist ideology for the abomination it was. His counter, much criticized in some circles, was a call for a return to a society's roots, to its indigenous sources of strength. In the case studies, particularly that of the Thai, we have seen a playing out of just such a scenario. A successful result from the standpoint of the state, however, has depended upon the degree to which this cultural essence has been linked to democratic action.

Therein lies the conclusion I have sought to emphasize: the primacy of democracy as the only viable approach to counterinsurgency. It bears emphasis that democracy is not merely a matter of voting in elections. The case of Sri Lanka demonstrated well the profoundly undemocratic consequences of procedures that marginalized those who found themselves on the short end of a flawed electoral system. Riggs' use of the 'constitutive system' comes closest to describing the manner in which I see the process. There are any number of ways in which the popular will can be realized. The key, certainly, must be the institutionalization of whatever means allow the populace to shape the environment in ways it chooses, social, economic, and political — and which attempt to safeguard minority concerns. To return to the Philippine case as an illustration, the base community form was correct, as was its popular inspiration. It sought to organize the masses for the pursuit of *their* goals. These, stripped to their essence, boiled down to the organization of society so that justice might prevail. The trick would be to tap such a manifestation and institutionalize its role. Federal systems have proved more adept at this than unitary, centralized polities.

Certainly none of this brief discussion should be interpreted to mean that voting in elections is not crucial, only to say that it is not the end in itself. The point is that it is only a means to an end. To wit, since justice is a relative term and can come only from the individuals concerned, there simply is no other way to discern their conception of 'the good life' save to ask them. Having determined their desires, however, there must be means whereby those desires can be implemented, with all appropriate safeguards for those not in the majority. This is democracy. Its purpose, whatever its precise forms — parliamentary, republican, or otherwise — is to reflect the desires of the people.

Maoist insurgency, in contrast, seeks popular feedback through the 'mass line' for the purpose of organizational mobilization in support of the revolution. It seeks to broaden the pool of prospective recruits by using the 'united front'. And it forges the power thus awakened into a weapon through 'people's war'. Governments can mobilize, too, as Chiang Kai–shek demonstrated well in the Five Encirclement Campaigns (1930–34) which resulted in the destruction of the Jiangxi (Kiangsi) soviets. But only where the mobilization is rooted in democratic impulse is the approach viable and of such substance that it does not guarantee a new round in the conflict as contradictions again surface.

What should be plain is that democracy — and particularly its mobilization in cultural particulars — can have its dark side. Plato, it will be recalled, was terrified of the beast. In each case study, when democratic action has been unleashed in the form of countermobilization to revolutionary mobilization, the results have included abuses. In some instances, such as those of Thailand and the Philippines, I will argue that these were kept under control, particularly when viewed in comparative perspective; in the others, Sri Lanka and Peru, passions have all too often run amok. The passions are inevitable, as Saiyud Kerdphol noted in Thailand — only effective organization can control them. But this organization is often beyond the capabilities of many weak states.

It is the final irony that Maoist insurgency, 'people's war', can only be met by a democratic response, true 'people's war'. And war, as Mao stated plainly, though in different words, is never anything but ugly. If it results in a better world, then we accept the cost. Maoist insurgency promises such a better world, but only democracy can deliver it.

NOTES

1. Mark Selden, 'People's War and the Transformation of Peasant Society: China and Vietnam', in Mark Selden and Edward Freedman (eds.), *America's Asia*, offprint (nfd).
2. This is a conclusion reached by Roy Hofheinz, Jr. in his 'The Ecology of Chinese Communist Success: Rural Influence Patterns, 1923–45', in A. Doak Barnett (ed.), *Chinese Communist Politics in Action* (Seattle, WA: Univ. of Washington Press, 1969), pp.3–77. He finds the most significant factor in explaining whether an area became involved in the insurgency to be the presence of CCP cadre themselves. William Wei agrees with this in his 'Insurgency by the Numbers: A Reconsideration of the Ecology of Communist Success in Jiangxi' (n.18, Introduction) but emphasizes, too, the role of structural factors. He points out that the importance of these factors becomes evident when statistical measures are used to analyze available data, as he has done, rather than relying solely upon map comparison, as in Hofheinz. I have questioned the viability of ecological explanation in my 'Insurgency by the Numbers II: The Search for a Quantitative Relationship Between Agrarian Revolution and Land Tenure in South and Southeast Asia', *Small Wars and Insurgencies*, 5/2 (Autumn 1994), pp. 218–91.
3. I have discussed this point at length previously; cf. my '"The History of Our Sewage Disposal System": Solzhenitsyn's Conception of Stalinism as a Necessary Product of Lenin's Thinking', *Issues & Studies*, 14/5 (May 1978), pp.65–89.

Index

Note: Thai and Chinese personal names are indexed under the first name.